DEVELOPMENT PERSPECTIVES

DEVELOPMENT PERSPECTIVES

Paul Streeten

First published 1981 by
THE MACMILLAN PRESS LTD
London and Basingstoke
Companies and representatives
throughout the world

ISBN O 333 28567 0

Printed in Hong Kong

Contents

v

Part I Concepts, Values and Methods

1 Programmes and Prognoses[1]

COLBY   That's not what I meant.
I meant, there's no end to understanding a person.
All one can do is to understand them better,
To keep up with them; so that as the other changes
You can understand the change as soon as it happens,
Though you could not have predicted it.

LUCASTA   I think I am changing.
I've changed quite a lot in the last two hours.

COLBY
And I think I am changing too. But perhaps what we call change . . .

LUCASTA
Is understanding better what one really is.
And the reason why that comes about perhaps . . .

COLBY
Is beginning to understand another person.

T. S. Eliot, *The Confidential Clerk* (p. 67)[2]

3

1 IS AND OUGHT

One of the peculiarities of political economy is the clash between the words and deeds of its protagonists. For over a century, economists have repeatedly declared that economic science is concerned only with observing, describing, analysing, and predicting events, and never with recommending, giving advice, or prescribing. Senior, John Stuart Mill, Cairnes, Bagehot, Sidgwick, John Neville Keynes, J. B. Clark[3] and in our times Professors Pigou and Robbins, as well as almost any textbook on economics, have affirmed that economics is about what *is* and *could* or *might* be, never about what *ought* to be.

Yet, in spite of these declarations of the scientific, neutral character of economics, virtually all economists have in fact advised, recommended, exhorted, warned, etc.—and all this with the aid of arguments derived directly from the 'science' of economics.

It is possible to argue that for the economists in the great utilitarian tradition the distinction between *is* and *ought* is not fundamental. Like other rationalist systems of philosophy, utilitarianism holds that *ought* can be deduced from *is* and *could be*. There is, indeed, evidence that the distinction between science and politics (or ethics) was thought to be merely classificatory. Economics as a *science* (in the narrow sense) is about facts; economics as an *art* is about values and policies. If this interpretation is adopted, the declarations as to the scientific character of economics amount to no more than a convenient classification into 'pure' or 'theoretical', and 'applied' or 'practical', economics.[4]

The difficulty that stands in the way of accepting this interpretation is the extreme importance which authors attach to the value-free character of economics, and the fervour with which they denounce in their methodological introductions any attempts to derive recommendations from the analysis of facts. I think they mean what they say, yet they never practise it.

The sharp division between *is* and *ought*, between positive and normative pursuits, is so widely accepted today that the inconsistency of the writers in the classical tradition might strike one as either gross carelessness or dishonesty. But one must remember that the habits of rationalistic philosophies, particularly those of the philosophy of natural law and of utilitarianism, according to which values and rules are either identical with, or can be derived from, facts, have deep and tough roots. Neither Adam Smith nor James Mill believed that there is anything improper in formulating a *science* of values and rules, and some of the confusion today may be merely the reflection of an ideological lag between words and deeds.

On the other hand, today we accept perhaps too easily the belief that the distinction between *is* and *ought* is always obvious, clear-cut, and easy to draw.[5]

Gunnar Myrdal's views on this issue have undergone a gradual change. There are passages in the *Political Element*, which imply that an honest effort and hard work can always sort out the values from the facts. The smuggling in of the value premises is done, on this view, at a rather superficial level. But there is a gradual shift from this *psychological* view (which, as Myrdal says in his 1953 Preface, implies a naive empiricism) to a more complicated analysis of the entry of value judgements. In the *Crux of All Science* the values enter, not as wishes distorting thought, but as essential principles, forming the structure of theoretical thought, giving it meaning and direction. But if values enter inevitably into the way in which we attempt to analyse reality, good will and honesty have nothing to contribute to the clarification at this deeper level. The whole conception of scientific analysis is changed. Values are not something to be discarded, nor even something to be made explicit in order to be separated from empirical matter, but are ever-present and permeate empirical analysis through and through.

2 PROGRAMME AND PROGNOSIS

In Appendix 2 of *An American Dilemma*, entitled 'Note on Facts and Valuations',[6] Myrdal draws a distinction between 'programmes' and 'prognoses'. These two key concepts open the door to his approach to the whole problem of value and I shall attempt to use them here for this purpose.

'Programme' should be understood as a plan of intended action, e.g., a party programme, the objectives of trade unions, farmers' or traders' associations, etc. A programme is the formulation of a policy. It consists of certain objectives or ends, and rules about the manner in which these objectives are to be pursued.

By 'prognosis' is meant a forecast of the probable or possible course of events. A prognosis is based on observation and analysis, and consists of the application to particular instances of generalizations about the actual and hypothetical connections between facts and events.

This distinction is related to the more familiar one between *analysis* and *policy*. 'Prognosis' stresses the predictive character of analysis; 'programme' is a concrete formulation of policy. The distinction is also related to the familiar *means–ends* dichotomy, but it is not the same. The means–ends model was constructed in order to salvage something of what appeared to be a normative science, in an age when the rationalistic faith in discoverable values had declined, and scepticism and relativism had grown stronger. If the dichotomy is tenable, a teleological argument can be conducted on objective lines, as long as the hypothetical clause about ends is inserted. All valuations are bundled together under the rubric 'ends', and the appropriateness of means can then be discussed 'scientifically'.

But people attach value not merely to 'ends', in the sense of the desired ultimate results of a course of events, but also to the means by which ends are achieved. This complex of desired ends, means and procedures, and effects other than ends which may be inevitable outcomes, all of which is conditioned by valuations, one may call 'programme'.

In terms of the distinction between programme and prognosis much of social analysis looks like the attempt to derive programmes directly from analysis and prognosis. Critics have repeatedly pointed out that such attempts stem from a confusion, and that clear thinking requires that ends (which are a part of programmes) be separated from means (analysis and prediction). The most recent formulation of this view can be found in the theory of the *social welfare function*.[7] The social welfare function is a hold-all for all valuations, set out in a definite order, a device which is supposed to purify economic investigation of all vestiges of unscientific matter. But the interdependence of programme and prognosis is in the nature of social theory, and the obstacle to their separation is not just muddle-headedness.

The purists claim that it is possible and desirable to separate sharply (*a*) the prognosis based on an objective analysis of a situation in which programmes are taken as data, from (*b*) the programme based on this analysis. In fact, there is mutual interaction, and each is partly determined and modified by the other.

The criticism of the view that independent prognosis is possible is similar, as far as I can see, to the criticism of modern physicists of the assumption that observer and observed do not affect each other. It has been found that it is inherently impossible to observe exactly both the position and the velocity of a particle, even if all experimental errors are eliminated.

This discovery did not lead to the abandonment of observation, but to a reformulation of the model used. Similarly, the fact that programme and prognosis affect each other forces us to abandon such models as "economics is the science of the allocation of scarce means with alternative uses between competing ends" and to replace them by more appropriate models, which take account of this interaction.

3 PROGRAMME DETERMINED BY PROGNOSIS

Pigou prefaced his *Wealth and Welfare* with a quotation from Charles Booth: 'discontent, to be effective, must be shot through with the colours of hope.' He was convinced that in his analysis hope could be found. A programme, to be effective, must take account of the probable and possible future course of events; in other words, it must be based on analysis and prognosis. Programmes are altered in the light of new knowledge about the facts. Programmes without prognoses are idle wish-dreams or empty protests.

More particularly, analysis and prognosis can point out the implications of alternative choices, and the consistency or inconsistency of objectives contained in a programme. They may indicate the proper policies for achieving given objectives, in so far as values are not attached to the policies as such, and the probable consequences of given policies. They may show to what extent the short-term interests manifested in a programme are compatible with the long-term interests of a group, to what extent the objectives expressed in a programme diverge from the actual conduct of the group in question (pointing out rationalizations and hypocrisy), and to what extent this conduct is consistent.

It appears therefore that the ends are never given, in the sense required by those who believe in the possibility of a neutral welfare theory. Ends are modified:

(1) In the light of fuller knowledge of the facts.
(2) In the light of what is believed can, and what cannot, be altered. But amongst these 'data' are the ends of other people; therefore ends are altered in the light of the programmes, and the power behind the programmes, of others. Many conservative recommendations rest on the conviction that 'you can't change human nature', whereas socialists derive hope from the belief that institutions can sometimes do so. Disputes between revolutionaries and reformists are often about whether certain institutions can be changed. Opinions as to the factual problem of what are the constants will condition men's moral and political convictions.[8]
(3) In the light of other ends which develop as one set of ends is explored, and in the light of undesirable, previously unforeseen, results which clash either with the 'given', or with the newly discovered, ends.

To put the same thing another way, analysis and prognosis modify programmes in the following ways:

(1) Programmes may become more consistent through being better informed, and thus more effective.

(2) Value standards, previously only implicit, or altogether absent, may be activated as a result of the facts turned up by analysis (see Section 5).

(3) Confusions not only about the relations of facts, but also about one's own desires may be cleared up. Rationalizations and pseudo-interests may give place to knowledge of real interests.

(4) Divergencies between words and deeds, action and belief, may become apparent.

For any of these reasons, programmes may be altered as a result of the clarification of certain facts. This relationship, however, is complicated because there is no *logical* connection between false beliefs about the world and valuations based on them, on the one hand, and correct beliefs and valuations based on them, on the other hand. If it were not for this complication, it might still be possible to maintain the dichotomy between ends and means. If we were given programmes based on erroneous factual beliefs, we might be able to deduce logically what programmes would be pursued if the errors were corrected. This is the view expressed by Max Weber in his discussion of the objectivity of social science.[9] In fact, this is impossible. The question, how do individuals and groups react to changing insight into reality, can be answered only by psychology and sociology, not by logic.

4 PROGNOSIS DETERMINED BY PROGRAMME

It is obvious that a programme is based on, and modified in the light of, analysis and prognosis, though not always logically. A programme without prognosis is an impotent utopian dream. On the other hand, a prognosis without programmes is necessarily incomplete. Prognosis depends upon programmes in two distinct ways. First and obviously, the programmes of *others* are data for the social observer and theorist. What physical facts and events are to the natural scientist, that valuations, beliefs and programmes, however wrong-headed or ill-conceived, are to the social scientist. Second, and perhaps less obviously, the observer and theorist himself has something like a programme which determines his analysis and prognosis.

(a) PROGRAMMES AS SOCIAL DATA

Social analysis treats the intentions and plans of individuals and groups as the most important part of its data. We can forecast what is likely to happen under specified conditions only if we know what certain people will want to do in those conditions and how successfully they will act. Not value systems in the abstract, not given sets of ends, but programmes, in so far as they are backed by power, are an essential element in analysis and prognosis.

Prognostic disputes have raged over the question of whether the removal of food subsidies, or a rise in rents, or devaluation, would have inflationary or deflationary effects. Yet, the answer hinges almost entirely on the programme and power of trade unions. If workers attempt to fix real wages, money wages will rise as a result of the above policies, and the effect will be inflationary. If they fix wages in money terms (either because they suffer from a 'money illusion', or because they are relatively weak) the effect may be deflationary.

(b) SELECTION AND RELEVANCE

The selection of empirical data relevant to any question under examination is subject to a judgement as to what *ought* to be admitted as good evidence. Factual propositions imply injunctions about what kind of events we *should* expect if we accept certain views about the real world, and valuations about the credit-*worthiness* of beliefs. Clearly these judgements are not moral or political value judgements (although they may be connected with these). This is not the place for a discussion of the nature of these judgements and rules, but they appear to be in some respects like moral value judgements and imperatives. They, too, require a decision, imply a choice, and cannot be subsumed under clearly definable general canons. Above all, they cannot be derived from the facts, because there are no facts without them.

Moreover, the element in these judgements which resembles value judgements is particularly prevalent in social studies. Here evidence cannot always be provided at will; situations are complex and often unique, and scientific experiment almost impossible. Hence the scope for appraisal and judgement is much wider than in many of the natural sciences.[10]

The importance of valuations in the formation of empirical hypotheses is brought out even more clearly when we consider probability prognoses in the form of statistical propositions. First, the decision as to what deviations in any given set of observations from a probability hypothesis should be considered as refuting this hypothesis, is quite independent of the observations, and determined entirely by the use to which we put the hypothesis. The purpose of our investigation thus determines the decision to accept or reject an empirical theory.

Second, when we are faced with a choice between alternative statistical prognoses, we require a programme to select the best one. One such programme is that formulated by Wald, which is equivalent to a Neumann–Morgenstern theorem in the theory of games, according to which we choose that hypothetical prognosis on which we are likely to lose least if it turns out to be false. *Safety first* bids us minimize the maximum of possible losses. By looking upon uncertain future natural events as if they were a partner in a game, we can apply the Neumann–Morgenstern strategy to the selection of empirical prognoses. Thus an evaluation of gains and losses is an essential prerequisite for prediction, where alternative probability hypotheses are available. In the words of R. B. Braithwaite, ‘ . . . we cannot be good, or at least deliberately good, without being wise. The modern principles of statistical inference show that, *vice versa*, judgements of value are, in the last analysis, inextricably involved in choosing the best way to scientific knowledge: we cannot be wise without making judgements of good and evil.’[11]

(c) MODELS AND CONCEPTS: THE INDEX NUMBER PROBLEM

All concepts are abstractions. They are normative, not only in the sense much discussed recently, that they may have emotive connotations and may be used to persuade or to commend, as well as to describe, but also in the more fundamental sense that a rule or judgement is required to determine what particular objects or experiences should be lumped together under any given concept. What is known in economics and statistics as the index number problem is a problem common to all thinking. But the difficulties become particularly glaring in the social sciences. Trouble arises when we mistake for concrete things what in fact are theories or models, and thus forget that there is usually a *choice* of alternative theories or models to explain a given set of experiences.

Examples of the muddles caused by this mistake are such models as ‘Man v Nature’, ‘Real Social Income’, ‘Consumption’, ‘the Economy’, etc. A particularly apt example is the means–ends model itself. By arranging and presenting the facts in a certain way, policy questions are already implied, which would not have arisen if a different model had been chosen (see Section (d)).

The same is true of all important concepts in economics. To say anything, not merely about prices, real wages, national income, etc., but, e.g., about the economic consequences of the war, about the economic prospects of a country, almost anything about capital—ideas with normally little emotive content—implies nevertheless *choosing*, hence *valuing*, although this fact is often concealed by our mistaking models for concrete objects.

The literature is replete with declarations that comparisons between the utilities of different men cannot be made by positive economists because such comparisons are value judgements. Yet, by using appropriately question-begging pseudo-positive terms—i.e., models with implicit valuations disguised as descriptive concepts—the valuations reappear. Thus shortly after Jevons says solemnly 'there is never, in any single instance, an attempt made to compare the amount of feeling in one mind with that in another' (*Theory of Political Economy*, p. 14) he speaks ingenuously of aggregate and average psychological functions, belonging to groups of people, nations, or trading bodies, as if the impossible were possible after all. Similarly, modern welfare economists speak of increases in social income and welfare after having declared firmly that interpersonal comparisons of real income and welfare are impossible.

In some instances it is, of course, possible to lay down a definite rule to eliminate ambiguity. But even then the decision will be guided by the *purpose* of our investigation, by the *question* we are asking. We shall be prepared to modify the rule according to what our *interest* requires. The point is that the concepts and propositions of even the most purely empirical investigation derive their meaning and significance from a purpose, an interest, and involve choice and, therefore, valuation.

'National income' has no meaning, unless we specify whether we are interested in an underdeveloped or a developed society, in one with little or much state activity, in a nation's productive capacity, its standard of living, or its equality, etc. 'Capital' has no meaning unless we know whether the enquirer is an accountant, a businessman, or a pure theorist who postulates equilibrium. Yet, many speak of 'national income', 'capital', etc., as if they were speaking of gallons of water.

All this may sound too obvious to be worth saying. Yet the belief is widespread that we can confine ourselves to the discovery of facts and thus avoid choice and valuation.

(d) INADEQUACY OF THE MEANS–ENDS SCHEME

In social analysis valuations enter not only at the ultimate (or initial) stage in decisions about sets of given ends, but at every stage. People do not attach value only to ultimate ends (whatever this may mean); and they are not indifferent between the means which promote these ends, even where the means are technically and otherwise exactly equivalent.

It is important to avoid a terminological confusion here. It is, of course, possible to *define* anything to which value is attached as an 'end'. But such a trick would not meet the purpose for which the means–ends dichotomy was constructed. As we have seen, it was meant to circumscribe a neutral sphere in which objective statements can be made, and into which no valuations enter. But if values are attached to means, the qualifications required by the acceptance of the ends become necessary at every stage. If end *E* can be brought about by courses *a*, *b*, and *c*, and if no direct values are attached to *a*, *b*, and *c*, a scientific discussion of these courses, which abstracts entirely from valuations, is possible: how long they take, how effectively they promote *E*, what other results E_1, E_2, etc., besides *E* they are likely to have, etc. It is then possible to arrive at the conclusion, say, that *a* is the most effective course, *if E* is desired and if E_1, E_2, etc. are insufficient deterrents (or welcome by-products). This is the model commonly envisaged by practitioners of economics.

But this procedure is no longer open if direct values are attached to *a*, *b*, and *c* themselves. For then we can only say, tautologically, choose *a if* you want *a*, choose *b*, *if* you want *b*, etc.: whereas before we could say, choose *a*, but not *b* or *c*, if you want *E*. Since the hypothetical clause referring to valuation has to be introduced at every stage, empirical analysis disappears altogether.

The following quite unwarranted assumptions would be required if we were to discuss objectively means in relation to 'given' ends:

(1) People attach to means no direct value, but only instrumental value.
(2) People attach to ends direct value only, and never consider them as means to other ends.
(3) No other effects of means than the 'given' ends have direct value.

Very rarely can one reach exactly the same end by alternative, politically entirely indifferent, means. The means affect the 'end' in the wider sense. Whereas the means–end model, to be useful, must assume that the same place can be reached by alternative paths (see Section (e)), in fact different paths usually lead to different places in this field. This fact greatly restricts the sphere in which prognosis can progress without assuming or committing itself to specific valuations almost all the time. It narrows the realm of 'neutrality' and 'objectivity', as defined by the means–ends protagonists.

To illustrate: If consumption were the only end, and if production and exchange were only means to its achievement certain rules about the optimum conditions of production and exchange could be laid down. The formulation of these rules has been the aim of an important branch of traditional welfare economics. But the disturbing fact is that neither the conditions in which production is carried on, nor the relationships generated by exchange are purely instrumental. They are *human* conditions and *human* relations, which are valued as much as, and in some cases more strongly than, the end of consumption. Nor, of course, is consumption *simply* a given end. Not only are there good and bad ways of earning money, but there are also good and bad ways of spending it.

The foregoing was an attempt to criticize the means–ends model in its own terminology. A different approach, pointing to the same conclusion, may bring out the argument more clearly.[12] Somebody may at this stage of the argument reply: 'Granted that problems of policy as a whole cannot be reduced to a means–ends model. Nevertheless, means–ends problems are ubiquitous, though always involving abstractions from the total situation, and they are the only ones which an economist as such is competent to deal with. Furthermore, surely not all the deliverances of an economist will be policy deliverances. If so, how are the purely descriptive parts of his analysis related to the policy part?'

Those who find the means–ends model helpful look upon problems of economic policy as if they were, in principle, like puzzles. There is the obvious difference that puzzles are constructed by some people in order to be solved by others, whereas problems of policy usually are not. But in both cases, granted consistent premises, there is always a "correct" solution. There is always an unambiguous 'scientific' test of whether we have solved the puzzle. Thus if the end is, say, the avoidance of more than 2 per cent unemployment for five years, statisticians can tell us whether we have succeeded or not. No doubt, many problems of economic policy are of this type.

If all policy problems were of this kind, not much more could be said in principle. Some people, perhaps the technocrats, believe that they are. It is certainly tempting to assimilate all problems to this type, and to say that a problem has been solved when certain ideal rules are obeyed. But the question, e.g., whether the avoidance of unemployment should be a primary objective of policy is altogether different. We might indeed say that absence of unemployment diminishes the chances of social rebellion and is to be commended solely on this ground. Thus considered as a mere means, statisticians could presumably again tell us whether this is correct or not. Many ends are, at least partly, intermediate ends in this sense. And some theories maintain that all problems could be subsumed under one single ultimate end. But this is not a plausible view.

If we believe that unemployment spells misery and loss of human dignity, and that it violates our belief in the brotherhood of men, but that some of it may at times be necessary to prevent greater evil, no simple criterion could be formulated, which would show whether, by avoiding unemployment, we have done the right thing. However, although we cannot apply simple and definite tests and present a 'scientific' solution, the answer is not arbitrary. Through observation, conversation, and experience we can learn to *judge* and *appraise* these matters.

Although value judgements enter into our judgement of the situation, they are not of the type of 'ends' as in the puzzle-solving model. A good deal of political and economic discourse is neither purely descriptive, nor just rhetorical emotive persuasion, nor a combination of the two. It is more like the exercise of a skill, or an art, like playing the piano, or giving a lecture, or writing a poem. The strictly scientific aspect of political discussion, as defined by the means–ends dichotomists, is comparable to the theory of the skill: it lays down precise rules, clear tests. But the best theory can produce neither a skilful performance nor good judgement of a performance. A skilful performance can neither be tested by hard and fast standards, nor is it merely an arbitrary or subjective decision whether we judge it good or bad.

An economist, like a novelist, is good not because (a) he knows the facts, and (b) has the right value judgements (political or literary). The answer to the question, 'How do we know that he is a good economist or novelist?', whatever it may be (and it is not an easy one), will certainly not be, 'Because his work follows certain definite canons.'

Analysis and prognosis and their appraisal are skills, which cannot always be subjected to the rules of the means–ends game. Although they inevitably involve judgements which have some of the characteristics of valuations, they are not for that reason 'subjective', arbitrary, or mere matters of taste.

(e) IMPLICATIONS FOR WELFARE ECONOMICS

There are, roughly speaking, two modern versions of welfare economics, the Paretian and the Bergsonian. Both versions depend, to some extent, on the validity of the means–ends model. The Paretian optimum conditions of production and exchange are claimed to be—in the more modest formulations—necessary, though not sufficient, conditions for an economic optimum, on certain additional assumptions which it is not necessary to enumerate.

If the puzzle-solving model is rejected, according to which recommendations of means become a merely *technical* matter, and if the more empirical approach suggested in the previous section is adopted, it becomes pointless to speak of a social or of an economic *optimum* which is achieved if certain specifiable conditions are fulfilled; and yet it is meaningful and important to speak of *improvements*.

But only if we are prepared to speak of an 'optimum' are the Paretian conditions *necessary* conditions (on certain assumptions). If we reject the applicability of an 'optimum', it is perfectly possible, even granted the stringent assumptions about values and facts of this theory, to envisage all kinds of improvements which do not meet the Paretian criteria. All desirable redistributions of wealth which would not allow compensation of the losers would be such improvements. The Pareto criteria would turn out to be not only insufficient, but also unnecessary.

Similarly, the social welfare function is a device which makes an ordering of all possible states necessary. Given a social welfare function, the solution of the optimum is like the solution of a puzzle though it may require great technical virtuosity. But no social welfare function is ever given, at any rate in a democratic society. We never order all possible total situations according to a system of values, but have rather muddled preferences for aspects and features of a limited number of actual and possible situations. These preferences change as a result of the discussion and adoption of policies intended to minister to them.

If the economist is to give advice in concrete situations, it is more helpful for him to think in terms of *improvements* than in terms of ideals or *optima*. Nobody really knows what an optimum economic system is like (or what the optimum degree of equality would look like), but many can make wise proposals for betterment. The fallacy of the means–end pattern of thinking lies in the belief that 'improvement' always logically implies an 'optimum' or 'ideal'. It may, if we judge the change with reference to a given ideal, such as the number of correct answers in a quiz where the only alternatives are 'Yes' or 'No'. But 'improvement' need not imply 'optimum', as may be illustrated in the example of writing a good article. An article is never completed; there is *always* scope for improvement. Nobody can lay down criteria and say: 'This is what the end-product ought to be like.' Yet it would be foolish to deny that there are ways of knowing when it has been improved. The mistake of fitting the 'good article' into the quiz schema is analogous to the mistake of fitting all economic policies into the means–ends pattern.

(f) BIAS

So far we have discussed some of the ways in which analysis and prognosis depend upon and presuppose judgements, valuations, and programmes, without, however, necessarily being distorted by them. But there are numerous interpretations of facts in social theory whose function it is not to clear up muddles or to show up inconsistencies, but, on the contrary, to justify inconsistent beliefs, to bridge over contradictions. Many well-known types of social prognosis are biased in a more or less conscious way, so as to justify valuations and the behaviour that springs from them.

When contradictions within a programme, or between the programme and certain facts, are pointed out, two reactions are possible: either the programme is altered in accordance with fuller, more rational understanding, or the belief about the facts is adjusted to fit the programme. Prognoses that are used to justify programmes in this manner may be manifestations of 'blind spots', prejudices, biases, or, more grandiosely, ideologies. The distortion may range from blatant lies to the very categories of thought, which, if the sociologists of knowledge are right, are conditioned by our interests and valuations.

At this stage, the philosophies of natural law and of utilitarianism are turned upside down. According to these two philosophies, values and rules can be derived from a contemplation of the facts, the natural order according to the former, happiness or welfare according to the latter. But today we are more inclined to believe that it is possible, and perhaps inevitable, that our values and rules determine the manner in which we approach, see, arrange, and interpret, the facts. It is not so much that values follow from 'the nature of the case', as that what we believe to be the nature of the case follows from our values.

Although in some cases a rational examination of political ideas may make them more effective by grounding them on a better knowledge of the facts, in other cases rational or rather pseudo-rational examination makes them into sterile ideologies. But their power over the irrational nature of men may be thereby increased. One of the most important facts of social life is that people are often highly irrational.

The critics of abstract, rationalistic systems in economics have, for over a hundred years, pointed out the historical and political value premises which underlie this type of theorizing, without, however, clarifying where they seek the Archimedean point from which to lift their own theory—the institutional or historical criticism—beyond ideology. It appears that the way towards a bias-free study of economics lies in the awareness of one's historical, political, institutional and moral valuations, and thus in an open recognition of the limitations of any theory, including one's own. Paradoxically, by abandoning the claim to absolutism, universality, and "pure" science, a way is opened to a more limited but also more rational, to a more modest but also more objective, approach to the study of society. Some of the problems raised by ideologies are more fully discussed in Section 7.

5 INTERDEPENDENCE BETWEEN PROGRAMME AND PROGNOSIS

It appears therefore that programmes are modified in the light of prognoses, but prognoses also depend upon, and are altered with, changing programmes. Valuations depend on what changes we believe to be feasible. But the 'constants' which determine what is feasible may in turn be altered by people's valuations. Faith can move mountains.

It is therefore impossible to take either the ends, in so far as they enter into programmes, as 'given' independently of the analysis of means, or to postulate a 'pure' analysis of means, a science of social engineering. Programmes depend on prognoses, which in turn depend on programmes, etc. It has been said that public knowledge of Keynesian analysis removes the world which Keynes analysed, and that successful practice of Marxism removes the conditions to which Marxian analysis applies.

In the following I shall try to give a few illustrations of the way in which prognosis alters programmes, the transformation of which in turn modifies prognosis.

(a) PROPHECIES: CURE THROUGH PROGNOSIS

Prognosis may serve the programme of changing the way of life (the programmes) of others. The oldest illustrations of this are the reform endeavours of the prophets of the Old Testament. Jonah's prognosis was the destruction of Nineveh in 40 days. God's programme for Jonah was not to make him into a successful forecaster, but to mend the ways of the people of Nineveh. As a result of Jonah's prognosis, this programme was achieved. Incidentally, Jonah's prognosis was falsified, which may have contributed to his anger.

In the same tradition of cure through prognosis stand the interpretations of history of Hegel, Marx, Spengler, and perhaps Toynbee. In some cases the cure lies in the fulfilment of the prognosis (Hegel, Marx), in others it lies in its falsification (Spengler, Toynbee). These interpretations contain analysis and prognosis, which are both determined by, and, in turn, determine social programmes.

The prognosis need not be guided primarily by the intention of improvement, but may have that effect nevertheless. The studies of Booth and Rowntree stated certain facts about poverty in England. As a result of this knowledge, consciences were stirred into action. But the measures which were taken to alleviate poverty, together with the general rise in the standard of living, led to a new interpretation of poverty. The poverty line, i.e., the standard set by public opinion, rose with rising living standards. Or, to put the matter another way, analysis and action to relieve poverty brought out a new aspect of poverty: it was considered to lie not merely in destitution, i.e., inability to afford the physically essential minimum, but also in what is regarded as socially decent. Poverty, it has become clear, is partly relative, though not entirely, for it is possible for all to be *equally* poor. The idea of what constitutes poverty has changed as a result of inquiring into poverty and of attempting to reduce it.

Other examples of the same process are Myrdal's study of the conditions of Negroes in the United States, Ferguson's and Cunnison's study of juvenile delinquency in Glasgow,[13] and reports on living conditions in poor countries.

(b) DANGEROUS THOUGHT: DESTRUCTION THROUGH PROGNOSIS

In other instances prognosis has the effect of destroying some of the values, and hence some of the social relations, upon which it is based. This is often neither foreseen nor desired by the prognosticators. Indeed, proposals based on prognosis often fail to produce the intended results, just because the prognosis alters the data on which it is based.

A simple illustration would be those theories that assume the 'money illusion' on the part of wage earners. Workers are supposed to object to a reduction in money wages while prices are constant, but not to a rise in prices with money wages constant. Such a theory in itself may make workers more real-wage conscious.

There is an element of erosion in almost all growth of knowledge on social relations. A good deal of our behaviour is habitual, semi-instinctive, subject to taboos and conventions. Analysis, which is based on the assumption that people behave in this way, brings taboos and conventions into the open, increases people's awareness of them, and leads to the desire for conscious manipulation. But the manipulation destroys the fabric on which, according to the initial prognosis, it is supposed to work. The price for eating of the tree of knowledge is the loss of Paradise.

Some objections to too much knowledge of the working of one's psyche have been raised on those grounds. In economics, the knowledge of the irrational, quasi-conventional character of competition led to monopolistic agreements; knowledge of the outwardly imposed rules of the gold-standard game led to a desire of every nation to be master of its own fate; and generally, greater awareness of the network of economic relations led to a desire to manipulate it, and thus to its disintegration. Increased organization by individuals and groups led to increased disorganization at large.

The social effects of birth control, of divorce, of control of property, markets, prices, currencies, and the use of propaganda, all result from growing knowledge and sophistication. The automatic adjustments of liberal society presupposed acceptance of traditional behaviour, and absence of the desire to question, experiment, and control rationally. Successful prognosis seemed to make it unnecessary to adjust ourselves to the world, and created the desire to adjust the world to our desires. But the cumulative effect was to produce an altogether new social situation, adjustment to which is more problematic than ever.[14]

We have seen above that Marxist theory, like prophecy, is a prognosis intended to create action. The theory and practice of modern state planning, on the other hand, is an attempt to meet the disintegrating pulls of a growing number of increasingly self-conscious, rational planning units. (Some of these pulls are themselves state interventions.)

It is possible to draw different conclusions from this tendency. Some might argue that 'too much knowledge is a bad thing.' There are various versions of the Japanese concept of 'dangerous thought', and almost every society attempts to protect itself to some extent by restricting open discussion of its most sacred institutions. Others might argue that the trend is both inevitable and desirable. What is required is more knowledge, i.e., knowledge that takes these socially disintegrating effects of partial knowledge into account.[15] But these questions are not my concern here.

(c) HARMONY THROUGH PROGNOSIS

In many theories a fuller understanding of the facts is believed to lead to greater social harmony. This is obviously so in all theories which consider evil as a form of ignorance. But although many believe implicitly in such a theory, few do so now when it is stated explicitly.

Yet, it is clear that knowledge *may* contribute to social harmony, and often does. It can remove opposition based on false views about reality, and a good deal of opposition does in fact have this origin. It can bring out more clearly the implications of commonly accepted standards,[16] and it can help to contribute to the formulation of common standards (respect for honest research, tolerance, etc.). In many situations, even where short-term interests clash, it can be shown that it is in everybody's interest to cooperate, because large potential gains could thereby be realized, out of which all members to the agreement could benefit.[17] A whole theory of welfare economics has been constructed on this argument.

On the other hand, fuller knowledge may also sharpen conflicts. Harmony may rest on muddled thinking, and conflicts may be brought to light by clarification. In particular, the reluctance to make sacrifices to achieve accepted objectives may be increased. Everybody wants peace, full employment, happiness and prosperity for all. But not everybody is prepared to do what is required to achieve these goals.

Moreover, knowledge of appropriate means gives power. Given divergent values, a clearer view on policies may therefore sharpen conflicts. Programmes backed by knowledge will be more powerful and, for those who do not share them, more dangerous.

Public opinion polls are a simple illustration of how a certain kind of knowledge (namely, of other people's opinions) may either increase or reduce agreement. Knowledge as to how votes are distributed may make some people switch their votes to the majority, and may induce others to back a minority.

To say more about the relation between social knowledge and social harmony would require specific sociological assumptions. Here it must suffice to note that totalitarian philosophies postulate a single rigid programme which must not be subject to modifications. Prognosis will tend to take the form of ideology: it will not show up, but rather will plaster over cracks in the analysis in order to justify the programme.

But this view is not confined to totalitarian philosophies. Programmes that cannot be modified by prognosis are to be found in any utopian system of political theory. The means–ends pattern fits best into these views. According to the liberal doctrine of the ultimate harmony of interests, either in its natural law version or as utilitarianism, conflicts result from ignorance; knowledge must promote harmony.

But closer inspection shows that the harmony aspect of these theories is in fact ideology. They are usually the formulation of the aspirations of a *particular* group (exporters, manufacturers, e.g., advocating free trade) put forward as in the *general* interest. Ideological concepts such as utilities, pleasures, social income, etc., are used in order to postulate a harmony where in fact there is conflict.

In times of crisis or war, even in a political democracy, the situation of a single, generally agreed, programme is approximated, and the means–ends dichotomy becomes a plausible assumption. But in a democratic society, in times of peace and at least moderate prosperity, programmes and the power behind them are conflicting and dispersed; and prognoses and programmes become intricately interconnected in a way which cannot be fitted into the means–end pattern. In a society that values independent research and programmes based on this research, and in which knowledge is widely disseminated, prevailing programmes will be modified in the direction of greater efficiency and consistency, though not necessarily greater harmony. As a result, probable future social trends are altered and prognoses will have to be modified. In the light of this revised knowledge, programmes will again be altered, some tensions will be resolved, others created.

All groups will be aware of the possibility that their programmes may have to be altered by new situations, and that they must be limited by the aspirations of others. Dictatorial programmes may be justly reflected in a means–end pattern. But democratic programmes are piecemeal, empirical, and elastic. The means–end pattern does not fit them.

(d) SPECULATION AND OLIGOPOLY

The strictly economic activities which illustrate this interdependence most clearly are speculation and oligopoly. The programme here is to make profits. The prognosis is the intentions and the behaviour of others (rival speculators, or rival sellers). Every sound speculator and oligopolist takes into account the manner in which the expectations of others (their prognoses) are affected by the intentions of others (their programmes), including his own. A's prognosis, hence A's programme, is a function of B's, C's, D's, etc., prognoses and programmes, B's prognosis and programme are a function of A's, C's, D's, etc., and so on. Any prognosis affects programmes, and any programme affects prognoses. Policies are sensible if certain facts are true; but whether they are true depends on whether people pursue certain policies.[18]

6 THE TASK OF THE SOCIAL SCIENCES

What follows from all this with respect to the task of the social scientist? It does not follow that social science is impossible, or that it must plunge at once into valuations and ideologies. On the contrary. To be useful and truthful, the social scientist, and in particular the economist, should start with actual political attitudes of people, or groups of people, not with their rationalizations and pseudo-theoretical ideologies. He should abandon speculation about 'general welfare', 'maximum satisfactions', etc., for at least two reasons: first, because these concepts have no clear implications and lend themselves easily to implicit interpretations and persuasive definitions; second, because, even if they had clear implications, actual concrete valuations are not concerned with them at all.

Concrete valuations in concrete historical situations, or in possible situations that might arise, and the attitudes which reflect them, should form the starting point of analysis. Political programmes are not good enough. They too contain empty rationalizations such as 'general welfare'; and they are conditioned by the desire to reach 'agreed formulae' and gloss over disagreement. Neither the party programmes in the United States, nor those of the parties in Britain would provide a sufficiently concrete basis for analysis.

On the other hand, the social scientist must not 'go behaviourist' either. The observed behaviour of groups in actual situations is not a sufficient guide to the formulation of concrete political attitudes. It is certainly a partial way of discovering attitudes, but it does not tell the whole story. The relevant attitudes to be discovered must also refer to readiness to act in certain ways in the future, and under different conditions. And since these potential reactions cannot be deduced *logically* from present reactions, an altogether different method suggests itself. It is the task of social or group psychology to attempt to unify group reactions under something which is analogous to character or personality in individual psychology. No anthropomorphism is involved here if it is possible to discover and predict regularities and unity in the reactions of groups to different actual and potential situations. The political attitudes thus mapped out can then yield value premises which are sufficiently concrete to be used for analysis and prognosis.

To map out this unity is obviously not a matter of looking for 'given' welfare functions, sets of ends, etc. It is more like the exercise of artistic imagination and sympathetic understanding than like solving puzzles, though puzzle-solving will have a part to play. The conclusions of Section 4 (d) are thus confirmed: problems of economic policy have a good deal in common with problems of artistic workmanship, as well as with problems of engineering.

Some of the difficulties discussed in the preceding sections would still remain, in particular:

(1) Values are attached to means, and to incidental consequences, as well as to ends.

(2) It may be difficult to separate professed valuations from actual ones.

(3) The transition must be made from valuations derived from false beliefs about reality to valuations derived from correct beliefs.

Thus ideology may creep into the theory of the personality, or the character of groups. Since the unity of group personality is neither one of deductive logic nor one of complete observation, but partly at least one of intuitive understanding, the scope for bias and controversy is enlarged. Yet an inadequate theory based on a correct view of social attitudes seems preferable to a logically perfect theory based on an altogether false view, i.e., the means–end dichotomy.

The growing complexity of social life, and the increasing importance of controlling groups, such as monopolies, public corporations, trade unions, planning bodies of various types, etc., whose activities are replacing the more conventional and automatic adjustments of the past, make it more important to study the valuations that underlie the actions of these bodies. In this analysis account should be taken of the probable reception of new theories and their social repercussions.

Once we have mapped out the valuations of different groups in society, two types of interconnected study can be pursued. First, one might pose the question: what policies are appropriate to these concrete valuations? And second: what social factors determine the formation and the strength of these valuations? It will be necessary to revise continually the results of the enquiry into one of these two questions in the light of the results of the other.

The main thread in Myrdal's thought that links the *Political Element in the Development of Economic Theory* with *Economic Theory and Under-Developed Regions*[19] is the idea that the fundamental presuppositions in which we attempt to understand society must be transformed if, as a result of the changes and new techniques of control, we are to make possible a new epoch of development. He showed in the *Political Element* that our thinking about society is invalidated by relics of old systems of thought (harmony, analysis of stable equilibrium, utility, welfare); he criticized the separation of means from ends as a doctrinal bias of the same origin in the 1933 article;[20] he gradually evolved and used presuppositions and models (in *Monetary Equilibrium, An American Dilemma, An International Economy*) more appropriate to an age in which the policies of integrated nation states have reduced some inequalities but given rise to new internal and international tensions, in which the basic work of industrialization has benefited only a few countries, in which the state and large private institutions have assumed power, and public and quasi-public relations have replaced private relations, in which science has been institutionalized, in which rational questioning of accepted ways has been extended, and in which Western ideals have spread throughout the world; and he is now using these new presuppositions of social thought (cumulative causation, integration of economic and non-economic forces, value premises from concrete aspirations of important groups) to understand the problems and to further the aspirations of our age.

7 IDEOLOGIES

In a previous section (4(f)) I have indicated that analysis and prognosis may be distorted by valuations and programmes. A somewhat fuller treatment of this problem may be forgiven, both because it is central in Myrdal's essays and also because discussion in general in this field is obscured by a reluctance of many writers who insist that valuations somehow seep into social analysis to state clearly (a) where precisely this seepage occurs, and (b) how the Archimedean point[21] can be found from which their own theory is lifted into objectivity.

Without entering into a discussion of these problems themselves, it may be useful to compile, in note form, a short list of some of the ways in which valuations may be thought to affect analysis and to consider the change in Myrdal's thought in the light of this classification. There appear to be roughly four possibilities:

1 Valuations determine the *content*, and thus the *validity*, of the analysis *psychologically*. (Views of this kind were held by Bacon, Nietzsche, Sorel and Pareto.)

(a) The analysis is consciously false; the propositions are lies.
(b) The distortion is semi-conscious : wishful thinking; special pleading.
(c) The distortion is unconscious; the conclusions are rationalizations.

It may, of course, be that one group of men implant what they know to be false notions into the minds of others by manipulative efforts. If the victims are not aware of being manipulated, their beliefs would fall under 1(c), whilst the activity of the manipulators (propaganda, conditioning) falls under 1(a), at least as long as they have not fallen victims to their own devices.

Freudian rationalization is a method of resolving conflicts peculiar to the individual, whereas rationalization here considered serves to resolve social conflicts. Ideology is for society what guilt and self-justification are for an individual. But tensions in the structure of society will tend to manifest themselves in the psychological problems of individuals and the two spheres are not strictly separable.[22]

In all cases, (a), (b) and (c) only *false* statements are contaminated. Ideology is defined as 'false consciousness'. Valuations may provide a motive for finding a *logical* (as well as an illogical) basis for a desired conclusion, but the analysis is not then distorted. There is a sphere of objective thought.

The Archimedean point is given by exposing the motives. (There is, however, a danger that this effort itself is contaminated by unexpressed valuations.)

2 Valuations determine the *content* and thus the *validity* of analysis by affecting the structure (categories, presuppositions, premises, etc.) of thought. (Hegel's and Marx's theories are not psychological but epistemological in this sense.) Contamination is not a matter of individual or even social psychology, but everyone in a given situation who thinks at all has to think in a certain value-determined way. Probing of motives cannot eliminate implicit valuations, for they are an essential condition of all thought.

Nowadays, a similar point is made by stressing the manner in which language influences the way we see, select, and analyse events, and thus opens the door to bias. First, it enters not only—as is generally recognized—into the selection and criticism of evidence, but also into our classifications and frames of reference. Particularly in social studies do we take our vocabulary from the field of study itself.[23] Thus the valuations of the market place and of the political arena are carried unobtrusively into scientific analysis.

Second, language introduces a bias by adopting identical terms for situations that are similar in some respects, dissimilar in others. To use the same concept, or model, or metaphor to refer to different situations is a source of both danger and opportunity: danger, because the reference may distort or misrepresent the facts; opportunity, because it may enlarge our vision by drawing attention to hitherto unnoticed features.

Third, there is the danger of seeing real essences behind terms of mere classification.[24]

In whatever manner we analyse the seepage of valuations into analysis, it follows that not only false but all statements under this second heading are 'ideological' and hence logically suspect, unless areas are cleared which are claimed to be exempt from bias. Thus some writers say that

(a) only at certain historical *periods* (e.g. in a class society), others that
(b) only certain *fields of study* (e.g. social studies), others that
(c) only certain *classes* (e.g. the bourgeoisie) are subject to contamination, have 'false consciousness'[25].

But the corollary that only certain periods, fields of study, classes, or men are free from bias, can, of course, itself be a fruitful source of ideology. Combining (a), (b) and (c), we arrive at the Marxist view that there is a proletarian social science in the late stages of capitalism to which truth is guaranteed. Particularly Georg Lukács has argued that only proletarian class-conscious thought represents reality 'adequately'. Mannheim (in his earlier work) believed that only the 'socially unattached' (i.e. radical) intellectuals can seek the required 'dynamic synthesis', a 'total perspective', that overcomes the inadequate, partial and biased conceptions of other groups. Hegel thought that reason revealed itself to philosophers (particularly Hegelian philosophers) at a certain stage of history. Nearer home, Marshall, Pigou and others in the tradition of Benthamism imply that in the midst of interest conflicts only the state is an agency that can see and promote disinterestedly the public good.

On the other hand, some authors argue that it is not only valuations, but other extraneous spheres that determine thought, e.g., social or economic *conditions* (as contrasted with *interests, aspirations, valuations*), natural environment, nationality, race, generation. This determination may be conceived as either causal, or as an expression of some kind of unity.

The Archimedean point cannot be reached empirically, nor logically, but only metaphysically. The 'intellectuals', 'the working class', or 'action', 'commitment', 'a synthesis' or 'an absolute sphere of values', guarantee objectivity. Or, using the linguistic approach, only a 'perfect language' that exactly fits the facts, could enable us to pull ourselves up by our own shoestrings. The attempt to save the theory from self-contradiction succeeds only through an arbitrary step into metaphysics. The choice lies between dogmatism and absurdity.

3 Valuations have merely *selective* significance. They do not affect the content or validity of thought, but its direction.

(a) They may be *positively selective*: valuations determine *that* a proposition is made then and there. The questions asked are value-determined, but not the answers. The relation between values and theories is not causal, but like the kind of determination by which a question 'determines' an answer.

(b) They may be *negatively selective*, preventing certain propositions from being made in certain situations. (Max Scheler suggested this, although his views are not consistent.)

Thus the Ricardian theory of distribution, the Malthusian theory of population, the Marxist theory of the increasing misery of the masses, the Keynesian theory of employment, and the various theories of secular stagnation, secular inflation, and secular dollar shortage, may all be projections on to a vast historical screen of the snapshots of a few years or decades and the magnified protests to which these short-run experiences gave rise.

An Archimedean point is not here required, for validity is independent of valuations. The distinction, however, between type 3 and type 2 ideology is blurred when we remember that an inadequate, partial conception of reality may lead to bias not by commission but by omission. The Archimedean point would consist in scaling down the claims of the theory to less generality; but it then often loses all interest.

4 Valuations determine whether certain propositions are understood, recognized, publicly accepted.[26] Again, no Archimedean point is required.

According to which of these views is held, the role of criticism is (1) to show up the more or less sinister motives in the false explanations of the opponents, or to psychoanalyse their theories; (2) to analyse the structure of their throught; (3) to fill in gaps in the selection; or (4) to relate ideas to their social setting. It is also obvious that these four views have radically different implications for the question as to what extent unexpressed value premises invalidate social theories. Yet, eminent exponents of these theories of ideology have shifted uneasily between self-destructive and fairly obvious positions. To say that the tests of logic change with one's values is open to the old objection to scepticism: if the theory is untrue, no more is to be said; if true, its own objectivity must be denied. On the other hand, to say that we meet with obstacles in our attempts to be impartial in thinking about political matters serves as a useful reminder that scientists, too, are human. But the ambiguity between these two views lends apparent force to many theories.

Unlike many methodologists who are quite naive about their own theory, Myrdal gradually develops a kind of methodology of methodology—a critical theory that criticizes itself. Myrdal started with a largely psychological approach. In the *Political Element* there is the suggestion (recanted in the 1953 Preface) that if economic theory were stripped of its implicit valuations, a corpus of hard facts and relations would remain that could then be successfully harnessed to any set of valuations explicitly introduced from sociological and psychological research.

In his later writings the epistemological approach gains ground, until, in the *Crux of All Science* the structural interdependence of valuations and facts is presented as a necessary condition of *all*—sound and unsound—theory and research, of both logical and illogical conclusions. His view seems to shift towards the selective role of value judgements—category 3(a) and resembles Schumpeter's. According to Schumpeter, scientific procedure

> starts from the perception of a set of related phenomena which we wish to analyse and ends up—for the time being—with a scientific model in which these phenomena are conceptualized and the relations between them explicitly formulated, either as assumptions or as propositions (theorems) . . . that perception of a set of related phenomena is a pre-scientific act. It must be performed in order to give to our minds something to do scientific work on—to indicate an object of research—but it is not scientific in itself. But though pre-scientific, it is not pre-analytic. It does not simply consist in perceiving facts by one or two of our senses. These facts must be recognized as having some meaning or relevance that justifies our interest in them and they must be recognized as related—so that we might separate them from others—which involves some analytic work by our fancy or common sense. This mixture of perceptions and pre-scientific analysis we shall call the research worker's Vision or Intuition.[27]

Like Myrdal, Schumpeter stressed the 'endless give and take' between theory and facts.

> This work [of model-building] consists in picking out certain facts rather than others, in pinning them down by labelling them, in accumulating further facts in order not only to supplement but in part also to replace those originally fastened upon, in formulating and improving the relations perceived—briefly in 'factual' and 'theoretical' research that go on in an endless chain of give and take, the facts suggesting new analytic instruments (theories) and these in turn carrying us towards the recognition of new facts.[28]

On Schumpeter's view, as on Myrdal's, the source of ideological bias is the initial vision of the phenomena we propose to treat scientifically.

But for Schumpeter the vision is, on the one hand, either corrected or ignored by sound analysis (as in Adam Smith), or, on the other, it dominates and sterilizes analysis (as in Marx). For Myrdal the vision plays a more constructive part. It is not merely the starter (as for Schumpeter) but the driving power of the analytical engine.

Myrdal never identifies valuations simply with the interests, ambitions or aspirations of a group. He is too subtle a psychologist for that. The valuations that he claims should form the bases of social theories are more like the complex of attitudes that unify a personality or a style. The beliefs, moral principles, sympathies, preferences, ideals and actions that characterize a group cannot be deduced logically from a set of abstract premises, nor are they the mechanical product of certain interests. And they are never 'given' once and for all, but change under the strains and stresses to which their relations to each other and to experience give rise. Although many prognoses are formulated to justify programmes, the relation between them is not static but one of cumulative interaction.

An attempt to explore the values underlying Myrdal's own persistent demands for the discussion of the role of values would show an increasing emancipation from liberal pre-suppositions in his own criticism of liberalism.

The strict separation of *ought* from *is*, which dominates modern liberal economic theory (and, in different versions, modern philosophy) is not, as it claims to be, morally neutral, nor simply a discovery of philosophical analysis. For no observation or logical analysis can *discover* that we *ought to* separate values from facts, or ends from means. No amount of description or deduction can show that we can fully analyse actual political and moral choices without introducing values into our analysis. Since most people act on the belief that only when objective criteria for choice hold is choice worthy of serious attention, the denial of any objective basis, if accepted widely, will radically influence people's choices.

The philosophy which denies the logical connection between facts and values and deduces from this denial its own moral neutrality (suppressing a series of necessary unwarranted premises) suits admirably a liberal philosophy of tolerance, in which different political views have an equal right to exist, though it is not explicit whence it derives this claim. (The liberalism may have radical connotations as in utilitarianism and logical positivism, or a conservative slant as in the philosophy of linguistic analysis.)

In his article on ends and means[29] Myrdal abandons the belief in the possibility or desirability of a strict separation of ends from means, which still underlay the criticism in the *Political Element*. Myrdal shows not merely the impossibility of this separation but also its ideological function.[30]

Once the dichotomy between values and facts is rejected, all kinds of questions about Myrdal's own method arise.

1 Since the choice of value premises in social analysis is itself a moral and political decision, why are we told to confine ourselves to those of actual and powerful groups as psychology and sociology formulate them? To admit *any* premises as equally valid would be to fall victim to relativist liberalism—itself a political theory. But to admit those only that are 'practicable', 'significant', 'relevant', 'real', etc., may lead into another trap. True, having shown the fallacies in the claims for a strict separation of facts from values, Myrdal has opened the door to a new connection between them. But has the criticism of the 'naturalistic fallacy' in utilitarianism only led to its substitution by pragmatism? The reasons that Myrdal gives for his selection of value premises—'the rule of economy', 'relevance', 'significance'—may not convince those who choose their premises on different principles.

2 Is it necessary that the analysis of stable equilibria must lead to laissez-faire conclusions, whilst the analysis of cumulative causation leads to policies that are both anti-laissez-faire and against 'one-factor-theories'? 'Equilibrium is just equlibrium', and to remove *bad* stable equilibrium overwhelming government action may be thought desirable. On the other hand, the spiral, if virtuous, may make government action unnecessary; and if government action is directed at one strategic factor, the inter-action of others may make one-cause remedies suitable.

3 Whence the characteristic blend of optimism and pessimism that pervades Myrdal's writings and that once led him to describe himself as a cheerful pessimist?

Starting with a vision of a world of free and equal men, he warns us against confusing hopes and prospects. He is pessimistic with respect to the latter and untiringly cheerful in attempting to make true the former. Is his pessimism educational, a caution against disappointments and despair, and a call for courage in the face of failure? Is his optimism a reminder that the unexpected may happen, that cheerful programmes may alter the gloomiest prognoses, a conclusion from the doctrine of the vicious circle turned virtuous, or a moral protest against fatalistic determinism? Myrdal combines the ideals that were common to nineteenth-century liberalism and socialism with an opposition to their doctrine of 'inevitable progress' as much as to the more modern doctrine of 'inevitable decline'. He unites emphasis on the need for the scientific analysis of society and on the presence and positive function of value clashes that is reminiscent of Marx, with a faith in a better society whose shape the imagination of free men can design, that recalls the Utopian Socialists.

8 SUMMARY

Analysis and prognosis cannot be neutral, in the sense that they belong to a sphere of actual and possible causal relations which can be permanently separated from valuations and the programmes which they inspire.

1 Analysis and prognosis pre-suppose programmes in the sense of interests which determine selection and appraisal of evidence. To ignore this side of the picture is analogous to adhering to naive empiricism in the theory of knowledge.

2 The relation between analysis and policy, and that between prognosis and programme, cannot always be adequately analysed in terms of means and ends. The application of analysis to policy is a matter of skill, not one of subsumption under given canons.

3 Modern welfare economics, in both its Paretian and Bergsonian versions, misapplies the means–ends model to social situations. It thus mistakenly holds that 'optima' must be sought where 'improvements' are appropriate and logically sufficient, and that valuations must be 'given' from outside, although in fact they may result from empirical appraisals.

4 Analysis and prognosis may harbour ideologies. They may be formulated in a manner that does not bring out the facts, but that rather attempts to reconcile conflicts in beliefs and valuations. Awareness of his own valuations, and of the limitations of his conclusions, are among the theorist's safeguards against falling into the ideological trap.

5 Although analysis and prognosis must take the actual or possible beliefs and valuations of people as data, by analysing them and bringing them into the open, they tend to change them. A fuller analysis and prognosis will take cognizance of these changes, but the interconnection is a continuous process. Prognosis must therefore be subject to continuous revision.

6 Social scientists should attempt to base their prognoses on concrete actual or potential valuations of groups in concrete situations. An understanding of the unity of complex attitudes is the task of social psychology or sociology.

7 As a result of social change, the presuppositions in terms of which we attempt to understand it, must be transformed if, by the achievement of new techniques of control, we are to make possible a new epoch of development. For the new programmes of our times, new theoretical prognoses are needed.

NOTES

1. This chapter, reprinted from "Introduction to Gunnar Myrdal", *Value in Social Theory*, ed. Paul Streeten, Routledge & Kegan Paul, London (1958) is a revised and expanded version of an article that appeared in the *Quarterly Journal of Economics*, vol. 68 (August 1954).
2. *The Confidential Clerk*, 1954, by T. S. Eliot. Reprinted by permission of Harcourt, Brace & Co., Inc.
3. For references see Gunnar Myrdal, *The Political Element in the Development of Economic Theory*, Routledge & Kegan Paul, London (1953), pp. 3f.
4. See, e.g., J. N. Keynes, *Scope and Method of Political Economy*, p.39. 'The problem whether political economy is to be regarded as a positive science, or as a normative science, or as an art, or as a combination of these, is to a certain extent a question merely of nomenclature and classification.' See also *Political Element*, pp. 8 and 219.
5. Hume's complaint was that:
   in every system of morality which I have hitherto met with, I have always remarked, that the author proceeds for some time in the ordinary way of reasoning, and establishes the being of a God, or makes some observations concerning human affairs; when of a sudden I am surprised to find that instead of the usual copulations of propositions, *is*, and *is not*, I meet with no proposition that is not connected with an *ought*, or an *ought not*. This change is imperceptible; but is, however, of the last consequence. For as this *ought*, or *ought not*, expresses some new relation or affirmation, it is necessary that it should be observed and explained; and at the same time, that a reason should be given, for what seems altogether inconceivable, how this new relation can be a deduction from others, which are entirely different from it.
   A Treatise of Human Nature, Book III, Part I, end of Section II.
6. Chapter 7 in *Value in Social Theory*.
7. A. Bergson (Burk), 'A Reformulation of Certain Aspects of Welfare Economics', *Quarterly Journal of Economics*, vol. 52 (February 1938), pp. 310–34; P. A. Samuelson, *Foundations of Economic Analysis*, Ch. 8; K. J. Arrow, *Social Choice and Individual Values*; A. Bergson, 'On the Concept of Social Welfare', *Quarterly Journal of Economics* (May 1954).
8. But the convictions may also colour their view of the 'facts'. See below.
9. Max Weber, *Gesammelte Aufsätze zur Soziologie und Sozialpolitik*, p. 416; *Political Element*, pp. 202–3.
10. These differences are, however, sometimes exaggerated. In astronomy, experiments are not possible; meteorology deals with complicated forces; and the

objections to controlled human experiments are partly moral, and not in the nature of society.

11. R. B. Braithwaite, 'Moral Principles and Inductive Policies', *Proceedings of the British Academy*, vol. 36 (1950), pp. 65f.

12. See T. D. Weldon, *The Vocabulary of Politics*, Penguin, Harmondsworth (1953), esp. Ch. 3, Section 7 and Ch. 5.

13. T. Ferguson and J. Cunnison, *The Young Wage-Earner: A Study of Glasgow Boys*, Oxford University Press (1951).

14. See Myrdal: "The Trend towards Economic Planning", *Manchester School* (January 1951).

15. Socially sophisticated countries like England, where people know that institutions can be eroded, often refuse to allow rational considerations to erode them.

16. For a recent expression of this view see Milton Friedman, in *A Survey of Contemporary Economics*, vol. 2, p. 456: 'I venture the judgement that currently in the Western world, and especially in the United States, differences about economic policy among disinterested citizens derive predominantly from different predictions about the consequences of taking action, differences that can in principle be eliminated by the progress of positive economics—rather than from fundamental differences in basic values, differences about which men can ultimately only fight.'

17. This, of course, is the classical argument for the greatest happiness principle, for free trade, etc. In commenting on his terms of trade argument for the imposition of a tariff, Edgeworth quoted with approval a remark by J. S. Nicholson that some demonstrations are 'part of the casuistry of economics, like the discussions of moral philosophers concerning the occasional justification of mendacity. Free trade, like honesty, is still the best policy.' R. W. Stevens, 'New Ideas in International Trade Theory', *American Economic Review* (June 1951), p. 375, note.

18. The common sense view that people's reactions to prognoses (that are made public) may, but do not necessarily, falsify all such prognoses, and that social scientists therefore may hope to predict, at least sometimes, and perhaps normally, both in public and correctly (although these predictions may be different from private ones because they have to take their own effects on people's actions into account) has been proved rigorously and elegantly by Emile Grunberg and Franco Modigliani in 'Predictability of Social Events', *Journal of Political Economy* (December 1954).

19. Duckworth, London (1957).

20. Chapter 10 in *Value in Social Theory*.

21. The expression is E. Grünwald's. Cf. *Das Problem der Soziologie des Wissens*, Wien-Leipzig (1934), p. 206.

22. Thus guilt can be a symptom of personal conflicts which, however, may reflect social forces. The connection between Protestantism and the rise of capitalism has been discussed by Weber and Tawney. Guilt over enjoyment may be connected with capital accumulation by men who valued thrift, hard work, and self-denial. The secularized guilt feelings of many modern Americans at not getting the most out of life may be similarly connected with a later stage of capitalism at which the problems of excess capacity and surplus production have replaced that of capital accumulation.

23. Cf. the perceptive reflections of Marc Bloch, *The Historian's Craft*, Manchester University Press (1954).
24. In so far as only the *emotive* use of words is stressed, the linguistic analysis should be classified under 1. Valuations enter at the psychological level and could be eliminated by a purged language.
25. The expression occurs in one of Engels's letters to Mehring. Cf. Franz Mehring, *Geschichte der deutschen Sozialdemokratie*, vol. 1 (1921), p. 386.
26. E.g., it could be argued that the appeal of Keynes's theory to the public resulted from protests against the Depression.
27. 'Science and Ideology', *The American Economic Review* (March 1949), p. 350.
28. *Ibid.*
29. Chapter 10 in *Value in Social Theory*.
30. In the *Political Element* Myrdal showed how the philosophy of natural law harboured a contradiction and a compromise between a radical and a conservative strand. In a different connection, Ernst Troeltsch suggested that the Christian idea of natural law fulfilled a similar function for the thought of the Church, enabling it to come to terms with non-Christian social facts and ideals. (Cf. *Aufsätze zur Geistesgeschichte und Religionssoziologie*, vol. 4, Tübingen (1925), pp. 156–180.) Similarly, the "naturalistic" relic in the modern, post-Humean, juxtaposition of ends and means serves to reconcile the rigorous demands of scientific neutrality with the ethics of liberalism. Can political thought ever be purged of all "naturalism"?

2 Values, Facts and the Compensation Principle[1]

CRITICISMS OF THE COMPENSATION PRINCIPLE

The so-called New Welfare Economics sprang from the desire to allow the economist to make policy recommendations without committing him to interpersonal comparisons of satisfactions. It attempted to do this by announcing an unambiguous criterion for an increase in social income or an improvement in welfare, which was believed to be free of the taint of interpersonal comparisons.

Since interpersonal comparisons of satisfactions were generally believed to involve value judgements, these doctrines can also be described as attempts to purge normative economics of value judgements. It has been said that the New Welfare Economics tried to elevate a set of *necessary* conditions for an optimum (from the point of view of a value system in which people's preferences are respected) into a *wertfrei* system of economics.[2] I shall examine whether these attempts were successful.

I should begin by saying that I do not believe that interpersonal comparisons of utility, satisfaction or happiness are, or logically involve, value judgements. People can agree on an ideal distribution but disagree on the facts, and *vice versa*. But since economists have normally not confined themselves to comparing, but have also recommended, value judgements arising from factual comparisons appear to be involved. The question therefore is: Can we make economic recommendations without making value judgements about distribution?

The Kaldor–Hicks criterion for an increase in social income ("economic welfare", "social welfare" or "welfare" have been used synonymously by the authors) states that social income has risen, even though some members are worse off than they were before, if those members who are better off could compensate the losers and still remain better off. This criterion has been criticized on the following grounds:

(1) Contradictions may arise when an attempt is made to arrange

35

economic situations in an order of preference. (T. Scitovsky and, more generally, K. J. Arrow and P. A. Samuelson)

(2) The criterion is not a *necessary* condition for an *improvement*.[3] It would define, were it not for criticism (3), improvements only relatively to the initial income distribution. Measures which harm some people may still be improvements, even though the gainers could not overcompensate the losers (e.g., progressive taxation, Marshall Aid).

(3) The criterion is not a *sufficient* condition, for the compensation which *might* be paid does not determine the welfare which *does* exist. Potentially better situations may be actually worse. (Baumol, Samuelson, Reder, Little, Robertson, and others.)

Some of these criticisms were, of course, seen, admitted and, indeed, stressed by the proponents of the compensation principle. Criticism (1), brought to light by Professor Scitovsky, was met by his own suggestion that only if both the Kaldor–Hicks condition (that the gainers could overcompensate the losers) and his own condition (that the losers could not overcompensate the gainers) are fulfilled should we speak of an unequivocal improvement.

No defence against criticism (2) is required, for nobody claimed that policies which did not conform to the principle could never lead to improvements, though some would deny them the title "economic" improvements.

DEFENCE OF THE COMPENSATION PRINCIPLE

Three arguments were (or could be) advanced in defence of the principle against criticism (3). They are the following:

(a) It is true that in particular cases the result of following the principle might be a worse state. But if the principle were accepted as a general guide consistently and over a sufficiently long period of time, everybody would most probably gain and hardly anybody would lose.

(b) It is true that potential overcompensation does not guarantee an actual improvement. Let us therefore require not potential but actual compensation of all losers. The principle would then be a sufficient (though, of course, not a necessary) condition for an improvement on some widely accepted value premises. A situation in which everybody is in fact either equally well or better off is surely an improvement.

(c) The principle does not claim to be a categorical command. Let politicians, governments, public opinion, reformers, or the common man decide on how to correct faulty, or restore desirable distribution. The principle merely brings out the "economic" *aspect* of changes in which other aspects play an important part. But these are not the economist's business.

JUSTIFICATION IN THE LONG RUN

Defences (a) and (c) are, of course, of ancient and respectable lineage (just as the attempt to distinguish between production or efficiency and distribution or justice, and to confine economic recommendations to the former sphere dates back at least to J. S. Mill). Arguments of the type (a) were used by the free traders. They freely admitted that there are cases in which theoretical analysis could show that free trade is not the best policy; but by and large, if it were accepted as a general principle, the results would be better than if we took any other course. We find a similar argument used by Edgeworth in favour of the greatest happiness principle.

> Moreover, each party may reflect that, in the long run of various cases, the maximum sum-total utility corresponds to the maximum individual utility. He cannot expect in the long run to obtain the larger share of the total welfare. But of all principles of distribution which would afford him now a greater, now a smaller proportion of the sum-total utility obtainable on each occasion, the principle that the collective utility should be on each occasion a maximum is most likely to afford the greatest utility in the long run to him individually.[4]

Professor Hicks, following the classical tradition, argued that "there would be a strong probability that almost all [inhabitants] would be better off after the lapse of a sufficient length of time if "the economic activities of a community were organized on the principle of making no alterations in the organization of production which were not improvements in this sense (i.e., potential overcompensation), and making all alterations which were improvements . . . "[5]. Against the classical argument Mr Little has pointed out that there is no reason to believe that the effects on distributions will be random, and Dr Myrdal that they are often likely to obey the principle "to those who have shall be given, and from those who have not shall be taken away." But if the effects are not random, and, worse still, if they are cumulative, we cannot assume that everyone will be better off after a sufficient length of time.[6] Second, this defence entails those interpersonal comparisons which the criterion is intended to eliminate. For if the time is long the individuals in the community will have changed and we would have to compare the welfare of individuals of different generations. Even if we look at one and the same generation inter-temporal comparisons for the same individual give rise to similar difficulties as interpersonal comparisons. Furthermore, to say that most people will have gained after a time and that the losses of those who have not will be negligible, involves both interpersonal comparisons and a value judgement. If it is meaningless to compare gains and losses, the smallest loss of even one individual would invalidate the recommendation. If, on the other hand, such comparisons are meaningful, other comparisons, involving more people and larger losses, are meaningful too, though agreement may be rarer. But in that case the *raison d'être* of the compensation principle disappears.

ACTUAL COMPENSATION

The criticism of defence (a) suggests defence (b). Changes in which some people gain and no one loses must surely be improvements.[7]

In spite of its plausibility this defence is not valid. In the first place, actual compensation is impracticable. We do not know enough about individuals' preferences. Even if we knew everything it would be administratively impossible. Not only would it be costly but it would cause further changes which would lead to some losses which again would have to be compensated for, etc. But even if we could ignore these objections, there are difficulties of applying the rule of *actual* compensation which lie deeper. Professor Scitovsky has argued that such a requirement would betray "a conservative bias", i.e., a bias in favour of the *status quo* distribution.[8] This does not seem to be true on the face of it, if the condition is claimed to be sufficient but not necessary. For it is not denied that many improvements may be brought about without actual compensation. It is merely asserted that if there is actual compensation, so that no one is worse off and some are better off, that in itself is an improvement, though perhaps not the best improvement.[9]

Yet, it is true that although it is a sufficient condition for an improvement, the criterion does betray a conservative bias if it were to be used as a basis for recommendations. Its bias is conservative because the basis of comparison is the *status quo*. A policy guided by the criterion may involve changes of a kind which would preclude other changes which would have been more desirable on distributional grounds. In other words, an improvement of a (distributionally) bad situation, such that every individual is made better off, may bar other improvements (both in income distribution and productive factor allocation) which would have been possible had it not been for the initial improvement and which would have been better still.

This can best be illustrated with the aid of utility–possibility curves.[10] The formal device of a utility–possibility locus has been used in order to separate analytically distribution from potential real income. A utility–possibility locus is defined as the locus of all combinations of the utilities of several individuals, which could be reached if the optimum conditions of production and exchange were fulfilled. In the simple case of two individuals, A and B, the locus is a curve (U curve) which is usually assumed to slope downwards to the right, as in Fig. 2.1.[11] A shift of the curve from UU to U_1U_1 makes it possible for both individuals A and B to be better off, and yet the shift may be undesirable. At point T both *are actually* better off than at S. But if we consider R to be better than T on *distributional grounds*, the shift to T *may* be undesirable because R can no longer be reached on U_1U_1. It definitely *is* undesirable if R is, on balance, better than T, i.e. if other considerations do not more than offset the distributional merits of R.

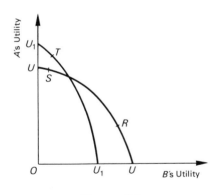

FIGURE 2.1

In order to arrive at a proper judgement we should not compare a new situation with the situation before the change only. If we wanted to refrain from interpersonal comparisons and were content to formulate conditions of potential improvements, we might compare the totality of *all* possible situations which could be reached without the change, with the totality of *all* possible situations which could be reached with the change.[12] But such a comparison would not tell us anything about which situations are *actually* better. It would yield information only about *potential* improvements. Before we could say anything definite about desirable policies we would have to make value judgements on distribution. And unless the *status quo* distribution is ideal the basis for comparison must be a different income distribution.

DIVISION OF LABOUR

It is possible to defend the compensation principle on other grounds than either (a) confidence in probable long-run *actual* compensation of all losers if all "improvements" allowing *hypothetical* compensation were carried out; or (b) the requirement of actual compensation of all losers every time. One could argue that whenever economists recommend changes that make compensation possible, it is up to other people to decide on what distributional corrections are indicated. There should be a division of labour between economists and those others, the former recommending improvements in "efficiency" and the latter correcting inequity and injustice which arise from the economists' recommendations.

The division of labour may take either of two forms. We may say that the recommendations of the economists stand without qualifications if we can be certain that those concerned with correcting the distribution have the will and the power always to act appropriately. This may be called the *institutional defence*. Or we may say that the "recommendations" of economists are concerned only with one aspect of complex problems and that the acceptance of those recommendations depends upon judgements of all relevant aspects, giving each its due weight. Only after those competent to judge distributional and other value aspects have made their contribution can the qualified "economic" recommendations become full-blooded recommendations. This may be called the "*economic aspect*" defence.

It seems that the new welfare economists may have meant to say something like what is implied by either of these two defences. Professor Sir Dennis Robertson pleads that they may have known all the time that they were discussing *potential* rather than *actual* increases of economic welfare.[13] Their recommendations were meant to be conditional upon the sanction of those able to correct, or fit to judge, distribution.

The institutional defence Professor Scitovsky ascribes to Kaldor, and he himself subscribes to it. If institutional arrangements can be relied on to prevent bad distributional effects, economists as "scientists" need not pronounce on the correct income distribution.

Those who rely on this argument are free to admit that "efficiency" and "justice" are not two separate things, that the question-begging analogy of the cake (production) and the slices (distribution) is misleading, and that "economic welfare" or "social income" embraces both. But they can still insist that economists can neglect one aspect of an indivisible whole as long as somebody else looks after it.

The institutional defence of the compensation principle has, however, its own difficulties. In the first place, to delegate authority for equitable arrangements to politicians implies itself a value judgement: the judgement that their will should be done. Scitovsky believes that socialist economies, and Britain under the Labour government in particular, are probably instances in which Parliament can be relied on to maintain equity and promote justice by correcting distributional evils brought about by the market mechanism.[14] But there are many people (including economists), both inside and outside Britain, who would dispute this statement. Some believe that distributional corrections are inequitable, others that legislation is not truly guided by the principle of equity but is, at best, stupid, at worst the tool of self-seeking pressure groups. The economist who is asked to replace a judgement about correct distribution by a judgement about the proper institutional arrangements to bring about correct distribution is not on safer, more neutral or more scientific ground. Even an ideal socialist government would act against the convictions of those whose ideal is not the socialist principle of distribution. The belief that such satisfactory institutions are possible is just a more sophisticated faith in the fallacious doctrine of the harmony of interests.

THE "ECONOMIC ASPECT"

These objections do not hold against the "economic aspect" version. There is indeed an apparent difficulty. If we could agree upon a body of men who are "experts" on distributional justice (the "experts" may be common men) economists could enter upon a symbiosis with them. A recommendation should be carried out only if both economists (judging the efficiency *aspect*) and distributional "experts" (judging the *aspect* of justice) have ratified it. The difficulty is that agreement on such a body of men is not easier to reach than agreement on the distributional maxims themselves. But this is no fatal obstacle. The recommendation is explicitly qualified by a value judgement about desirable distribution and anyone is free to reject it. The economist could leave the matter to be decided by his readers as long as he makes it quite clear that he is recommending only subject to their value judgements about distribution. Or interest groups, irreconcilably divided on questions of distribution, could consult economists about the "economic aspects" of their programmes. Trade unions, employers, and consumers whose interests in distribution diverge, may seek advice from economists as to how their real income would change if, say, the general level of prices fell, without committing these economists to desiring any of these results.

Somebody might object at this point that precisely the same difficulty arises when we try to compare distributional "aspects" of "different real income situations", as when we try to separate distribution from efficiency. Surely it is meaningless to speak of "the same" distribution of a larger or smaller social income if the amount and composition of goods (or of factors) has changed.

The utility possibility locus enables us to separate analytically these two aspects. If the whole U curve is shifted outwards (from UU to U_1U_1 in Fig. 2.2) it is *possible* to make both A and B better off, no matter what distribution of utility between A and B we deem right. But, without committing ourselves to distributional value judgements,[15] we cannot recommend a measure which would thus shift the curve. For the *actual* movement might be from a point on UU with a better distribution to one on U_1U_1 with a worse distribution.

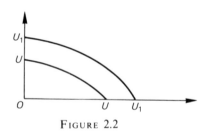

FIGURE 2.2

In the realm of pure abstraction it would, however, seem possible to connect all points which are deemed to be equally good on distributional grounds by series of lines (or possibly areas). These lines could be ordered according to some value standard about distribution. Let us call these lines D and let D_1 represent the best distribution, D_2 the second best, etc. These "equally-good-distribution lines" (isodiks) are drawn in Fig. 2.3 on an egalitarian value standard, but others could be adopted. These D lines, like the U curves, do not imply that the same indices are used for the utilities of different individuals. Since these utilities are assumed to be incomparable, no index can be reduced to any other. Nevertheless, any point on one index

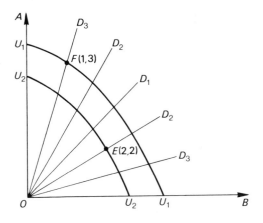

FIGURE 2.3

together with some other point on the other index can be judged to be as just (i.e. good on distributional grounds) as some other pair of points on the two indices.[16]

We are now in a position to make recommendations about some types of change, but not all. Clearly, a movement to a point on the same or on a higher D line and on a higher U curve is desirable.[17] But what are we to say about moves to points on lower D lines, though on higher U curves, or to points on higher D lines but lower U curves?

The answer of those using the "economic aspect defence" would be this: although we cannot make recommendations, our analysis may help others to arrive at decisions. We are, as it were, laying bare the aspects of a situation which are relevant for decision-taking. Although we cannot make up the mind of the individual (or policy-maker) who has to make the choice, we can help him to think clearly about what is involved in his decision. Although we cannot tell him which of two situations is better, we can throw some light on certain features which will help him to make his choice. Obviously potentialities are relevant to policy.

In a sense this very formal approach enables us to separate the distributional aspect from the "potential real income" or "potential utility" aspect. A movement from E to F in Fig. 2.3 would be bad (unjust) on distributional grounds. But somebody might judge that the gain in A's utility is worth the loss of justice. An indifference map between utility and justice may be said to reflect these preferences.

One of the merits of this analysis is that it removes the ambiguities, implicit in the compensation principle, of the notion of "equally good distribution", when real income has increased, but nothing is known about the valuation of the distribution of the *increment*. If the (sufficient) condition for an improvement were that no one should be worse off and some should be better off, we might get a situation as illustrated in Fig. 2.4. At *F* individual *B* is considerably better off, whereas *A* is not harmed. But distribution at *F* is clearly not equally good as at *E*, as those imply who believe that the sufficient condition (that nobody should be harmed) eschews distributional value judgements. If we believe in equality (in some sense), or in the right of *A* to get a fair share of any *gain* we shall deplore the movement from *E* to *F* on distributional grounds. This is brought out by the fact that *F* lies on D_3 which is worse than D_2, the *D* line on which *E* lies. The *D* lines enable us to pay attention not merely to the distribution in situation *E* and to the condition that neither individual should be harmed absolutely, but also to the valuation of the distribution of the *increment* in utility. Many increases in real income and utility might be considered bad, *although nobody is harmed* absolutely, because they increase inequality, or because they accrue largely to the undeserving.

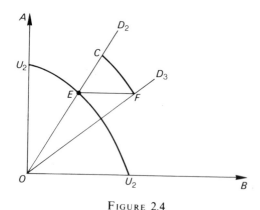

FIGURE 2.4

We have seen that this analysis, although it brings out certain features of different situations, does not tell us their relative merits.[18] Thus it does not reveal how we should rank situations *E*, *F* and *C* in Fig. 2.5. On distributional grounds *C* is better than *F* and *F* better than *E*. But we do not know whether the gain in utility to individual *B* at *F* is worth the loss in distributional justice, or whether a movement to *E* might not be desirable, in spite of its distributional drawbacks. Distributional objectives compete with others and, unless they are made the overriding consideration, some undesirable distributional effects are usually considered to be a sacrifice worth paying for "real income gains".[19] Thus many people who would,

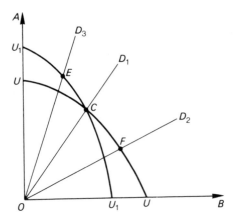

FIGURE 2.5

ceteris paribus, prefer an equal income distribution, condone some inequality because they fear that equal distribution would reduce incentives and hence available resources too much.

This defence of the compensation principle depends upon a formidable list of unrealistic assumptions.[20] But even if those assumptions were granted, there is a flaw in it. It is *illegitimate* to assume that the *D* and the *U* curves are independent of each other. Distributional value judgements depend on the amount available for distribution, and satisfactions derived from a collection of goods depend on the desires generated by a particular distribution. Thus equality may be considered imperative in siege conditions, or in a lifeboat, but may be a matter of indifference or even undesirable if there is abundance.[21] Many believe that some inequality in distribution adds to the variety and colour of life but should only be fostered when there is more than a minimum. Such perfectly sensible value judgements would lead to intersecting *D* curves.

Moreover, judgements about distribution are not independent of the path by which a situation is reached. This is another reason for the interdependence of *U* and *D* curves. The very fact that people have enjoyed certain things in the past and have built expectations on this enjoyment, or that they have acquired them by legitimate methods, even though it may be judged to be wrong on distributional grounds, renders the situation different from one in which they never enjoyed, or were not entitled to, these things. The trouble is that distributional ranking, even more than utility ranking, largely depends upon what *others* enjoy and what anyone has come to expect as his due in the *past*.

Not only the *D* curves depend upon *U* curves, but also *vice versa*. Many enjoyments above the minimum subsistence requirements depend on the social structure of a society. Distribution may, in many cases, be taken as an index of this structure. The U curves which spring from an equal distribution are quite different from those generated by an unequal one. It is impossible to rank situations merely according to their "utility" or "economic" aspect apart from the "distributional" aspects. The attempt to isolate aspects of "utility", "satisfaction", "welfare","happiness", etc., from the social setting which determines them may be for some purposes heuristically useful, but as a basis for prescriptions it is misleading.

The recognition that wants and desires are not ultimate, independent, autonomous data, but the product of social relations[22] also casts doubt on the belief that the more fully desires are met by an economic system, the more efficient it is. The optimum, even in the wider sense of a utility *possibility* curve or an Edgeworth contract curve, is an optimum only in a very limited and trivial sense. Although institutions which would yield positions on the contract curve could meet *given* wants most efficiently, the wants to which they pander are largely their own creation. A different product, produced in a different manner, would result in a different set of wants and hence would also be an optimum if it met those new wants fully.[23] In other words, the whole U curve shifts when we move from one point of it to another.

Sociologists have observed and common experience confirms that it is true not only that we do, and try to get, what we like, but also that we like what we have to do and what we get. "The facts of life and situations come first, and attitudes are simply ways of adjustment and adaptation."[24]

All this is still based on the value judgement that individual wants only ought to count. Even on that postulate, the "optimum" (defined as that organization of production in which there is no further opportunity of "improvements" according to the compensation principle) is ambiguous for two reasons: first, because there is an infinite number of optima according to the initial income distribution, even if wants were constant; second, because there is an infinite number of sets of wants, each created by the economic set-up (distribution and social factors) which also serves them.

In order to rank situations in an order of better and worse, we would next have to value and appraise these wants. Then an additional range of possible optima is opened up according to the values postulated. A policy which frustrates individual wants might maximize the war potential; or a policy which maximizes the manifest satisfactions of individuals might also result in neuroses, breakdowns, suicides and road deaths which may be deemed too heavy a price for the benefits.

It would be a misundersanding to interpret this argument as a justification for controls or as a threat to liberty. For a society which imposes restrictions will, of course, not merely remove some but also create new wants, e.g., the desire for a removal of restrictions. This would lead to new conflicts. Nothing can be said unless the desires themselves are judged (good, urgent, or bad, unimportant). The argument merely shows that it is entirely arbitrary and circular to select one set of desires which are largely moulded by the prevailing social setting as an ethical premise to justify this setting.

It appears, therefore, that even the most hopeful attempt to salvage the compensation criterion, namely, that the "economic aspects" should be laid bare, is bound to fail because these aspects are not independent of other aspects.

We have so far discussed two attempts to justify the compensation principle, both of which purport to avoid distributional value judgements. The first was the justification by probable long-run actual compensation, the other by "let others concern themselves with distribution". The latter comprises two sub-groups, according to whether the "others" are appropriate institutions or separate judgements on other "aspects". According to the former appropriate institutional authorities with will and power to act see to it that maldistributions are corrected. In this case economic recommendations are said to stand without qualifications. According to the latter the recommendations are conditional, bringing out certain features of a situation which are relevant for reaching a decision. Both these attempts proved unsatisfactory.

VALUE JUDGEMENTS ON DISTRIBUTION ADMITTED

If we admit the necessity for value judgements on distribution, there are further possible ways of defending the compensation principle. One can say that *distribution does not matter*; that any distribution (within a range) is as good as any other. It is likely that this value judgement is frequently implicit in some of the "neutral" defences of the compensation principle, particularly when it is argued that the distributional changes will be "negligible" (i.e., ought to be neglected). Hardly anybody would seriously and explicitly advocate such a value judgement for all possible changes without qualification. But many would say that too much preoccupation with distributional issues in times when we ought to concentrate our efforts on increasing "production" (whatever that may mean) is harmful. The injunction not to worry and waste time over distributional reforms but to get on with production may (though it need not) spring from a value judgement of this type.[25]

The other possibility is to allow interpersonal comparisons of utility and value judgements based on such comparisons. Indeed, an assumption frequently made by those in the Pigovian tradition (i.e., those who believe that interpersonal comparisons are possible) is that the marginal utility of income *is* the same to everybody over the relevant range. If we postulate also that the marginal utility of income *ought* to be the same to everybody,[26] then, over that range, shifts in distribution will not worsen the situation. The conclusions will be the same as if we postulated that distribution does not matter.

The upshot of the discussion about the compensation principle and the new welfare economics is that "efficiency", "wealth", "real income", "economic welfare" etc., cannot be separated from equity, justice or distributional value judgements. Income refers to a collection of hetero-geneous goods which we render homogeneous by weighting them by their market prices. Any change in this collection (except in the trivial and unimportant case where there is more of all or at least no less of any good, or in a one-commodity world) involves weighting. But prices, which are normally used as weights, are the result of income distribution. Efficiency is meaningless apart from the question "efficiency for whom"? And judge-ments based on the assumption of a harmony of interests and values (objective, scientific, unequivocal judgements) are not possible except in the most trivial cases. To say that the conditions for optimum efficiency should be fulfilled but that interpersonal comparisons are meaningless is, in the words of Samuelson, like saying "that it does not matter whether or not a man has hair, as long as it is curly".[27]

NOTES

1. From: *Probleme der normativen Ökonomik und der wirtschaftspolitischen Beratung*, ed. von Beckerath and Giersch, Berlin (1963).
2. P. A. Samuelson in his review of Graaff's *Theoretical Welfare Economics, Economic Journal* (September 1958), p. 540.
3. It is, however, on certain value premises, a necessary condition of an optimum.
4. F. Y. Edgeworth, *Papers Relating to Political Economy*, vol. 2, pp. 102–3.
5. J. R. Hicks, "The Rehabilitation of Consumer's Surplus", *Review of Economic Studies*, vol. 8 (1940–2), p. 111.
6. It has been argued that even though they may not be random, there is no reason to assume that they will be biased in favour of a deterioration rather than an improvement of the income distribution. But such complete ignorance would form a most unsatisfactory basis for policy recommendations. Moreover, even

if they were biased in the favourable direction an even more favourable distribution might have been brought about by forgoing the change. But there are good grounds for holding that they will be cumulative in the direction of greater inequality: a higher income makes possible not only absolutely but proportionately higher savings and thus a higher rate of growth of future income. It also enables a man to benefit from education and training, to improve his health and his credit-worthiness, etc. All these raise his and his children's earning power in a cumulative process.

7. Cf. J. R. Hicks, *loc. cit.*, p. 111.

8. T. Scitovsky, "A Note on Welfare Propositions in Economics", *Review of Economic Studies* (1940–1), p. 108.

9. To be better off is not necessarily the same thing as to have more goods than are wanted if external diseconomies of consumption are present. If an individual has more goods but his rival has more still, the first individual may be worse off. Compensation for external diseconomies would have to be paid too. This would make the simple index number measures inapplicable.

10. P. A. Samuelson, "Evaluation of Real National Income", *Oxford Economic Papers* (January 1950) and *Foundations*, Ch. 8. J. de V. Graaff, *Theoretical Welfare Economics* (1957).

11. This implies certain assumptions about consistent behaviour, absence of certain types of social determination of desires, some similarity of tastes, factor transferability, etc. Few of these assumptions can withstand a more searching critique. But it should be noted that only ordinal utility is involved. With ordinal and interpersonally non-comparable utility the scale used on each axis is arbitrary. Only more or less is registered. The curvature of the curves is therefore also arbitrary. If individual *A* derives considerable satisfaction from *B* being better off and *vice versa*, the curve could slope upwards to the right (Fig. 2.1a). If one man's meat is another man's poison, and if factors producing meat and poison are specific, the curve would take the form of two rectangular lines (Fig. 2.1b). Dog-in-the-manger types of external diseconomies (the sin of envy) would be consistent with the normal shape (Fig. 2.1c).

12. An increase in *potential* real income would be illustrated by a shift of the *UU* curve to U_1U_1 in Fig. 2.2.

   An increase in some goods without a reduction in any would be, in the absence of strong external diseconomies of consumption, a sufficient condition for such a shift, though not a necessary one.

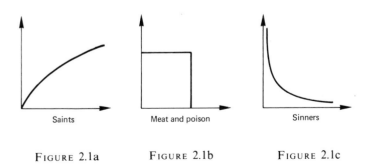

| Saints | Meat and poison | Sinners |

FIGURE 2.1a   FIGURE 2.1b   FIGURE 2.1c

13. D. H. Robertson, "Utility and all that", *Manchester School* (May 1951), p. 134, reprinted in *Utility and All That* (1952).

14. "I would conclude, therefore, that while the new welfare economics has, in Kaldor's argument, provided the economist with a guide to policy in some communities, this guide has no universal validity." T. Scitovsky, "The State of Welfare Economics", *American Economic Review* (June 1951).

15. And to the view that the possibilities are also feasible. In fact, Pareto's optimum conditions are *never* feasible.

16. In other words, relative income distributions, on present assumptions, cannot be described, but can only be judged. In order to define the same relative distribution of utility, the utility indices would have to be unique with respect to proportional transformations. The oddity of having to say that we can judge states which can be neither defined nor described is one reason for believing that interpersonal utility comparisons are not simply value judgements.

17. Always with the important proviso that the possible is also feasible, or at any rate that the movement on the relevant feasibility curves is equivalent to that on the possibility curves, and that it does not prejudice an even more desirable move. The economics of the feasible *first* best is different from the economics of the *second* best.

18. If we are prepared to commit ourselves, at least to a partial social welfare function, the situations can be ranked in a definite order. The two aspects could formally be integrated in an indifference map between utility and justice, as in Fig. 2.3a, where $F(1,3)$ is judged equal to $E(2,2)$, the first figure standing for the utility–possibility index and the second for the "isodik" index. These indifference curves may be said to reflect value judgements between different utility–possibility and justice combinations. With opportunity curves indicating constraints on these $U-D$ combinations, allowing, say, for effects on incentives, optimum tangency solutions can be found. In this way the transition from the "economic aspect" or "piecemeal" approach to the social welfare function or "all or nothing" approach could, formally, be made.

19. More accurately, the contrast is not, as used to be said, between "real income" and "economic welfare", but between potential utility combinations and distributional value judgements.

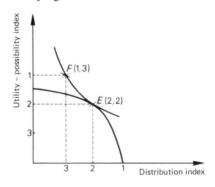

FIGURE 2.3a

20. See notes 11 and 17. In particular, the construction of U curves presupposes the possibility of "ideal" lump-sum transfers between individuals which do not violate the optimum conditions of production and exchange.
21. Alternatively, it could be argued that those who are rowing in the lifeboat must be given more food to keep them fit than others who may have to die, whereas greater abundance makes it worth sacrificing a good deal of efficiency for greater justice.
22. In particular the "insatiability of wants", almost axiomatic in welfare economics, is the product of a certain culture.
23. There is the quite separate point that one may agree that unfulfilled desire is an evil and yet believe that the best solution is, not to satisfy, but to kill it.
24. F. Zweig, *Women's Life and Labour* (1952). "You might just as well say", added the March Hare, "that 'I like what I get' is the same thing as 'I get what I like!'" Lewis Caroll, *Alice's Adventures in Wonderland*, p. 98.
25. It may be objected that this assumption contradicts the argument that changes in real income cannot be defined apart from positive value judgements about distribution, i.e., definite preferences for one over another. But no stand need be taken on preferred distribution if the whole utility–possibility locus shifts outwards, at any rate in the neighbourhood of the position from which we start. It is possible to hold that any point on $U_1 U_1$ in Fig. 2.6 is distributionally as good as any point on UU. If, however, the curve is twisted as in Fig. 2.7, so that it intersects UU, the value judgement that distribution does not matter cannot supplement the potential compensation criterion, for compensation is no longer possible at all points. But one can still say that in the neighbourhood of E the double criterion holds good. We may be satisfied to know that after a change from E to F the loser *could* be compensated, though we do not think it important to compensate him, not because we believe that he ought to lose but because we hold that the change in distribution does not matter.
26. This assumption, with some important qualifications, has been made by R. F. Kahn, "Notes on Ideal Output", *Economic Journal* (1935), p. 1; and recently by J. M. Fleming, "On Making the Best of Balance of Payments Restrictions on Imports", *Economic Journal* (March 1951), p. 49.
27. Samuelson, *Foundations*, p. 250.

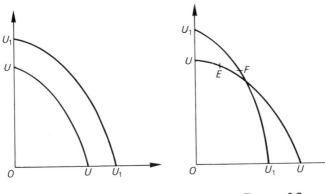

FIGURE 2.6   FIGURE 2.7

3 The Meaning and Purpose of Interdisciplinary Studies[1]

SUMMARY

There are three distinct reasons for interdisciplinary work in development studies. First, specialists in different disciplines may work together on a specific practical planning problem. Second, assumptions, concepts or methods evolved in one discipline may yield fruitful results when applied to the problems previously treated by another. Third, the concepts, models and paradigms may have to be recast so as to encompass variables previously separated in distinct disciplines because of the demands of the social reality of a different culture. This is illustrated with the concept 'capital'. There is a conservative and a radical version. In the former, new wine can be poured into old bottles; in the latter, wholly new concepts and models must be constructed.

With almost monotonous repetition, we hear calls for interdisciplinary studies, or, more accurately, for the breakdown of boundaries between disciplines, at conferences, in papers and in books about the problems of development in the Third World. Yet, relatively little is done to achieve this breakdown. This is partly due to lack of clarity about what is meant by the plea and partly due to the fact that the only forum where interdisciplinary studies in depth can be conducted successfully is under one skull, and that such skulls are scarce.

There are three quite distinct reasons for interdisciplinary, multidisciplinary, transdisciplinary or supradisciplinary work.[2] Each has different methodological implications. First, a practical problem like improving nutrition, introducing new varieties of crops, controlling population growth, reducing pollution, planning a town, may call for drawing on and applying several disciplines. In the cooperative effort the disciplines are not transcended but brought together to solve a particular set of practical problems. The prevalence of planning at all levels has contributed to the cooperation between different disciplines. The planner has to draw on all relevant knowledge and skills. This practical need to bring all relevant methods, data and information to bear on the solution of a specific problem does not affect the methods used in the contributing disciplines. On the contrary, it is just because they are specialists in their fields that the different members of the team have a contribution to make to an integrated solution. We might think of them as members of a Royal Commission investigating problems of controlling environmental pollution, deciding on a family-planning programme or planning a new town.

Second, it may be the case that certain assumptions, concepts or methods, hitherto applied only to one sphere of activity, yield illuminating results when applied to another, previously analysed in quite different ways. There has been some invasion by economic concepts and methods into the territory of political scientists and sociologists. Thus, the assumption of maximizing behaviour has been fruitful, up to a point, in analysing the behaviour of consumers, firms and farms. Its success has encouraged its application to political activities such as voting and party formation. It has also been applied to the exploration of politically feasible income distributions. Calculations of economic returns have been extended from profit-making investments to education, health, birth control and the allocation of time between work and leisure and of leisure time itself. Occasionally, though much less frequently, concepts used in political theory have been applied to economic problems. Albert Hirschman's use of 'voice' as an alternative to 'exit' is an interesting example.[3]

INTERACTION AND INTERDEPENDENCE

There is a third, and deeper, reason for interdisciplinary work. It may be that for a particular time or region the justification for having a separate discipline does not hold. This justification for a discipline consists in the empirical fact that between the variables encompassed by this discipline and those treated by another, there are few interactions and the effects of any existing interaction are weak and damped. Only then are we justified in analysing causal sequences in one field, without always and fully taking into account those in others.

We may all agree that society is a system and that all social variables are related, but with growing differentiation of functions and standards, some relationships are stronger than others. This justifies us in separating, say, business responses from family responses, or economics from anthropology. As Michael Lipton has argued in a stimulating and valuable article, the need for interdisciplinary studies does not arise because people in underdeveloped countries, particularly in subsistence households, perform many functions normally separated in rich countries, but because there is interdependence between variables normally analysed separately. 'Lack of specialization among the people being studied in no way justifies lack of specialization among the students. A student of Michelangelo could well confine attention to his sculpture, while caring little for the architecture and painting in which Michelangelo also excelled.'[4] The fact that functions in underdeveloped societies are less differentiated does, of course, have a bearing on the interdependence.

The situation can be illustrated diagrammatically. Figure 3.1 depicts the absence of interdependence between the variables X and Y. Figure 3.2 shows interdependence, but it is weak and damped, so that if one variable diverges from the stable equilibrium point S, the system will tend to return to it. Whether we are justified in neglecting such interdependence will depend on the size of the reaction coefficients, the comparative slopes of the lines, and on the time lags in the adjustment

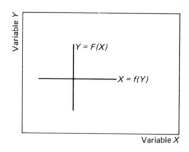

FIGURE 3.1   Non-interdependence

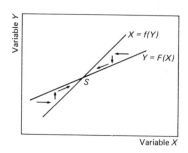

FIGURE 3.2   Damped interdependence

process. Figure 3.3 shows a cumulative process away from the unstable equilibrium at *U*. Clearly, we must not neglect such interdependence in our studies. Figure 3.4 shows that stability and instability may be the function of the size of the move, so that for small moves interdependence is damped and for large ones explosive. Theories of the large push or the critical minimum effort are based on such non-linear relationships.

There are numerous illustrations of such interdependence in the field of development studies. One is the relationship between income per head and population growth. High rates of population growth may be presumed to reduce income per head and higher income per head may be presumed, in certain conditions—but only in those conditions—to reduce population growth.[5] Or take the relationship between the level of living of a deprived minority group, for example a low caste or a racial minority, and an index of prejudice against it. Prejudice will be a function of the level of living—the less educated, the less healthy, the stronger the grounds for prejudice—and the level of living will be a function of prejudice—the stronger prejudice, the stronger discrimination in jobs, education, and so forth.[6]

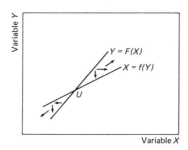

FIGURE 3.3   Explosive interdependence

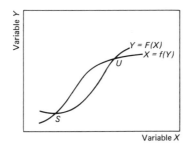

FIGURE 3.4   Non-linear interdependence

Or consider the relationship between productivity per man and the investment/income ratio. The higher the productivity, the higher will tend to be the savings and hence the investment ratio, but the higher the investment ratio the more capital per man and hence the higher productivity. There is also interdependence between the quality of interdisciplinary studies and the quality of the scholars they attract. One can continue.

If interdependence between variables normally studied separately is strong, or, though weak, if reaction coefficients are large, or, though small, if they change size for moves above a critical level, there is a case for breaking down the boundaries between disciplines. This is sometimes called transforming parameters into dependent variables. Family ties and economic calculus, land tenure and responses to incentives, religious beliefs and commercial motivation may interact in this way. When interdependence of this kind occurs and when the interdependent variables belong to different disciplines, there is a case for interdisciplinary work.[7]

CAPITAL AND INVESTMENT

It is possible to draw two quite different conclusions from such interaction. First, it might be said that what is called for are not interdisciplinary studies, but *a new discipline* that constructs concepts and builds models appropriate to the conditions of underdeveloped societies. In this case, we should have to discard concepts such as employment, unemployment, underemployment, income, savings, investment and construct altogether new terms.

Second, and less radically, the existing concepts and models may continue to be used, but their content may have to be changed or their definition modified.

The difference can be illustrated with the concepts "capital" and "investment". Conventionally, "investment" is defined as the addition of physical pieces of equipment, plant or stocks in order to raise the future flow of products or services above what it would have been otherwise. "Capital" is the stock of these items that has resulted from past flows minus depreciation through use of obsolescence.

Now it is possible to enlarge this concept so as to cover all forms of expenditure that lead to a larger flow of future output, not only those that result in physical items of machinery, constructions or inventories. This would include "investment in human capital", such as education, health and, at low income levels, nutrition; possibly expenditure on birth control, if we are concerned with raising income per head; it would also include investment in productive knowledge that is not incorporated in machinery or in people; it would further include expenditure on building social institutions and on shaping human attitudes.

All this can, in principle, be covered by an enlarged concept of "capital" and "investment", as long as one condition is fulfilled: there must be a fairly systematic connection between the devotion of current resources, that might otherwise be used for unproductive current consumption, and the resulting flow of extra output. These resources need not be the only condition for the enlarged flow of output, but they must be systematically linked to this output by a fixed set of technical coefficients, or at least by a range that is not too wide.

But if the link between the devotion of current resources and extra output is only tenuous, so that a given result can be achieved with widely varying inputs, or the same inputs can lead to widely varying results, or if the results can be achieved without using any current inputs, or if in spite of large current inputs, no results can in principle ensue, the notions of "capital" and "investment" become inapplicable and we have to focus on those factors on which the outcome systematically depends.[8]

The output of a factory may be within wide limits a function of the degree of capacity utilization which, in turn, will depend on the quality of the management; the result of a family-planning programme may be only tenuously linked to the money spent on clinics, doctors, nurses and contraceptives, but largely depend upon changeable economic, social, cultural and religious attitudes of couples. The quality of the administration, the system of land tenure, the solidarity between different classes, the ethnic origin of the entrepreneurs, their power over the workers, the history of the country may be more important determinants than the amount of resources. If this is so, no new wine can be poured into old bottles; the bottles themselves must be changed.

In either case, in the process of analysing social phenomena in underdeveloped countries, we may incidentally gain new insights into those in advanced industrial countries. Studies of the caste system in India may illuminate trade union behaviour and demarcation (jurisdiction) disputes in England or the rôle of women in Western Europe; scrutiny of the capital/output ratio may change our view of the production function. Research into small-scale, intermediate technology may be useful for reducing environmental damage in advanced countries; research on the social services may teach us how to improve our own; a wider concept of capital may throw new light on our own problems of industrial management. If this happens it will be a bonus over and above what we had bargained for. Research can thus be made not only co-operative but also mutually enlightening.

ECONOMICS AND ANTHROPOLOGY

Let us illustrate how this would work out between, say, economics and anthropology. In the first case of interdisciplinary work—the team approach—anthropologists will be used for their traditional training. If a land reform or a birth-control programme or a tourist project or even a research project is proposed, they will be able to point to "constraints" in the beliefs and mores of the people, or they will be able to point to beliefs or institutions that can be mobilized and on which the proposed reforms or projects can be built. Nothing new or radical is required here.

The second case is more interesting. I suspect that economic method could illuminate some anthropological work and probably the converse too. While I know of some cross-disciplinary work of this kind between economics and political science, I do not know of any between economics and anthropology.

The most interesting possibilities are opened up by the third case, whether in its reformist or radical version. It is quite clear, for example, that an agricultural production function in many underdeveloped countries should count among its inputs, not only the conventional factors, land, labour, fertilizers, water and power, but also levels of education of the farmers, nutritional standards, distance from town, health, systems of land tenure and of family kinship. All these variables are likely, in some societies, to be systematically related to agricultural production.

Still, while we adhere to the notion of a "production function", a status-conscious anthropologist will complain that he is being used only to provide fodder for the cannons of the economist. A self-respecting anthropologist might refuse to have all the important questions asked by the economist and to be reduced to a handmaiden, supplying low-class empirical material for the high-class analytical structure of another discipline. Questions of status and precedence are, of course, not of concern to serious scholars; on the contrary. John Maynard Keynes looked forward to the day when economists would have become like mechanics, when they could "get themselves thought of as humble, competent people, on a level with dentists . . .".[9]

But it may turn out that the whole notion of a production function is wrong or misleading. Perhaps there is no systematic relationship between inputs, whether of fertilized, irrigated land, physical capital, or of educated farmers, human capital, and crops. It may be that output depends upon variables that have been constructed and analysed by anthropologists: the relationship between majority and minority groups; religious beliefs, the Protestant ethic; or kinship systems.

Or again, at a different level of discourse, it may be that large increases in output beyond a decent minimum are not a crucial component of development either at this stage or ever. The society may have opted for an alternative style of development, in which the ever-growing production of material goods is rejected. It prefers containment of wants and aspirations to increasing production to satisfy ever-growing wants and infinite aspirations. Or, through a shift in valuations, unemployment may be converted into leisure. If this is the case, the crucial questions will have to be asked by the anthropologist or the sociologist. He has to construct the concepts and it may be that it is then the economist's turn to fill the boxes constructed by the anthropologist. Which of these possibilities should be realized, will depend partly upon empirical conditions, but ultimately upon valuations and the choice of a style of life.

CONCLUSION

What is the conclusion for those dispensing money for policy-oriented research? The first case, members of each discipline solving a practical problem together, presents no problem. Teams can be, and have been, assembled who put their heads together to solve a particular problem, each member bringing his expertise with him. Interesting organizational, managerial and administrative problems arise about the levels and the forms in which the heads should be brought together, and about the relative weight to be given to each in the light of possibly controversial objectives, but this is not our concern here.

The second and third cases (extension of methods to other fields and changing concepts and models to include "outside" variables) are much more difficult. The only solution is to back individuals and groups of individuals who are interested in and excited by this work, who read each other's drafts and discuss their ideas among themselves, and who are sensitive to the limits of the techniques in which they were educated, in spite of having acquired a certain vested intellectual interest in them. I suspect that such backing will be more successful than backing chairs, institutes or projects that declare, programmatically, that they are committed to interdisciplinary work, though institutional change clearly must accompany psychological change.

A modest practical proposal is to give grants to scholars for the purpose of reading and catching up in fields outside their narrow professional expertise, so as to familiarize them with what has happened in these fields. Problem-orientated survey articles, critically summarizing the literature and pointing to gaps, without respect for the traditional boundaries between disciplines, can also be a help initially in introducing outsiders to the work done by groups of workers.

Interdisciplinary work raises some of the same issues as collaboration between scholars from different countries, as is shown by our use of language: the "frontiers" of development economics, "poaching" on other people's territory, intellectual "imperialism" as an attempt to extend the "frontiers", etc. Here, as for international collaboration, considerations of sovereignty, status, power and legitimacy are out of place. The language of research should be quite different from the language of diplomacy or power politics and should have no room for "legitimacy" or "sovereignty".

Applied development economics clearly is a service discipline: it draws its inputs from engineers, scientists, agronomists, technologists; it delivers its output to policy-makers. It is noteworthy that research on the "inputs", essentially research in the natural sciences, has been more readily welcomed by the developing countries than the research at the next stage of processing. This is so because, as we approach the final use of the product, namely policy, both valuations and biases are more likely to colour the analysis. Problem-orientated applied, usable research can overcome these objections, not by emulating the natural sciences in being "value-free", but by making the valuations explicit.

Economic analysis has found certain assumptions convenient. Among these may be included optimizing behaviour of atomistic units; convexity, for example absence of increasing returns and of indivisibilities, diminishing marginal utility; constancy of certain determinants such as tastes, knowledge, institutions; absence of uncertainty or the construction of certainty equivalents or of "contingent commodities", the prices of which are all known; fragmentation of power, hence inability of any one unit to affect the behaviour of other units and therefore exclusion of problems of bargaining, alliances and interdependence.

These assumptions, while convenient for yielding determinate equilibrium solutions, have been criticized and have occasionally been relaxed. Some of these relaxations amount to breaking down the barriers between disciplines, for example stepping from economics into politics. The only criterion for this must be the realism and relevance of the resulting research and, beyond that, direct and indirect implementation of the results of research for the benefit of mankind.

NOTES

1. *Interdisciplinary Science Reviews*, vol. 1, no. 2 (1976).
2. Some people object to terms like "multidisciplinary" or "interdisciplinary". It is true that they sound somewhat pretentious and abstract. I have not been able to think of a better expression for this type of work.
3. A. O. Hirschman, *Exit, Voice and Loyalty*, Harvard University Press (1970).
4. Michael Lipton, "Interdisciplinary Studies in Less Developed Countries", *J. Development Studies*, vol. 9 (October 1970).
5. See H. Leibenstein, *Economic Backwardness and Economic Growth*, John Wiley, New York (1963).
6. See G. Myrdal, *An American Dilemma*, Harper & Row, New York (1944).
7. An important attempt to discover which variables and interactions may be appropriate under which circumstances is to be found in I. Adelman and C. T. Morris, *Society, Politics and Economic Development*, Johns Hopkins Press, Baltimore (1967).
8. "As Voltaire said, an incantation will destroy a flock of sheep if it is accompanied by a sufficient dose of arsenic." A. Marshall, *Official Papers*, Macmillan, London (1926), p. 40.
9. J. M. Keynes, "Economic Possibilities for our Grand-Children", reprinted in *Essays in Persuasion*, Macmillan, London (1931), p. 373.

4 The Limits of Development Research[1]

SUMMARY

The scope and the limits of the use and transfer of development research are discussed and the question is raised what social, political, philosophical and moral problems arise when scholars from rich countries, with well-endowed centres of learning, carry out research on and in substantially poorer countries. The charges are examined that have been made by developing countries against research on their problems and in their territory, and in particular the charge of intellectual imperialism. Different arguments for collaboration in research between rich and poor countries are distinguished. The question is raised whether research in rich countries should confine itself to the 'interface' of rich–poor relations or whether development research is an indivisible whole.

1 INTRODUCTION AND SUMMARY

In this paper I examine some of the problems that arise when research on social and economic development is carried out by scholars from rich countries with established and comparatively well-endowed centres of learning. Research is itself a social activity, though social scientists tend to neglect the analysis of their own activities.[2] In this paper the social sciences will be treated as a form of (intellectual) technology.

Technology has been defined as the 'skills, knowledge and procedures for making, using and doing useful things'.[3] In spite of this broad definition, which covers, in addition to technical knowledge, knowledge of organization, administration and management, the concept is not entirely appropriate for applied social science. While there are some similarities with commercial technologies, there are also important differences. I shall ask what are the scope and the limits of the use and transfer of development research and what social, political, philosophical and moral problems arise

62

when scholars from one set of countries carry out social research on and in substantially poorer foreign countries. The paper is an exercise on the sociology of research and of international relations. As an economist, I have no particular advantage in writing about these issues. I am aware of the philosophical shortcomings of my argument and of the lack of thorough empirical evidence to support some of my suggestions.

In the second section I examine critically the charges that have been made by developing countries against research on their problems and in their territory by scholars from rich countries. The five main charges are (1) academic imperialism; (2) irrelevance, inappropriateness and bias of concepts, models and theories; (3) research in the service of exploitation; (4) domination through a superior and self-reinforcing research infrastructure; and (5) illegitimacy.

I conclude that basic knowledge is a common good in use but not in production. Its pursuit unites scholars across national frontiers. Truth cannot be nationalized but there exists bias, distortion and intellectual imperialism in a quite different sense from the one often decried, the correction of which is demanded by true scholarship. Scholarship rejects diplomacy and tact, though sensitivity is essential in social studies and tactics are in order if implementation is desired. The infrastructure of research is subject to increasing returns (both physical and intellectual), so that polarization, dominance and dependence will tend to be established. There is an infant-industry argument for encouraging research in developing countries even, initially, at lower standards. This argument should, however, be clearly distinguished from arguments for parcelling up what is the unity of scholarship. All ideas should be exposed to world-wide scrutiny and criticism.

In the third section I distinguish between different arguments for collaboration in research between rich and poor countries and try to separate different reasons for such collaboration. These motives range from using the local institute in a subservient capacity to participatory theory construction. Collaboration between rich and poor country scholars, like joint business ventures, may be merely a facade for domination but this can be avoided by first building up research capacity and then entering into genuine joint ventures. But the choice between capacity and quality raises difficult problems of objectives, time, discount rates and risk. As there are grounds for collaboration, there are also grounds for specialization. But the economically appealing rule that countries should specialize according to their relative intellectual and physical factor endowments cannot be applied to research.

The fourth section discusses the question whether research in rich countries should confine itself to the interface of rich – poor relations or whether development research is an indivisible whole. The arguments for confining it to the interface are (1) that this is an area in which rich countries can act; (2) that this escapes the charge of academic imperialism; (3) that it avoids the paradox of rich-country institutions propagating indigenous capacity building, and (4) that it avoids the impropriety and counter-productivity of advocating radical solutions for others. Objections to confinement to the interface are (1) since not everyone can be prevented from doing research on the domestic issues of the poor countries, balance demands that anyone should be free to correct a possible imbalance; (2) attention by foreigners to domestic issues of poor countries may be a correction to internal brain drain and encourage domestic work on relevant issues; (3) international and internal variables interact and a division is methodologically impossible; (4) free research should not be limited by national boundaries. In spite of these objections, interface issues are in the present climate particularly suited for rich-country research. The section also discusses, as part of the interface, research on questions of international cooperation, confrontation (conflict) and LDC self-reliance.

The fifth section deals with problems arising from the origin and organization of research funds, the questions whether and when money is tainted, whether there should be concentration or dispersal of sources of funds, and how to bridge the gap between the requirements of policy-makers and the freedom of academic research. It warns against sacrificing the important to the urgent.

The sixth section contains a brief warning against over-simple quantification in an attempt to emulate the 'hard' sciences. It ends on the sceptical note that we still do not know what are the springs of development, and a warning that we should not sacrifice the important to the manageable.

An appendix reproduces a review of a book on Project Camelot, a research project that sparked off some of the fire of the debate and that contributed to the difficulties scholars nowadays face in their work in developing countries.

2 THE ROLE OF THE SOCIAL SCIENCES AND THE SOCIAL SCIENTIST IN DEVELOPMENT STUDIES

The shift in our perception of development from the linear view to the interdependent view discussed in chapter 5, pp 103–8, also affected the view of the role of research. On the linear, missing-components view, research in rich countries or by rich-country scholars can contribute bits of knowledge and thereby remove a particular constraint. On the neo-Marxian view, research may itself be part and parcel of the international oppressive or at least impeding system, depriving the developing countries of brains, or diverting the attention of their brains to irrelevant problems or inducing them to produce apologias for their ruling class and the unjustifiable world system. The new view has been reflected in growing tensions and difficulties encountered in research relationships and resistance to the admission of social science researchers to developing countries.

In several places in this paper I shall try to analyse how this shift of perception affects the role of the research donor. What should be noted here is that, irrespective of the scientific status of the new view, the mere fact that influential people in developing countries hold it is bound to make a difference to the research relationship between rich and poor.

Development research in the developed countries has been criticized on several grounds.

(1) First, there is the charge of academic, scientific, intellectual or cultural imperialism or colonialism.[4] The critics see a close parallel between the operations of the more ruthless mining companies and the developed-country research teams. They move into the country with their already designed research projects, trying to 'mine' for data and statistics, using locals for semi-skilled activities such as interviewing, filling out forms, interpreting, but preserve for themselves at headquarters the monopoly-rent-earning activities of basic research design, processing and publishing. The 'researched' country, having been stripped of its data, suffers the humiliation of seeing the results published in the journals or books of the advanced industrial countries, adding prestige and glory to the foreign professors and their institutions. Sometimes, as in the case of certain multi-national firms and the CIA, mining is combined with undermining; the research is used to interfere with the democratic processes of the country and to further the aims of foreign powers.[5]

(2) Second, there is the charge that 'Western' concepts, models, paradigms and the questions asked—both the agenda for research and the filing cabinets—are inappropriate for understanding the utterly different circumstances of developing societies. Here again, an analogy is drawn between the inappropriate industrial and agricultural techniques and the concepts, models and methods of economics and other social sciences. These alien concepts and models determine inappropriate policies and either divert attention from the real problems (e.g.,

corruption) or become apologies for existing power structures—when the charge becomes the one discussed under (3). Excessive sophistication, esoteric irrelevance, ignorance and false beliefs conveyed by these doctrines are opportunistic and serve vested interests. Heavy emphasis on capital/output ratios, savings and investment ratios, the notion of unemployment and employment, aggregate income, and others have, it is argued, misled policy-makers (or strengthened them in their narrow class interests) and have concealed the importance of institutional and other structural changes, such as land reform, corporate reform, tax reform, credit and banking reform, the creation or strengthening of an independent, honest and efficient administrative service, or an egalitarian educational system. The paradigms of 'Western' social science serve as blinkers or escape mechanisms, preventing scholars and policy-makers from seeing and acting on the strategic fronts.

(3) A stronger version of the charge of opportunistic irrelevance is the view that advanced-country research is part of the system of international capitalism, in which underdevelopment makes possible the growth of the capitalist countries of the West. Private foreign investment, the multi-national enterprise, international trade, international monetary arrangements, universities and, indeed, research itself, all reinforce the position of the advanced, industrial countries, together with a small class of privileged people in the underdeveloped countries and serve the exploitation and the continuing underdevelopment of the majority of people in the poor countries. The framework of research is essentially an apology and justification for the neo-colonial apparatus of exploitation.

(4) Fourth, there is the charge of domination and dependence in a rather different sense. The complaint here is not that the developing countries are exploited (as in the charge of intellectual imperialism or neo-colonialism), nor that the concepts and models are inappropriate or ideological. The trouble is simply that, as a result of the concentration of funds, greater scope for specialization and the accumulation of skills, the scholars from the developed countries have gained a superiority and that this superiority, combined with the institutions and attitudes derived from it and reinforcing it, prevent research institutions and attitudes in the developing countries from growing to strong and independent status. Both the incentive and the capacity to generate new ideas and to carry out indigenous research on relevant problems are weakened by the operations of the foreign scholars and institutes. The relationship between the foreign professor and the local workers is often that of

patron and protégé. The patron will try to get jobs, write references, arrange a fellowship to the metropolitan country for his protégé. But the relation is one of dependence of the developing-country researcher on the favours of the foreign patron. Only more inward-looking policies towards research (it is argued), more cooperation with countries at similar levels of development and the pulling down of a curtain against the stunting influence from outside, hold out hope for the growth of realistic and relevant research, based on self-reliance, self-confidence and autonomy. It is a kind of intellectual infant-industry argument.

The economic analogy can be extended. What is needed (it has been argued) is import substitution in research, the elimination of stultifying foreign competition, the establishment of a temporary domestic monopoly.

(5) Fifth, there is the charge of illegitimacy. If this amounted merely to saying that scholarship should be confined to the territory within a scholar's national boundaries, it could be dismissed without further discussion. But a question of moral (though not intellectual) legitimacy is raised when research leads to the recommendation of actions, the cost of which is borne entirely by other people. There is something, if not illegitimate, at any rate distasteful in people from safe and comfortable positions recommending revolutions or painful reforms, or, for that matter, the maintenance of the *status quo*, to others.[6] This is, of course, a much more general point, not confined to research on poor countries. It raises the much discussed question of the moral responsibilities of the scientist. But it arises in particularly acute form if the subjects of investigation are countries on the government of which we have no influence.

To what extent are these five charges justified? The analogy between mining or quarrying and searching for knowledge is surely false. The more nickel, copper or gold I have, the less is left over for you. This is not so with knowledge. We all can draw on the stock of knowledge and my discovery does not normally deprive you of intellectual profits from it, though it may deprive you of recognition for the discovery.

More important, there are common standards of scholarship, which assert its universality and the solidarity of any one scholar with the international fraternity of other scholars. Commitment to the search for knowledge, to scientific objectivity and to telling the truth as one sees it, knows no national frontiers. In addition to the intrinsic value of this commitment, loyalties to universal values that cut across frontiers have their political value in an age when nationalism, a powerful Christian heresy, and ideologies have become dominant secular religions. In this sense, therefore, there cannot be African, Asian and Latin American criteria for truth or validity. Mining companies can be nationalized; criteria for truth cannot.[7]

The problem is, however, complicated and sometimes confused by people mistaking economics for a form of logic, truth for logical validity and criteria of truth for its empirical content. For if economics is equated with a form of logic ('the logic of choice'), it would follow that there is only a single, universal economic science from China to Peru and no separate economics for Africa, Asia or Latin America.[8] Yet clearly, if we turn from the standards and criteria by which we judge evidence, methods and conclusions to the content of our work, it should be plain that very different propositions are likely to be true for different societies. In this sense, it is perfectly legitimate to speak of 'African', 'Asian' or 'Latin American' economics or politics or sociology. It is this confusion between logical validity and truth, to which some economists have themselves contributed, which is partly responsible for what appear to be nationalistic attacks on the 'legitimacy' of 'Western' social science.

It is part of scholarship to recognize the limitations of the propositions established and possibly applicable to one region (or period) but not, or not without modification, to another. It is understandable that territorial and temporal claims of the validity of certain theories have tended to be excessive and that there is, for this reason, an element of 'imperialism' in the generalizations of social science. But this sense of 'imperialism' is, of course, entirely different from the one discussed above. Thus, it can be argued that important elements of 'scientific socialism' are an extrapolation and universalization of the experience of industrial England between 1780 and 1840, when inequalities increased and when, in the midst of fairly rapid industrial progress, the poor may, for a time, have become poorer. Ricardo and Malthus universalized the temporary pressures on land of the rapidly growing population of England, while technical progress lagged behind. The so-called General Theory of Employment, Interest and Money is a rather special theory, applicable to the grossly underutilized resources in industrial countries during the depression of the 1930s. Neo-classical economics, with its nicely calculated little more and little less, its assumptions of maximizing behaviour and atomistic competition, may be regarded as a generalization of certain principles of petit-bourgeois housekeeping. And so one could go on. Not only the Ricardian theory of distribution, the Malthusian theory of population, the Marxist theory of the increasing misery of the masses, the Keynesian theory of employment, but also various theories of secular stagnation, secular inflation, secular shortages of dollars, food or raw materials, or secular doom, may all be projections on to a vast historical screen of the snapshots of a few years or decades and the magnified protests and responses to which these short-run experiences give rise. The designers of these theories suffer from a high elasticity of expectations, or, less politely expressed, hysterical reactions.

If these doctrines had made more limited territorial and chronological claims, if they had confined themselves to their time and their place, nobody would have paid much attention. They derive their interest and their significance from the grand design, the magnificent extrapolation, the large screen, from magnifying the trivial into the false. But it is quite legitimate (in the service of universal truth) to criticize orthodox Western models for their excessive claims, for their 'intellectual imperialism'. It is in the interst of honest work to assert that in Africa, Asia, Latin America, at very low levels of development, in another demographic setting, in tropical climates, in a different international system, etc., they order things differently.

Yet, such limitation of excess claims, if it is legitimate, is such that it must be recognized as legitimate by scholars wherever they may be. There have been sociologists (like Karl Mannheim), anthropologists (like Lucien Lévy-Bruhl), linguists (like Benjamin Lee Whorf), and philosophers of science (like Thomas Kuhn) who have argued that the criteria of truth and validity themselves vary from time to time and place to place, according to their context. But I believe it can be shown that at least some criteria of truth and validity cannot be dependent on social, cultural, linguistic or other existential factors, indeed that even asking questions about differences between beliefs and theories presupposes logically universal and fundamental criteria of truth.[9]

Those who claim that bias enters into social paradigms and theories and that 'Western' social science is an apology of exploitation or a diversion manoeuvre are not always clear about the precise manner and form of entry.[10]

It is likely that the limitations shown up by those combatting the excess claims and correcting the distortions of biased ideologies will ultimately benefit work in and on the developed countries themselves.[11] There is mutual illumination which a shutting-off and 'going it alone' would impede. This is a bonus, but even if it were not so, theories with excess claims are not 'true for Europe but not true for Africa': they are simply not true.

I conclude that, although the laws of logic and the criteria for truth must be universal, the concepts, models, premises, assumptions, paradigms, theories or questions in the social sciences are in some respects peculiar.

*There may be an African economics, distinct from a European economics;
there can be no African truth.*[12] By rigorous analysis, by accumulation of
evidence and by bringing out explicitly value premises, errors and biases
can be reduced. But there will always remain a residual of ideology. And
this residual.element may be particularly misleading if transferred from the
experience of industrial countries to developing countries. It is for this
reason that the assertion of the universality of the criteria for truth must be
qualified, although the remedy cannot be found in 'indigenous' theory
construction or in erecting a barrier against 'alien' doctrines.

One important element of truth in the charge of 'Western' intellectual
domination is the ideological component of 'Western' theories just
discussed. There is a second element of truth in these charges.

While the stock of fundamental knowledge is a public good, to be drawn
on by anyone anywhere, the resources that enable scholars to conduct
research are, of course, scarce and the recognition, prestige and fame that
are the reward of successful work are competitive and by no means a free
good. A scientific discovery can be used by anyone, but only one man can
make it. And he reaps the monopoly rent of recognition.[13] Moreover,
recognition attracts funds and funds make it possible to gain recognition: a
cumulative process that will tend to penalize ill-endowed centres of
learning. No money: no ability to train and attract a high quality and a
large quantity of scholars: no scope for specialization and for good work:
no recognition: no money. It is then understandable if institutions starved
of funds in the developing countries should resent the well-endowed
foreigners who use their work in the developing country to gain further
recognition and hence even more funds, to attract more and even better
scholars. If this invasion is then accompanied by concepts, models and
paradigms that are irrelevant, unrealistic or ideologically biased, if these
concepts , models and paradigms make excess claims, if the behaviour of
the foreigners is tactless, insensitive or patronizing, it is understandable
that the indigenous scholars will charge the foreigners and their doctrines
with being dominant and arrogant and that they will wish to bar them.

There is also a feeling that opportunities to present, exchange, develop
and communicate ideas and to implement them are much greater in the
developed countries. Doers and thinkers meet at beautiful country houses
like the Villa Serbelloni in Bellagio or in Ditchley Park or in Bürgenstock or
in Königswinter or at Wilton Park, and from these meetings clusters of
ideas and policies emerge.[14] In rich countries, there is a continuing
generation and exchange of ideas between policy-makers and scholars
from which paradigms and programmes are crystallized. Nothing comparable exists in the Third World. Different paradigms, incorporating

variables that are omitted, especially political and social factors, would create a different picture of reality and different programmes for action. It is felt that existing opportunities for such a crystallization are inadequate or absent and that, in particular, the United Nations bodies have failed to generate the ideas on which policy-makers could draw.

All this constitutes an argument for institution-building in the Third World, to which I shall return. But the analogy with international trade, just as the analogy with quarrying and mining, is surely false. 'Import substitution', the exclusion of foreign competition and the establishment of a local monopoly in research, even if they were feasible, would not generate the kind of ideas that could eventually face international competition. The pursuit of knowledge is not like the pursuit of profits.

Finally, there is clearly some justification in the fifth charge, moral illegitimacy, though the term 'illegitimacy' is unfortunate. It is all too easy, and, therefore, for those who take their social responsibility seriously, exceedingly difficult, to be a radical, a revolutionary, a reformer, or, for that matter, a conservative, for another country.[15] The moral commitment to objective research may conflict with the non-commitment to action or the commitment to non-action.

But there is another side to it. Foreign support, whether financial or intellectual, is often welcome to scholars in developing countries because it gives them greater independence from the pressures of their own governments. What may appear from outside as illegitimate interference is then regarded, from inside, as a basis for autonomy, for critical detachment. It has been reported that authoritarian governments which applied strict political standards to the research financed by themselves, did not interfere with externally financed research, even when it was critical. The universal commitment to scientific research and to presenting its conclusions as one sees them, is not only fundamental to all scholarship but its institutional expression through foreign support for research also has a political aspect. It may be one way in which critical and uncongenial views can be developed and expressed in a repressive regime. It follows from the commitment to objective research that the scholar, in presenting the results of his work, will not be concerned with tact, tactics or diplomacy. He will not keep silent merely to spare feelings and he will not mince words. It would be a form of inverted snobbery and condescension if scholars from developed countries thought it necessary to treat 'sensitive' problems of the developing countries with kid gloves, although this is what has largely happened, even in the very terminology of this sentence. Such diplomacy and inverted snobbery have reduced the intellectual standard of work in this field. Tact and diplomacy are, of course, necessary if recommendations are to be adopted by governments. But this must not affect the content and presentation of basic research, partly because it offends against the principles of scholarship and partly because policies based on blinkered analysis are bound to fail.

Such frankness and even bluntness is entirely consistent with, indeed is demanded by, empathy with, and imaginative understanding of the problems analysed, though not necessarily sympathy for all that is done. Some outside criticisms have, it is true, failed in their sensitivity to the social complexity. But equally, some sycophantic or 'diplomatic' work is at bottom patronizing and hence equally insensitive.

Are Western scholars more liable to impose biased or inappropriate concepts and models than scholars from the developing countries? Many of the 'alternative' models used by Third World intellectuals have, of course, Western origins. Marxism is a Western doctrine. So are Intermediate Technology, Structuralism, Planning, Cumulative Causation and Growth Poles.

Myrdal, Singer, Perroux, Ivan Illich and Fritz Schumacher are all 'Western' thinkers and Prebisch is only marginally an 'underdeveloped' scholar. Padma Desai quotes as illustrations of 'innovative economic contributions based on indigenous conditions and talent' the early Soviet economists, Evgenii Preobrazhensky and G.A. Fe'ldman; the Chinese shift from the Marxist emphasis on the revolutionary potential of the industrial proletariat to that of the rural masses;[16] and the Indian efforts at evolving an intermediate technology such as the Ambar Charkha and the Chinese campaign to produce steel from backyard blast furnaces, though both attempts were unsuccessful.[17] These are not altogether good examples of indigenous innovations of ideas and, in any case, the social science research content of the Chinese and Indian innovations is small, whereas the Russians are surely for this purpose 'Western'.

Perhaps more relevant are the studies carried out by the Economic Commission for Latin America (ECLA) in the 1950s on import substitution, the structural theory of inflation, the relations between the 'centre' and the 'periphery' and *dependencia*.

But with these exceptions, the new patterns have grown more out of *praxis* and experience than out of systematic research. Indeed, those who take a non-Keynesian view of the relation between the power of ideas and the good sense of practical experience see evidence that solutions to social problems are worked out by men and women going about their daily work, by politicians, party officials, farmers, businessmen, union officials, administrators, teachers, extension workers, and that the grand theories distill these practical experiences.[18] It would be arrogant, as well as wrong, to believe that only research is the source of new knowledge.

Paradoxically, the doctrine of the limits of transference may itself be regarded as a typically Western product and therefore as non-transferable.[19] This line leads us to the dilemma of the Cretan liar. More sinister, there is a short step (it might be argued) from the doctrine of the need to evolve alternative styles of thinking to the doctrine of 'separate and equal' and from there to apartheid. It is quite easy to give the call for alternative systems of thought a nasty racialist ring.[20] The doctrine of non-transferability may be interpreted as an unpleasant form of Western neo-colonialism. But, at least logically, this trap holds no danger. If non-transference must not be transferred because it is Western, Transference is OK. Rejection leads to acceptance.

I conclude that knowledge itself is a common good and that its pursuit unites scholars across the world;[21] that scholarship rejects diplomacy and tact, though sensitivity and imaginative understanding are essential in social studies and tactics are in order if implementation is desired; but that the concepts, models and theories are often partial, inadequate, irrelevant, or biased in a manner which ignores or distorts the relevant problems; that, while the *consumption* of knowledge is free, its *production* can be monopolized; and that the infrastructure of research: seminars, conferences, country houses, institutes, universities, travel, grants, sabbaticals, etc., is subject to increasing returns, so that polarization, dominance and dependence will tend to be established and reinforced. There is an intellectual and economic infant-industry argument for encouraging research in the weak periphery, even if it is initially of a lower standard than research carried out in established centres, but there is no argument for a local monopoly and against exposing ideas to world-wide scrutiny and criticism.

3 EQUAL OR UNEQUAL PARTNERS IN RESEARCH

Clearly the commitment to universal standards of scholarship in no way reduces the need to encourage the growth and self-confidence of indigenous research institutes. It is now a cliché to say that research in developing countries must be sensitive and must be collaborative.

Although research links with departments or institutes in LDCs are now generally advocated and, less widely, adopted, it is not always clear what the purpose of these links is. One might distinguish between the following objectives *from the point of view of the scholar in the developed country*. (Different objectives would be listed if we looked at joint ventures from the point of view of the developing country or its scholars.)

(1) In order to carry out research on a particular country and its problems, a link with a local institute is helpful because it provides a source of data collectors, interviewers, interpreters, contactmen and other useful local resources. These are essentially ancillary services. When in Rome, don't do as the Romans do; get a Roman to do it! More important, the costs of hiring local people are often lower and one can draw on their special skills and knowledge and improve the quality of research.

(2) The link may be useful for more or less blatantly political and tactical purposes. It may facilitate getting approval for conducting the project from the authorities; it may remove criticism in the local press or by public opinion; it may make it easier to gain access to sources of information; it may even be a necessary condition for government approval.

(3) A link may be necessary in assisting in the dissemination and implementation of policy-oriented research. Domestic institutes in developing countries have often special links with government agencies or other policy-making bodies and the dissemination of research conducted in advanced industrial countries is facilitated when it is channelled through these institutes and when they, or the policy-making bodies, are involved in the design and implementation of the research project.

(4) The prestige of a link with an institute in a developed country may add "respectability" and acceptability to the work of a local institute, even though the link is only tenuous: perhaps confined to occasional visits or only a letterhead. Such added prestige may help the institute in raising funds from other sources and recruiting better people.

(5) The link may be intended to build up and strengthen indigenous research capacity both of individual skills and of institutions. It is generally recognized that such capacity is highly desirable in itself and is a necessary condition for development. If it were objected that this could be done better by teaching and helping in curriculum design, the reply would be that research is best learned by doing. Teaching of how to do research by itself (without research) is less effective, and would also attract less well qualified people.

(6) This leads to the sixth objective. A link may be desired in order to improve the teaching and training capacity of the local and of the sponsoring institution.

(7) Finally and ideally, the local institute may contribute professional

expertise at the highest level. This objective might be called *institution-linking,* in contrast to *institution-building.* The indigenous scholars, being more familiar with their society and its problems, may improve the design of the research project, may help to ask the right questions and formulate the right hypotheses, may contribute to the right balance and emphasis and may prevent errors and omissions. They may, even more ambitiously, through what Susanne Hoeber Rudolph has called "participatory theory construction" help to correct the biases and partial visions of economists trained in a certain tradition and subject to the influences of their culture. A "Western" approach would be complemented by an "Eastern"; a "white" by a "black" and "brown"[22]. If what I have said about the imperialist claims of partial social theories is correct, such "participatory theory construction" has remedial value and can contribute to a more comprehensive theory of society and development. Just as the view of a mountain changes according to the point from which it is observed, so African, Asian, Latin American, North American or European perspectives may be brought together into a more universal vision. Participation in this area may be the cure not only for political discord but also for intellectual distortion or partiality. It may be a cure for arrogance and may teach us humility. This approach is the opposite of making compromises in order to accommodate different points of view. The aim is genuine reciprocity and an improvement in the quality of the research, including greater awareness of the limits of our knowledge.

Some of these objectives may be pursued jointly, and may even gain strength from this. Objective (3), dissemination, for instance, may be much easier to achieve if the recipients are involved in the design—objective (7). But conflicts may arise. Collaboration agreements and joint ventures, in research as in business, may be forms of window-dressing. They may pretend to an equal partnerhsip when in fact subservience exists.

When the local institute lacks the capacity to achieve objective (7), objective (5)—help in building up research capacity—may have to precede objective (7), genuine collaboration. This may include help in reducing a heavy teaching load or help in reducing time spent on supervising and organizing research of others, or on raising money for it, by those who would be better employed in doing the research themselves.

This roundabout way of strengthening research capacity raises important and difficult issues. The problem is sometimes presented as a trade-off between strengthening indigenous research capacity and research quality. At least three questions arise.

(1) What precisely is the purpose of the link? Is it good research or is it training for research and strengthening of research capacity? If training, is the intention to create or improve the skills of individuals or of institutions? The answers to these questions will dictate different courses of action.

(2) What is the time horizon? Is it important to have results of the highest quality soon, or is it preferable to forgo speedy results for the sake of more and better results later? Are there strict deadlines that have to be adhered to, or does slippage not matter? Should the work be directly relevant to the sponsoring institution's interests, or do we value more indirect contributions to the understanding of the development process and the generation of ideas?

(3) What risks is the donor prepared to take? The results of all research are subject to uncertainty, but backing underdeveloped research in order to strengthen its capacity is more risky than conventional research. Some projects will fail or be disappointing in relation to the time, effort and resources devoted to them. Is there a case for diversifying risks or, resources being scarce, should they be concentrated in order to reduce the risk of failure?[23]

If the answers to these questions were merely a matter of timing or risk-taking, the problem would be relatively simple. The difficulty is that there is an inconsistency between the master–apprentice (or, worse, the master–servant) relationship and the equality implied in international collaboration. It is not arrogance, nor intellectual imperialism, nor the assumption of superiority, but the *fact of superiority* that is at the root of the trouble. No amount of sensitivity, tact and courtesy can get round this unpalatable fact, which may be more important in causing hostility and resentment, and perhaps even discouragement, than the propagation of objectionable biases or the disposal over superior material resources. Ironically, the contribution of researchers, where it is most realistic and relevant, may be most resented. For it is irritating to be told by foreigners what is right and to have one's errors corrected by them.[24]

The most fundamental argument for international co-operation in development is that human beings, wherever born, should be able to develop to the fullest extent their capacities, both in order to fulfil themselves and to contribute to the common heritage of civilization, of which the stock of knowledge is part. In the light of this, the so-called trade-off between building research capacity and carrying out research of high quality then appears as an inter-temporal choice with an element of risk. But, human beings and especially researchers being what they are, how the fact of initial superiority and inferiority can be acknowledged, tolerated and, eventually, removed, is a much more difficult question in research management than the approach outlined above would suggest.

One reason for this is that good research requires self-confidence and single-mindedness, both of which can be undermined by the feelings of inferiority bred by domination by a rich-country institution.

A possible response to this would be to advocate infant research protectionism, intellectual import substitution, or delinking. If, it might be argued, outsiders wish to make a contribution the best way of doing so is to provide untied money. (This might be used to attract drained brains back to their mother country, though this might constitute a form of linking.) Otherwise the indigenous institutions might be best advised to shut themselves off from foreign influences and to devote their attention and resources to problems of interest to them. Only in this way can confidence, strength and relevance be built up. I have discussed the objections to this argument on pp. 67–8.

But there is another side to this question. The development community's work has recently been increasingly concerned with problems of poverty, internal income distribution and basic needs. These are politically sensitive areas in which external intervention may be particularly resented. On the other hand, foreign support, whether financial or intellectual, is often welcome to researchers in developing countries because it gives them greater independence from the pressures of their own governments. What may be castigated by the government as illegitimate outside interference is regarded from inside as a basis for autonomy and critical independence. Here the donor's contribution may be to strengthen the independence of the researchers and their institutes. It has been reported that authoritarian governments which applied strict political standards to the research financed by themselves, did not interfere with externally financed research, even when it was critical of their policies. External support of this kind of research may thus be one way in which critical and sensitive research can be developed and disseminated in a repressive regime.

In addition, governments are not monolithic. Outside support of research may encourage and back up the progressive groups within the government apparatus who wish to implement rational policies. On the other hand, collaboration with a foreign institution can be a fatal embrace, when the opponents use it as an accusation of "collaboration".

For the achievement of objectives (1)–(4) collaboration is often more honest and more practical if both partners get something out of it. The introduction of an element of trading can be a useful way of making the relationship more acceptable. You help me in collecting data and I help you with designing. a curriculum or in giving lectures or in reducing your administrative work load. Arrangements for mutual benefit, not all of which need directly relate to the research project, are possible and often desirable.

A practical conclusion that helps to take the neo-colonial, *dependencia* sting out of cooperative research and to make the relationship symmetrical would be to encourage and finance researchers from developing countries to conduct research on the problems of the developed countries, or of international relations. Such reciprocal and symmetrical arrangements can give reality to the idea of international cooperation of equal partners in research. To take an illustration, if the impact on internal income distribution in developing countries of resource transfers from developed countries is at issue, it is morally legitimate to enquire into the impact on internal income distribution of the transfer in the developed donor countries. Whose income is reduced by the extra tax required for the transfer, or who would be relieved by avoiding the transfer? Such questions are just as legitimate as those referring to the consequences inside recipient countries. The obvious place for conducting such research is, of course, the developed donor country, but it would strengthen the sense of partnership if developing country institutions were drawn into this type of work.

Are there certain areas of research which are more suited than others for collaborative research? Research work on development may be classified for this purpose in the following way:

(1) research on matters of narrow interest to the donor institution;
(2) research on methodology and other basic research;
(3) research on specific country problems—including poverty, income distribution, and basic needs; work involving large-scale data collection;
(4) work on sectors and projects;
(5) comparative studies and international issues such as international trade, foreign investment, international migration, international monetary issues and aid.

Are there principles according to which we can divide work between that which is best carried out in developed countries and that which is done best by local institutes? An obvious answer would be that work on local problems should be done locally; work of specific donor interest, work on general and basic problems, and comparative work, in the developed country. Since basic research is a human-capital-intensive and often also equipment-intensive activity, it might be argued that most of it should be conducted in a place where the critical mass of human capital is assembled, and that developing country institutions should confine themselves to adopting and adapting basic research and direct their own efforts at work that can be applied quickly and can be used locally.

Yet such a conclusion could be misleading. First, the ability to adopt and adapt intelligently, to appraise the scope as well as the limits of the basic work for purposes of application, requires a research capacity not too dissimilar from that needed for the basic research. Workers must be able to appraise critically what is useful and what is not, and how the useful can be adapted. This ability requires research capacity of a similar order and depth to that of the original workers.

Second, in view of the international market in the skills of professional social scientists, developing countries may have to attempt to match, or nearly match, if not the salaries at least the research opportunities their best brains are offered abroad if they wish to keep them.[25] And keeping them may be a necessary condition for carrying out useful applied research with quick-yielding results. For both these reasons—the need of an indigenous research capacity in order to select and adapt, and the need to plug the brain drain—developing countries cannot simply confine themselves to applied, quick-yielding, locally relevant research plus adaptation of research from rich countries.

Assuming the objective of building and strengthening research capacity in developing member countries is accepted as a primary objective for an institution, how does it select countries and institutions for support? Questions similar to those in aid allocation arise here. Some might argue that the weakest, poorest, most neglected are those most worthy of support; others that the optimum strategy is to lift those nearest equal capacity into the international community of scholarship: in this way could support most effectively strengthen global research capacity and ultimately and indirectly also contribute more to raising the capacity of the weakest.

But as in the case of financial aid, the old dilemma between the "needy" and the "speedy" is a false one. The criterion for allocation should be neither weakness nor strength, neither the worst nor the best, but, within the resources allocated for this purpose, the greatest improvers for a given expenditure. It is institutes to whose capacity support would make the greatest difference. Unfortunately, these magnitudes are not quantifiable, and even if they were, we should want a discount rate and the equivalent of poverty weights in order to determine the present value of the stream of the difference between what research would be with support and without.

Nevertheless, the criterion does provide a rough guide line.

If we measure graduates in the social sciences per thousand of population on one axis and the number of projects, or the amount of money spent in a given country on the other, the best place is likely to be the middle range. At the top end, what might well be needed is expensive equipment to match the facilities in the advanced countries. At the bottom end, long and thorough training of people, either in their own country or abroad, is needed. For neither of these may the institute be particularly suited. In the middle, a relatively small sum may be sufficient to divert already trained manpower either from other domestic, private or public activities, or drained brains from abroad to domestic research. The gap may be one of budgetary resources to top up salaries rather than much larger expenditures on facilities or training.

A practical conclusion emerges from the discussion. Time and people would have to be devoted to consultation and preparing the ground for cooperative research. Suitable researchers and institutes would have to be found, and the precise conditions for collaboration would have to be discussed. Such feasibility or pre-investment studies are essential if the selection is to be fruitful. If researchers are brought to the rich country, additional staff time will be required to work with them.

In deciding on the difference the role of the developed country institute could make in strengthening indigenous research capacity of developing countries, it is important to analyse in each particular case the factors that are responsible for the present "underdeveloped" state of research in the poor countries. The needs will be different for different countries and different institutions. for unless these factors are clearly identified, and other constraints removed, the donor's effort may be wasted.

A full list of such constraints would be impossible to compile, but among them will figure such items as:

—too small a size of staff, so that there is less than the minimum critical mass to produce results;
—too great a distance from centres of policy-making and intellectual life;
—too few opportunities to exchange ideas between researchers and policy-makers; lack of access to conferences, seminars, workshops;
—too little money to attract good people, provide adequate equipment, an adequate library; and adequate opportunities for sabbaticals;
—excessive load on staff members in teaching, administration or outside activities;
—poor direction of the institution, inefficient management; lack of organization;

—a host of cultural factors, including attitudes to research, recognition of research, outlets for publication, etc.;

—political factors which militate against objective research, ranging from low prestige to suppression of results, imprisonment and death.

In choosing an institute for research-capacity strengthening, the presence or absence of these factors is a crucial consideration. Only when these other constraints are absent or weak, or can be removed or weakened through donor action, or will be removed in the course of time, will the specific contribution be effective.

So far, I have talked about links in general. Should there be *specific* links between *particular* universities or departments and institutes in developing countries? There are arguments for and against. The case for such links is that there is stronger commitment, a clear responsibility, advantages of continuity and of getting to know one another well. On the other hand, it may mean reduced flexibility, so that one is bound to accept students or staff members from the linked institutions to the exclusion of others who might contribute more, or that one engages in a series of joint research projects for which other partners would have been more suitable.

There remains the question of balance and direction. If scholars are induced not to leave the country but carry out the kind of irrelevant, esoteric, excessively sophisticated, abstract work that gains prestige in the centres of learning of the developed countries, little is gained. To re-channel the external brain drain into an internal brain drain brings no benefit to the community. How this can be prevented raises difficult questions of academic prestige, social concern, conflicts between social and professional priorities and individual motivation. On these grounds a case might be made out for some closing in of the scholars of the developing countries, for reduced contacts with the international community of scholars, if such turning away encourages attitudes more in line with social priorities. On the other hand, if the scholars in the developed countries recognize that what is regarded as 'the best' in one setting might be the enemy of the good in another and adjust, not only their research priorities, but also their pecking order of recognition and prestige, the objections to international cooperation across wide open frontiers are weakened or removed. Paradoxically, by lowering the claims of prestigious subjects and 'standards of excellence', by making analysis more flexible, standards less universal and policy recommendations more diverse, greater universality and better international collaboration can be achieved.

4 IMPLICATIONS FOR RESEARCH PRIORITIES

What are areas suited for joint research projects? According to one view, purely domestic issues should not be on the research agenda of rich-country scholars and institutes for four reasons. First, there is little rich countries can do to implement policies for wholly domestic matters of the developing countries, whereas rich countries *can* act in the international arena. Second, research on purely domestic issues gives rise to the charges of mining and, possibly, undermining, discussed on p. 65. I have argued that such charges are often based on a confusion, but the political and psychological obstacles are nonetheless real.

Third, there is something paradoxical (though not contradictory) in foundations, agencies or institutes from rich countries advocating the need to strengthen indigenous research capacity as an important ingredient in development and then doing the work themselves. I have argued that a somewhat Böhm-Bawerkian approach[26] can make the two consistent, but again some resistance may remain.

The fourth objection is the most serious one and I am schizophrenic about it. It links up with the discussion of 'legitimacy' in Section 3. Assume a careful analysis leads to the conclusion that a radical redistribution of assets and power is a condition of progress. Can we then tell citizens of other countries to adopt these radical changes which may require a revolution? At the level of independent, objective analysis, there is nothing wrong with saying such changes are necessary, where they are seen to be.[27] But for an outsider to say this may be condemned not only as an easy option (I have already said that nothing is easier than to be radical for another country), but also as counter-productive. These changes, by definition, are going to hurt some people. If these people can point to the outside agency as the source of inspiration of these changes, this may make it more difficult for the progressive groups to carry out their intentions. What some may regard as supporting and well-wishing outside pressures, others will, as I have already said, see as the kiss of death, or at least an embarrassing embrace. So here is the dilemma. Honest research bids us expose the political constraints and point to the radical solutions, but it may be both improper and counter-productive for foreigners to recommend painful and possibly bloody domestic reform.

Equally, if the analysis were to lead to the conclusion that the costs of a revolution in terms of human suffering are too great and that reforms should be brought about gradually, can we then tell the country to refrain from violent change, even if this means that many will continue to suffer extreme poverty and deprivation? May not again such recommendations be both facile and counter-productive, by encouraging the advocates of violent change to say that foreign research supports the existing power structure?

Some of the issues raised here are just part of those usually discussed under the heading 'the moral responsibilities of scientists' and are not different from those faced by atomic or genetic scientists. But the dividing line between the subject of research and its application is less sharply drawn in the social sciences. The subject matter itself is influenced by the study and the interaction between academic and moral considerations is therefore closer. Further, scientists can influence actions of their own governments as citizens – but much less the actions of other countries' governments.

A second school of thought rules out domestic issues and concludes that the appropriate area for research by scholars from rich countries, whether they work on their own or jointly with scholars from the developing countries, is where the actions of rich countries impinge on the poor countries, what in the current jargon is called the interface: international trade, including adjustment assistance, aid, capital movements, the multinational enterprise, international monetary reform, energy, the environment, the sea and the sea-bed, migration, transfer of technology, the direction of research and development expenditure in rich countries, science policy, international taxation. These are areas in which data are available without intrusion and in which analysis and concern by the rich can lead to action and improvement by the rich. International issues could therefore be regarded as those suited *par excellence* for development research in and by developed countries.

There are objections to such an ordinance of self-restraint. The self-restraint can work properly only if it is obeyed universally. For if scholars not obeying the ordinance move into a developing country, advocating a partial solution, without stressing the other components of a strategy, they might inflict more harm than good.[28] Balancing action to neutralize such damage might then be needed. Since not everybody can be prevented from working on internal problems of the developing countries, anybody must be free to do so, if only to counteract one-sided and biased research.[29]

Second, if, as has been argued, preoccupation with prestige-endowed topics that are irrelevant to the development efforts of the developing countries leads to internal brain drain,[30] attention to relevant, though domestic, topics by scholars from rich countries may stimulate interest in these topics and attach indigenous prestige to them. Work by a foreign scholar on income distribution in Brazil has, if not initiated, certainly provoked, a good deal of excellent domestic work.

Third, foreign observers are often much more illuminating than those submerged in their own societies. Probably the best book on the British economy is that written by a group of American scholars and edited by Richard Caves.[31] Outsiders can bring a freshness of perception to bear on a country's problem that nationals of that country cannot.

Fourth, the distinction between international and internal topics is analytically untenable. The international system penetrates national affairs and *vice versa*.[32]

Fifth, the best research is inspired by what the researchers think they can do best and what interests them. It would be a pity if there were no funds to back these efforts.

Finally, I have argued that scholarship has its standards, which ignore the maxims of etiquette, diplomacy and tact. If, after honest research, in the light of the evidence, politically sensitive conclusions emerge, they should not be suppressed, dressed up or softened. But it is well to remember that cooperative research calls for standards of cooperation.[33] Jagdish Bhagwati, in his contribution to the panel discussion on 'What we need to know' at the Princeton Conference on International Trade and Finance (March 1973), tells the story of how Frazer, the great anthropologist from the pre-Malinowski, pre-Radcliffe-Brown era, when asked if he had ever visited the exotic areas he wrote about, replied: 'I only write about savages, I don't mix with them.' Bhagwati goes on to note that the foundations, AID and the World Bank, supported by the jet, had removed any obstacles and Frazerian inhibitions to the pursuit of knowledge, if not pleasure. But there may be a conflict between opportunities and objectives. Just as the hordes of tourists in search of exotic sights destroy the very mysteries they have come to see, so scholars may interfere harmfully with the processes they have come to study.

In addition, there is a certain process of selection at work, encouraged by high living standards abroad, and the relative absence of equally high academic standards. Some years ago, Dudley Seers wrote a memorable article on 'Why Visiting Economists Fail'. Perhaps the time has come to write a companion piece on 'Why Failed Economists Visit'. T. N. Srinivasan, in his already-quoted Belgrade paper on 'The State of Development Economics' notes, rather generously and politely, that 'there are situations in which the value of the contribution of the resident foreign economist covers his marginal cost'.[34]

I find it difficult to give a clear answer to the questions about the limits of research by scholars from rich countries, except that research into international issues, and particularly those areas in which action by rich countries can contribute to development, is in some respects more appropriate and safer, in spite of the objections mentioned, than research into entirely domestic issues of the poor countries. The 'adjustees' of adjustment assistance are more appropriate subjects for research than the victims of a foreign revolution. But if the 'interface' penetrates into largely domestic issues, no barrier can halt the progress of research.

Yet, there is another problem. Even where national interests coincide, and where appropriate policies would lead to common gains (such as access to imports from LDCs), there is a question about the division of these gains. In other areas, national interests may clash. Certain gains for the developing countries may be available only at the expense of developed countries. Are such problems of bargaining and possibly confrontation and conflict appropriate areas for rich-country research? Alternatively, there might be schemes of self-help, where the best policy would be for developing countries to turn away from the rich and encourage arrangements among themselves (regional integration, payments unions, etc.). Could such problems be studied in developed countries?

In spite of the suspicion that such research may be nationally biased and self-interested, I can see good reasons why it could be usefully conducted by rich countries in cooperation with poor. First, until the work has been done, it is not always clear whether the game is a zero sum one or whether positive sums may be available for distribution. It is quite legitimate to investigate the conditions in which private foreign investment, freeing trade or permitting immigration help both groups of countries and when they are beneficial to one at the expense of the other.

Second, even where interests clearly conflict, informed bargaining is often to the advantage of both partners. Representatives of multi-national enterprises often insist that they prefer to negotiate with well-informed, hard-headed officials from developing countries to having to face ignorant and incompetent ones (though OPEC may have gone too far for them). The short-term advantages that may be gained from the latter, they argue, are not worth the recriminations, regrets and retaliatory actions that spring from the later reactions to ill-informed bargains.

Third, developed-country scholars are quite capable of detaching themselves from the narrow national interest of their own country and of analysing conflict situations that can be resolved to the advantage of the developing countries. Some of them are eager to do this. The exploration of areas of potential bargaining power is only beginning.

One would hope, however, that areas of cooperation will give more scope than areas of confrontation and conflict. There are ways in which the talk of international cooperation can be backed by action. One way to give reality to this notion is for the rich countries to encourage exchange of ideas and experience between developing countries. In many respects they can teach one another more than developed countries can in such areas as export promotion of labour-intensive products, family-planning programmes, rural development, including smallholder schemes. Countries which have recently undergone an experience are much better equipped to communicate it than countries that went through this experience decades or hundreds of years earlier, in quite different demographic, climatic, international and social conditions. This is another important argument for the encouragement and finance by developed countries of 'offshore' research on an international or inter-regional basis.

The upshot of this discussion is that international and 'interface' issues are more appropriate items on the agenda for research of rich-country institutions than purely LDC domestic ones, but that this is subject to a number of qualifications. More particularly, (a) development is a complex process in which international relations cannot be severed from domestic ones; (b) self-restraint will never be universal and if one group of researchers (possibly belonging to the same school of thought) occupies itself with these issues, balanced scholarship requires that their work be subject to the criticism of others in the profession; (c) focusing interest in high-prestige centres of learning (the USA, Europe) on purely LDC domestic issues may correct the internal brain drain (the diversion of efforts to irrelevant prestige topics) and stimulate indigenous, relevant research in the developing countries; (d) outside observers have often a better insight, and (e) the universality of scholarship draws no political frontiers, though the existence of such frontiers may impede the work and colour the outlook of scholars. On the other hand, work on international issues may be as suspect as work on domestic issues, precisely because the national self-interest of rich countries is involved. In spite of these qualifications, I would conclude that the emphasis of rich-country research in rich countries should be on 'interface' issues.

5 MONEY: THE ROOT OF ALL GOOD

Quoting proverbs is like reading tea leaves: you can always find what you are looking for. Proverbial wisdom is wise because it hedges its bets. It is irrefutable, because it is self-contradictory. 'Many hands make light work' seems to offer advice to a personnel catering manager wishing to determine the number of staff he should recruit. But proverbial wisdom protects itself by coupling with the proverb its antidote: 'Many cooks spoil the broth.' Similarly, the impecunious scholar turning his troubled conscience to sources of finance finds ambiguous advice from '*pecunia non olet*' and 'he who pays the piper calls the tune.' In principle, it should make no difference where research money comes from, as long as no intellectual, moral or political conditions are attached to the methods and conclusions of the work. In practice, what matters is not only freedom from ties but also whether outsiders, on whose cooperation the work depends, see it in this light. However self-effacing the CIA or the US Defense Department or, indeed, any American source may be, many Latin Americans regard *all* US money as tainted. Yet, the rational reaction to suspect sources is not to reject them but to demand full and open disclosure of the purpose, methods and origins.

At one time, it was possible to distinguish between public and private (charitable) sources of finance. Public sources clearly insisted on, or were thought to insist on, returns on their money, which meant support for their policies. Private charitable sources were regarded as more disinterested, more prepared to support genuinely independent research. This distinction, if it existed, broke down with the revelation of the various private foundations that the CIA had used for channelling funds for its purposes. On the other hand, government departments may genuinely divest themselves by channelling their funds through independent bodies, such as the University Grants Committee in Britain or the various science research councils, so that academic freedom and public accountability are reconciled. For reasons such as these, the public–private distinction does not coincide with that between heteronomy and autonomy.

Another distinction may be drawn between national and international sources. National sources might be thought to be concerned with promoting the interests of the nation; international sources those of the world community. But international organizations have their own partial and vested interests and it is doubtful whether they are inclined to support more independent research than some national bodies; and some national bodies may take a genuinely international view.

More important, in my view, than the source or channel of funds, namely whether they come from public or private bodies, from national or international ones, or whether they are channelled directly or indirectly (through intermediate bodies), is the question whether they are highly concentrated or whether there is genuine, not just legal or formal, dispersal. There are obvious advantages in concentration. Wasteful duplication of effort and overlaps can be avoided; attention can be drawn to gaps in our knowledge; data, concepts and methods can be standardized. But there are also dangers in concentration. The principal danger of heavy concentration and centralization of research funds is that diversity, originality, criticism and heterodoxy are liable to be discouraged in favour of a uniform and possibly premature orthodoxy or a swinging with fads and fashions. The pressures of the professionalization of a subject in the direction of confirmity to the standards evolved by the profession are, in any case, powerful. If they are further strengthened by a single grant-dispensing research council, the chances for critical, independent work are weakened.

Against the obvious benefits of concentration and centralization must be set the less obvious losses resulting from weaker questioning of the prevailing orthodoxies. The safeguard of original, independent, critical research must therefore be sought in a multiplication of channels of funds between which the applicant has a choice and an encouragement of small, independent, uninhibited scholars. An additional safeguard is not to entrust the decisions solely to established academics working in the same field as the applicant. Academics from other fields, officials, politicians and other laymen may be useful members of grant-awarding bodies and appointments committees. They can help to break through the crust of conformity. Multiplication of channels in turn calls for a single place where these sources are listed, so that potential applicants are fully aware of the opportunities.

Should research be commissioned by grant-giving, policy-making bodies, according to their needs and priorities as they see them, or should the initiative come from the researchers? The arguments are by now well-rehearsed. On the one hand, the flicker of original, first-class ideas is such a rare thing and depends so much on individuality and autonomy, that any spark that is struck should be carefully fanned. Interference or even requests that impose conditions may extinguish these precarious and precious flames. Again, innovation and originality do not usually thrive under the strait-jacket of officially commissioned projects. Donors are preoccupied with the urgent problems of the day and the near future; researchers are better at raising more fundamental issues of greater importance in the more distant future. The conflict is between the urgent and the important, between the short-term and the long-term, between the simple rule of thumb and the complex web and between getting answers and raising questions. Further, useful and applicable knowledge often grows unexpectedly out of what may at first appear esoteric and useless knowledge. For these reasons the purposes of policy are often best served by leaving scholars free to identify the problems and set about solving them in their own way. At least there should be an area in which such free pursuit is vouchsafed.

On the other hand, problems of action *are* urgent and data and analysis are needed for informed policy. Unless the donor and customer (the policy-making department) can specify what precisely he requires from the contractor, there will be waste, gaps and a failure to focus on what is usable.

This dilemma can be overstated. There is no need to opt between, on the one hand, a clearly specified take-it-or-leave-it attitude, when the customer lays down clear specifications, and, on the other hand, complete *laissez-faire*. If universities and research institutes are represented on the grant-giving bodies or their committees by men and women who understand the needs and attitudes of scholars and if the needs and priorities of the policy-making bodies are spelled out clearly, the gap can be greatly reduced. Many good, competent scholars and even more graduate students look for appropriate topics to work on and if ministries, councils, international agencies or foundations make it known on what topics they require more information and analysis, many are eager to respond. Letting priorities be known and continuing a dialogue between policy-makers and researchers, perhaps on joint committees and through informal contacts, will greatly contribute to bridging the gap between the needs of policy-makers and the incentives and temperaments of independent scholars.

6 SCIENCE AND CRYPTO-SCIENCE

If the social sciences are a 'soft' technology compared with the 'hard' technology of the natural sciences, development studies have been regarded as the soft underbelly of 'economic science'. I have heard it equated to economics minus logic. In the attempt to emulate the colleagues practising 'hard' economics, mathematical methods have sometimes been brought to bear on issues for which they were not appropriate.

In his Romanes Lectures, Sir Isaiah Berlin illustrates how what was once revolutionary doctrine has become establishment doctrine, by Turgenev's *Fathers and Children*.

> The victorious advance of quantitative methods, belief in the organisation of human lives by technological organisation, reliance on nothing but calculation of utilitarian consequences in evaluating policies that affect vast numbers of human beings, this is Bazarov, not the Kirsanovs. The triumphs of the moral arithmetic of cost effectiveness which liberates decent men from qualms, because they no longer think of the entities to which they apply their scientific computations as human beings . . . this today is rather more typical of the establishment than of the opposition.

Growing concern with social objectives: employment, equality, the environment, has led to calls for the "dethronement of GNP" which (erroneously) has been regarded as an *economic* objective. But if there was a fault in the preoccupation with GNP, it was excessive attention to a simple quantitative index, irrespective of the valuation implicit in its sets of weights, i.e. of its composition, distribution and the manner in which it was produced. We are in danger of repeating this very same fault in attempting to extract simple indexes for the social objectives. The proportion of the GNP earned by the bottom 40 per cent, or the Gini coefficient are just as inadequate and, by themselves, misleading measures of what we are getting at when we try to reduce inequality or eradicate poverty, as GNP is an inadequate measure of productive capacity. Inequality of income distribution touches only a small portion of the vast, multi-dimensional problem of inequality. There is inequality of ownership of assets, of access to earning opportunities, of satisfaction from work, of recognition, of ability to enjoy consumption, of access to power, of participation in decision-making. The call for greater equality, for a genuine community of equals cannot be answered simply by measures that reduce the Gini coefficient or any other simple measure of inequality, which are inadequate even in expressing what concerns us in unequal income distributions. It is possible to envisage a technocratic society, where decisions are highly centralized and in which a few enjoy the satisfaction from power and creativity while the many carry out boring and disagreeable tasks in a hierarchic structure and in which the Gini coefficient is zero.

The danger of social science research that attempts to emulate the "hard" sciences is that it focuses on the measurable and neglects the rest, that only what can be counted counts. Some of the most important obstacles to the eradication of poverty and the promotion of greater equality lie in areas in which measurement is still very difficult or perhaps impossible.

The important question is: What are the springs of development? Many would stress the importance of entrepreneurial and managerial motivation, attitudes and education. We do not know what characteristics make for the social selection of an innovating, entrepreneurial group. Neither innate characteristics nor education nor religion can explain why some societies at certain periods are better and quicker at innovating than others at other times. Innate characteristics are distributed according to normal distribution curves; the level of scientific education is quite high in many societies in which innovation is poor and *vice versa*; and all kinds of religion have proved to be consistent with innovation. What we need is an explanation of why, with the right education, innate characteristics and religion, the ablest and fittest, the "best and the brightest", the creative innovators, are not attracted to business but, instead, to politics, universities or the civil service.

Economists have chased for hundreds of years the sources of economic growth and development. Land and natural resources (the physiocrats), labour (John Locke and the classical economists), capital (Marx, Harrod, Domar), education (T. W. Schultz, Gary Becker), achievement motivation (David McClelland) and most recently research and development have, in turn, been scrutinized and, when examined in detail, found wanting. The experts looking at the facts tell us in each case that the factor they investigated is not very important for development. At the end of the day (and of this paper) we must confess that we do not know what causes development and therefore lack a clear agenda for research. But we must try to resist the temptation to behave like the drunk who has lost his key and looks for it not where he dropped it but under the street lamp – because this is where the light is.

APPENDIX

Review of Irving Louis Horowitz, *The Rise and Fall of Project Camelot*, MIT Press, from *New Society* (11 January 1968).

In December 1964 the American Army and the Department of Defense launched Project Camelot. It proved far the largest grant ever handed out for research in the social sciences: $4 to $7 million for three to four years and, as this was to be only a feasibility study, with expenditure of perhaps $50 million to follow. A number of international scholars received a letter telling them that "Project Camelot is a study whose objective is to determine the feasibility of developing a general social systems model which would make it possible to predict and influence politically significant aspects of social change in the developing nations of the world."

What interested the army, translated from the tortuous deodorized jargon, was why revolutions happen ("the predisposing conditions and the precipitants of the potential for internal war") and how to prevent or stop them ("counter-insurgent prophylaxis"). Seven months later the exercise was called off, not because it was intellectually ill-conceived and unscholarly, but because it had caused a row in Chile and threatened to upset United States relations with Latin America. The craft union demarcation (= jurisdiction) dispute between the State and Defense Departments over political and military competence, the politicians' contempt for social studies and the army's doubt about the ability of this type of software to support their hardware, all contributed to the final Presidential veto prohibiting goverment-sponsored research which, in the opinion of the Secretary of State, would be bad for foreign relations. Even the scholars were less concerned with criticizing the design and method of the project than with the degree of military supervision and the method of channelling research funds. Professor Horowitz has assembled in this fascinating volume some of the contributions, academic, political and official, to the debate on the affair and has written a stimulating account and evaluation.

The main methodological faults of the project were the implicit value premises: the identification of revolution and radical social change with social pathology, and of order and stability with social health. Revolutionary movements became "anti-systems activities", indications of "severe disintegration" and "destabilizing processes". Abt associates, one of the consultants, suggested that techniques developed for reliability and quality control could, by analogy, be applied to social systems: rebellious groups then become failures in a particular component of the system. Professor Horowitz is right in saying that " . . . the preeminence of a 'systems' approach rather than a 'problems' approach led to exaggerated model building techniques that obfuscated rather than clarified major issues."

But the central issue, on which the contributors express a wide variety of views, is this: should social scientists accept money from the governmnet or government agencies in return for work on foreign countries for the government? It seems that at least five distinct questions arise: the *source*, the *terms*, the *use*, the *area* and the *conjuncture*.

As to source, some contributors think it is so tainted that the autonomy and integrity of scholarship is threatened by the bargain. This position seems to me to be untenable, partly because all sources are potentially tainted (more about this later) and partly because it remains true that *pecunia non olet*: he who pays the piper may call the tune, but not the way in which it is played. If the scholar, while disclosing the source of his funds, is left free to pursue truth, there can be no objection to the source. The safeguards of this freedom include the availability of a multiplicity of alternative sources, a high proportion of "untied" grants free from specific contractual obligations, fair chances for individual workers as well as teams. It is neither direct government grants nor government requests for specific pieces of research that constitute threats to academic integrity, but the *terms* on which the money is given. If these permit the scholar to reach the conclusions to which his clearly stated assumptions and the evidence lead him, there can be no objection to the selection of the topic of research by the sponsor. Several contributors argue, to my mind unconvincingly, that agency-financed research is necessarily corrupting.

Professor Horowitz, on the other hand, thinks that the important question of integrity arises from the purpose and ultimate *use* of the findings. But since any piece of applied knowledge can be put to bad use (for if you know how to improve, you also know how to impede improvement) the rule that the scientist must not be instrumental to abuse, strictly interpreted, implies intellectual abstinence. Horowitz limits his rule to *intended* use. But unintended, though foreseeable, or even unforeseeable, use may be more objectionable, and the intention may fail.

As to the *area*, many contributors consider government-sponsored research on and in foreign countries, without the host government's agreement, not only unwise and inexpedient, but ethically and scientifically wrong. Some go further and say that research conducted in foreign countries must be, and must be seen to be, in the service of the host country and its people. But surely the primary obligation is to advance the subject, and is therefore to the international fraternity of scholars, whether inside or outside the host country. The Norwegian Professor Galtung, who was responsible for exposing the project in Chile (there was nothing secret or classified about it), in a searching essay, coins the phrase "scientific colonialism". The Chileans certainly felt that, just as foreign copper companies were mining and remitting profits, so American social scientists were threatening to mine and undermine Chilean society in its most private recesses and to remit the material to the Pentagon. The correct answer to this question was given by Dudley Seers, in a different context. In his article on "Why Visiting Economists Fail", he wrote that "the conscious and public definition of one's role is essential in work overseas". Although this is not always easy, the social scientist must try to make clear in precisely what capacity he is acting.

Finally, and perhaps most difficult, the scholar may have to judge the political *conjuncture* in which his work is done and published. The American intervention in the Dominican Republic may have made a difference to joining in a study by the American Army of counter-insurrection, even if the *terms* were consistent with freedom and no direct *use* was intended or possible.

Some of the radical critics of Camelot, such as Professor Blumer, write as if only government contracts pose problems of integrity. As Professor Boguslaw points out in a sensible apologetic, these critics ignore the pressures (of business, of the foundations and of the universities themselves) to bend the scholar's work towards bias, compromise and conformity. It is surely naive to say, as Professor Kalman Silvert does, that "no problem of integrity exists for two polar groups of social scientists: those who work inside governments . . . and those who . . . stay entirely inside the university world. . . . It is the social scientist working both fields who is in danger of betraying both his masters through the loss of his power of independent analysis." The temptations of betrayal in order to gain an appointment or promotion at a university, or in order to placate courts or boards of governors of academic institutions, are more corrupting than political temptations. On the contrary, government sponsorship and patronage can be a countervailing power against the temptations and pressures of the academic establishment. The contrast, drawn by Silvert, Blumer and others, between the pure groves of Academe and the sullied corridors of power, not only reveals an ideology shared by radicals and reactionaries, but is also false.

This is not to say that there is a harmony of interests or of approach between politicians and administrators on the one hand and scholars on the other. Camelot was an offspring of the army's Special Operations Research Office (SORO), a tail which wags the body of American University to the extent that on the stationery SORO was set in larger type than American University. The director of this organization, writing, as it were, more in SORO than in anger, makes the point that conflict arises if research has to be justified by a government agency both as immediately useful and as basic and independent. But no contributor to the volume analyses the differences between the approach of the scholar and the official, although Professor William Polk, in a thoughtful and perceptive essay, discusses related issues. The scholar brings out value premises explicitly, in order to gain clarity and objectivity, the official tends to suppress them in order to get agreement on action; the scholar wishes to sharpen and refine distinctions, the official to reduce and blur them; the scholar is suspicious of "wide agreement", the official of "controversy"; when the scholar says the same thing twice, he begins to doubt it; when the official says it twice he begins to believe it; the scholar has time, the official is in a hurry; when the official asks, what shall I do now? The scholar replies, you are trying to change the world; the point is first to understand it. The research proposal of Camelot, obviously drawn up by officials, talked of "orientation" that "is scientific, offering a balanced course between theoretical and empirical work", bringing to bear "all the relevant disciplines and talents required". Camelot was a beast designed by a committee.

One result of Camelot, as Professor Kalman Silvert says in an interesting contribution, is to accelerate the Latin American desire to diversify academic contacts. Although American social scientists are, by and large, professionally better, the American Department of State and the American foundations have responded to this desire, and it is for the Parry centres and others in this country to respond to the opportunity and to learn from past mistakes. Professor Silvert says that Latin America is not only a neglected area of study but also an exceptionally difficult and diverse one. But it would seem that it is a particularly rewarding one for a scholar interested in comparative politics.

Professor Horowitz subtitles his book "Studies in the Relationship between Social Science and Practical Politics". But the affair raises also another interesting question: is more money for social research *always* better than less (which is not the same as: is more knowledge always better than less?)? "Most of the men viewed Camelot as a bona fide opportunity to do unrestricted fundamental research with relatively unlimited funds at their disposal." These are described and generally accepted as optimal conditions. Yet there are disadvantages of size. First, abundance discourages discrimination and the weighing of priorities, while financial constraints impose the need for selection. Economy in thought is encouraged by financial economy. Financial stringency, like hanging, focuses the mind.

Second, large sums of money shift the emphasis of research from the construction of theories to the colletion and manipulation of data, because original ideas are scarce, while data collection can always be expanded. In spite of a widely held view that social scientists need more data rather than more theories, the opposite is true, particularly in the field of development. Too much money chasing too few ideas debauches the value of intellectual currency. Foundation grants, research councils, computerization are encouraging the accumulation of data, while reflection on their significance is neglected.

Third, large sums of money encourage the mounting of projects by teams, with their accompanying strengths and weaknesses (bureaucratic attitudes and mediocrity) and transform scholars into executives, diverting their talents from doing research to organizing and coordinating it. The lone wolf is losing out if only because of the economies of scale of grant administration.

Fourth, if the handing out of big money is concentrated in one body, however independent and fair-minded, the "premature crystallization of spurious orthodoxies" (in the memorable words of the Clapham Committee) can be encouraged. The sums disbursed by our own Social Science Research Council (which spent in 1967 on *all* forms of research in the social sciences about the same as feasibility Project Camelot budgeted for one year, though this in turn is trifling compared with the $80 million spent on military hardware) have not yet reached a scale to raise these

questions, but the time will come when they do. On a longer view, the threat
to learning from an independent, grant-channelling large monopoly is
greater than that from agencies of a democratically elected government.

NOTES

1. From: *World Development*, vol. 2, no. 10–12 (October–December 1974), pp.
   11–34. I have benefited from comments and criticisms of an earlier draft by
   Irma Adelman, Peter Balacs, Ronald Dore, Edgar Edwards, Unni Eradi,
   Michael Faber, Anne Gordon, Keith Griffin, Seev Hirsch, Jill Rubery, Ernest
   Stern, Frances Stewart, Hugh Stretton, B. R. Virmani, Gordon Winston and
   Howard Wriggins. To these, and to a research seminar at Queen Elizabeth
   House, I am very grateful. I am also grateful to the Economic Development
   Institute of the World Bank and its director, Mr Andrew Kamarck, for having
   provided the facilities and stimulating atmosphere for the early stages of this
   work.
       An earlier version of this paper was presented at a conference in Bellagio on
   the financing of social science research for development, 12–16 February 1974,
   sponsored by the Ford Foundation, the Canadian International Development
   Research Centre, the Rockefeller Foundation, USAID and the World Bank.
2. While it may appear odd of social scientists not to examine the social origins
   and implications of their own activities, it is quite consistent with what might be
   called the blind spot of auto-professionalism (or, by Gunnar Myrdal, 'the beam
   in our eyes'): psychologists' children are crazy mixed-up kids, and the suicide
   rate among psychiatrists is the highest; dentists have bad teeth; experts on
   management cannot manage their affairs nor marriage counsellors their
   marriages; planners are quite incapable of planning their own lives; and the
   London School of Economics, that power house of social science, was in
   difficulty about its own structure. So it should not surprise us that social
   scientists have somewhat neglected the social determination and implications
   of their own professional activities.
3. Frances Stewart, 'Technology and employment in LDCs', Paper for Ford
   Foundation Conference on Technology and Employment in New Delhi, 1973,
   where she quotes R. S. Merrill, 'The Study of Technology' in the *Encyclopaedia
   of Social Sciences*.
4. This charge can be interpreted broadly, when it covers also the subsequent two
   charges, or narrowly, when it is confined to 'mining'.
5. See Appendix.
6. Ronald Dore remembers 'being at a conference in Singapore when the
   sociologist Wertheim gave a paper on the obstacles to development, which he
   identified as landlords and capitalists, ending with the stirring prediction that
   the masses were already awakening and that the duty of the scholar was to help
   them sweep away their enemies. An Indonesian there was somewhat indignant.
   'Fine for you, Professor Wertheim. But I'm the sausage that's going to be fried
   in the fire—though I'm neither landlord nor capitalist.' Ronald Dore goes on to
   say (in private communication) how the same point arises when we preach
   income redistribution in even a mild form to our colleagues from poor

countries, whose reference group is the international academic community
rather than peasant incomes in their own countries.

7. Michael Faber reminded me of John Austin's '*In vino*, possibly, '*veritas*', but in
a sober symposium '*verum*'. What needs discussing rather is the use, or certain
uses, of the word 'true'.' J. L. Austin, *Philosophical Papers*, ed. J. O. Urmson
and G. J. Warnock, Oxford Clarendon Press, (1961), p. 85. But for the sense in
which I use it, Pilate's question holds no terror; 'true' will do for my purposes.

8. This is the view of, e.g., Lionel Robbins. 'It has sometimes been asserted that
the generalisations of Economics are essentially "historico-relative" in
character, that their validity is limited to certain historical conditions, and that
outside these they have no relevance to the analysis of social phenomena. This
view is a dangerous misapprehension.' *An Essay on the Nature and Significance
of Economic Science*, Macmillan, London (1st ed., 1932, 2nd ed., 1946), pp. 80–
81. See also Ludwig von Mises, *Human Action*, Hodge (1949). Sir Geoffrey
Wilson tells me that about 20 years ago, when he was in Ceylon starting up the
Colombo Plan, he sent to Sydney Caine, who was then Vice-Chancellor of the
University of Singapore, a memo suggesting that the economics of the
countries of South-East Asia might better be studied locally than at the London
School of Economics and that an institute might be set up for the purpose in
South India where, incidentally, foreign scholars might find a home and see
what it was like to work in local conditions. Caine's reply 'led me to think that I
had blasphemed in church – economics was economics, whether in London,
Delhi, Tokyo or the moon, etc., and I retired covered in confusion at ever
having had such an unclean thought'.

9. See Steven Lukes 'On the social determination of truth', in *Modes of Thought:
Essays on Thinking in Western and Non-Western Societies*, ed. Robin Horton
and Ruth Finnegan, Faber & Faber, London (1973).

10. See Chapter 1, Section 7.

11. See pp. 57–8.

12. Spelt out less aphoristically, this means: there exists a set of propositions about
social and economic phenomena and their relations which is generally true of
Africa (at least for the time being), but not generally true elsewhere; but there
can be no set of exclusively African criteria for what is true.

13. 'The comparison that Lagrange made of Newton is worth repeating in this
connection: assuredly Newton was the greatest man of science, but also the
luckiest. For there is but one system of the world and Newton was the one who
found it. Similarly, there is but one grand concept of general equilibrium and
it was Walras who had the insight (and luck) to find it.' P. A. Samuelson,
'Economists and the history of ideas', *American Economic Review*, vol. 52, no. 1
(March 1962) pp. 3–4.

14. Michael Faber tells me that 'when Danilo Dolci held a conference of notables
on his problems of development, he chose Palma di Montechiaro (the true
home of the fictional Gattopardo), where the heat was intolerable, the village
hall was filled with the stench from the open gutters outside, the din from the
square made the speakers inaudible, and the fragile electricity supply could be
counted upon to break down.'

15. See below, p. 82.

16. But Bakunin, a thinker with intuition in many respects superior to Marx's
(though greatly inferior as a theorist), had seen the revolutionary potential of

the peasants and predicted revolutions not in the most industrialized countries, but in underdeveloped rural societies such as Spain, Russia and China.

17. Padma Desai, 'Third World social scientists in Santiago', *World Development*, vol. 1 no. 9 (September 1973), pp. 63–4.

18. A synthesis of the Marxian and Keynesian view of the respective influence of interests and ideas is presented by Max Weber: 'Interests (material and ideal), not ideas, dominate directly the actions of men. Yet the 'images of the world' created by these ideas have often served as switches determining the track on which the dynamism of interests kept the action going.' *From Max Weber: Essays in Sociology*, Oxford University Press, New York, (1947), p. 280.

19. In an interesting report on a seminar in Poona, Andrew Shonfield reported that he 'was frankly surprised at the violence of the antipathy shown by the Westerners towards the Western way of life' compared with the enthusiasm for large-scale facilities to produce cement, electricity and steel of many 'Easterners'. Fritz Schumacher 'emphasized the need to protect, above all else, the process of 'organic growth'. Planning of development on this view would be as much concerned to avoid the introduction of new manufactured products . . . which would put the established [producers] in the villages out of business.' 'Whereas Schumacher foresees spiritual disaster in any attempt to speed up development through a programme of large-scale industrialisation [Colin] Clark asserts flatly that it cannot be hurried up at all.' 'Alternatives to Backwardness', *Encounter*, no. 99 (December 1961).

Similarly, the 'decision to introduce English education was taken not without an acute controversy. The story of this controversy, known as the controversy between the Orientalists and the Anglicists, is quite familiar to all students of the history of Indian education. The curious fact is that the Orientalists were almost all Englishmen in the service of the Company, whereas almost all Indians of repute were Anglicists. . . . It was the strong position taken up by Macaulay that forced the issue in favour of the Anglicists.' G. Ramanathan, *Educational Planning and National Integration*, Asian Publishing House (1963), p. 21. And Macaulay wrote in his famous Minute on Education: 'I am quite ready to take the oriental learning at the valuation of the orientalists themselves. I have never found one among them, who could deny that a single shelf of a good European library was worth the whole native literature of India and Arabia.' From Macaulay's Minute on Education, in *Sources of Indian Tradition*, by Theodore de Bary, Stephen Hay, R. Weiler and Andrew Yarrow, Columbia University Press, (1958) published in Britain by OUP, London.

In spite of some Western critics of Western modernization (since joined by Ivan Illich), Max Weber identifies the claim to a single universal future as an important characteristic of Western civilization. 'A product of modern European civilisation, studying any problem of universal history, is bound to ask himself to what combination of circumstances the fact should be attributed that in Western civilisation, and in Western civilisation only, cultural phenomena have appeared which (as we like to think) lie in a line of development having *universal* significance and value.' Max Weber, *The Protestant Ethic and the Spirit of Capitalism* George Allen & Unwin, London (1930) Charles Scribner, New York (1958).

20. See Ch. 7, 'Alternatives in Development'.

21. It is this unity of scholarship that gives us the right, beyond a general appeal to

human rights, to send petitions to foreign governments to protect the life and work of colleagues in danger of being imprisoned or tortured for their ideas. If this were not so, such petitions, based on professional solidarity rather than human rights, would be a form of intellectual imperialism.

22. 'Reflection of an Indian Scholar' (mimeo).

23. In his discussion of this problem, Edgar Edwards makes the additional point that policy-makers in developing countries should regard research by their own nationals, particularly on sensitive issues, as being better grounded in local knowledge and possibly more concerned with national welfare and long-term implications than research conducted abroad or by visiting scholars 'Employment in Developing Countries', mimeo, p. 75.

24. One is reminded of the lady who went to a psychiatrist, complaining that she suffered from an inferiority complex. The (sensible) psychiatrist, after examining her, replied: 'Madam, you do not have an inferiority complex: you *are* inferior.'

25. Research contacts with the donor institute will often lead to developing country researchers seeking jobs with it. The economics and ethics of the brain drain are controversial.

26. Böhm-Bawerk was a famous Austrian economist who reasoned that greater production later resulted from devoting current resources to more 'roundabout' methods of production, e.g. rather than training students, training trainers of students.

27. There is a school of thought that advocates 'participatory observation', 'participant intervention', the role of 'militant cum observer' and 'liberation anthropology'. Without going into the merits of this case, such activities are bound to remain a minority interest.

28. For an illustration of the need for a multi-pronged attack, where single prongs can do harm, see Chapter 8.

29. Another example is some of the currently fashionable doctrines of project appraisal. These profess to cover domestic social objectives, such as reducing inequality in income redistribution and raising savings rates. Yet, if propagation of these doctrines were to proceed, while the critics of these methods kept silent, the analysis and policy would be one-sided and biased.

30. T. N. Srinivasan, 'The State of Development Economics', *Planning Income Distribution Private Foreign Investment*, International Meeting of Directors of Development Research and Training Institutes, Belgrade, Yugoslavia (28–30 August 1972), Development Centre of the Organization for Economic Cooperation and Development, Paris (1974), pp. 189–90.

31. Caves and others, *Britain's Economic Prospects*, Brookings Institution (1968).

32. Thus British aid to overseas education can be analysed only in the context of the educational systems of the developing countries. International trade policy cannot be isolated from the domestic allocation of resources, etc.

33. Here again, work on the Brazilian data of income distribution has a moral. The complaint in Brazil is that officials sympathetic to a critical analysis provided a foreign scholar with the data but that he, without reference to them and without consulting them, published them speedily in a foreign journal. Revolutionary or radical mining and imperialism are regarded as just as objectionable as conservative mining.

34. *Ibid.*, p. 191.

5 Development Ideas in Historical Perspective[1]

THE NEW INTEREST IN DEVELOPMENT

Development economics is a new branch of economics. There was little that went under this name before the Second World War, though many of the same problems were dealt with by members of the colonial services, anthropologists, and others. Since much of economics is a response to current political and social problems, it is pertinent to ask what new conditions gave rise to the new and rapidly growing interest in development.

First, there was a new awareness that poverty is not the inevitable fate of the majority of mankind. This new awareness was itself the result of the achievement of affluence for the masses in the West; the high economic growth rates of countries in Western Europe, of North America, of the Soviet Union, and of Japan; and the improvement in mass communications which brought events in the rich North to the consciousness of the poor South, and more specifically to the consciousness of the new élites there. As a result of the propaganda of politicians and economists, aided by the transistor radio, television, and jet planes, economic growth came to be regarded as a human right.

A second source was the Cold War, in which East and West competed in attracting the attention of the Third World. Both the capitalist, mixed economies of the West, and especially the USA, and the planned economy of the Soviet Union attempted to win friends and influence people by showing that their economic performance was superior, by holding up their respective regimes as ideals to be imitated and by giving development aid. It is interesting to note that with the thawing of the Cold War (if this is the right metaphor) and with the relatively reduced significance of military expenditure, the expectations of those who thought that this would make more resources available for international aid were disappointed: the flow of aid levelled off and shrank as a proportion of national income. It not only shows up the limits of economics but illustrates the principle of the irrelevant alternative, according to which a boy comes home and tells his father proudly that he had saved 10 pence by walking and not taking a bus. To this the father replies contemptuously: "You fool; why did you not save £1 by not taking a taxi?"

A third factor was the population explosion. When population was kept at a fairly constant level as a result of high mortality rates, poverty was bearable. There was no growing pressure on scarce resources, son followed father in his occupation and traditional ways continued. But a growing population requires production increases simply in order to maintain the level of living. The maintenance of "traditional ways" and freedom from the pollution and rapaciousness of modern civilization presents an attractive, romantic picture, but it is unrealistic. Admittedly, it was the introduction of modern medical and other scientific technology that reduced spectacularly mortality rates, while no equally cheap and effective method to reduce traditionally high birth rates was available. But it remains true that, without development and the disruption it brings, societies could not continue to enjoy the happy existence presented by some romantic anthropologists, but would be faced with growing misery.

The fourth source is the large number of countries that attained independence after the Second World War. Decolonization is the most important effect of the last war. More than 100 countries have achieved independence in the last 30 years. Membership of the United Nations has increased from 51 to 147 (and the total number of countries is 153). Development and planning for development were written on the banners of the governments of these countries.

An understanding of the reasons for the rapid growth of interest in development economics is both interesting in itself, and helpful in identifying possible biases and omissions in our work. Gunnar Myrdal, who has consistently tried to remain aware of these influences, wrote:

For social scientists it is a sobering and useful exercise in self-understanding to attempt to see clearly how the direction of our scientific exertions, particularly in economics, is conditioned by the society in which we live, and most directly by the political climate (which, in turn, is related to all other changes in society). Rarely, if ever, has the development of economics by its own force blazed the way to new perspectives. The cue to the continual reorientation of our work has normally come from the sphere of politics; responding to that cue, students are launched, data collected, and the literature on the "new" problems expands. By its cumulative results, this research activity, which mirrors the political strivings of the time, may eventually contribute to a rationalization of these strivings and even give them a different turn.

So it has always been. The major recastings of economic thought that we connect with the names of Adam Smith, Malthus, Ricardo, List, Marx, John Stuart Mill, Jevons and Walras, Wicksell and Keynes, were all responses to changing political conditions and opportunities.[2]

It is not easy to convey, in the present atmosphere of gloom, boredom and indifference surrounding discussions of development problems, what an exciting time of ferment these early years were.

The excitement arose both from the challenge and the vision of eradicating poverty and opening up new lives and opportunities for hundreds of millions of people, and from the new ideas to which this challenge gave rise. These ideas were a revolt against the traditional, conventional views of the profession.

Albert Hirschman recently pointed to the importance, in the history of development economics, of Samuelson's proof of factor price equalization in 1948–9.[3] The articles proved that, on certain assumptions conventionally accepted in the theory of international trade, free trade would equalize wages throughout the world, so that a US worker and an Indian worker would be paid the same, and trade could therefore perform precisely the same function as free international movement of factors. In a world in which people became increasingly aware of wide and widening international income gaps this was a brilliant and startling conclusion. As Albert Hirschman says, here the neoclassical paradigm was not undermined by the accumulation of contradictory evidence, as Thomas Kuhn's scientific revolutionary sequence would lead us to expect, but "the theory contributed to the contradiction by resolutely walking away from the facts".[4]

Raúl Prebisch, Hans Singer and Gunnar Myrdal, less elegantly but more realistically, challenged not only Samuelson's findings but the more general view that equilibrating forces meant that the fruits of economic progress would be widely and, after a time-lag, evenly shared.

At the same time, the Harrod–Domar model, according to which the rate of growth of output equals the ratio of savings to income divided by the capital–output ratio, though formulated for different conditions than those of underdevelopment, added output-generation to the Keynesian income-generation of investment, and thereby provided the principal pillar for the analysis of development and for many development plans.[5] Capital accumulation became, if not the necessary and sufficient condition for development, at any rate the main strategic variable, and the propensity to save and the capital/output ratio became the basic equipment of development analysts, planners and aid officials. The notion that capital was scarce and savings difficult to raise in poor countries was qualified by pointing to the opportunities of attracting them from abroad, from the capital-rich countries, which would find new profitable investment opportunities in the countries to be developed. Notions like those of Balanced Growth (Ragnar Nurkse), the "critical minimum effort", and the Big Push (Paul Rosenstein-Rodan) threw new light on the role of market forces and planning.

From the beginning there were critics. Paul Baran argued that the political power structure in the poor countries prevented adequate and productive investment and that foreign investment and aid reinforced social and political systems hostile to development.[6] And between the position that development was ensured by adequate amounts of capital accumulation, and the conviction that the political power structure made development impossible, there were many intermediate positions. It soon became evident that some development was taking place in some places, but that it was not always simply a matter of capital.

The analysis was refined, qualified, criticized. Albert Hirschman emphasized entrepreneurial incentives, appropriate sequences of motivational pressures and linkages. Other writers attempted to introduce in addition to total income the distribution of this income as an important force determining subsequent investment. A more equal distribution was thought to be necessary in order to generate the mass markets which could exploit economies of scale; a less equal income distribution was thought to be conducive to higher savings. The choice of techniques was discussed in both its productive and distributional aspects.[7] What is remarkable about these early discussions is the proliferation of ideas, criticisms, and qualifications which contrasts sharply with the monolithic view that a single paradigm existed. This view is an optical illusion created by looking back from later vantage points. In subsequent sections, I may be guilty of such simplifications, but it should always be borne in mind that the early days of development economics were a time of intellectual pioneering, of considerable excitement, of the opening of new geographical and intellectual frontiers, of optimism and confidence.

Bliss was it in that dawn to be alive,
But to be young was very heaven!

CONTRASTING PERCEPTIONS OF DEVELOPMENT

Somewhat over-simplifying, we can identify five recent changes in the perception of the development process. "Perception" is intended to convey modesty and lack of pretension. Others might prefer terms like models, frameworks, or paradigms. Dudley Seers has suggested a hybrid between perceptions and perspectives: "perspections". Whatever name we give them, they certainly colour the way in which questions are asked, empirical evidence is collected, selected and used, and solutions are presented.

Although the shift in perceptions has been described as "recent", some of these changes go back a considerable time. Indeed, hardly any of the features of the "old" perception were generally accepted at any stage and qualifications, criticisms and alternative perceptions were put forward almost as soon as the "orthodox" perception had been formulated.

1 The first change between our perception of development until about 1970 and after can be traced to differences of view between the First World and the Third World, and the Right and the Left, although there are all kinds of cross-alignments. The more popular (though not the academic) thinking of the 1950s and 1960s, codified in the Pearson Report, was dominated by W. W. Rostow's doctrine of the stages of growth.[8] This perspective was, partly, superseded in the early 1970s by what has sometimes been called a "dependencia" interpretation of international economic relationships. To illuminate the shift in perceptions from the first of these views to the second, let us review briefly each in turn.

According to Rostow's doctrine, development is a linear path along which all countries travel. The advanced countries had, at various times, passed the stage of "take-off", and the developing countries are now following them. Development "was seen primarily as a matter of 'economic growth', and secondarily as a problem of securing social changes necessarily associated with growth. It was taken for granted that organizing the march along the development path was the prime concern of governments."[9]

The linear view begged a host of questions about the nature, causes and objectives of development. It tended to focus on constraints or obstacles (particularly lack of capital), the removal of which would set free the "natural" forces making for the steady move towards ever higher incomes.

Applied to the area of international relations, this view calls on the rich countries to supply the "missing components" to the developing countries and thereby to help them break bottlenecks or remove obstacles. These missing components may be capital, foreign exchange, skills or management. The doctrine provides a rationale for international capital aid, technical assistance, trade, private foreign investment. By breaking bottlenecks, rich countries can contribute to development efforts a multiple of what it costs them and thus speed up the development process in underdeveloped countries. Models pointing to gaps between required and available savings or foreign exchange are a rationalization of foreign assistance. The ultimate purpose of aid is to be rid of aid.

This linear or stages-of-growth view has come under heavy fire. It was criticized on logical, moral, political, historical and economic grounds. Logically, it should have been clear that the coexistence of more and less advanced countries is bound to make a difference (for better or worse) to the development efforts and prospects of the less advanced, compared with a situation in which no other country was ahead or the distance was not very large. The larger the gap and the more interdependent the components of the international system, the less relevant are the lessons to be learned from the early starters. Morally and politically, the linear view ruled out options of different styles of development. Inexorably, we were all bound to pass through the Rostovian stages, in the words of the famous limerick, like a tram, not a bus. Historically, the view can be criticized as excessively determinist. Economically, it is deficient because it ignores the fact that the propagation of impulses from the rich to the poor countries alters the nature of the development process; that late-comers face problems essentially different from the early starters, and that "late late-comers" again find themselves in a world with a range of demonstration effects and other impulses, both from the advanced countries and from other late-comers, which present opportunities and obstacles quite different from those that England or even Germany, France and Russia, faced in their pre-industrialization phase.

Summarized briefly, it may be thought that too much weight is given to Rostow and to the linear view of the development. The "stages of growth" were criticized from the beginning, by Kuznets, Gerschenkron and others. The heavy concentration on physical capital was criticized by Cairncross, Hirschman and the human capital school of T. W. Schultz. There were many non-linear theorists, from Schumpeter to Rosenstein-Rodan and Nurkse. The whole debate on balanced *versus* unbalanced growth does not fit into the linear perception. But it remains true that outside academic circles the Rostow model had a powerful grip on the imagination of policy-makers, planners and aid officials and that it was this view that gave rise to a reaction.

Succeeding the linear development perspective in popularity in the early 1970s was a second view, according to which the international system of rich–poor relationships produces and maintains the underdevelopment of the poor countries (the rich "underdevelop" the poor, in André Gunder Frank's phrase).[10] In various ways, malignly exploitative or benignly neglectful or simply as a result of the unintended impact of events and policies in rich countries, the coexistence of rich and poor societies renders the efforts of the poor societies to choose their style of development more difficult or impossible. Certain groups in the developing countries— entrepreneurs, salaried officials, employees—enjoy high incomes, wealth and status and, constituting the ruling class, they perpetuate the international system of inequality and conformity. Not only Marxists but also a growing number of non-Marxists have come to attribute a large part of underdevelopment and of the obstacles encountered in the process of development to the existence and the policies of the industrial countries of the West, including Japan and the Soviet Union.

This new perception is succinctly expressed in President Nyerere's address to the Royal Commonwealth Society in November 1975.

> In one world, as in one state, when I am rich because you are poor, and I am poor because you are rich, the transfer of wealth from the rich to the poor is a matter of right: it is not an appropriate matter for charity. . . . If the rich nations go on getting richer and richer at the expense of the poor, the poor of the world must demand a change, in the same way as the proletariat demanded change in the past. And we do demand change. As far as we are concerned, the only question at issue is whether the change comes by dialogue or confrontation.

According to one line of this second view, aid is not a transitional phenomenon to be ended after "take-off", but a permanent feature, like an international income tax. According to a more radical line, aid is itself part of the international system of exploitation, and self-reliant, independent development has to get rid of it.

The conclusion drawn from this perception is that the developing countries should put up barriers between themselves and the destructive intrusions of trade, technology, trans-national corporations, and educational and ideological influences, and should aim at "delinking" or "decoupling", at pulling down a bamboo or poverty curtain, at insulating and isolating themselves from the international system.[11]

W. W. Rostow for the first kind of perception, and André Gunder Frank for the second, are the popular rather than the academic models. Balogh,[12] Prebisch, Singer, Myrdal,[13] Hirschman,[14] and Perroux, not to say anything of Marx and List, had long ago developed approaches to development that separated "spread" or "trickle-down" effects from "polarization", "backwash" or "dominance" effects. And many had raised doubts as to whether everything would be fine if all countries only pursued free trade policies and established competitive markets. But probably because of their more careful formulations, the impact of their thinking, important though it was, remained "peripheral", not "mainstream", and sales of their books did not reach the figures of A. G. Frank's.

Irrespective of whether the "new" perception is true, what matters is that many developing countries see their place in the international system in this way and their perception is a political fact to be reckoned with. This clearly does not mean that the perception should not be subjected to a critical analysis.

The transition between the two perceptions has been overdrawn. Perceptions alternate, points emphasized change and there is no rapid, large-scale conversion. At about the same time that the critics of the international economic order became more vocal, and advocated "delinking", there took place a rebirth of orthodox thinking. The work on effective protection by Johnson, Corden and Balassa, the OECD studies of industrialization and trade centring on the work by Little, Scitovsky and Scott, research by the Brookings Institution and the World Bank, and the doctrines of the Chicago School that influenced many Latin American policy-makers reflected a recoil against inefficient protectionism and "inward-looking" planning. The conclusions pointed to more "outward-looking" policies. These changing analyses and perceptions alternate and interact.[15]

A reconciliation between the two perceptions, namely, that development can be speeded up by the international "system" and that under-development is caused by it, is possible along the following lines.[16] The advanced industrial countries emit a large number of impulses of two kinds: those that present opportunities for faster and better development than would otherwise have been possible, and those that present obstacles to development, those that stunt growth. Arthur Lewis invited us in 1974 to imagine that the developed countries were to sink under the sea in 1984. (He gave us ten years in order to allow time for adjustments. He felt it necessary to add that this was not a recommendation.) He then posed the question: are the developing countries better off, worse off, or would it make little difference?

The answer to the question neatly separates the adherents of different "paradigms". The upholders of the first "paradigm" would say "worse" (pointing to South Korea, Singapore, and Hong Kong as beneficiaries from the international system and Burma and Uganda as losers from "closing themselves off"), those of the second "better", and Sir Arthur thought it would make little difference. But I submit that, whichever answer one is inclined to give, this is not a helpful way of presenting the problem, however useful it is as a litmus test for ideologies. The developed countries propagate a large number of impulses to the developing countries. Reasonable men may differ about the net balance of these impulses, e.g., whether the exploitation by ruthless trans-national companies offsets the availability of a stock of scientific, technological and organizational knowledge, or whether the harm done by the brain drain is greater or less than the benefits from foreign technical assistance, or whether the inflow of grants and loans at concessionary interest rates is counterbalanced by aid-tying and capital flight, etc.[17] The interesting question then is not "do the developing countries benefit or lose from their coexistence with developed countries?" but: "how can they pursue selective policies that permit them to derive the benefits of the positive forces, without simultaneously exposing themselves to the harm of the detrimental forces?" Looked at in this way, the question becomes one of designing selective policies for aid, trade, foreign investment, trans-national companies, technology,[18] foreign education, movements of people, etc.

2 The shift from a linear theory of missing components to some version of a theory of neo-colonialism and dependence was accompanied by another change. It amounted to a change in emphasis of what constitutes the meaning and measure of development.

   Early thinking and policy-making was dominated by economic growth as the principal performance criterion of development, not so much because growth was regarded as an appropriate objective in itself, but because it was thought either that its fruits would rapidly "trickle down" to the poor, or that corrective government action could be relied upon to redistribute them, or that inequality and poverty are essential for growth (which, through accumulation by the rich, would first have to create the productive base from which to launch the attack on poverty). But it was soon evident that none of these three assumptions was valid. It became clear that growth in many countries remained concentrated on a narrow enclave of modern, organized, urban industry; that governments often were unwilling or incapable of using taxes and social services to offset growing inequalities; and that the concentration of income in the hands of the rich was not a necessary condition of development (e.g., research has disclosed that small farmers with access to improved agricultural technologies save as high a proportion of their incomes as large farmers and are often more efficient in terms of yield per acre).

The expected absorption of the rapidly growing labour force from the subsistence sector into the modern, industrial sector was considerably slower than expected. Dualism in many countries was marked and prolonged. The golden age of growth with greater equality, ushered in after a period of growing inequality, when labour from the subsistence sector has been fully absorbed by the modern sector, seemed, with a few important exceptions, to move into the distant future. This awareness led to a new emphasis on rural development and "employment". It was soon seen, however, that the problem was not "unemployment", which is a Western concept that presupposes modern sector wage employment, labour markets, labour exchanges and social security payments in the form of unemployment benefits. (Only those relatively well-off who had some other means of support can afford to be unemployed.) The problem was rather unremunerative, unproductive work of the poor, particularly of the rural poor. The ILO Kenya mission suggested the "informal sector" as not just another name for disguised unemployment but as a potentially productive labour force. The new emphasis on the "working poor" led to a concern for redistribution of productive assets as a path to reduced inequality. The relation between the increased concern for equity and conventionally measured economic growth presented a dilemma. On the one hand, it was accepted that in poor societies poverty can be eradicated only through increased production. On the other hand, the growth experience in some countries (though not in all) had shown that growth had reinforced inequalities in income, asset and power distribution which made it more difficult or impossible, both economically and politically, for its benefits to be spread widely. Attention, therefore, shifted to the conditions under which "redistribution with growth" is possible and desirable.[19]

The next step was to realize that what was needed was a more effective and speedier attack on deprivation. Reductions in inequality do not necessarily reduce poverty. It was not just inequality as such that was offensive, but also the fate of the destitute, whether working, incapable of working, whether unemployed, underemployed or unemployable. The objective narrowed down to "meeting basic human needs",[20] which covers not only adequate earning opportunities to purchase the necessities of life, but also access to the provision of public services for basic education and health. The progress was from highly aggregated magnitudes like "national income" and "growth rates" to increasingly disaggregated objectives, like different types of "employment" (e.g., for the young, for recent migrants) and reduced inequality, to meeting highly specific human needs of particular poverty groups: young children, women, people in distant regions.

In focusing on these needs, it became clear that measured income and its growth is only a part of basic needs. Adequate nutrition and safe water at hand, continuing employment, secure and adequate livelihoods for the self-employed, more and better schooling for their children, better preventive medical services, adequate shelter, cheap transport and (but not only) a higher and growing level of measured income: some or all of these would figure on the list of urgently felt needs of poor people.

In addition to these specific "economic" objectives, a new emphasis was laid on "non-material" needs that cannot be dispensed, but, in addition to being valued in their own right, may be the conditions for meeting "material" needs, such as self-determination, self-reliance, political freedom and security, participation in making the decisions that affect workers and citizens, national and cultural identity, and a sense of purpose in life and work. This was accompanied by attempts to evolve human and social indicators of development that would reflect the extent to which some of these needs were met.[21]

3 A third shift in interest and emphasis was away from the specific economic problems of development and towards the world's common problems and shared constraints: resources and, in particular, energy, the environment and its global pollution, the sea and the sea bed, and world population. The new emphasis was on scarcity and interdependence.

The new emphasis on interdependence was regarded by some as calling for greater solidarity and cooperation ("spaceship earth", "one world"), and for the exploration of positive-sum games, by others such as the advocates of *triage*, and of the lifeboat philosophy, as calling for partial contracting-out of human obligations, and by others again as a shift of attention from positive-sum to zero-sum games. The renewed emphasis after 1972 on scarcities of resources and exhaustion of raw materials extended not only to food, energy and certain metals, but also to some previously free goods, such as clean air and clean water, with the resulting concern for environmental protection.

Interdependence does not necessarily point to solidarity; on the contrary, it may give rise to threats, "blackmail", the demand for ransoms, and attempts at isolation. But whatever the response, the fact is that many problems are now global and are shared by all men. Whereas, with the growing interest in different societies in the 1960s, many had argued that there is no single, universal "science" of economics, applicable from China to Peru, and Dudley Seers wrote a critique of universalist economics on "the economics of the special case", the wheel has now turned full circle and we (with Dudley Seers in the lead) now acknowledge that many of the issues that we had considered as belonging to the poor countries are seen to be global, of concern to the rich, too. Alienation, pollution and crime can spring from underdevelopment as well as from overdevelopment; "intermediate technology" is just as relevant to high-income societies suffering from unemployment in the face of resource limitations, pollution and alienation from work; all states confront the new phenomenon of the trans-national corporation; we are all affected by the energy crisis; there are diseases of affluence as well as diseases of poverty; migration of workers and professionals affects rich and poor countries; there is global experimentation with new life-styles; there is a heritage common to all mankind and the unexploited resources of the sea and the sea bed can be allocated according to world-wide priorities.

4 A fourth and closely related change is that from a tacitly or explicitly assumed international harmony of interests (which was built into the stages-of-growth model) and positive-sum games, to greater emphasis on actual or potential conflict and zero-sum games. There was much talk of cooperation versus confrontation. The new perception was brought out vividly by the actions of OPEC and by CIPEC as well as similar attempts with bauxite, phosphate and iron ore; by attempts or threats of the developing countries to use bargaining power in other fields such as refusal to participate in drug control, or the control of nuclear weapons or patent conventions; by threats to expropriate, or tougher terms for trans-national companies; and by the support by a few governments of terrorists and hijackers. As the old harmony had benefited the haves, the new confrontation was intended to be used to change the "rules of the game" in favour of the have-nots.

The fact that economists point to potential joint gains from, say, trade liberalization or commodity-price stabilization, and thus to positive-sum games does not, of course, mean that governments perceive such policies as in their national interest. Policies are shaped by pressure groups and lobbies and the ubiquity of protection testifies to the power of these interests. On the other hand, developing countries may on occasion have an interest in "show-downs" rather than negotiations of common interest. There are political advantages in the publicity of such confrontations. In any case, sovereign political power in situations of conflict is in its nature a zero-sum game and the added strength of one country is often perceived *ipso facto* as a defeat for a rival.

At the same time, negotiations do appeal, if not to common interests, at least to common norms and to acceptable rules. Most nations realize that a world in which each nation and group of allied nations exercises to the full its bargaining power to extract maximum concessions from others is a world in which most nations will be worse off. Bargaining must, therefore, appeal not only to national self-interest but also to widely acceptable principles, rules, and norms on which tacit agreement can either be assumed or assumed to be more readily reached than is possible with selfish demands and threats. If bargaining is seen and conducted in this light, its power to disintegrate the world community is greatly weakened, even if the game is, in economic terms, a zero-sum one. Properly used, bargaining can strengthen world cooperation through joint attempts to evolve a more acceptable set of rules and institutions.[22]

5 A fifth change was that from treating the "Third World" as a homogeneous group of countries with common interests to the acknowledgement of the wide variety of experiences, interests and stakes in the world order—in spite of the growth of solidarity of the "Group of 77" at UNCTAD and other international forums. "Gaps" in income per head opened up more widely within the "Third World" than between the developed and the developing countries.

The distribution of the benefits of the commodity boom, especially the oil price rise, and the incidence of the damage done by the world recession were highly uneven and further sharpened differences within the Third World. The hoped-for benefits of the new international economic order also are likely to be very unequally distributed.

6 The sixth change in the perception of the development process, closely related to the other five changes, is that from abounding optimism[23] about development prospects and the contribution to them by the rich (through aid, trade and private investment) and by economic analysis, which dominated the 1950s and 1960s, to the deep pessimism of the 1970s. Both optimism and pessimism have their social origins. The optimism of the early decades, as Gunnar Myrdal has pointed out, had its origin not only in the excitement of the discovery of new problem areas but also in the desire of the governments in the industrial countries to please the élites in the newly independent countries and to reinforce the view that transfer of capital, skills and technology from rich to poor countries will soon lead to "self-sustained" growth and thereby get rid of the need for future aid. When faced with the real problems and difficulties of development, which transcended the "economic" variables, and at the same time, in their own

countries, with what has come to be known as "stagflation" together with a host of new problems such as urban ghettoes, student unrest, a growing number of industrial strikes, drug addiction, racial tensions, etc., the pessimism of the rich countries was a convenient excuse for falling and failing commitments to development cooperation and for contracting out of or for reducing contributions.

As far as economic theory was concerned, neither the Keynesian nor the monetarist approaches had much to offer in analysing and solving the problems of inflation accompanied by an intractable form of unemployment, the energy crisis, pollution, and the dwindling consensus underlying a social order.

In addition to these six fundamental shifts in perceptions, there have been shifts in fads and fashions. Just as fashion-setters emphasize, display and conceal at different times different parts of the female anatomy (though presumably all are there all the time), so economic and social research tends to be preoccupied at different times with different aspects of the variables in the social system, to the neglect of others. Certain subjects or views, at any given time have "sex appeal". The emphasis on industrial import substitution, followed by recommendations of industrial export promotion and, now, the beginings of some disenchantment with industrial export-led growth and a new turn to primary export restrictions is one illustration. Another fashion cycle is the switch from investment in physical capital to investment in formal education and a turn to informal education and motivation; from emphasis on output growth to calculations of the social costs and benefits of birth control; also the swings between functional-literacy and mass-literacy campaigns. Yet another cycle is that between pessimism and euphoria about world food production. The debates on agriculture versus industry,[24] large-scale versus small-scale techniques, formal versus "informal" sector, deteriorating versus improving terms of trade, material versus social objectives, growth versus the environment, and others have found in turn a clustering of views round alternating sides of the pendulum. The importance and the irrelevance or damage of development aid, as viewed by both donors and recipients, represents yet another swing. One could go on and to some of these debates I shall return later.

To the extent that these swings of the pendulum are indications of important underlying forces, they clearly raise important questions. But often, they by-pass the important issues and, looking back only a few years, or even months, one is astonished at the problems that vexed the profession and by the absence of the discussion of problems that vex us today. With the wisdom of hindsight it is now clear that the really important issues lay elsewhere. It would be nice to be able to predict where the next breakthrough in research is going to be, so that we can prepare ourselves for it. Yet, such a forecast would involve a logical contradiction. If I, or anyone else, knew where the *next* breakthrough was going to be, we should already have performed it and it would be the *latest* breakthrough.

Very few indeed would have predicted in 1950 that the preoccupations of the mid-1970s would be trans-national companies, "stagflation", protection of the environment, energy shortages, and the intractable nature of the development process. One safe prediction is that few, if any, of the problems that concern us now will stand high on the agenda in the year 2000.

KEY ISSUES

Another useful way to trace changes in thinking about development during the last 30 years is to select certain "key" concepts and examine how they have provided a focus for development thinking and policy-making. This section reviews some of these key concepts and their impact on the study of development.

CAPITAL

In the early literature, capital was regarded as the key to development and lack of it as an essential or the main or even the only constraint. Nurkse[25] argued that poor countries were poor because they were poor. Behind this apparent tautology lies a theory of the vicious circle of poverty or the low level equilibrium trap. Poor people can save only a small proportion of their income, if anything at all. As a result, there is little capital to invest. This in turn keeps the productivity of workers low and leads to low incomes per head.

This view of capital as the "missing component" fitted well into the linear stages-of-growth doctrine: "[I]n technical discussions and writings, in analytical models as well as in policy papers, the relationship between capital formation and economic development is stressed to the exclusion of all other causal factors and relations."[26]

A powerful influence was Arthur Lewis' model of the dual economy.[27] A rise in the savings and investment ratio from about 5 per cent to about 15 per cent and the accumulation of capital, combined with unlimited amounts of labour drawn from the traditional, subsistence sector, are the necessary and sufficient conditions of development according to this model. The model re-established a classical mechanism of reinvested profits by capitalists who save, and justified urban industrialization up to the point when the reserve army of labour is exhausted and neo-classical principles come into their own.

The strategic role of capital was questioned both by theory and by statistical findings. Theoretical analysis showed that there is no reason to expect poor people to save a lower proportion of their income than the rich. The relative preference of future consumption over present consumption is not necessarily affected by the current level of income.[28] It was also observed that even quite poor people saved in the form of holding gold and silver ornaments. Furthermore, Abramovitz and Solow[29] showed that capital, as measured, played only a relatively small part in the growth of output and a substantial part must be attributed to the residual or the "coefficient of ignorance". A. K. Cairncross[30] and Albert O. Hirschman[31] had questioned early the strategic or autonomous importance of capital, compared with techniques, attitudes, institutions and entrepreneurial motivation. Likewise, T. W. Schultz and others had extended the concept "capital" first to investment in human beings and later to other fields.

At the same time, experience showed that a good deal of productive capital was underutilized, and that capital was not as scarce as the above analysis had led one to expect. Moreover, the capital/output ratio in manufacturing industry turned out to be considerably lower than expected, partly because of the transfer and adaptation of existing, very productive technology from advanced countries, partly because capital-intensive infrastructure with excess capacity already existed in some areas, and where it did not, expenditure on housing and capital-intensive public services was kept low, and partly because countries with uncultivated but fertile land could simply bring more land under cultivation. Rostow had argued that "take-off into self-sustained growth" would require raising the savings ratio from 5 to 10 per cent, yet countries with low levels of income succeeded in saving, on average, 15 per cent of their income (though developed countries saved 22 per cent).

Not only was capital more plentiful and more productive than anticipated, but foreign aid, a post-war innovation in international relations, was substantial compared with earlier periods and contributed to capital accumulation. On a very crude calculation, using the Harrod–Domar model, the savings and investment ratio of 15 per cent was made up of 1 per cent official aid, 2 per cent private foreign investment, and 12 per cent domestic savings. With a capital/output ratio of 3, this yielded an annual growth rate of 5 per cent, to which external resources contributed one-fifth. (This contribution was gradually reduced in later years to one-tenth.) Such a model does, of course, assume that capital is the mainspring of economic growth, that foreign contributions are additional to domestic savings and that the capital/output ratio is low and constant. All three assumptions were later questioned.

As both theoretical reasoning and empirical evidence showed that capital does not play the crucial role that had been allotted to it, the debate about "missing components" broadened. The importance of physical capital was down-graded and other missing components were added, such as foreign exchange, entrepreneurship, skills, investment in "human capital", innovation, know-how, technology, institutions, and even birth control.

ENTREPRENEURSHIP

It was difficult to maintain that entrepreneurship, as such, or the willingness to take risks or the desire to make more money were absent in the underdeveloped countries, for there was considerable evidence to show that plenty of entrepreneurial talent was applied to trade, to small-scale industry and to gambling, and that farmers do respond to price incentives and profit opportunities. It was misdirection and lack of opportunities, rather than absence, that seemed to be the trouble. In particular, large-scale manufacturing enterprise was missing. This gap was filled in many countries by state and foreign enterprises. But these presented their own problems. State enterprises were subjected to political pressure to keep prices of their products and services down. Under the guise of rendering a social service, they merely subsidized the private sector, strengthening monopoly power. At the same time, salaries were kept low and retired civil servants or other worthy claimants for patronage were appointed as managers. This did not help efficient management.

Foreign enterprises were more efficient, but the desire to maintain control over indigenous resources and for economic, as well as political, independence of foreign decision-makers conflicted with the admission and expansion of foreign firms. In some countries the most enterprising groups were ethnic minorities which attracted the envy and hatred of the indigenous population. The Chinese in South-East Asia, the Asians in East Africa, the Ibos in Nigeria were maltreated, discriminated against or exiled.

SKILLS AND EDUCATION

As attention shifted from physical to human capital,[32] excessively aggregate treatment soon showed up a difficulty. In many countries there were not too few but too many educated. But they either had the wrong kind of education, or the wrong location from the point of view of contributing to development. (England's industrialization took place before the Education Act when the country had a much smaller proportion of literate people in the labour force than many developing countries today.) The problem in Asia was too many educated unemployed who had received a university education of low quality (though some of them had been educated in developed countries) which had contributed to aspirations that could not be fulfilled. Nor could it be argued that the fault lay with the *content* of education, e.g., too much Sanskrit, law or ancient languages and too little science and technology. India had 40,000 unemployed engineers.

In Africa there was excessive stress on primary education which contributed to a flight from the land to the towns. Skilled manpower was needed in the rural sector, but the aspiration of those who had learned to read and write was to become clerks in the civil service. The difficulty was not to educate more people, but to keep schooling and motivation in step with the changes in the rest of the economy. As in the previously false stress on capital, against the evidence of physical capacity standing idle and underutilized, so the emphasis on formal school education was accompanied by a growing army of unemployed school-leavers. There was also too much emphasis on acquired learning, compared with the capacity to enquire and add to knowledge.

FOREIGN TRADE

The early period was steeped in trade pessimism. It was thought that foreign trade had ceased to be an "engine of growth", as protectionist policies in industrial countries and the thrust of science and technology made exporting natural primary products increasingly difficult and unprofitable. In fact, trade grew at quite high rates. The exports of LDCs in the 1960s grew by 7 per cent per annum (though those of the developed countries grew by 9 per cent). The exports of manufactured goods grew even faster. Between 1960 and 1966 they grew at a rate of 12 per cent per annum, and between 1966 and 1973 at 25 per cent per annum, compared with a rate of growth of 17 per cent per annum for the developed countries. (These rates are in money terms.) Nevertheless, the relative share in world trade of the LDCs fell from 30 per cent in 1948 to 18 per cent in 1969. If petroleum exporters are excluded, the share of the developing countries in world exports fell from 24·3 per cent in 1950 to 14·7 in 1960 to 11·7 in 1969 and to 9·7 in 1975. This gave rise to complaints. Yet, it is not clear why shares should matter. The criterion should be import requirements rather than shares in world trade, which are bound to change with changing incomes and technology.

A good test of "obstacles to development" came in 1973 when the oil-exporting countries enjoyed large increases in financial resources, foreign exchange and government revenue.[33] The constraints that earlier writers on development had seen in the way of the "big push" advocated by others were suddenly removed, and it became possible to invest à la Nurkse and Rosenstein-Rodan, on a broad front. Mutually supporting investments could be carried out, in principle, so that the demand by industries for one another's products could be generated and supply bottlenecks could be eliminated by complementary investments or imports.

In spite of this great opportunity, development did not occur as swiftly and as harmoniously as the doctrine of the big push would have predicted. New types of imbalances became evident. Administrative, organizational and technological skills and appropriate institutions to direct them to the required areas were lacking, and the surplus oil revenues did little to stimulate or create them swiftly. Finance, foreign exchange and government revenue are not substitutes for all required inputs, and a large advance in foreign-exchange spending generates bottlenecks in complementary resources, such as non-tradable goods.

More subtly, it was discovered that "resources" are not just an abstract entity, but it matters how they are generated, earned and used. Oil revenue depends on the actions of governments and is not linked to the responses and motivations of farmers, businessmen, workers or households. And the imbalances that it creates, between tradable and non-tradable goods, between high and low incomes, between income generation and its distribution, between present strength and future vulnerability, between finance and administration, between wealth and underdevelopment, present constraints and create tensions of a different kind from those normally considered by economists.

Even before the opportunity to test the doctrine of the big push presented by the large increase in oil earnings and revenues, attention of some development economists had shifted increasingly to variables not previously emphasized by mainstream economists. Among these new concerns were human attitudes, social institutions, power structures, cultural and religious beliefs and the impulses enjoyed or suffered that originated in the advanced countries. The "new" problems on which work was now focused were population growth, unemployment, inequality, and rural underdevelopment.

POPULATION

From the beginning of history until 1850, world population rose slowly to 1000 million. (It is estimated that at the end of the last Ice Age, about 10,000 BC, it was less than 10 million and AD 250 it was between 200 and 250 million.) By 1960 it had more than trebled to over 3000 million, and by the year 2000 it will be about 6000 million. It has been pointed out that the present world population could all find standing room, though somewhat uncomfortably packed, on the 147 square miles of the Isle of Wight. At the present rate of increase of 1·7 per cent per year, in 850 years the whole 196,836,000 square miles of the world land surface would be needed to provide standing room on the same cramped scale for a population of 4×10^{15}.[34]

The rapid growth of the population has, however, slowed down, and we now talk of the "demographic transition". Successful programmes of limiting population growth were launched in South Korea, Taiwan, Singapore and Hong Kong. The precise relationships between higher income levels, social services, government expenditure on family planning, attitudes to birth control and availability of appropriate techniques are still highly controversial, but there is no doubt that there are statistical correlations between success in other fields (such as income growth, reduced inequality, export performance and, more specifically, women's education, reduced infant mortality and other health measures) and success in bringing down fertility rates.

Nor was it entirely clear or non-controversial why precisely it was desired to bring down birth rates. Malthusian limitations of food and land played a less important part as it was found that there are large potential reserves of both. Attention shifted to savings and it was argued that a rapidly growing population (or, more correctly, a population growing at an accelerating rate) generates lower savings and, of what savings there are, a higher proportion has to be devoted to welfare rather than productive investment. It was also thought that rapidly growing populations presented more serious employment problems and made policies aimed at reducing inequality more difficult. The most convincing arguments are possibly not to be found in macroeconomics, but in the reduced burden on mothers and the improved quality of family life.

UNEMPLOYMENT

However successful population policy is in reducing population growth, the employment problem remains, because the entrants into the labour force in 14 years' time have already been born. The sources of the problem were identified as (1) the high rate of growth of the labour force; (2) the high wages in the organized, urban sector; (3) its small initial size in most developing countries; (4) the absence of appropriate technologies for low-income countries. To this, some authors added (5) the limitations on international trade of labour-intensive products.

The analysis of unemployment and underemployment was refined as it was found that the standard categories and measurements of employment, unemployment and labour force did not apply to the developing countries. Gunnar Myrdal, who found that the obstacles lay as much on the side of supply as on that of demand, though he also questioned the basis of this distinction, pleaded for the replacement of the misleading concept "employment" by "labour utilization", which draws attention to the multi-dimensional obstacles to mobilizing labour. Obstacles were to be found in bad health, malnutrition, poor education, caste prejudice, attitudes to women, absence of labour markets, etc., as well as absence of effective demand and equipment. Levels of living, attitudes and institutions largely determined the degree of labour utilization.

RURAL UNDERDEVELOPMENT

Agricultural growth was, until the middle 1960s, the main brake on economic growth. This was the result partly of low growth in agricultural productivity and partly of the sheer size of the agricultural sector in low-income countries. Even spectacularly high rates of urban, industrial growth could not absorb the growing numbers in the rural sector because the starting base of the industrial sector was so small. This led to a revision of the early fallacy that industrialization is the remedy for underdevelopment, indeed is almost synonymous with development. So strong was the hold of this myth that Myrdal regarded his view in 1960s that "the employment effects of industrialization cannot be expected to be large for several decades" as "unorthodox". Eighteen years ago, Folke Dovring had shown that the size of agriculture relative to the rest of the economy imposes a ceiling on the rate at which labour can be absorbed outside agriculture, and he predicted that in most developing countries a continued increase in the size of the agricultural population could be expected for a considerable time.[35]

The majority of the poorest people in the world—the sharecropper, the peasant with a tiny plot, the landless labourer—lived on the land and were bound to continue living there for some time. The Green Revolution, on which the technocratically-minded had pinned so much hope, benefited often the large and rich farmers, occasionally at the expense of the small, poor farmers and the landless labourers. In any case, since it is a seed, water, fertilizer revolution, it applies only to the wet tropics where water is available and its supply can be controlled: 75 per cent of India and 50 per cent of Pakistan are without irrigation. No technology has yet been found that can increase yields in the arid tropics. Such a technology (combined, of course, with the other necessary measures such as land reform, incentives, institutions, information, provision of inputs, access to markets, improvement of health, education and nutrition) would make an important contribution to eradicating poverty in the Third World.

THE DISTRESSING POLITICAL RECORD AND OTHER NEGLECTED OBSTACLES

Side by side with the new "economic" focus on poverty, underemployment and inequality went certain political developments. In the international debates on the widening income "gap" between rich and poor countries and in the domestic debates on growing inequality, inequality stood to some extent as a proxy for discontent with political (or tribal or ethnic) results. Systematic denial of dignity or freedom to certain groups reinforced disadvantages of low incomes and denial of access to public services. Both domestically and internationally, the uneven process of development had important, and in some cases, disastrous, side effects. The development disasters of the Nigerian civil war and the war of the cessation of Bangladesh are extreme instances of the discontent and frustration generated by unequal access to the opportunities offered by development and growing intolerance of this inequality.[36] The same forces encouraged a turn towards greater authoritarianism and military dictatorships.[37] While the aggregate growth record, therefore, has been spectacular and the evidence on distribution ambiguous, the political record has been distressing.

Moreover, there are important areas for analysis which tend to be either neglected ("opportunistic ignorance"), treated in separate compartments as "exogenous" variables, not integrated into development analysis and policy, or dismissed as biased partisan views. Yet, any serious, objective analysis of development ought to incorporate them, because they are closely linked to the development process. Here they can only be enumerated.

(1) The unwillingness of governments to grasp firmly the political nettles: land reform; taxation, especially of large landowners; excessive protection; labour mobilization.

(2) Linked with the first, nepotism and corruption.

(3) Behind these, again, various forms of oligopoly and monopoly power: the power of large landowners; of big industrialists; and of the trans-national enterprises.

(4) In a different field, but often equally disruptive to development efforts, the power of organized urban labour unions and the obstacles to an incomes policy and to a wider spread of employment opportunities, particularly to the rural poor.

(5) Restricted access to educational opportunities and the resulting job certification that both reflect and reinforce the unequal structure of power and wealth. Similar restrictions in access to health, housing and other public services, the incidence of which often reinforces the inequality of the distribution of private income.

(6) Weak entrepreneurship and defective management and adminis-tration of public-sector enterprises, of the civil service and of private firms granted protection or other forms of monopoly power.

(7) Lack of coordination between central plans and executing ministries, central plans and regional, local and project plans, and between the activities of different ministries.

(8) The weakness of the structure, areas of competence, recruitment, training and administration of the UN specialized agencies charged with development, combined, too often, with a narrowly technocratic approach, encouraged by the historical origin and organization of these agencies and their politically "non-controversial" approach.

(9) There are also the terrible facts of mass slaughter, expulsion of ethnic minorities (often entrepreneurial and therefore hated) and political opponents, imprisonment without trial, torture, and other violations of basic human rights, and the $370 billion spent annually on armaments, compared with $17 billion on net concessional transfers (in 1975).

The list is not exhaustive but merely illustrative. It is intended to indicate some of the obstacles to human and social development in the full sense and to pinpoint some of the reasons for the disenchantment with what has turned out to be, by narrow economic criteria, unexpectedly and unpre-cedentedly high growth.

DISCARDED IDEAS

Let us summarize the elements in earlier thinking on development which have largely been discarded.

(1) Analysis and policy were originally dominated by the experience of the rapid recovery from the war, supported by Marshall Aid, of the industrial countries of Western Europe, by the high post-war rates of economic growth and the scientific and technological triumphs of post-war reconstruction. The problem of development is, however, fundamentally different from the problem of reconstructing war-damaged advanced economies.

(2) Priority was given to industrialization and infrastructure (power and transport) which came to be almost synonymous with development. Hence, also, the strong emphasis on capital accumulation as the strategic variable in development. The savings ratio and the capital/output ratio together were thought to determine the rate of growth of output, which was the main objective of development. It was found, however, that capital accounted for only a relatively small portion of growth, and that growth was not synonymous with development.

(3) Central government planning from the top down and the need for a "big push" dominated thinking and policy-making, and the limitations of administrative capacity, of human and institutional constraints, and the need for participation, decentralization and mobilization of local labour were not recognized.

(4) Policies were dominated by the reaction to colonialism. The governments of many newly independent states wanted to do what the colonial powers had neglected to do. This reinforced the desire for planning, for industrialization and for import substitution. It also fed the desire, after the achievement of political independence, for economic independence, which was often equated (wrongly) with a high degree of economic self-sufficiency. Latin American countries, which had been independent for a long time, felt that economic independence, which did not follow from political independence, was elusive.

(5) Thinking was deeply influenced by foreign trade pessimism, which led to the formulation of two-gap models. Pessimism about export prospects and the terms of trade reinforced policies of import-substituting industrialization, which in turn created strongly entrenched vested urban interests that resisted efforts to liberalize trade.

(6) There was a belief that high average growth rates of production will lead to reduced poverty either as a result of trickle down or of government policies: that the best way to attack poverty was indirectly, by supporting growth, and that the spin-offs would, after a time-lag, benefit the poor.

(7) The rate of population growth and the problems generated by it were

underestimated, and diplomacy ruled out the topic for both bilateral and multilateral development agencies.

(8) The goals of development were defined narrowly in terms of GNP and its growth, and other goals such as greater equality, eradication of poverty, meeting basic human needs, conservation of natural resources, abating pollution, and the enhancement of the environment, as well as non-material goals, were neglected or not emphasized sufficiently.

(9) The contribution by the developed countries was seen too narrowly in terms of capital aid and technical assistance, instead of as the impact of all policies pursued by the rich countries, whether or not they were pursued with the express purpose of assisting development efforts. These would include science policies, the thrust of research and development expenditure, policies towards trans-national companies, migration policy, monetary policy, regional policy, trade and employment policies, agricultural policy, as well as foreign policy and military actions.

(10) The "Third World" was considered, rather monolithically, as an area with common problems, whereas it became increasingly clear that some of the differences within the group of developing countries were at least as great as those between them and the developed countries.

(11) Development was considered exclusively a problem of under-developed countries becoming less so. In contrast, development is now beginning to be viewed as a problem common to the whole world: it gives rise to problems that are shared by the rich and by the poor, with some interests in common, others conflicting.

THE NEW STRATEGY

The new development strategy which reflects a fair degree of consensus among scholars, may be summarized in the following way:

(1) We must start with meeting the basic needs of the majority of the people who are very poor. These needs are more and better food, safe water at hand, security of livelihood, health, sanitation, education, decent shelter, adequate transport. In addition there are "non-material" needs such as self-confidence, self-reliance, dignity, capacity to make one's own decisions, to participate in the decisions that affect one's life and work, and to develop fully one's talents, all of which interact in a variety of ways with "material" needs.

(2) Meeting the basic needs of the billion poor people requires changes

not only in the income distribution, but also in the structure of production (including distribution and foreign trade.) It calls for increases in basic goods bought in the market, as well as in the purchasing power to buy them, and for an expansion and redesign of public services. To ensure that these actually reach the poor, restructuring public services will be necessary, as well as greater participation at the local level, better access to these services, and an appropriate delivery system.

(3) Since the majority of the poor live (and will continue to live for some time) by agriculture in the countryside, priority has to be given to growing food for domestic consumption. Agriculture has been the lagging sector; it has been holding up development and its produce has been unevenly spread. Agriculture also forms an important potential mass market for industrial goods.

(4) In order to meet the needs of the rural population, credit, extension services, fertilizer, water, power, seeds must be made available so that these reach the small farmer. He must also be given security of tenure or secure ownership of his land and a guarantee that he gains from the improvements that he makes. He needs inputs including information, appropriate institutions and incentives.

(5) The small farmer must also be provided with access to markets in market towns and regional cities through feeder roads and marketing facilities.

(6) A group of smallholdings should be serviced by modern centres of processing, marketing, financial services and extension services, but this must be done in a way which does not call excessively for scarce managerial resources.

(7) Efforts should be made to develop efficient labour-intensive technologies or, more accurately, technologies that economize in the use of capital and sophisticated skills and management and are appropriate for the social, cultural and climatic conditions of developing countries. Construction with appropriate building materials also offers opportunities for creating efficient employment.

(8) The rural towns should provide middle-level social services, such as health and family clinics, secondary schools and technical colleges.

(9) The new structure will reduce the rush to the large cities, economize in the heavy costs of certain services, and will increase the scope for regional and local participation.

(10) The whole process should embrace human and social, as well as economic development. More particularly, hundreds of millions of people will not be more productive, for some time to come. They need social help.

All policies, such as price controls, allocation of inputs, financial and fiscal measure, credit control, foreign exchange controls, etc., should be scrutinized with respect to their final impact on the specified goals. Although some increase in inequality may be inevitable in the early stages, as long as it does not impoverish the poor, those measures whose incidence is to benefit the rich at the expense of the poor should be abandoned or redesigned.

GENERAL CONCLUSIONS

No doubt there were errors, false starts and dead ends in the development story of the last three decades. In accounting for these, there are Keynesians and Marxians. Keynes attributed (at least in a much-quoted passage in the *General Theory*) the errors of "practical men, who believe themselves quite exempt from any intellectual influences" to "some defunct economist". He thought "that the power of vested interests is vastly exaggerated compared with the gradual encroachment of ideas". On this interpretation it was the mistaken doctrines of Nurkse, Singer and Rosenstein-Rodan that led governments to subsidize industrial capital equipment, support high urban wages, overvalue exchange rates, raise the costs of farm inputs by protecting domestic manufacturing industry, lower the prices of farm outputs and generally neglect or, worse, exploit, agriculture and the rural poor.

Marxians believe that it is the power of class interests that is reflected in ideas. The above-mentioned doctrines, on this view, are merely an ideological superstructure, reflecting the powerful vested interests of the urban industrialists and their workers.[38]

But there is a third way of looking at the succession of problems and difficulties: there is a Hydra-like aspect to development (and perhaps to all human endeavour). Many of the difficulties encountered in the path of development were neither the result of economic errors, not attributable to vested interests, but were the offspring of the successful solution of previous problems. Scientific confidence asserts that there is a solution to every problem, but history (and not only the obstructionist official) teaches us that there is a problem to every solution.

The solution of one problem creates a series of new ones. Success in manufacturing industry has brought out the lag in agriculture. The need to expand the production of food for domestic consumption became so acute partly because of the remarkable growth of industrial output. The seed–fertilizer revolution has spawned a collection of new problems about plant diseases, inequality, unemployment and the other so-called second-generation problems. The need for population control arose from the successful attack on mortality and the resulting extension of life expectancy through cheap and efficient methods of disease eradication. Growing unemployment is (partly) the result of high productivity and growth of manufacturing investment. Education raises excessive aspirations and contributes to the movement to the cities and the consequent unemployment of the educated. The success and the attractions of urban development have shown up the need to accelerate rural development, which by the turmoil it creates, may further accelerate the migration to the cities.

This Hirschmanesque generalized doctrine of unbalanced growth cannot, of course, be used to justify and legitimize errors in development thinking and policy. Of these there were plenty. But, on the other hand, not all difficulties are the result of past mistakes, and some are the consequences of the successful solution of preceding problems.

"Hydra" may be the wrong metaphor, for it suggests the hopelessness of all endeavours. "Second-generation" problems, on the other hand, may be too optimistic a term. The question is whether, in spite of the subsequent emergence of new problems, the series converges to, or diverges from, a solution. While some solutions are worse than the problems, others represent progress. It is important to bear in mind that solutions are not readily transferable between places and periods.

Another lesson is what more sophisticated colleagues like to call "the counter-intuitive character of systems analysis". Things are not necessarily true because they are paradoxical, but in development studies, as in other fields, common sense does not always lead to the correct answer. Job creation may cause more, rather than less unemployment. Import restrictions and physical allocations, intended to reduce inequalities may strengthen monopoly power. A strategy that sacrifices economic growth of consumption in order to create more jobs may require *faster*, not slower, growth. Policies designed to help the poor may benefit the middle and upper classes, and so on. As these illustrations show, the implications of this view can be profoundly conservative or startlingly revolutionary. In a given power structure, attempts at piecemeal reform *may* be self-cancelling and the system will then tend to re-establish the initial wealth and power distribution. Only a deep, structural change *may* enable reform to take root.

On the other hand, piecemeal reform *may* trigger pressures that lead to further reforms, whereas revolutionary change, as the many revolutions that failed show, may fail to achieve its objective.

A third lesson is that in many areas only a concerted, properly phased, attack on several fronts yields the desired result and the application of some measures without certain others may make things worse. "Correct" prices in a society with a fairly equal distribution of assets and available appropriate technologies may raise efficiency and reduce inequality, but to use "correct" prices in a society with very unequal ownership of assets will change only the manifestation of inequality.

Not only are there Myrdalian cumulative processes, but the processes require packages; the causation is cumulative and joint. The appropriate metaphor is the jigsaw puzzle, the fitting together of different parts, not the toothpaste or the sausage machine which responds to pressures with homogeneous outputs. To do something in a certain sequence, together with other things, brings success; to do it in isolation may be worse than doing nothing. A programme of education without employment opportunities will only accelerate the brain drain. What is needed is a range of interrelated, properly phased, measures. There are no simple remedies. The solution of underdevelopment is not to be found in making the soil more, and women less, fertile, in a combination of fertilizer and pill (the technocratic solution); nor, for that matter, by staging a revolution (the revolutionary solution), or implementing a radical land reform (the radical solution), nor by "getting prices right" (the economist's solution), though each, in conjunction with the others, may have something to contribute to a total solution.[39]

A fourth lesson is that few problems are narrowly economic ones. The difficulties often lie with human attitudes, social institutions and political power structures, more than, or as well as, with scarcities of productive inputs and their correct allocation. Scarce inputs—capital and skills—will probably also be needed to attack social and political obstacles but the link between resources and outcomes is a tenuous one: there are no fixed capital coefficients between resources spent and an effective land reform, or between money and a successful birth-control campaign.

Finally, the response of the rich countries to the challenge of development is not to be found in development aid alone, whether it consists of capital or brains, even if it were 2 per cent instead of 1/3 per cent of GNP, or in freer access to the markets of the rich countries. It is the *total* relationship, the impact of *all policies* of the rich countries, that is relevant, and that has to be our concern if we are serious about international cooperation.

NOTES

1. This paper was commissioned by the Rothko Chapel and read at a conference

at Houston, Texas, on 3–5 February 1977. I am grateful to Ajit Ghose and Jeffrey James for assistance in preparing it, and to Albert Hirschman, Dudley Seers, Karsten Laursen and J. C. Voorhoeve for helpful comments.

2. Gunnar Myrdal, *Asian Drama*, vol. 1, Penguin Press (1968), p. 9.
3. Albert O. Hirschman, "A Generalized Linkage Approach to Development, with Special Reference to Staples", *Essays on Economic Development and Cultural Change in Honor of Bert F. Hoselitz, Economic Development and Cultural Change*, vol. 25, Supplement (1977), ed. Manning Nash. The two articles by Paul A. Samuelson were "International Trade and the Equalization of Factor Prices", *Economic Journal*, vol. 58 (June 1948), pp. 163–84; and "International Factor-Price Equalization Once Again", *ibid.* (June 1949), pp. 181–97.
4. *Ibid.*, p. 68.
5. Paul Streeten, "A Critique of the 'Capital/Output Ratio' and Its Application to Development Planning", in *The Frontiers of Development Studies*, Macmillan, London (1972), Ch. 6.
6. Paul A. Baran, "On the Political Economy of Backwardness", *Manchester School of Economic and Social Studies*, vol. 20 (January 1952), pp. 66–84.
7. Walter Galenson and Harvey Leibenstein, "Investment Criteria, Productivity and Economic Development", *Quarterly Journal of Economics*, vol. 69 (August 1955), pp. 343–70.
8. Since W. W. Rostow's *The Stages of Economic Growth*, Cambridge University Press (1960) veers between the tautologically trivial and the historically false it could be said of the tautology that it was not even wrong. See also "The Take-off into Self-Sustained Growth", *Economic Journal*, vol. 66 (March 1956), pp. 25–48.
9. Colin Leys, "The Role of the University in an Underdeveloped Country", *Education News* (April 1971), Department of Education and Science, Canberra. For a critique of the linear theory, see Ch. 2 of *Development in a Divided World*, ed. Dudley Seers and Leonard Joy, Penguin (1971). See also my "Changing Perceptions of Development", *Finance and Development* (September 1977).
10. André Gunder Frank, "The Development of Underdevelopment", *Monthly Review* (September 1966), pp. 17–31, and *Capitalism and Underdevelopment in Latin America*, Monthly Review Press, New York (1967).
11. It is paradoxical that the socialist or radical advocates of "delinking propose something that was triggered off by capitalist hostility to the USSR, the People's Republic of China, and Cuba. A similar paradox arises from the fact that the burning of wheat and the dumping into the sea of coffee in the 1930s brought home to many the irrationalities of capitalism, whilst similar restriction schemes are advocated in the 1970s by socialists.
12. Thomas Balogh, *The Economics of Poverty*, M. E. Sharpe, New York, 2nd ed. (1974) and *Unequal Partners*, Blackwell, Oxford (1963).
13. Gunnar Myrdal, *Economic Theory and Under-developed Regions*, Duckworth, London (1957).
14. Albert O. Hirschman, *The Strategy of Economic Development*, Ch. 10.
15. See Harry G. Johnson, *Economic Policies Toward Less Developed Countries*, Brookings, Washington, DC (1967). Ian Little, Tibor Scitovsky and Maurice Scott, *Industry and Trade in Some Developing Countries*, published for the

OECD by Oxford University Press (1970). Some of the country studies on which this work was supposed to be based are considerably less critical of the policies criticized in the main report. See e.g., Joel Bergsman, Brazil: *Industrialization and Trade Policies*, OECD, Oxford University Press (1970). Another important study in the same vein is Bela Balassa and Associates, *The Structure of Protection in Developing Countries*, Johns Hopkins University Press, Baltimore (1971), sponsored by the World Bank and the Inter-American Development Bank.

16. A different kind of reconciliation has been proposed by Albert Hirschman as long ago as 1957, at a conference of the International Economic Association in Rio, where he advocated that an *alternation* of close contact with the centre and of enforced isolation from it may be the most effective way for the periphery to develop. More recently, he set down his reasons for this point of view in the following terms:

A discussion has long been raging about whether close contact by means of trade and capital flows with the advanced industrial countries is beneficial or harmful to the less developed countries. Some authors have been able to cite important static and dynamic, direct and indirect benefits that accrue to these countries from close contact. Others have shown that close contact had a number of exploitative, retarding, stunting, and corrupting effects on the underdeveloped countries and that spurts of development in the periphery have often been associated with periods of interruption of contact, such as world wars and depressions. To neither of these two warring parties has it apparently occurred that they may quite conceivably both be right. In order to maximize growth the developing countries could need an appropriate alternation of contact and insulation, of openness to the trade and capital of the developed countries, to be followed by a period of nationalism and withdrawnness. In the period of openness, crucial learning processes take place, but many are of the latent kind and remain unnoticed and misperceived. They come to fruition only once contact is interrupted or severely restricted: the previous misperceptions are then forcibly swept away. Thus both contact and insulation have essential roles to play, one after the other." *A Bias for Hope: Essays on Development and Latin America*, Yale University Press, New Haven (1971), pp. 25–6.

As Albert Hirschman adds on another occasion, "Unfortunately it is not easy to spell out the correct phasing of such an alternation." Recent events in China appear to confirm this view.

17. For a list of harmful impulses, see Paul Streeten, *The Frontiers of Development Studies*, pp. 5–12.

18. For an analysis of the conflict between closing the "Communications Gap", because of lack of external contact, and closing the "Suitability Gap", because of excessive external contact, see Chapter 22 of *The Frontiers of Development Studies*.

19. For a fuller discussion, see Ch. 18.

20. Here again, as in the evolution of thought on "delinking" discussed earlier, undercurrents and cross-currents present a more complex picture. The Indian planners and particularly Pitambar Pant from the beginning were concerned with the fate of the poor, with "Basic" or "Minimum Human Needs" and the much criticized community development programme was directed at the

welfare of the rural poor. The first World Bank mission, led by Lauchlin Currie, in its report in 1950 also put primary emphasis in meeting basic needs in Colombia. But the strategies were quite different from the basic-needs approach.

21. For an excellent survey of the change in objectives on which the above paragraphs have drawn, see H. W. Singer, "Poverty, Income Distribution and Levels of Living: Thirty Years of Changing Thought on Development Problems", in *Essays in Honor of V. K. R. V. Rao*.

22. See Chs. 9 and 13.

23. There were, of course, also pessimistic threads in the fabric of thought of earlier years. The doctrine of the vicious circle of poverty can hardly be called optimistic. At the same time, the seeds of optimism were there: vicious circles could be transformed into virtuous circles, and the same forces that cumulatively prevent progress in one constellation can reinforce it in another. More specifically, the solution pointed to more foreign aid as a solvent of the obstacles to progress. For a different view of cycles of optimism and pessimism see H. W. Singer, "Recent Trends in Economic Thought on Underdeveloped Countries", in *International Development, Growth and Change*, McGraw-Hill (1968), Ch. 1.

24. While a good deal of the debate on agriculture *versus* industry is a sham dispute, Michael Lipton has made a powerful case that "urban bias" has systematically neglected or exploited the rural sector for the benefit of the urban sector. See his *Why Poor People Stay Poor, Urban Bias in World Development*, Temple Smith (1977).

25. R. Nurkse, *Problems of Capital Formation in Underdeveloped Countries*, Oxford (1953).

26. J. Adler and S. K. Krishnaswamy, "Comments on Professor Bye's Paper", in *Economic Development for Latin America*, ed. H. S. Ellis, St Martin's Press (1961).

27. W. A. Lewis, "Economic Development with Unlimited Supplies of Labour", *The Manchester School of Economic and Social Studies*, vol. 22, no. 2 (May 1954), pp. 139–91.

28. M. Friedman, *A Theory of the Consumption Function*, National Bureau of Research, New York (1955).

29. M. Abramovitz, "Resources and Output Trends in the United States since 1870", *Papers and Proceedings of the American Economic Association* (May 1965); R. Solow, "Technical Progress and Productivity Change", *Review of Economics and Statistics* (1957), reprinted in Amartya Sen (ed.), *Growth Economics*, Penguin, Harmondsworth (1960).

30. A. K. Cairncross, *Factors in Economic Development*.

31. Albert O. Hirschman, *The Strategy of Economic Development*.

32. T. W. Schultz, "Investment in Human Capital in Poor Countries", in *Foreign Trade and Human Capital*, ed. Paul D. Zook, Southern Methodist University Press, Dallas (1962), pp. 7–14.

33. Robert E. Mabro, "Aspects of Economic Development in Iran", mimeo for The Royal Institute of International Affairs, *Iran, 1980–85: Problems and Challenges of Development*, Chatham House Conference (7 December 1976).

34. James Meade, "Population Explosion, The Standard of Living and Social Conflict", *Economic Journal* (June 1967), p. 233.

35. F. Dovring, "The Share of Agriculture in a Growing Population", *Monthly Bulletin of Agricultural Economics and Statistics* (September 1959).
36. See Albert O. Hirschman, "Changing Tolerance for Inequality in Development", *World Development* (1974).
37. It would be quite erroneous to equate this trend towards authoritarianism with a turn away from what Myrdal has called "the soft state". Violence is not hardness, though some of the regimes came to power with the pretence to eradicate "softness", like corruption. See Gunnar Myrdal, *Asian Drama*, Penguin, Harmondsworth (1968), vol. 2.
38. See also n. 18, Ch. 4.
39. See Ch. 8.

Part II   Strategies

6 How have the Poor Fared?

In the foregoing chapter I discussed the evolution of new ideas on, and responses to, the development process. One may, however, ask the questions: how have the poor in fact fared in the last 15–25 years? Before answering it, certain preliminary questions have to be asked, if not answered.

First, there is the question: how should the poor be identified? The common practice of using deciles (or quintiles or quartiles) of income recipients has serious defects. Should they be identified by social and economic classes? Or by residence (rural versus urban)? Or, a somewhat neglected approach, by ethnic groups or by regions? Or by the stage in the age cycle (the very young and old), or by family size and age of head of the family? Or as particular members of families, such as children under five or women? Poverty has many dimensions and concentration on deciles, even if adjusted for relative price changes, post-tax incomes and social services, may obscure some of these.

Second, is poverty absolute or relative? Clearly poverty lines vary between climates, cultures and social environments. But is there a component which has to be defined in relation to the mean, or to the bottom of the 80 per cent above the lowest 20 per cent, or to some other standard of what is regarded as a minimum decent standard in a society? The need to relate poverty to some acceptable social standard or some reference group is partly psychological and partly arises from the nature of economic progress (see below). It may even be asked whether the distinction between relative and absolute poverty is valid. If it is valid, which should be our main concern?

Third, it may be asked whether the absolute number of poor or the proportion of poor in the total population has increased. With rapidly growing populations, it may be thought that the relevant concept in judging the success of strategies in eliminating poverty should be the proportion of poor.

Fourth, we must ask how we proceed from money income shares, on which we have data, but which are irrelevant, to real income shares or income levels, which are relevant but unknown, in assessing inequality and poverty? Ideally, we should have an index of the minimum needs cost of living, allowing for price changes and consequential substitution between items in the basket. We might then make estimates for what Seebohm Rowntree, many decades ago in his research on poverty in York, called 'secondary' poverty—real incomes adequate to buy the minimum needs basket, allowing for the fact that people, for a variety of reasons, do not spend their incomes exclusively on minimum needs. General consumer price indexes are not relevant to poverty indexes. There are three distinct issues.

(1) In developing countries, even more than in developed countries, different groups do not face the same prices for the same goods. The urban cost-of-living is higher than the rural, and regional costs vary. For this reason money income shares may overstate inequalities and rural poverty.

(2) Different groups consume different goods, and the same goods in different proportions. Prices do not rise proportionately for all groups. Food forms a higher proportion of total expenditure for the poor, and if its price rises by more than average prices, poverty is underestimated by money income shares. The same problem arises for both cross-section and time series data.

(3) With rising average standards, certain items especially important to the poor may cease to be available and be replaced by more expensive items, and the same items may be subject to more sophisticated treatment through more packaging, higher degrees of processing, or types of 'improvement' which raise the costs to the poor, especially the urban poor or subsistence farmers switching to cash crops.

Some items counted as final goods and therefore part of income may be more properly regarded as intermediate goods – like the journey to work, or urban requirements of "proper" dress.

Fifth, we may ask whether consumption or income is the appropriate measure. Data for consumption and for income are sometimes inconsistent. Consumption may be thought to be the appropriate welfare concept. There is always an advantage if we can supplement income measures by measures of physical volume, e.g. of food consumption. There are several layers to penetrate, each of which may give different results. Behind money income there is real income; instead of real income we may wish to measure consumption; behind consumption, nutritious food; behind nutritious food, calories and proteins; and behind these health levels reflected in morbidity and longevity.

Sixth, there is the question of mobility, both in the social and economic scale and by residence. It is, for example, possible for the proportion of the rural poor to increase, without anybody becoming worse off, simply because some of the rural better off move to the towns, or for the urban poor to increase because the rural poor have moved to towns. The evaluation of poverty will also be different according to the length of time members of poverty groups stay in them.

It may also be asked whether the members (and families) of the group have largely remained the same or whether the composition has changed? Are their expectations of improving their lot the same or are there some identifiable groups who feel that opportunities are barred?

Seventh, should we use cross-country regressions or time series? Cross-country evidence tends to neglect policy options but time series data (a) are unreliable and (b), if general conclusions are drawn from them, may also encourage undue determinism. The twentieth century is different from the nineteenth, and its last quarter may turn out to be different from its third. Taiwan is different from Brazil.

Finally, it might be asked whether it is important to know the facts. We may say 'Yes', because what we know, or think we know, enters into our models and policies. On the other hand, firm knowledge is very hard to gain. The fate of the English poor during the Industrial Revolution is still an unsettled issue. Action cannot wait for the results of research.

Bearing these preliminary questions in mind, we can next turn to the two main questions: how has inequality and how has absolute poverty changed over the last 20 years? The question of inequality raises, in turn, two distinct questions: (1) how is inequality at any given time related to growth, and (2) how are changes in inequality related to growth?

The main lesson, bearing in mind the unreliability of the figures, is that there is no correlation between either point inequality or changes in inequality and rates of growth. There is a vast variety of experience.

(1) There are fast growers with equality: Taiwan 1964–8, later Korea. And there are fast growers with inequality: Puerto Rico, Colombia, Philippines.
(2) There are fast growers that have become more equal: Taiwan 1959–64 and since 1968, and Korea in the earlier period; and there are fast

growers that have become less equal: Mexico, Brazil, Peru, Argentina, Malaysia.

(3) There are slow growers that have been unequal and slow growers that remained unequal (India).

(4) Finally there are slow growers that have become more equal, such as Sri Lanka (though the evidence is controversial) and slow growers that have become less equal (some states in India).

Perhaps more interesting, what has happened to absolute poverty?

In one group of countries, including South Korea, Taiwan, Hong Kong, Singapore, the People's Republic of China, rapid growth was combined with a substantial reduction in poverty. This group covers 1 billion people or 35 per cent of the population of the Third World. But the figures depend crucially on the high growth rates of China, which are controversial. The evidence for South Korea and Taiwan has also been questioned.

In a second group of countries, including the Philippines, Malaysia, Turkey, Argentina, Mexico, Brazil, rapid or moderate growth was accompanied by growing inequality but not by absolute impoverishment, though also not by spectacular progress of the poor. This group comprises 25 per cent of the population of the Third World.

In a third group of countries, including Bangladesh and the poorer African countries, slow growth was accompanied by absolute impoverishment. The evidence on India, Indonesia, Pakistan is disputed. In India, periods of high agricultural growth were accompanied by improvement of the lot of the poor, except in the Punjab, where high growth appears to have left the proportion of the poor unchanged. Even in these poor countries indicators for health and education of the poor show improvements, so that on that score the poor are better off. Since this group contains some very large countries and comprises 40 per cent of the population of the Third World, it is crucial for any general lessons. Yet, the evidence is inconclusive and disputed. There is no doubt that there are absolutely more poor, but whether the proportion is larger is less certain.

When we examine *causes*, a wide variety of explanations are offered. Policies obviously play an important part, but the social and political structure, cultural factors, the amount of human capital formation, especially education, the initial distribution of assets, especially land, and foreign trade, are all powerful determinants of the link between growth and poverty reduction, though the relative importance of each of these factors is controversial.

On the question of remedies, an important conclusion of several studies appears to be that both micro- and macro-tinkering are likely to fail. Some models confirm that responses of income distribution to piece-meal intervention are sluggish. There is evidence that even in developed countries redistribution to the poor occurs only after civil or foreign wars (e.g. in Britain after the last war). This raises the question whether structural change can ever be gradual. Israel seems to be an exception. Japan took a very long time to achieve greater equality. There seems to be general agreement that the option 'grow first and redistribute later' is not a realistic one.[1]

NOTES

1. For a fuller treatment of some of these issues, see David Morawetz, *Twenty-Five Years of Economic Development: 1950–1975*, The World Bank (1977) and *World Development*, Special number on 'Poverty and Inequality' vol. 6, no. 3 (March 1978).

7 Alternatives in Development

My daughter uses a *Directory of Alternative Work*. This poorly duplicated document used to be called rather more attractively *Uncareers* and "is about the idea that you may be able to do something full time (or at least most of the time) that you want to do, that you enjoy, and see some purpose in. Things you can *do*, rather than what you can get a job as!" We also hear of the "alternative society", "alternative cultures" and "alternative life-styles". Some advocate the legalization for alternative forms of marriage, like group marriage. The Vienna Institute of Development has a programme called "Alternatives in Development".[1]

On the other hand, there is a good deal of discussion of the scope for transferring "Western" institutions and standards to underdeveloped countries, perhaps with some adaptation. What do we mean when we talk of alternatives in development or of transfer, adaptation or innovation?

While our scientific and technological imagination has leaped ahead, putting man on the moon, deciphering the genetic code, discovering new sub-atomic worlds and probing the recesses of inner space and the farthest reaches of outer space, our institutional and social imagination has lagged inertly behind. Our styles and institutions of living together—the nation state, the city, the village, private property, public enterprise—are ill-adapted to meet the challenges of rapid scientific and technical progress. Dissatisfaction with this dissonance between science and technology on the one hand and the desire for more satisfactory styles of development on the other has raised the question of alternatives in development. In this short note I should like to ask three questions. First, what is meant by "alternatives in development"? Second, why should we be concerned with thinking about and planning for such alternatives? Third, what are the possible objections to our search for alternatives?

What, then, is meant by "alternatives in development"?[2]

First, the alternatives may refer to different political, ideological or social systems: capitalism, fascism, socialism; freedom versus planning; secular *versus* theocratic societies. The option here is between total ideological systems. Detailed technical discussion and design of specific institutions does not contribute to such total choices and commitments.

Second, the alternative may refer to strategies and be concerned with technical issues: agriculture *versus* industry; import substitution *versus* export promotion; outward-looking *versus* invard-looking policies; capital-intensive *versus* labour-intensive techniques; growth *versus* equality; employment *versus* output—such choices combine different value judgements with differences in the analysis of causal sequences.

There is some overlap between the first and the second meaning. Thus, the choice between "outward-looking" and "inward-looking" industrialization and trade strategies has some ideological components and some purely technical economic ones. On the other hand, the debate agriculture *versus* industry took place both within the capitalist and the socialist ideological option and is largely technical.

A third meaning is implicit in the notion of a "Third World", in which things are done differently from the way they are done in the other two worlds. Critics have pointed to the fact that in some countries there has been "growth without development". On the other hand, there are those who advocate "development without growth" (or without modernization), at any rate for an initial period when the institutional foundations are being laid, or as an option against the sort of growth that is measured by aggregate figures of commodity production irrespective of who benefitts from the production, in what conditions it is produced and what forms it takes. A more appropriate definition of "development" would begin by identifying basic needs. In many underdeveloped countries the objective of development would be defined as raising the level of living of the masses of the people. This implies meeting such needs as continuous employment or secure livelihoods, more and better schooling for the children, better medical services, pure water at hand, cheap transport and, of course (but by no means only) a somewhat higher income. Much of this can be achieved in ways which do not register a high index number for measured output of commodities, while a high and growing index number is consistent with leaving these needs unsatisfied. Both the aims of development and the initial conditions in the now developing countries are different from what they were in the industrial countries in their pre-industrial phase or what they are in the industrial countries now.

This third meaning implies a rejection of certain "Western" institutions and standards and a call for the development of "appropriate" alternatives. It is important to be clear about the motivation for this call. A good deal of the emotional force behind such calls is simply the reaction against the former colonial power: let us see how they've done it and let's do the opposite. Some aspects of development in newly independent states can be understood only in terms of such a reaction. "If colonial rule supplied administration without policy, the post colonial era risks offering policy without administration."[3] Another illustration of this reaction (also mentioned by Barber) is the reaction against *primary* production for *export* (mines and plantations), which took the form of often very inefficient and costly *secondary* production (industrialization) for *import substitution*. Such motivation of alternatives is not a response to felt needs in the light of available resources, but an emotional (though understandable) reaction. It may be necessary in the search for national identity to reject material benefits (what are often wrongly called "economic objectives"), but a recipe of rejecting all "Western" ways, and always doing the opposite of what the ex-colonial powers did, is not a sound basis for the kinds of alternative which are called for by the need to feed and clothe a rapidly growing, largely rural, population.

As Professor Berger says, there are two possibilities for this positive approach to alternatives. Either one might call for a return to or a reconstruction of traditional indigenous institutions, standards and customs, or one might think of the creation of entirely new models. In addition to these two possibilities, traditional features and modern features transferred or adapted from the West or newly designed might form new combinations presenting genuine alternatives. There is now mounting evidence that some of the most successful development stories combine traditional and modern features.

Having distinguished between the possible meanings of "alternatives in development" we may ask why should we be concerned with this question?

Perhaps the most important reason is that the transfer of Western institutions and standards has been disappointing and, indeed, in some cases has created or aggravated obstacles to development.[4] I have discussed these problems in relation to the educational system, trade unions and labour legislation, social and particularly health services and technology.[5] Others have discussed them with reference to bureaucracies, political and party systems, the family, land tenure, military institutions, means of transport and communication, consumption standards and other areas. The criticism of these transfers need not spring, as Professor Berger puts it, from a "masochistic self-denigration that has been fashionable among European and North American intellectuals in recent years", though it is ironical that those who reject "Western" ways are often Westerners and those who wish to emulate "cement, steel and electricity", high industrialization, material incentives and expanding aspirations are the Buddhists, Hindus, and traditionalists or at least the vocal élites of countries in which these beliefs are indigenous. Without any anti-Western animus, it is reasonable to argue that models that have been evolved in different historical and physical settings cannot be directly transplanted into entirely different cultures, or can be transplanted only at a cost. In particular, European institutions and attitudes were developed in societies in which, until relatively recently, population increased rather slowly and labour was scarce, whereas today the labour force is growing at unprecedentedly high rates; in societies from which emigration was often possible, in which a good deal of differentiation had already taken place, in which the agricultural revolution had preceded the industrial revolution, which lie in the temperate zone, and where incomes and savings are high. The differences in both initial conditions and current conditions call for different responses, though the history of the now developed economies clearly has something to teach.

The second reason for why we should be concerned with alternatives, put forward by Professor Berger, is more ideological. "It is related to respect for diversity and richness of human cultures and revulsion at the thought that all this must be sacrificed on the altar of development."

Additional significance is given to the reason for exploring alternatives by the fact that precisely those institutions and models which are avidly adopted by the élites in the Third World are being rejected by the young in the advanced countries of the West and for all we know in the Soviet world. Indeed, one often finds the same action groups deploring the fact that the gap between rich and poor countries is growing ever wider and, in the same breath, announcing that we, the rich, have not really enjoyed economic growth but have poisoned ourselves with the pollutants of industrial so-called progress. But while such collision of bandwagons testifies more to the hearts than to the heads of these young activists, there is a real problem in the simultaneous rejection of "Western" industrial progress by the group in the "West" and its enthusiastic adoption by the "Eastern" élites. While the Indians and Africans are adopting our methods of schooling, Ivan Illich calls for de-schooling society. Western students wish to drop out; the greatest ambition of African students is to drop in. The same goes for the motor car, the symbol of modern industrial life. Industries that the "West" finds grubby, the "South" finds groovy.

The search for alternatives may ultimately teach us to mend our own ways. It has been said that the study of history is not a way to help us understand the present, but our knowledge of the present helps us understand history. In studying underdeveloped societies the reverse is true: self-knowledge is not a way to understand societies with different attitudes and institutions but the study of alternatives for them helps us to understand and reform ourselves.

What are the possible objections to a search for alternatives? First, it has been argued that development inexorably proceeds through certain stages and that there is no point in attempting to interfere with the flow of history. The stage theorists from Auguste Comte and Karl Marx to Walt Rostow would regard it as utopian romanticism to plan for "alternatives". While such deterministic theories have been subjected to a good deal of criticism, the possibility cannot be ruled out that the range of alternatives is pretty circumscribed and largely dictated by certain broadly accepted goals of the application of science and technology to production and by the evolution of a differentiated society built on the division of labour and specialization.

Related to this first criticism is the view that innovation cannot be done piecemeal, sector by sector, institution by institution. Those who advocate total change, the ideologues, and those who say everything depends on everything else, the systems analysts, argue that partial change is bound to be ineffective. The attempt to reform the educational system, or the shape of companies, or the social service, or the means of transport, or the administration, in a society in which the rest remains subject to a different system and different standards, is doomed to failure. The reform will, they argue, soon be absorbed by and made to serve the established ruling groups and reinforce the *status quo*. Whether they are right or not is an empirical question. Within a system it is, in principle, possible to select those loops which have the most powerful repercussions on the other variables in the system and thus change the whole system, rather than permit the variables to be modified in the conventional direction by the system. Or again, it is possible to make use of certain features of the "traditional" society (the extended family, the hierarchical factory organization, traditional religion, caste, traditionally determined consumption standards) and use them in the service of modernization, as well as letting modernization serve them.

But those who do not accept the possibility of such piecemeal reform or of making use of traditional elements in the process of modernization say that what matters is liberation from oppression through revolution and the assertion of genuine independence. Unless this is done, all the other reforms will come to nought; if it is done, the rest will follow. But revolution, while it may be necessary, is not sufficient. Even revolutionary juntas must exercise their institutional imagination and plan institutional change in considerable detail. It is paradoxical that Marxist (though not utopian) socialist theory is naively utopian in its vision of a planned society.

Engels believed that "government of persons is replaced by the administration of things". Lenin thought that one would have to "organize the whole national economy like the postal system". The problem of running the state would be "simply one of registering, filing, checking . . . so simplified and reduced . . . [as] to be quite within the reach of every literate person." The French anarchist Georges Sorel once quoted Marx as saying "Anyone who makes plans for after the revolution is a reactionary". The revolutionary young stand in this tradition of naive utopianism.

A third criticism (discussed by Berger) is the view that institutional reform cannot be dreamed up but must evolve through experience and practice. This criticism is often linked with the argument that developing societies must evolve "their own" solutions and that people from other countries and cultures have nothing to contribute. Even where we might evolve alternatives, they will remain steeped in alien soil and the roots will not "take" when transplanted. Paradoxically, the doctrine of the limits of transference may itself be regarded as non-transferable. More sinister, there is a short step (it might be argued) from the doctrine of the need to evolve alternatives, to the doctrine of "separate and equal" and from there to apartheid. It is quite easy to give the philosophy of the need for alternatives a nasty racialist ring.[6] The conclusion need not be the call for importing "Western" ways but the impossibility of foreigners meddling in the evolution of indigenous ways.

The reply to this criticism can be given on two levels. On one level, one must assert the universal community of scholarship and the impossibility to nationalize truth. But scholarship and the search for truth are quite consistent with arrogance. At the second level, the test is whether the common pursuit in the Republic of Knowledge is done in a genuine spirit of human brotherhood or whether it is motivated by cultural imperialism or a feeling of arrogant superiority.

Some of the discussions here suffer from a confusion. It is perfectly sensible to deny the possibility of a universal science of economics, which applies from China to Peru. The assertion of such universality derives from mistaking economics for logic and validity for truth. But while different economic and social principles may apply to Africa, South Asia and Latin America, there can be no African, South Asian and Latin American truth. The criteria of truth are universal and the principles of African or Asian economics must be accepted by rational American, Japanese or English economists.[7]

A fourth type of criticism objects to the call for alternatives on the ground that it is an attempt to serve up second- and third-best options: in schooling, in universities, in technology, in health services. "What is good enough for you will do us fine." With this goes the call for "centres of excellence" with internationally acceptable standards, for the most modern production methods, for heart transplant surgery, aerodynamics and pure welfare economics, contributing to an internal brain drain that is more damaging than the external one. Again, this criticism appears more plausible when one remembers the methods by which the South African government wishes to preserve traditional ways for the Africans. But there are two rejoinders to this criticism. First, it is by no means clear that all Western ways are *ipso facto* superior and we have already seen how they have come under attack from those concerned with the protection of the environment and a more human style of living and working. Indeed, technologies appropriate for underdeveloped countries may then be transferred to the industrial countries because they may prove to be environmentally or humanly preferable. Second, even where they are superior, in one setting, they may be inferior in a different setting. To adopt products that have been evolved in high-income, high-savings economies in low-income, low-savings societies must mean meeting the demands of a small, rich clique and letting the basic needs of the masses go unsatisfied, and/or oversatisfying a few needs of many at the expense of not satisfying a range of their more basic needs. What are claimed to be centres of excellence are often really pockets of privilege. What is claimed to be free consumers' choice is really depriving the vast majority of any choice at all.

I have often thought that what is needed is an exercise of our institutional imagination to evolve, in considerable detail, institutions more appropriate to the needs of the developing world than existing ones; to break away from the models handed to us from the past and to innovate in the social realm. But Professor Berger, at the end of his paper, puts the point so vividly that I can do no better than paraphrase him.

Humanity, and social scientists, and in particular those concerned with development, can be divided into two groups. First, there are those who pay close attention to what the world is like. This group either has no interest in even imagining how the world might be different, or it insists that such visions must be excluded from the field of the social sciences. They are the conservative pedants. Second, there is a group, smaller but often very noisy, who present us with utopian visions of different possibilities of social life. They equally passionately dislike precision and attention to detail, both in what exists today and in their ideas of the imagined future. This dichotomy between pedantry and utopianism is deplorable. It should be replaced by informed fantasy—by pedantic utopianism or utopian pedantry—imaginative visions of alternative possibilities with close and precise attention to detail.

NOTES

1. Professor Peter L. Berger's Paper "On the Concept of Alternatives in Development", drafted for this programme, has stimulated my thoughts on this subject and this paper is indebted to him.
2. "The notion that because it is derived from the Latin *alter* (one or other of two) *alternative* cannot properly be used of a choice between more than two possibilities is a FETISH." *Fowler's Modern English Usage.*
3. William J. Barber, "The Colonial Hangover", *The Yale Review* (Winter 1969).
4. In some instances the transfer, while itself desirable, has created new problems. The transfer of modern methods of death control (e.g. malaria eradication) without the provision of equally cheap and effective means of birth control, and without the provision of adequate food, clothing and shelter for the extra population is the most striking example of transfer creating new problems.
5. Paul Streeten, *The Frontiers of Development Studies*, Macmillan, London (1972), Chs. 9 and 22.
6. See Ch. 4, p. 73.
7. For some qualifications, see Ch. 4.

8 New Strategies for Development: Poverty, Income Distribution, and Growth[1]

Frances Stewart and Paul Streeten

It is now widely acknowledged that growth of GNP, conventionally measured, is unsatisfactory as the main target of development strategy and as the sole criterion of its success or failure. Among the many reasons why this is accepted, two have been singled out. First, many developing countries that have experienced rapid rates of growth of GNP have also and simultaneously generated increasing amounts of unemployment and underemployment. The growth rate of employment in the modern sector has been much slower than the growth rate of GNP, and much slower than the growth in numbers seeking modern sector jobs. Secondly, rapid growth in GNP has often been accompanied by a more unequal income distribution and increasing relative and, in some cases, absolute impoverishment of sections of the community. GNP has been 'dethroned' mainly because it fails to incorporate any measure of a country's success in achieving fuller employment and a more even income distribution.

These two phenomena—growing unemployment and increasingly unequal income distribution—are connected, in that lower (relative and/or absolute) income levels are to be found mainly among those who fail to find modern sector employment, while the gains from growth of GNP have been concentrated on the employed. A measure of open unemployment is not a satisfactory proxy for poverty, because the openly unemployed are generally better off, since the really poor cannot afford to be unemployed. However, poverty (relative and absolute) may be a satisfactory proxy for at least part of the 'employment' problem, since excess supply of people seeking modern-sector jobs is reflected in low incomes arising from complete lack of employment (open unemployment), partial lack of work

148

(few hours), or work of very low productivity (insufficient complementary resources or low productivity caused by low levels or living). It has therefore been suggested that the elimination of poverty and the achievé-ment of greater equality in income distribution should at least supplement, if not replace, growth of GNP as a target of development. Indeed, in a formulation of policies that aim at meeting the basic needs of the poor people and at an appropriate inter-temporal allocation of these improvements, growth will turn out to be the *result*, not the *aim*, of economic policy. This paper aims at exploring the various meanings which may be attached to these new targets, and the strategies that have been proposed for their achievement.

DEFINING THE NEW TARGETS

We shall skate rapidly over those problems of definition and measurement that arise in the comparison of real income levels between different groups in the same society at the same time, different groups in different societies, and the same groups at different times, when the groups to be compared do not consume the same goods in the same proportions but spend differing proportions of their incomes on each of the goods. In such situations, a comparison of real income levels depends on the value attributed to each good. The market price is no guide since, apart from other difficulties, the use of price as a welfare weight is legitimate only if income distribution is considered optimal, and it is precisely income distribution that is in question. When the bundle of commodities alters, as it does over time, there are further problems, which might make the purist give up altogether at this stage. But this is to be too finicky. Clearly income levels do differ in a way that is not simply in the eye of the beholder (i.e. the weight fixer); crude measures such as calorie consumption could be used as a start. Generally, money income (within a society at one time) is taken as the measure: if this is the measure adopted, then changes in the prices of the commodities consumed by the different groups must be included for a measure of changing income distribution over time. In fact this is rarely done.[2]

Most measures of income distribution over time do not include changes in relative prices of the goods consumed by different income groups. More specifically, money measures are used to prove points about real income distribution, without these adjustments.

Let us suppose we have a satisfactory measure of real income levels in different groups in society. This is a big supposition (a) because there are aggregation problems within groups, just as there are within societies; (b) because theorists may be able to devise measures that are conceptually workable, but statisticians may not be able to provide the necessary data; and (c) because, since the whole point of shifting from GNP to some new measure is to improve targets and achievement criteria, it is important that they should be consistent criteria. There remains the problem of defining more precisely the suggested targets of eliminating poverty and/or increasing the equality of income distribution. The first, most obvious, point is that there is a difference between these two suggested targets— elimination of poverty and reduced inequality. The first *appears* to be about the absolute income levels of certain (as yet undefined) sections of society; the second is unambiguously about the relative, not the absolute, level of income of the poor. The second might be achieved by reducing incomes throughout society, but reducing the incomes of those above the average most. Here the two targets would appear to be in conflict, since this sort of strategy would actually increase absolute poverty amongst the poorest. An alternative strategy of raising all incomes, but raising those of the poor least, would contribute to achievement of the first target, elimination or reduction of poverty, but would actually worsen the situation vis-à-vis the second target. It is therefore important to be clear which of the two targets the revised strategy follows.

There are powerful arguments in favour of each. On the one hand, absolute poverty, malnutrition, poor health, bad housing would seem to be among the main evils of underdevelopment, and their eradication is what development should be about. On the other hand, people mind about their relative position in society; while it may be difficult to argue in overdeveloped societies that rising average income levels in fact improve anyone's welfare all that much, it remains true within those societies that relative improvements are strongly desired, and probably do increase the welfare of those who benefit from them.[3] By definition of course, relative improvements cannot be shared by all. Equality, for some at least, is an important end in itself, and some would be prepared to accept reductions in average levels, and even, up to a point, in all levels of income, to achieve greater equality. Concern with the employment problem, and the use of income distribution as a proxy for its measurement, also is mainly a matter of relative, not absolute, poverty: the problem arises because of vast *differences* between income-earning opportunities in different parts of society, as well as because of absolutely low income levels.

People mind not only about their *individual* relative position, but also about the average relative position *of a group* to which they belong: a class, region, or country. In comparing distribution between groups, some measure of the average income of the group is appropriate. Thus, when making international income comparisons, we usually compare income per head for different countries. Now it is possible for income distribution between groups to become more equal while distribution within groups becomes less equal, and *vice versa*. More particularly, policies that emphasize greater equality within low-income countries may widen the gap in incomes between rich and poor countries; while policies that aim at reducing the international gap often widen the domestic one.

The two objectives—poverty eradication and reduced inequality—may not be in as sharp opposition as might appear because the income level and size of the group singled out as below that absolute poverty line, the growth of whose incomes would be the prime target in a strategy for the eradication of absolute poverty, itself generally depends on their position *relative* to those in the rest of the population. What is to count as absolute poverty tends to be relative to average standards in the society in question. Contrast, for example, the kind of income level Abel-Smith and Townsend[4] consider to be a minimum (below which people are in poverty) in the UK or in the USA (see Harrington (1962)), with the levels considered to be a minimum in India by Dandekar and Rath (1971). Interpreted in this way, the target poverty group depends on how the incomes of the poorest move, in relation to those of the society as a whole, and in this case much of the conflict between the two objectives is eliminated. However, to deal with it in this way, though convenient, conceals important differences in the way in which the objectives may be achieved. We shall therefore assume that the revised strategy may consist, in the short run at least, of two different objectives:

Revised strategy:
Objective A—elimination of poverty;
Objective B—reduced inequality in income distribution.

There are problems about both objectives. If for the objective of poverty elimination (as argued above) poverty is defined in relation to the average standard, it comes closer to the objective of reduced inequality. For the moment we assume it is not, but is independently identifiable. The objective of reduced inequality is subject to all the difficulties of defining what is to count as reduced inequality of income distribution.[5] It might be thought that a shift of the Lorenz curve entirely to the north-west can be described unambiguously as one of reduced inequality. When the two Lorenz curves cross, as is the case with measures designed to help the poor which do so at the expense of middle-income groups but also redistribute something to the rich, the change is ambiguous. But even a non-crossing Lorenz curve gives an ambiguous result. By redistributing income from the richest man to anyone other than the poorest man, inequality between the poorest and the recipient is increased.[6] Only if every one is moved nearer the average is the move unambiguously one towards greater equality.

In keeping with the spirit of the revised strategy, we may argue that the relative position of the poorest must improve, which rules out a situation in which income is transferred from the rich and the poor to middle-income receivers. But ambiguity remains. The position of the poorest may improve in relation to some groups, and worsen in relation to others. Perhaps the best we can do is to require that the incomes of the poor increase in relation to the average. This is consistent with increasing disparities above the average. As far as the employment problem is concerned it is disparities in earning opportunities which are at the heart of the problem. It is arguable that for the unskilled and semi-skilled these would be largely captured by a measure of the relation of the incomes of the poor to the average.[7]

Quite apart from the possibility of intersecting Lorenz curves, the social significance of situations with the same index of inequality will vary, according to a number of considerations, often neglected.[8] The same income may not be described as equal to another income, for which the earner has worked longer or more disagreeable hours, if the choice was open to both and if equality is related to desert. Second, allowance might be made for time spent previously in acquiring skills and forgoing earnings during training. Third, the same person's income may fluctuate between years and any one year's figure will then give a misleading impression of inequality. Fourth, adjustments may have to be made for age and non-registered incomes. If the young have no or lower incomes than the old, though lifetime earnings are the same, apparent differences in income distribution may be simply due to different age structures. If the services of housewives are not included in national-income calculations, apparent differences in distribution are due to this arbitrary convention. Fifth, the social significance is different according to the length of time persons remain in their income groups. Consider two societies. In one, the children of the rich become poor and those of the poor rich. In the other, subsequent generations stay in the same income group as their parents. We should describe the former as more egalitarian. Finally, one would want to know whether other dimensions of inequality coincide or cut across income inequalities: satisfaction from work, physical facilities, recognition, status, access to political power. A society in which inequalities are not only rigid and unchanging, but in which economic, social, and political inequalities coincide, is a more inegalitarian society than one in which the composition of the deciles is always changing and in which the different dimensions of inequality intersect, even though the Gini coefficients may be identical.

For both the objective of eradicating poverty and that of reducing inequality there remains, of course, the question of defining which groups at which income levels are to count as poor.

Ahluwalia and Chenery[9] have defined the revised strategy somewhat differently by focusing upon changes in income shares of different groups. They propose maximizing the weighted average of the *rate of growth* of the income of groups with different income levels—i.e. maximizing $G = w_1 g_1 + w_2 g_2 + w_3 g_3 + w_4 g_4$, where g_1, g_2, g_3, g_4 are the growth rates of incomes of different income groups in a society, and w_1, w_2, w_3, w_4 are the weights attributed to income growth at the different income levels. As they point out, GNP growth rate maximization consists of maximizing G, defining the w's as the initial share of each income group in the national income. An alternative strategy in which $w_1 = 0$, $w_2 = 0$, $w_3 = 0$, and w_4 (the weight of the poorest group) $= 1$ would amount to regarding only the incomes of the poorest group as an objective.[10] A third possibility is to weight each group equally, according to the number of people (or households, allowing for size and age composition) in it, so that a 1 per cent growth of the poorest 10 per cent has the same weight as a 1 per cent growth of the richest 10 per cent. Their approach is neat, as it enables one to continue to place some weight on income growth of sectors other than the poorest. In terms of our revised strategies, described above, in the special case where $w_4 = 1$, and $w_{1,2,3} = 0$, the Ahluwalia–Chenery strategy amounts to our objective A (poverty elimination). There is no way in which their approach can incorporate strictly distributional objectives—our objective B of reduced inequality.[11] We may thus distinguish a third possible objective of the revised strategy:

Objective C: the Ahluwalia–Chenery objective, or maximization of the weighted average of the growth rates of different income groups, with the stipulation that (a) $w_4 < 1$ (because where $w_4 = 1$ it becomes identical with our objective A of poverty elimination); and (b) the weights are not equal to the respective shares in the national income, but are less at above average, and more at below average income levels. This stipulation is necessary if more weight is to be attached to poverty elimination than under the older, unrevised strategy. This objective focuses on raising the *growth rate* of the income of the poor, instead of on B's *static* income inequality. However, the same weighted average growth rate has a different significance according to whether the initial situation is one of great or only mild inequality.

For completeness we define objective D as the unrevised strategy of GNP growth optimization (i.e. weights are shares in national income).

In the discussion so far, we have avoided the important question of *time*. Appropriate policies to meet the various objectives may differ considerably according to the time period to which the objective refers. At the most extreme, for example, if the time horizon were very short (say one year) then purely redistributive policies would be best for meeting any of the revised objectives. In the longer run, such policies could reduce the rate of growth of income of all groups including the poorest, and would thus be inappropriate as policies with longer time horizons. Alternatively, it might be possible to achieve *greater equality*, at a *higher level of living* for the bottom 10 per cent, after a period of time, only by increasing inequality for a limited period. If an economy consists of two sectors, one with high average incomes, the other with low average incomes, if there are not great inequalities within each sector, and if the high-income sector is initially small but absorbs an increasing number of workers from the low-income sector, until all are employed in the high-income sector, inequality is bound to increase in the transitional period, while everyone is becoming better off (absolutely) all the time. (The problem is more complicated if there are inequalities within the two sectors.) More generally, inter-temporal choices may have to be made with respect to degrees of equality at different times, and levels or growth rates of income of the poorest sections at different times. Some (but not all) of the conflicts between the various strategies turn out to be a question of differing time horizons. For each of the objectives, therefore, the time period and the inter-temporal value judgements have to be specified.

STRATEGIES

A number of different approaches have been proposed for meeting the revised objectives. Conflicts between these may partly (as argued above) be a question of inter-temporal value judgements, and judgements about inter-temporal trade-off opportunities, and partly of differences in objectives, since the objectives are rarely clearly defined, as between objectives A, B, and C above, but normally simply refer to giving more weight to distributional considerations. Here we need to define some of our terms. *Strategy* is often used to describe a set of policies towards development, but the term covers not only the policies but also the objectives they are intended to fulfil. Thus strategies differ because objectives differ as well as because proposed policies differ. We shall retain this meaning of strategy, using *objectives* to describe ends, and *programmes* to describe the *set of policies* designed to achieve the objectives.

In discussing strategies, there is a complex interaction between programmes and objectives.[12] As outside observers, we may be able to define our ultimate objectives (e.g. poverty elimination, reduced inequality, weighted growth and conventional growth) and maintain these (in theory), unaffected by the programmes. But in the actual economies under discussion, when the objectives are those of some group (or groups) within the society, the objectives are themselves a product of the situation of those defining the objectives, and this situation depends on past programmes. Let us assume the objectives in which we are interested are those of the official decision-makers—government and civil servants: we are concerned with them, because they make decisions and therefore policy can be affected only by them. The objectives of the decision-makers may be altered by past policies in four ways: first, they may change their objectives because their own *interests* alter as a result of past developments: for example, after a period of trade protection members of the government may acquire an interest in continued, or increased, protection; second, the *results* of past policies may make them change their objectives. For example, growing unemployment and poverty have brought increasing attention to their elimination as objectives; third, their *power* to bring different objectives about may alter, either through changes in the resistance to policies as a result of social, economic, and political factors (again a product in part of programmes), or through new techniques. Objectives respond to the possibility or impossibility of achievement. Putting a man on the moon was an objective of the 1960s, not the 1860s. Similarly, the political impossibility of achieving some end may rule it out as an objective. Fourthly, the social and political *composition* of the decision-makers—the interests they represent and consequently their objectives—may alter as a result of past programmes. Of course, individual decision-makers are continually changing. We are not concerned with that, but with changes in the social composition of the decision-makers and the interests they represent. Similarly, when we talk of the interests of the decision-makers we do not necessarily mean the actual interests of the individuals concerned (though this too is highly relevant) but the interests of the class (and region, tribe and race) from which they come, and whom (primarily) they represent.

It may be argued that though the day-to-day aims of decision-makers may respond in this way to past developments, this is not true of ultimate objectives—these are forged out of deep political discussion, and reflect the ultimate aims of mankind—for, e.g., freedom and happiness. It is perfectly true that most national plans lay down their objectives in this very general way; it is also true that, in a sense, all other objectives are only a means to achievement of these ultimate objectives. But the objectives that determine programmes are not of this kind; they are more of the A–D variety—derived objectives. There is a further distinction to be made.

Many governments pay lip service to objectives which they have no real intention of implementing; we shall describe these as *nominal* objectives to distinguish them from real objectives. A real objective is one for which the decision-makers will the means as well as the end. Indeed one can argue that real objectives by their nature are identified by revelation—by the policies adopted. Nominal objectives are to be identified by words; real, by deeds.[13]

We have defined programmes, and will be using the term in the discussion. But it is by no means clear that governments, as opposed to advisers, have programmes. Governments do have policies, but they are rarely undertaken as part of a coherent programme; *ex post*, it may be possible to identify the type of programme that a particular government's policies add up to; this does not mean that this was the *ex ante* intention of the government, nor indeed that, given the choice again, informed that it represents a particular programme, they would choose it again.

There are, then, a number of interacting elements that determine choice of strategy. Important among these are the initial situation, the nature of the decision-makers and their power and power base, and the technical possibilities. These interactions help determine the possibility (technically and politically) of the various revised strategies. These interactions should become clearer in the discussion that follows. The strategies we shall discuss can be categorized as follows:

high growth and 'trickle down'; redistribution;
  (i) radical,
 (ii) incremental,
(iii) redistribution through growth.

RELATIONSHIP BETWEEN STRATEGIES AND OBJECTIVES

The four strategies named above need little elaboration, as their content is self-evident.

The strategy of high growth plus trickle down is, crudely, the strategy that was followed in the 1950s and 1960s, aimed at objective D (high growth with conventional weighting). The strategy was not based on the premiss that the only thing that matters is growth of GNP, but rather on the assumption that either (a) the elimination of poverty can be left to the government via redistribution of the fruits of growth; or (b) without any active intervention of the government, high growth of GNP would automatically raise the levels of living of the poor through a trickle-down mechanism. Dissatisfaction with the achievements in eliminating poverty during the period in which this was the strategy suggests that these assumptions were incorrect. It is clear that the two assumptions above, (a) and (b), are very different. Failure to achieve (a)—redistribution of the fruits of growth—may, in our view, somewhat naively, be regarded as a failure of will on the part of the government. (Here 'will' includes the desire to implement a particular policy, and actual execution of the policy, given the apparent desire. The two cannot be distinguished completely since the reality of desires cannot be assessed independently of their execution.) In contrast, failure to fulfil assumption (b) is not a matter of will at all, but of misspecification of the mechanism of growth, the incorrect belief that rapid growth will be, broadly and after brief time lags, at least proportionate in all sectors and income levels. Failure in terms of assumption (a) may be due to belief in the validity of assumption (b)—i.e. the government feels no need to redistribute actively because it believes poverty will automatically be eliminated via trickle down, in the course of rapid growth. It is important to know what actually were the implicit assumptions during the past two decades, because the realism of much of the proposed revised strategies depends on it. If the failure was really a failure of will on the part of the government, then other policies which require similar acts of will may well fail too, unless we can find some distinguishing characteristic about them which makes this unlikely. It is therefore worth discussing the alternative assumptions and the nature of the failure more carefully.

It is obviously true that high growth was expected (at least initially) to increase incomes at all levels, which is one of the main reasons why the emphasis on GNP, a high savings rate, and a rapid growth rate were regarded as respectable. But it is also true (in many countries, and generalizing about the whole world there are always exceptions) that the combination of growing poverty and unemployment and growing GNP has been evident for some time; that most governments pay lip service to the need for redistributive policies, and that their policies continue to be predominantly protective of the haves and hostile to the have-nots. This is illustrated in tax policy, in public expenditure, government regulations and restrictions. Why is this? It seems to us three sets of reasons may be put forward, none of which really has much to do with *will*, which is why we reject the idea that failure of will is at the heart of the matter.

First, it is possible that governments lack the knowledge and/or the administrative power to redistribute effectively. It is true that public-expenditure programmes benefiting the poor in the rural areas are far more difficult to administer than those for the urban élite. Similarly, tax systems are notoriously inefficient. There may therefore be something in this argument, but probably not very much since the governments often seem capable of administering complex programmes of import restrictions or investment licensing, where the protection of the privileged is in question. The administrative weakness of governments in this connection is at least in part a matter of lack of a political base which will enable the government to carry out the policy effectively. The élite, against whom redistributive measures must be aimed, form the personnel who administer the measures; they capture the machine and render it ineffective. Thus in India, despite enormously high marginal tax rates, few pay them. Contrast the apparently similar machinery for rural administration in India and China. In India the machinery is taken over by the landlords and worked to their advantage; in China, with no landlords, it is not. The difference is not a matter of machinery, or institutions, but of how they are run, who runs them, and what they want.

Second, the kind of growth strategy pursued may have required the kind of inequality generated, as necessary for its achievement. This is partly (but only partly) the age-old question of incentives. It is also a matter of the requirements of modern technology. Modern technology requires—on the input side—labour and materials similar to those in the developed economies for which it was designed—i.e. a high proportion of highly skilled personnel, and high standards of literacy, discipline, and efficiency among the unskilled workers. For the required standards of efficiency, the workers must be fed, housed, educated more or less to Western standards; they need watches and bicycles to get to work on time; their clothes must be clean and neat. All these requirements mean that private and public expenditure must be disproportionately concentrated on the workers of modern industry, if it is to operate at all efficiently. So the uneven distribution of incomes (including public expenditure) is in part a necessary condition of a system which uses modern technology. In addition, the consumption goods produced by modern technology, also designed for the type of consumers typical of advanced countries, are suitable for consumers with much above average incomes in developing countries. To generate markets for these goods an unequal income distribution is needed. The high level of skills required by modern technology naturally leads to shortages of skilled workers and therefore tends to increase the quasi-rents of these workers; the opportunity of migration of these and higher-level workers to advanced countries provides further upward pressure on their incomes. Hence the inequalities generated can be seen, in part, as a necessary consequence of the adoption of modern technology, while this itself is an intrinsic part of any strategy involving rapid growth, given the absence of efficient alternative technologies.

Trans-national firms operating in developing countries contribute to this process. The excessive sophistication and over-elaboration of their products is, of course, partly the result of their having been developed in and initially for high-income, high-savings industrial countries. But this is not the whole story. Companies in search of profits should not find it difficult to invent and develop cheap, mass-produced consumer and producer products, appropriate for the lower incomes of the masses in the poor countries. But the *raison d'être* for trans-national enterprise investment is a special monopolistic or oligopolistic advantage, enjoyed by the firm over actual or potential local rivals. If imitation is easy and this advantage soon lost, the incentive is lacking. Possibilities of imitation are avoided if production is geared to sophisticated, changing, technological processes and products in the advanced countries, to which the trans-national companies have privileged access. It is therefore in the nature of the trans-national enterprise that its products and processes should be excessively sophisticated in relation to the needs of a poor country and it therefore tends to reinforce inequalities.[14]

Third, government policies are themselves in part determined by the strategy pursued and the consequent nature of development; they are not autonomously imposed on the strategy. The decision-makers in government in developing countries are themselves part of the élite who have benefited, directly and indirectly, from the high-growth strategy, and rising incomes at upper levels. The policies become self-reinforcing. Thus, for example, protection establishes interests in its continuation and indeed extension, and these interests then see that the policy continues. Inequalities tend to beget policies which lead to accentuation of inequalities; the riches of the *nouveaux riches* bestow power and influence; this power and influence is then exerted to enforce policies which extend their power and wealth, and to thwart policies which threaten them. Government policies become a product of the strategy pursued. There is a reinforcing cycle: high growth leads to the adoption of Western technology, which tends (for technical reasons) to generate inequalities; those who benefit also gain power and set in motion further policies reinforcing the inequalities and the pattern of development which gave rise to it.

The high-growth policy thus tends not only to generate inequalities, but also to establish positions of power that make it extremely difficult to combat these inequalities by government redistributive policies, and indeed make it likely that anti-egalitarian policies will be adopted. Thus invalidity of assumption (a) on p. 156 above itself leads to the invalidation of assumption (b).

The trickle-down strategy is one of pursuing objective D (high growth with conventional weighting)—in the earlier discussion—and aiming as a result also at achieving objective A—the elimination of poverty—as a consequence of rising absolute incomes throughout society, including the incomes of the poorest. It failed because in the event the poorest turned out in many cases (and, of course, there were exceptions) to receive a diminishing proportion of the growing income. This was partly because of the technical requirements of the high-growth strategy which resulted, at least initially, in growing inequality (e.g. the Green Revolution); and partly because of the political consequences of the strategy, which created a newly enriched class, including most of the significant decision-makers, who pursued policies which would preserve, and indeed increase, their privileges. It also failed because inequalities matter as well as income levels, which is not allowed for in objective D (high conventional growth).[15] Inequalities create the employment problem, not absolute poverty. And poverty is worse in a society in which others are getting richer—it is clearly worse psychologically, but it is also worse *materially*. This is because the type of services a society provides (and requires people to buy) changes in line with aggregate incomes, so that people with the same income, in terms of yesterday's goods, are worse off in terms of what is available today. For example, as societies grow richer, private cars replace buses, new buses replace old, cans and elaborate packages replace sacks, so that the poor become worse off because the products they once consumed are no longer available and their sophisticated substitutes are often more expensive. This changing composition of goods as average incomes rise refutes the belief—for developed countries as well as developing—that high growth is preferable to direct income redistribution, not only for the rich *but also for the poor*.

REDISTRIBUTION

The alternative to a 'trickle-down' strategy in dealing with poverty is one of deliberate intervention to redistribute resources to the poorest sections of society, thus raising their relative position (the objective of reduced inequality). In the short run, any policy of redistribution should also have the effect of raising the absolute income levels, unless the immediate effect of the redistribution is a loss in aggregate output so great, that with a higher weight, *per capita* incomes of the poor none the less decline. In the longer run, the level of incomes of the poor, as compared with what it would have been under alternative non-redistributing strategies, depends on growth in aggregate incomes, and the changing share of the poor under the alternative strategies. If, as appears to have been the case with some high-growth strategies, a high growth rate is accompanied by a falling share of income for the poorest categories of people, then redistribution can be accompanied by a reduction in the growth rate, without reducing the absolute level of income of the poor below what this would have been under the high-growth strategy. Given the relationship, discussed above, between the extent to which goods appropriate to the needs of the poor are available and growth in aggregate incomes, a lower apparent increase in low incomes may be consistent with a higher level of welfare in a slow-growth situation than in a fast-growth one.

A number of alternative forms of redistribution have been proposed.

NON-INCREMENTAL REDISTRIBUTION

This is a policy of redistributing existing assets. Redistribution of income without redistribution of assets—e.g. by progressive taxation of income—has not been notably successful. In countries as apparently dissimilar as the UK and Kenya the net effect of an apparently progressive tax system has been to leave real incomes much as they would be in a no-tax situation.[16] Redistribution of assets includes policies of land reform, and wider spread of ownership or nationalization of industrial property. It also includes radical reforms of institutions to give to the poor greater access to educational and health services, to credit and technology. Redistribution of income normally automatically follows redistribution of assets. Where the assets being nationalized were formerly in the hands of foreigners, nationalization does not necessarily lead to greater equality *within* the nation, but it may do so *between* nations. Substantial redistribution of assets within a nation involves such a break with the past that it both requires and constitutes a revolution. This type of redistribution is not therefore generally carried out by those who have gained from past inequalities.

INCREMENTAL REDISTRIBUTION, OR REDISTRIBUTION AT THE MARGIN

Because substantial and non-marginal redistribution, which we have described above as *radical* redistribution, is a revolutionary requirement, it does not normally form part of the advice given to existing governments and, from the point of view of *realism*, cannot do so. For this reason, given the need to alleviate poverty, incremental redistribution has been recommended. Such incremental redistribution involves taxing the better off to redistribute to the worse off. This has been the policy of democratic socialist regimes for a long time, rarely having marked effects on the distribution of income, precisely because the redistribution is marginal and if it threatens to become non-marginal, it is successfully resisted. Believing that resistance stems from people's dislike of having their absolute income levels cut, the latest version of incremental redistribution is redistribution through growth.

REDISTRIBUTION THROUGH GROWTH[17]

This policy involves taking the extra income that would accrue to the better off and redirecting it to the poor. As proposed the redistribution would take the form of providing *investment* resources to the poor, so that the redistribution would give them a permanent source of income rather than a temporary increase in consumption. If pursued over a long period redistribution through growth would, though it started by being incremental, end up by affecting the distribution of income and of assets substantially. The policy corresponds to objective C (raising the growth rate of the incomes of the poor) because it means a lower rate of growth of incomes at the upper end, and a higher rate of growth at the lower end, without any absolute reduction of income, as in other forms of redistribution. The ILO report on Kenya (ILO, 1972) was the forerunner and inspiration of the approach, which was developed and sophisticated by Chenery *et al.* (1974). *Cognoscenti* will recognize that there are some differences between the two, including significant differences in nomenclature. The ILO Kenya strategy was *redistribution from growth*, while the Chenery approach was termed *redistribution with growth*.

To be successful the strategy requires that the policies will not significantly reduce the growth rate of GNP as conventionally measured. This is of obvious importance to the Kenya strategy since redistribution from growth can occur only so long as there is growth, unlike other forms of redistribution. The Chenery strategy redefines the target growth rate to give a higher weight to growth of incomes of the poorer groups. But if redistributive policies are to lead to a higher growth of this redefined target than the conventional non-redistributive trickle-down strategy, then it is clear that the new redistributive strategy must not too adversely affect the conventional GNP growth rate. Moreover, if redistribution is to occur from extra incomes—explicitly the Kenya strategy, implicitly the Chenery strategy—and not by cutting into existing standards, then the extent of possible redistribution will be limited by the growth in incomes.

There are two major problems about the strategy. The first concerns the required assumption that such redistribution could occur without seriously affecting the growth rate. Redistribution—once it became more than trivial—would involve redirecting additional incomes from consumption of high-technology goods, and from production of such goods with advanced technology, to investment in small-scale activities, and production of investment and consumption goods for the worst off. But the bias of technological advance has been such that these latter areas have been almost entirely neglected. A policy which switched a substantial amount of resources to them would thus almost certainly reduce the rate of growth measured in conventional terms, at least for a time. While this would not matter at all as far as the objective of redistribution is concerned, it would matter as far as redistribution through growth is concerned because to the extent that the switch in resources was successful, the source of redistribution—the extra incomes generated by advanced technology among the élite—would dry up.

Second, the policy is probably as unrealistic politically as the earlier forms of redistribution. The trickle-down policy almost certainly failed because those who benefited from high growth did not wish to divert their gains to those who did not. The same applies to the redistribution through growth policy. The required restraint on incomes at the upper income end will be resisted just as previous redistribution was resisted—and resisted by the decision-makers who form part of that group. This appears to be the evidence from Kenya: in 1972 the ILO[18] recommended redistribution through growth—and gave detailed requirements in terms of incomes and tax policy. Despite lip service paid to the report at the time, there has been no serious attempt to put this part of the recommendations into effect.

Strategies towards poverty alleviation are easy to devise so long as the critical links between technology and income distribution, income distribution and decision-makers, and decision-makers and objectives, are ignored. Once made central, it seems difficult to avoid the conclusion that much wasted ingenuity has been put into devising *forms* of redistribution, when it is not lack of ingenious schemes but a basic political contradiction between the schemes and the real as opposed to nominal objectives of decision-makers, that is critical. Viewed in this light, trickle-down may offer a more realistic strategy for decision-makers than recently developed forms of redistribution.

THE STEADY TRIPOD

One may distinguish, very broadly, between three schools of thought, each advocating a different strategy to eradicate poverty and reduce inequality.[19] They may be called, for want of better names, the Price

Mechanists, the Radicals, and the Technologists.[20] The Price Mechanists argue that low production, low productivity, inequality and unemployment can be eliminated by setting the correct prices, which serve both as signals and as incentives.[21]

There is a powerful and vocal group of development economists who argue that many, if not all, of the disappointments with development efforts are the result of faulty price policies. Governments have set the wrong price for capital (too low and often rationed, encouraging excessive scale and under-utilization of capital, discriminating in favour of large firms and encouraging take-overs of local by foreign firms), for labour (too high, contributing to unemployment and under-utilized capacity and discouraging exports), for the foreign exchange rate (overvalued, discouraging labour-intensive exports and encouraging high-cost import substitution), for the products and services of public enterprises (too low, subsidizing the private modern sector). If only governments were to set the right prices, economic growth, as well as jobs and justice, would triumph. Indeed, this group argues, many of the evils attributed to foreign investment, the multi-national enterprise, the wrong technology, inappropriate products, the dominance of the developed country and the dependence of the underdeveloped country, the terms of trade, international inequality, etc., are *really* due to 'distortions', to faulty pricing policies, which convey the wrong signals and provide the wrong incentives.[22]

Most people would agree that 'getting prices right' is not enough. Some would say it would go a long way towards combining more growth (and more efficient growth) with greater equality, others would say that the contribution would be only marginal, but all would agree that other things would have to be done as well, if only additional marketing efforts for the extra exports generated by the 'right' price policies, or better facilities to improve the capital or labour markets. (But some would argue that the 'right' prices themselves would provide sufficient incentives for the creation or improvement of these institutions.)

But to say 'getting prices right is not enough' is open to two diametrically opposite interpretations. It might mean either that, by itself, it would make a contribution to the eradication of poverty and to greater equality, though this contribution would be greater if other things were done as well. But getting prices right is better than nothing. Alternatively, it might mean that while correct pricing policies *combined with* structural reforms, and in particular the redistribution of assets, would contribute to growth and equality, by themselves they might make matters worse or simply alter the manifestation of inequality.

No doubt, the 'wrong' price policies can impede development, reduce employment, strengthen monopoly and aggravate inequality. But it does not follow that the 'right' policies necessarily do the opposite. They might simply lead to *different* forms of the same evils. Let us assume that land and real capital equipment are scarce, while unskilled labour is plentiful. The supply of labour is growing faster than that of land and capital. We allow competition to prevail and factor rewards to be determined by marginal productivity. And we allow for a fair degree of substitution between labour and capital. Then rents per acre and real returns on capital will be high and rising (reflecting the growing relative scarcity of land and capital), while the wage rate will be low and falling (reflecting the growing abundance of labour). Producers will pay much to get hold of scarce resources of land and capital equipment and will offer little for the abundant supply of workers seeking jobs. Low wage costs will tend to expand employment and output, the extent depending on the elasticity of substitution. Processes, sectors, and products[23] that are labour-intensive will be encouraged and those requiring land and capital discouraged. Foreign capital will be attracted from higher-wage, lower-profit countries. High profits and low wages will tend to encourage domestic savings and hence increase the supply of capital inside the country. Moreover, there will be incentives to invent new methods and products that use labour and save land and capital. All this is fine and as it should be.

But these desirable incentives *depend on* wages being low (and, if labour grows faster than land and capital, falling), while rents, interest and profits are high (and rising). If in such a society the distribution of land and capital were to be very equal (peasant proprietors or socialized ownership of means of production, though the latter would raise questions as to how the state determines wages and the disposition of the surplus and also about the unequal distribution of power), the functional differences would not matter because personal or household equality would still prevail. What a family loses on labour income, it gains on property income. But if property (land) distribution is unequal, if the ownership of assets, including access to educational opportunities, is highly concentrated, inequality might increase, even if the share of wages went up as a result of a fairly high elasticity of substitution. The difference between a high-wage, low-interest and a low-wage, high-interest policy is that in the first case the evil takes the form of unemployment, in the second of inequality between wage earners and property owners. 'Getting prices right' may therefore transform inequality within the working class (between those with and without jobs) into inequality between workers and owners of assets.

To conclude: correct pricing is *certainly* not enough when ownership of assets is concentrated and, *by itself, may* make matters worse. This does not mean that correct pricing, combined with other policies, has not an important part to play.

This brings us to the second school of thought: the Radicals. This school believes that what matters is to redistribute assets, power, and access to income-earning opportunities. Only through such 'structural' and institutional reforms, whether peacefully and gradually or through revolution and quickly, can growth and equality be achieved. To some (extreme) members of this school, there is only one road to salvation. The whole revolting, suffocating mess must be flushed away. What is to take its place is irrelevant. Even to ask that question reveals a desire to preserve the Establishment. To destroy is also to create.

> The fiery anarchist agitator Bakunin . . . was saying something of this kind: the entire rotten structure, the corrupt old world, must be razed to the ground, before something new can be built upon it; what this is to be is not for us to say; we are revolutionaries, our business is to demolish. The new men, purified from the infection of the world of idlers and exploiters and its bogus values—these men will know what to do. The French anarchist Georges Sorel once quoted Marx as saying 'Anyone who makes plans for after the revolution is a reactionary.'[24]

Those advocating this line are open to the criticism advanced by an examiner of the development paper in the Oxford Final Honour School: 'Several candidates, having argued convincingly that a revolution would be a necessary condition of economic development, in a certain country, concluded that it would be a sufficient one.' Even, or rather especially, revolutionary juntas must plan signals and incentives[25] for development in considerable detail.[26]

Other less extreme members of this school advocate expropriation with compensation, though unless the compensation falls short of the initial value of the expropriated asset, there will be no redistribution. Others again would confine redistribution to *additional* assets as they accumulate over time, and would bring about a more gradual redistribution, say by the transfer of a certain proportion of annual savings and investment to low-income groups. Whether as argued above such incremental redistribution is possible in the face of an unequal power structure is controversial.

Both revolutionary and evolutionary, both average and incremental redistributive reforms have tended to fail because of a failure to provide the signals and incentives to make the assets now owned by the poor at least as productive as they were when owned by the rich. Soviet Russia had a long struggle with its peasants. The Soviet hammer has been more successful than the sickle, largely because of a failure of agricultural price incentives. In Cuba,

'Market anarchy' has been replaced . . . by the anarchy resulting from the interplay between chaotic decentralisation (chaotic because micro economic units, even if totally unselfish and devoted to collective welfare, have no accurate signals to guide their actions into socially optimal channels), and authoritarian centralization, which try as it may, is unable to coordinate and direct efficiently every decision involving resource allocation.[27]

Cuba's sugar estates and Chile's copper mines under Allende might have contributed more to the incomes of the poor had signals and incentives not been neglected.[28] Ironically some members of the Radical School commit the same error as the Price Mechanists: they mistake a necessary for a sufficient condition. In this way, they contribute to a redistribution of inequality, not to its reduction, to a perpetuation of poverty, not to its eradication.

Both the Price Mechanists and the Radicals are (often implicitly) optimistic about technology. They believe either that the technologies appropriate for the eradication of poverty and for the promotion of greater equality already exist, or that the 'right' prices or the redistribution of assets will automatically provide the incentives to invent them. The third school, the Technologists, are not so optimistic.

They approach the solution of the problem of poverty, unemployment, inequality and low productivity like that of putting a man on the moon, or, nearer home, discovering new high-yielding varieties of wheat, maize, and rice. Industrial technology, public health, low-cost housing, birth control, nutrition, crops for small farmers, urbanization, require the concentration of brain power and research resources. The Technologists are right, in so far as neither prices and incentives nor 'structural changes' can solve a problem where the appropriate technical solution just does not exist: where it has to be invented or discovered and where the incentives are too weak or too slow-working to produce 'automatically' the right solution.

Consider, by way of illustration, the need for a capital-saving, efficient technology to provide jobs for all willing and able to work. With existing technology transferred from the West, fixed technical coefficients, unchanged composition of products and unchanged sectoral distribution of investment, only between 1 and 2 per cent of the additions to the labour force can be employed, if we assume that the labour force in developing countries grows at 3 per cent compared with 1 per cent in developed countries, and that income per head is one-twentieth. An appropriate technology to employ only the extra workers entering the labour market each year would have to be such that the investable resources per worker would be only one-sixtieth of what they are in developed countries. Even allowing for some substitution between labour and capital (by changing the product mix, the sectoral distribution or techniques), this is a large hole in the production function to fill.

Technological innovation, in this context, should be interpreted broadly. It includes innovation in institutions. Just as the appropriate hardware may be non-existent, so appropriate institutions may have to be invented. Management, administration, organization, like physical techniques, have been developed in the West to solve labour scarcity, to meet the demand of high incomes, in an environment of temperate climate. Rural institutions to meet the needs of a large, rapidly growing, poor rural labour force make quite different demands on the institutional imagination than those we have tended to transfer from the developed countries.

The technological solution would appear to be particularly appealing both to researchers in the developed countries and to policy-makers in the developing countries, because, on the face of it, it does not violate vested interests and therefore seems to escape political opposition. It appears to lie beyond ideology: ideologies of both the "right" Price Mechanists and the "left" Radicals. It seems to tackle problems in a scientific, practical, workmanlike manner. Technology has been called the opium of the intellectuals.

But technology is both result and cause of income, asset, and power distribution in the national and international system. As the "Green Revolution" has shown, if the distribution of assets such as water, fertilizers, and credit is concentrated, it is the large farmers with controlled water supply who benefit, in some cases at the expense of the small farmers and landless labourers. A technology specifically invented to overcome food shortages for the growing number of poor people has reinforced and aggravated rural inequalities. Once again, the Technologists, like the Price Mechanists and the Radicals, may aggravate poverty and inequality or change its form.

Less than 2 per cent of total R & D is spent in the developing countries and only a fraction of this on the problems of poverty, even though the number of people is more than twice that in the developed countries. But even if a substantially larger proportion were spent, this would not mean that poverty would be eliminated, if the institutional arrangements and the power structure necessary for dissemination and application are weak or absent. And organized interests will oppose measures that hurt them.

The conclusion of the discussion is by now plain. We have an instance of the Theory of the Second Best, according to which $\alpha + \beta + \gamma$ yield the desired results, but α or β or γ by themselves, far from being "better than nothing", may move society away from the desired goal.[29] Only a three-pronged attack, combining signals and incentives, institutional reforms directed at the redistribution of assets (including access to education) and technical and institutional innovation, promises results. The precise combination of price policies, asset redistribution, and technological research will depend on a number of factors that will vary between countries: on the readiness of vested interests to yield, on the elasticity of substitution between factors, on the nature of the interdependence between sectors, on the degree of concentration of ownership, on the productivity of assets when redistributed, on the fiscal system, etc. But it is only on the three legs of this tripod that efficient redistribution can rest.

It may be objected that to demand a simultaneous attack on all three fronts is to ask for the impossible. This, it might be argued, is suggested by the frequent failure to meet any one of the three requirements. However, the relations between the three are such that failure to attempt change on one front only may prevent the change itself, or the desirable effects of the change. Hence the failure of one-prong attacks may actually be the result of confining attention to one aspect.

However, much may depend on the *order*[30] in which the policies are pursued. Taking one sequence may prevent the achievement of any or all of the targets. For example, price changes preceding income redistribution may establish patterns of production and consumption inimical to redistribution. Yet if redistribution precedes policy changes on technology and prices, it may establish pressures likely to bring them about. Irma Adelman concludes that the *sequence* of reform is critical to the relative success of some countries which have combined improvements in the incomes of the poor with accelerated growth.

Irma Adelman has argued that an "examination of the development process of those non-Communist countries which have recently successfully combined improvements in the incomes of the poor with accelerated growth (Israel, Japan, South Korea, Singapore and Taiwan) shows that they all followed a similar dynamic sequence of strategies . . . " (1975, pp. 307–8). Her strategies do not correspond precisely to ours, but the sequence is first, radical asset redistribution (sometimes accompanied by negative growth rates); second, massive accumulation of human capital and skill creation far in excess of current demand; and, third, economic policies directed at rapid, labour-intensive economic growth, with the development of appropriate technologies for large countries and foreign trade for small countries. Historically, the "grow now, redistribute and educate later" strategy has been followed by some capitalist economies, but the "redistribute and educate now and grow later" strategy is the one followed by the economies studied by Irma Adelman. It is more consistent with current demographic trends and time scales.[31]

In considering the correct sequence one must pay attention to the pressures which reform on one front will have in inducing or preventing reform on the other two, and the likely impact of the one reform taken by itself. From this point of view, it seems that radical redistribution should come first, then the other steps may follow. This reverses the sequence in the now developed countries which was "grow first, redistribute later". This took many decades to make the poor better off and bring about greater equality; and it contrasts with the "redistribute marginally *and* grow" policy, or "redistribution with growth", which is likely to fail in one or both aims.

NOTES

1. This chapter is reprinted from *Oxford Economic Papers*, vol. 28, no. 3 (November 1976). We are indebted to Wilfred Beckerman, Robert Cassen, Richard Jolly, Amartya Sen, and Hans Singer, and to a research seminar at Queen Elizabeth House, for helpful comments.

2. i.e. if (Y_{t10}/Y_{b10}) is taken as our measure of income distribution at time t' (Y_{t10}, Y_{b10} is the money income of the top tenth decile and the bottom tenth decile at time $'$), then at time t'', the relevant ratio for comparison is

$$\left(\frac{Y''_{t10}}{1 + \Delta p_{t10}} \div \frac{Y''_{b10}}{1 + \Delta p_{b10}} \right)$$

where Δp_{t10}, Δp_{b10} measure the change in prices of the goods consumed between t' and t'' and not (Y''_{t10}/Y''_{b10}) for a comparison of income distribution between the two dates. Δp, the change in prices, itself depends upon which quantities are taken as weights. The two usual measures, Paasche and Laspeyres, use current and base period quantities respectively. But other quantities could be used as weights. In the light of the subsequent discussion on p. 160 the customary use of base period weights underestimates the impoverishment of the poor as average income grows.

3. Further, as discussed more fully below, the welfare associated with any given purchasing power tends to decline as average incomes rise because of the changing nature of the goods available for purchase.

4. Abel-Smith and Townsend (1965) defined poverty in Britain as occuring when people's standards fell below the level at which National Assistance became payable. This standard is relative as they explicitly recognize: 'It must be recognised that any subsistence standard is inevitably influenced by current

living standards, and that we cannot define a poverty line in a vacuum but only in relation to the living standards of a particular society at a particular date' (p. 17). A similar definition is used by Atkinson (1969).

5. See Atkinson (1973) and Sen (1973a).
6. It could be argued that, although inequality between the poorest and the recipient is increased, that between the poorest and the richest diminishes by exactly the same amount, and in addition there is a reduction of the inequality between the recipient and the richest man. But this implies weighing increases and reductions in inequality against one another.
7. A measure of the relation of the incomes of the poor to the average is captured, corrected for inequality *among* the poor, in the measure suggested in equations 8 and 9 of A. K. Sen (1973b).
8. A good discussion is to be found in P. T. Bauer and A. R. Prest (1973).
9. M. Ahluwalia and H. Chenery, 'The Economic Framework', in Chenery *et al.* (1974). See also Simon Kuznets (1972):
10. This might be described as the Rawls Strategy, see Rawls (1972).
11. Distributional objectives mean that the *ratio* of measures of final to initial income distributions is an objective, not simply the absolute rates of growth of the incomes of different groups, as in the Ahluwalia–Chenery strategy.
12. See P. P. Streeten (1958), Ch. 1 of this volume.
13. If this position is taken to its extreme it becomes impossible to distinguish between objectives and policies and therefore to assess whether the right policies have been selected to meet a government's objectives, as Wilfred Beckerman has pointed out. However, it remains possible to assess policies in the light of declared or nominal objectives.
14. Langdon (1975) provides a fascinating case study of these effects for the soap industry in Kenya.
15. In some countries 'trickle-down' may have worked in raising incomes at most levels, but it was none the less *regarded* as a failure because of the *relative* impoverishment of some groups—in other words, whether it worked or not depended on whether our strategy of high growth and 'trickle-down' or redistribution was taken to be the objective. Possibly decision-makers considered high growth the objective, while critics considered redistribution.
16. See Westlake (1973).
17. See ILO (1972) and Chenery *et al.* (1974).
18. ILO, *op. cit.*, Ch. 20 on 'The Cost of Inaction' does, however, discuss some of the points raised here.
19. In line with most current discussions, we focus on inequality in the distribution of income and assets. But these are only a small part of the problem. More important are inequalities of power and access to power, status, prestige, recognition, satisfaction from and facilities at work, conditions of work, degree of participation, freedom of choice, and many other dimensions.
20. See F. Stewart (1974).
21. The function of prices to serve as signals and as incentives can, of course, be separated.
22. Some members of the school believe that all this results from lack of understanding of basic economic analysis, others that the 'distortions' serve entrenched vested interests. Which of these views is correct makes, of course, a difference to the policy prescriptions.

23. Usually, more attention is paid to processes than to sectors and products. But it may be more rewarding to encourage labour-intensive sectors, like the non-organized sector, and appropriate products, than processes which are often dictated by the choice of product and sector. Cf. Frances Stewart, *loc. cit.* (1974).

24. Isaiah Berlin (1970), p. 26.

25. Signals and incentives need not be material ones; they may be moral ones. But many socialist economists have argued that the price system comes into its own under socialism.

26. The methodological similarity of the Price Mechanists and the Revolutionary Marxists reveals their common origin in nineteenth-century liberalism. The early utopian socialists were more realistic and are more relevant today in their emphasis on detailed planning of institutions and incentives.

27. Carlos F. Díaz-Alejandro (1973), p. 92.

28. ' . . . Chile's resource situation has worsened under the impact of a drastic decline in aid from the West and virtual elimination of private inflow of foreign capital—so that the economic regime is under severe stress, calling particularly for improved export-performance, much the way we face this necessity. And yet Allende's advisers have given up the 'sliding' exchange rate scheme of the earlier Frei government, which worked so well, and the balance of payments situation in consequence has continued to deteriorate disastrously. On a recent visit to Santiago I found that the system had broken down to a point at which the divergence between the official and the unofficial parities was of the order of 1 to 10—thus resulting in a situation where selling foreign exchange at the official rate had become an act of honest idiocy that no one, including the distinguished members of the United Nations Secretariat in Santiago, was willing to perpetrate! Ironically, the resulting sabotage of the Allende regime's admirable efforts at socialist transformation has been far more effective than anything the ITT or the U.S. State Department could have planned or even implemented!' Jagdish N. Bhagwati, 'India in the International Economy: a Policy Framework for a Progressive Society', Lal Bahadur Shastri Lecture, delivered before the fall of the Allende government.

29. The three schools clearly do not cover all relevant issues. In particular, we have left out the school that advocates using fiscal policy to redistribute *consumption* goods and services to the poor. Disregarding the difficulty of differentiating at very low income levels between unproductive and productive consumption, such redistribution as the sole measure of eradicating poverty and promoting equality has serious drawbacks. First, developing countries do not have an adequate fiscal machinery. Second, in order to maintain equality, redistribution of consumption goods and services would have to grow not only in absolute terms, but also as a proportion of national income. This would raise administrative, economic and political difficulties. Third, people may wish to earn their income rather than have it doled out. None of this implies that subsidizing consumption of the poor has not a supplementary part to play. It is by now well known how public services, like health and education, without other reforms, largely benefit the middle class. Another area that we have neglected in this section is the international impact on strategies for equality. Can countries pursue policies for equality, while remaining wide open to communications, foreign investment, the trans-national enterprise, foreign

technology and foreign products, and the whole structure of international relations with advanced industrial countries? Also left out of the discussion in this section are intertemporal choices. By keeping the income of the lowest 40 per cent down for a number of years, a country (it has been argued) may be able to raise them to a higher level after a period than if it had raised them earlier. This is the proper formulation of the choice 'growth versus equity'. Formally, this can be solved by taking the net present value of the future flow of consumption of the bottom 40 per cent as the objective—though this would involve all the problems associated with the choice of the appropriate rate of discount. Nor have we discussed the important problem of how equality, once established, can be maintained in the presence of increasing returns, cumulative processes and unequal distribution of inherited characteristics. Finally, as Robert Cassen has reminded us, we have omitted the important problem of population policy. Redistributive and employment policies, through improved health and education, may reduce fertility and increase incomes per head, though reducing growth of total GNP. This is a powerful argument against the 'grow now, redistribute later' strategy and strengthens our case.

30. A point made by Hirschman in correspondence and Adelman (1975).
31. Irma Adelman concludes: 'There is also evidence that the entire package—resource redistribution, massive education and labour-intensive growth policies—must be adopted in that sequence to achieve rapid success. Incomplete versions of this program, such as land reform alone or education without labour-intensive growth, have not worked. For the advanced countries which followed a grow-first pattern, economic development did eventually benefit the poor, but the time it took to do so was much longer (roughly two or more generations) than in our five successful cases (where it took only two decades).'

REFERENCES

Abel-Smith, B., and Townsend, P., *The Poor and the Poorest*, Occasional Papers on Social Administration, no.17, G. Bell & Sons (1965).

Adelman, Irma, 'Development Economics—a Reassessment of Goals', *The American Economic Review*, Papers and Proceedings (May 1975), pp. 302–9.

Atkinson, A. B., *Poverty in Britain and the Reform of Social Security* (1969).

Atkinson, A. B., 'On the Measurement of Inequality', in Atkinson, A. B. (ed.) *Wealth, Income and Inequality*, Penguin, Harmondsworth (1973).

Bauer, P. T., and Prest, A.R., 'Income Differences and Inequalities', *Moorgate and Wall Street* (Autumn 1973).

Berlin, I., *Fathers and Children*, The Romanes Lecture, Oxford (1970).

Chenery, H., *et al., Redistribution with Growth*, Oxford University Press, 1974.

Dandekar, U. M., and Rath, N., 'Poverty in India', *Economic and Political Weekly*, vol. 6, no. 2 (1971).

Díaz-Alejandro, C. F., review of Bernardo, R. M., *The Theory of Moral Incentives in Cuba, Journal of Economic Literature*, vol. 9, no. 1 (March 1973).

Harrington, M., *The Other America—Poverty in the United States*, Macmillan, New York (1962).

ILO, *Employment Incomes and Equality: A Strategy for Increasing Productive Employment in Kenya*, Geneva (1972).

Kuznets, Simon, 'Problems in Comparing Recent Growth Rates in Developed and Less-Developed Countries', *Economic Development and Cultural Change*, vol. 20, no. 2 (January 1972), pp. 185–209, reprinted in *Population, Capital, and Growth*, Heinemann Educational Books, London (1974).

Langdon, S., 'Multinational Corporations, Taste Transfer and Underdevelopment: a Case Study for Kenya,' *Review of African Political Economy*, no. 2, (January–April 1975).

Myrdal, Gunnar, *Asian Drama*, The Twentieth Century Fund and Pelican Books (1968).

Rawls, J., *A Theory of Justice*, London (1972).

Sen, A. K. (a) *On Economic Inequality*, Oxford University Press (1973). (b) 'Poverty, Inequality and Unemployment: Some Conceptual Issues in Measurement', *The Economic and Political Weekly*, vol. 8, special no. 31–3, (August 1973)

Stewart, F., 'Technology and Employment in LDCs', *World Development*, (March 1974).

Streeten, P. P. 'Introduction to Gunnar Myrdal', *Value in Social Theory*, Routledge & Kegan Paul (1958).

Westlake, M. J., 'Tax evasion, Tax Incidence and the Distribution of Income in Kenya', *East African Economic Review*, vol. 5, no. 2 (December 1973).

9 The Dynamics of the New Poor Power[1]

Few would deny that the United Nations Conference on Trade and Development (UNCTAD) has, until recently, been a relative failure.[2] Many reasons have been advanced for this, but the main reason is surely that, from the developed countries' point of view, it seems all give and no take. The poor countries' moral appeals and appeals to distant and uncertain national self-interest of the rich, backed by masses of facts and figures, were not enough. There must also be appeals to the clear and imminent self-interest and backing by power.

Appeals to self-interest can be of two kinds: those that point to previously undisclosed, undiscovered or unexploited self-interest and those that create a nuisance or a threat for the removal of which concessions are extracted. An example of the first is trade liberalization, combined with adjustment assistance to those who are displaced by the new imports. There are wide areas in which negotiations that emphasize the common interest have a better chance of success than those based solely on moral appeals.

The archetype of the second kind of appeal is the blackmailer or the kidnapper, though these expressions beg the moral question. Ransoms demanded to correct previously committed inequities must be judged differently from those that destroy equity. Though two blacks do not make a white, blackmail against a blackmailer may be regarded as whitemail. An example would be the threat to withdraw from the control of narcotics traffic by permitting the growth of opium.

Appeals to self-interest or to the conscience of the rich must, then, be backed by power. In order to back moral appeals by power, three things are necessary: solidarity among partners; fragmentation among opponents; and information.

SOLIDARITY

Solidarity between sovereign nation states is difficult to achieve. The reasons for this are best illustrated by the case of a restrictive, price-raising

175

commodity cartel, but they apply with equal force to other exercises of joint bargaining power (see below).

Solidarity is difficult to achieve because the more effective a cartel or a cartel-like agreement, the greater the reward for any one member to break it. But the fear that anyone may break the agreement will induce those who would otherwise be willing to adhere, to prepare for the break-up. For sticking to an agreement while others abandon it makes the loyal members worse off than they would have been without any agreement. The potential defectors cherish the *hope* of operating *outside* the agreement. But this encourages on the part of the conformers the *fear* of a situation *without* the agreement. This fear is ever-present, even if there are no actual or potential defectors. The fear itself leads to actions that undermine the agreement. Action outside the agreement is an ever-present hope and action without the agreement an ever-present threat.

On the other hand, if buyers do not believe in the stability of the cartel, they will not take the actions they would have taken, had they expected prices to stay high (e.g., searching for substitutes or installing expensive equipment that economizes in the use of the imported material).

Agreements can be renegotiated and a partner will hope that, at the next round of negotiations, he will get a better deal, a larger share. The actions necessary to secure this are similar to those leading to defection or breach. Again, the knowledge that some will ask for a larger share puts others on the defensive. But defence is as disruptive as attack. Cartels are a continuation of competition by other means, as Clausewitz might well have said, and only error can arise from identifying them wholly with monopolies.

A cartel that restricts supply and raises prices must allocate quotas. (Since OPEC does not do so, it is not a cartel in the strict sense, though it is fortunate in that the exporters with large oil reserves, Saudi Arabia, Kuwait and Abu Dhabi, have limited absorptive capacity and an independent interest to curtail production, while those with a vociferous demand for imports have relatively small reserves.) Producers and countries have an interest in enlarging their quotas at the expense of other producers and countries. The power to negotiate for a larger quota depends, partly, on the capacity to fill it. Each country therefore has a strong interest in increasing this capacity by maintaining reserves, either in the form of productive excess capacity or stocks. In the International Coffee Agreement reserve stocks were feared to be ammunition of this kind. In the case of mineral agreements, the high fixed costs of mining, the equivalent of spare productive capacity, are a destabilizing factor.

The incentive to hold such reserves or excess capacity and the ability to do so are diametrically opposed to the conditions on which stability in the cartel can be maintained. For the fear that these reserves will be used will tend to undermine willingness to adhere to the restrictions necessary to maintain the cartel. The fear that the breakdown of the cartel will make everyone worse off is not a sufficient deterrent to prevent it, for any one member, in most cases rightly, believes that the threat of breakdown comes from others. The defensive response of each member, however, has the same effect as the aggressive undermining by defectors. It explains why, in spite of the obvious rational interest of the group, successful, lasting cartels are so rare, whether in the field of commodity prices or agreements to follow common policies towards foreign companies or boycotts or sanctions.

The prevalence of reserve stocks and reserve capacity is partly a function of the level of demand. When world demand is high and growing, stocks and excess capacity will tend to be low, compared with the desired level, making cartel agreements workable, but there will be less incentive to form them. On the other hand, when world demand is low and falling, and reserves and excess capacity are large, the need for cartels will be more urgent, but their chances of success reduced. The situation is like a leaking roof: in good weather there is no need to repair it, in bad weather no opportunity. When there is a will, there is no way; when there is a way, there is no will.

The problem of adherence to a cartel agreement is that of the prisoner's dilemma. Peter and Paul are arrested, but in separate cells, and not permitted to communicate. The prosecution knows that they have committed a crime but has not enough evidence for a conviction in a court. If neither confesses, they get a minor punishment on a trumped-up charge, say one year. If Peter confesses and Paul does not, Paul gets the maximum penalty, say ten years, and Peter only a light one, say three months, for turning queen's evidence. Similarly, the other way round. If both confess, they get some remission, say eight years. Though it is clearly in their interest that neither should confess, neither can rely on the other's not confessing and the result of (individual) rational action on the part of both is that both confess.

The general feature of such situations is that, (1) given the actions of other individuals, no matter what they are, the individual is better off choosing A rather than B; but, (2) given the choice between everyone doing A and everyone doing B, each individual prefers the latter to the former.

Sen shows that certain results follow from these two assumptions.[3] First, in the absence of collusion, each will prefer A to B, for no matter what others choose each is better off choosing A. As a result each will be worse off than had all chosen B. Second, the result is completely independent of each party's expectations of others' actions. Uncertainty does not enter. Third, even if all agreed on doing B, this would not come about (assuming self-seeking) except through compulsory enforcement. Every party would like others to do B, while it chooses A, so that even if a contract is drawn up, it will be in the interest of each to break it.

Sen distinguishes this case (the isolation paradox) from another case, where (2) above still holds (each individual prefers everyone doing B to everyone doing A) but (1) is modified to allow one exception: if everyone else does B, the individual prefers B. In all other cases, the individual prefers A to B, no matter what others do. The difference in this case, which Sen calls the assurance paradox, is that expectations must now be brought in and the need for enforcement no longer holds. If each can be assured that all others will do B, it is in his interest to stick to the contract.

The situation we are here concerned with, the cartel and cartel-like agreements, is of the type of the isolation paradox, not the assurance paradox. It is this type of situation which has provided the justification for collective coercion wholly in the interest of individual preferences.[4] Only a penalty as great as that imposed by the disastrous, though fully rational, option, will ensure that they are not driven to the 'stupid' result, that they avoid embarking on a negative-sum game. Coordinated rationality must be enforced to avoid the results of uncoordinated rationality.

An n-person analogy to the prisoner's dilemma, relevant in the present context, is price competition between sellers, where profits are eroded as a result of each trying to snatch a gain and rents are transferred to buyers as consumers' surplus. Competition results in the erosion of monopoly profits and therefore benefits the buyers of the product. The desirable outcome depends, *inter alia*, on producers and consumers forming part of the same community and income distribution being optimal. Clearly neither of these conditions is met in the relations between countries or between poor producers and rich consumers, and coordinated action can therefore improve the allocation and distribution of resources by conserving monopoly rents as poor producers' surplus instead of passing them on to rich consumers.

A cartel has, of course, greater coordination than the separated, non-communicating prisoners. But the penalties for defection are normally too weak to ensure adherence. Those emphasizing solidarity, joint actions, common fronts, which give rise to situations in which choices of the type of the prisoner's dilemma have to be made *should, therefore, pay attention to instituting a system of rewards and penalties that shifts the incentives so as to make the unstable optimum solution stable.*

An important source of rewards in commodity agreements are diversification funds and technical assistance to diversification. These have a double virtue. First, they compensate countries for restricting supplies and, second, when opportunity costs are positive, they absorb resources in alternative uses, thereby reducing the danger of erosion of the cartel. Through geographical and commodity diversification countries previously dependent on one or a few markets and one or a few crops or minerals or services can thereby be made more self-reliant and their loyalty to the cartel increased.

Another factor that will enhance the stability of the cartel is the ability of a supplier to do without any earnings, or with substantially reduced earnings, for a period. This is one of the forces that strengthens OPEC. Withholding supplies is a powerful weapon of the cartel. If a supplying country is not able to withhold supplies because it depends on earnings, the cartel can be strengthened by other members compensating the country for doing so.

Conflicts of interest arise both between countries and between producers. Thus a country with a small share in the total export market of a commodity has a stronger interest in increasing its supply *by a given absolute amount* (and *a fortiori* by a given percentage of its sales), because the main burden of the lower price will be borne by the exporter with the large share. Inducements will have to be provided to the exporter with the small share not to undermine the agreement. Of course, if there are several exporting countries each with a small share, the notion that each can cut price without damage will turn out to be an illusion. But the large exporter is less likely to suffer from such an illusion.

In order to raise the stability of cartel agreements there must exist not only rewards for adherence and penalties against defection, but also a sense of a fair distribution of the gains from the agreement between and within countries. This may require compensatory payments from large gainers to small gainers. Conflicts of interest arise not only between countries but also between producers inside countries. While it is in the interest of the cartel as a whole, whenever demand is less than infinitely elastic and supply more than zero elastic, to restrict supply below the level that would be reached under competition, it is in the interest of each country to increase supply in the face of the restrictions of others, and it is in the interest of each producer within each country to raise his supply, while others restrict theirs. The reconciliation of the pressures of producers on the country's negotiating position and the pressures of countries on the agreements reached in the cartel will be possible only if each party believes it has more to lose from breaking than from keeping the agreement.

The fair distribution of gains is further complicated by differences of view as to what constitutes fairness. There may be conflicts between fairness and bargaining power, and bargaining power may change over time. Here, a sense of solidarity derived from sources other than the cartel, e.g., ethnic, religious, ideological or linguistic unity, may be a help in achieving acceptance of a system of sharing, by inducing those with greater power to make sacrifices for those with less.

Further complications arise from differences over the time distribution of gains. Some partners may prefer short-term gains at the expense of longer-term ones, others the reverse. Different partners may have different preferences for independently given time distribution of gains and different capacities for reserves. In addition, the time distribution of gains may itself be partly determined by the actions of the cartel. Raising prices now tends to encourage speedier switches to or invention of substitutes, greater economies in the use of the product or loss of goodwill and thereby reduces prices later below what they would have been had prices not been raised. On the other hand, some members of the cartel may anticipate that their supply of a non-renewable resource will have been exhausted when lower prices prevail in the future, while others may anticipate continuing supplies. Successful cartel agreements would have to find methods of reconciling such conflicts of interest and would have to combat the attempts of buyers to nurse them.

It is sometimes argued against cartel agreements in commodities for which the demand is more elastic in the long run than in the short run that the gains are only short-term. But this is not an argument against a cartel. The short-term gains can be used to strengthen the base of action at a future time when the agreement will have been eroded (for example, by promoting diversification with the aid of the short-term gains from raising the price of a commodity for which short-term demand is inelastic). Or they may be used to push up demand through research and development or to make it less elastic through advertising. Only to the extent to which the agreement itself is responsible for shortening the period over which benefits can be derived, e.g., by encouraging production outside the cartel or by speeding up the search for substitutes or for economies in use, or by losing goodwill or by lowering future demand curves in other ways, should the longer-term losses be set against the short-term gains and such gains be moderated in the light of inter-temporal preferences.

Illustrations of a later collapse in price, resulting from a cartel that raises price, are the British rubber control scheme and the Brazilian attempt to raise coffee prices in the 1920s. The British rubber scheme was based on Malaya and Ceylon and succeeded, at first, spectacularly in raising the price of rubber, but investment in Indonesia was stimulated and led to a drastic fall in price. The Brazilian scheme was based on government stock holdings but the high price stimulated planting and led to a bumper crop that exceeded the government's financial stock-holding capacity.

A rise in export earnings resulting from restricting supplies has implications for employment. Many primary products are labour-intensive and production is often concentrated on certain regions. The increased export earnings would therefore have to be used so as to avoid any undesired consequences for employment and income distribution. No automatic mechanism will look after this and the operation requires careful planning.

If solidarity can be extended from members of one cartel to others, additional opportunities are presented. A successful cartel in one commodity can use part of its extra earnings to buy up surpluses in order to maintain or strengthen another cartel. OPEC funds could thus be used to buy up copper in order to raise its price. By reducing reserves, the successful cartel would also strengthen the potentially unstable cartel.

DIVISION AMONG OPPONENTS

Successful cartel action is derived from a degree of dependence of the purchasers which the cartel members exploit. One-sided, permanent dependence is very rare. It is not just a question of a low elasticity of demand. For, as we have argued above, the shift of the demand curve and its elasticities in the future may themselves be a function of the present rise in price. To define dependence precisely, we should have to combine ordinary demand elasticities with inter-temporal cross elasticities. Such a cross elasticity would be defined as the proportionate change in the quantity demanded at a given future date, resulting from small proportionate change in price now. But the precision of such a concept is a pseudo-precision, for inevitably a historical element will enter into the quantity demanded at any given time at any given price. It will depend, at least partly, on the memory of the history of prices charged in the past.

We explored briefly above the temporal aspect, i.e., the possibility that dependence can be reduced over time. We must now turn to the question whether dependence is not mutual. If there is *inter*dependence, there is the possibility of retaliation. Not always is it the case that the victims of a cartel can say: "Anything you can do, I can do better", but, on the other hand, there is usually some countervailing power. Using bargaining power by one group may invite retaliation by another. The recent US Trade Act refuses most-favoured-nation treatment to members of an export cartel. The USA also has refused to give trade preferences to all members of OPEC. If oil consumers depend on OPEC, food-grain consumers depend on the USA and the food producers' monopoly exceeds the oil producers' monopoly, as Assistant Secretary of State Thomas O. Enders said at the World Food Conference in November 1974. In a struggle of "agripower against petropower", many poor nations are liable to lose. When the knives are out, who can say who will win? To carry a gun when nobody else does gives the gunman extra power, but a world in which everyone carries a gun is liable to be worse than one in which nobody does.

There are four replies to this line of argument against the use of monopoly power by poor countries. First, common action by the rich already exists in many areas and joint action among the poor cannot therefore make things much worse then they are already. In the past, there was always the possibility of armed intervention. Until the October 1973 war, military intervention by the big powers was improbable. In the post-Suez, post-Vietnam world of the balance of nuclear terror, the use of military power seemed ruled out. But in the new situation, in which wages, employment and standards of living are endangered and whole economies may be "strangulated", the situation has changed. It is perhaps not quite so improbable as it was before 1973, though the super powers will probably find more effective and cheaper ways of safeguarding their supplies than armed intervention.

It is clear, therefore, that the big powers still have considerable latent bargaining power. But, military intervention apart, greater sophistication goes with better organization for national interests. Regional groupings such as the European Community, the policies of the governments of rich countries towards their trans-national companies, the policies pursued by the Group of Ten or by members of the General Agreement on Tariffs and Trade are, or were, to some extent, already in the nature of actions of "rich men's clubs". Collective action by the poor may be needed to catch up with these established policies.

Second, the ability of the rich to band together can itself, to some extent, be influenced by the poor. The far-sighted cartelier must give thought to how to prevent the rally of the forces of the opposition. Division and fragmentation of opponents is as useful to the cartel as *divide et impera!* is to the dictator. Whether by design or not, the result of discrimination against Holland and the USA and in favour of France and Britain, by the oil exporting countries during the cutback in 1973–4, may have been bad economics (because it seemed to neglect substitution), but it was good politics. An Organisation of Oil Importing Countries (OPIC) could have inflicted greater damage on the oil exporters than they inflicted on importers. But powerful divisive forces were at work and were nourished by OPEC, so that it never came to joint action by importers.[5]

In addition to fragmentation of opponents, the members of the cartel can weaken the power of the buyers by: (i) encouraging them in the belief that the price rise is only temporary, so that they do not embark on the investment and installation costs of inventing or using alternative sources of supply or of economising in the use of the imported material; (ii) depriving them of stocks, for stocks are an important weapon in resisting the demands of the cartel.

Third, if the *status quo* is quite intolerable for some countries, the result of an international free-for-all may be preferable for them, even though most countries would be worse off. The balance of power and the balance of advantage may, in some instances, lie with some of the poor. However strong the organizations of buyers, they may heavily depend, at least for a time, on certain raw materials or fuels of which the exporters are monopoly suppliers, or on certain areas for locating factories requiring cheap labour. Japan is heavily dependent on imported raw materials. The USA depends almost entirely on imports of manganese, tin and chromium. All industrial countries have shown themselves vulnerable in their dependence on cheap petroleum, though Japan and Western Europe more than the USA.

Fourth, and most important, the argument points not to a full use of the bargaining power by all countries. As I. G. Patel has said, "once you get into a mood of warfare in trade, it is going to be difficult to keep the firing within any prescribed limits."[6] The valid conclusion is that the situation calls for a new set of international rules and institutions enforcing these rules, which reflect a more even power distribution. It is this that lies behind the demand for a new international economic order. If the rules of the game have in the past been biased in favour of the rich countries, the solution is not to abandon all rules, but to change them. For this, reference to potential, latent, power constellations and power reserves on both sides is necessary, but the powers need not be exercised. The incentive for the rich countries to avoid a break-down of regulated international relations is that they may lose more from a situation without rules than they would lose from a set of rules that makes generous concessions to the poor. If the poor threaten to abandon the system of international rules unless their grievances are removed, a reformed system will then be preferable to breakdown.

Applied to the areas of cartels, this leads to the conclusion that there is a case for commodity agreements in which both producing and consuming countries participate. The previous discussion has been conducted for producers' associations, but there are common interests between producers and consumers, and there is scope for bargaining. Producers may, for example, agree on a lower price than they could otherwise impose, in return for some limitation on the introduction of substitutes for their exports. Consumers may guarantee a floor price in return for ensured supplies at not more than an agreed ceiling price. Cooperative agreements of this type have many advantages.

AREAS FOR BARGAINING

What are the areas in which there is a *prima facie* case for exploring the exercise of joint bargaining power? The classical case, on which much of this discussion has focused, is joint action to raise the prices of exports in inelastic demand and to restrict supplies: to transfer consumers' surpluses of the rich into producers' surpluses of the poor. Cartels will tend to be more successful in restricting the supply and raising the price of a commodity and thereby raising total earnings, the more price inelastic the demand for the commodity, and the more price inelastic (in response to a higher supply price) its supply in the medium and long term. Demand will be more inelastic:

(1) the higher the proportion of imports to total consumption of the commodity in importing countries;
(2) the fewer substitutes there are (i.e., the lower the elasticity of substitution between the cartelized commodity and its non-cartelized nearest substitutes, including scrap and other forms of re-usable materials), and the slower the rate of innovation in substitutes in response to the price rise;
(3) the more difficult it is to economize in the use of the commodity as an input into given products;
(4) the more difficult it is to switch to products using less of the commodity in question (i.e., the lower the elasticity of substitution between products using the commodity as inputs and products using less or none of it).

The medium- and long-term supply of the commodity will be more inelastic (in response to price increases):

(1) the fewer the countries in which the commodity is or can be produced and from which it is or can be exported;

(2) the stronger the solidarity among cartel members (i.e., the greater the rewards for adhering and the penalties for defecting); agreements between governments are likely to be more successful than those between producers; and agreements between politically friendly governments more successful than between hostile ones;

(3) the more commodities that are substitutes for one another are included in the cartel (e.g., *all* metals or *all* tropical beverages).

OPEC has been the most successful institution using collective bargaining power for transferring resources. Its stability has been strengthened, apart from political and ideological bonds, by the fortunate and fortuitous fact that member countries with large oil reserves (Kuwait and Saudi Arabia) had no need for immediate earnings, while those with the strongest and most urgent needs, because of large populations and ambitious development plans (Nigeria and Iran), had small reserves. Indeed, as the countries with relatively small reserves and large absorptive capacity pressed for price increases, the countries with large reserves and small absorptive capacity have an interest not only in not increasing production, but in actually reducing it, in order not to accumulate unwanted funds (which might depreciate in real value and reduce their future bargaining power). It is true that excessively high prices, by encouraging the search for substitutes, will lower future prices of oil, but this may be regarded as a lesser evil. However, this combination of forces making for stability depends on a level of total demand sufficiently high to accommodate the different countries' wishes. In addition, the oil companies implemented the cut-backs in production, which might have been more difficult if the countries had had to allocate quotas.

On the other hand, price increases due to the action of the cartel may have an inflationary impact on the general price level, and therefore on the prices of the imports of cartel members. To safeguard itself against such consequences, the cartel has to fix its price increases in real terms, e.g., by indexing. The same rules apply here as in the case of cartel action.

Even in this most successful case, restricting supplies and raising the price of oil is only part, and perhaps not the most significant part, of the bargain. In addition, there are the partial or total nationalization of the oil companies and the new terms for the flow of technical know-how from the companies to the host countries. There are also political pressures on policies towards Israel. Reducing or withholding supplies may be used for purposes other than maximizing the cartel's export earnings. They may be used to achieve economic advantages in other fields, or for political purposes.

This paper is concerned mainly with the *feasibility* of exercising joint bargaining power and hence with the stability of cartels. We are not here examining the *desirability* of commodity agreements as instruments to accelerate development in low-income countries and to reduce worldwide inequality. But it is worth remembering that commodity agreements, even if they could be made to work, have certain drawbacks.

First, there is the question of the internal and international distribution of gains from price increases. The beneficiaries of these cartels may be large farmers, plantation owners or mining companies who belong to the rich in poor countries, and the consumers hit by price increases may be the poor in rich countries. If these plantations or mines are owned by rich foreigners, e.g., by trans-national companies, the benefits take the form of aid or redistribution to the rich countries.

Second, many poor countries, the largest ones among them, have few commodities that lend themselves to successfull cartelization (tea and jute are poor commodities, produced by very poor countries) and rely heavily on imports of commodities more readily cartelized or on imports of manufactures which incorporate these materials and which are exported by relatively better-off countries. Unless development aid is concentrated on these importers or unless safeguards are built into the commodity agreements, divisions within the so-called Third World would be aggravated. In addition, many rich countries are exporters of commodities that would benefit from cartels. Developing countries account for only 30 per cent of world exports in non-fuel commodities.

The World Bank has calculated that developing countries containing about 300 million people are likely to benefit substantially from the rise in the price of oil, as a result of improved terms of trade in 1980, another 100 million mineral producers are unaffected and 1,600 million in developing countries are likely to suffer a serious deterioration. The poorest countries will be the most seriously affected. Table 9.1 gives the details.

Third, the developing countries most likely to benefit from commodity agreements will tend to be small countries in whose economy foreign trade plays a relatively important part. But it is precisely these countries that already get more aid per head than large countries. The so-called small-country effect of development aid would be reinforced by commodity agreements, unless the rise in import prices due to the cartelization of imported commodities wiped out any benefits they derived from rises in their export prices.

Fourth, where commodity agreements require quota arrangements (rather than buffer stocks) both between producing countries and within each country, high-cost producers are favoured over low-cost producers

TABLE 9.1 Terms of trade: 1973 v 1980 (1967–9 = 100)

Developing countries	Population (× 10⁶)	Terms of trade	
Major oil producers	300	140	350
Mineral producers	100	102	102
Other developing countries			
With per capita incomes over $200	600	104	95
With per capita incomes under $200	1000	95	77
TOTAL	2000	—	—
OECD Countries	600	99	89

Source: McNamara, Robert S., Address to the Board of Governors (Washington DC, 30 September 1974).

and the latter find it more difficult to expand their production. While the forces of competition continue to operate through a cartel, and to that extent make it less stable, in so far as it succeeds in achieving stability, it discriminates against low-cost producers and adaptation to technical change.

Fifth, such restrictions are not only inefficient but are also inequitable when they fall more severely on the supply of poorer producers within members countries (small farmers) and of poorer countries.

Sixth, while jacking up export receipts increases the *means* to diversification, industrialization and general development, it simultaneously reduces the *incentive* to do so. Successful cartelization may therefore delay or impede the growth of industrial exports in which the countries may have a long-term comparative advantage.

Not all commodity agreements aiming at higher average export prices (contrasted with those aiming merely at stabilization of prices) need take the form of a confrontation between exporting and importing countries. The USA used the threat of a grain cartel in an attempt to beat OPEC. But producers and consumers have cooperated on a sugar agreement, a coffee agreement, and others. The main interest of consumers in remunerative prices for producers is that these ensure higher levels of investment and therefore continuing supplies. Very low prices, on the other hand, tend to discourage investment and to lead to excessive dependence on imports. They carry the seeds of future shortages and deprivation of supplies. Short-term restrictions, leading to very high prices, tend to encourage the growth of substitutes and economies in the use of the product, and thereby carry the seeds of future surpluses. There is, therefore, an area in which producers' and consumers' interests coincide. Both will want to avoid setting a price that, though in their short-term interest, is self-defeating in the long run. A higher average level of prices, combined with a larger volume of production, can therefore be in the interest of both consumers and producers.

So much about the desirability and the feasibility of cartels. But there are other areas than commodity agreements in which the same or similar issues arise. The following list is illustrative.[7]

(1) The threat to expropriate foreign investments.

(2) The threat to default on foreign debts.

(3) Limitations on the repatriation of foreign profits and capital.

(4) The threat of the withdrawal of money balances or the demand of their conversion into gold.

(5) Joint action to improve the terms of contracts with trans-national enterprises (removal or reduction of tax concessions; demand for higher royalties; fewer direct or indirect subsidies; stronger demands for local participation or use of local materials, etc).

(6) Refusal to admit companies dependent on cheap labour or refusal to accept polluting factories.

(7) Trade discrimination against or boycott of exports from industrial countries.

(8) Refusal to sign trade mark, patent or copyright conventions.

(9) Demand of higher rents for granting military facilities.

(10) The denial of overflying rights.

(11) Non-cooperation in the control of drug growing and drug traffic, the use of nuclear waste, nuclear plants or nuclear weapons as bargaining instruments, etc.

(12) The use of bargaining power based on the ability to prohibit the presence or passage of troops.

It must be emphasized again that this is not a list of recommended actions but an attempt to sketch areas of potential reserves of power which might be used to formulate a fairer set of international rules and institutions.

INFORMATION

Solidarity and strength among protagonists and division and weakness among antagonists is not enough for the success of the cartel. Knowledge and information are also needed in order to use effective bargaining power. In the case of commodity agreements, it is important to know about alternative sources of supply, about research and development directed at the production of substitutes, about the scope for economies in the use of the material, and about the tendency to switch demand to products using less of the material. Knowledge of competition between buyers, their financial strength, their profit rates, etc, is also useful. In the case of negotiations with trans-national enterprises, it is important to know about accounting methods, about transfer pricing, over-invoicing of imported inputs and under-invoicing of exported outputs, about realistic figures for management fees, royalties and interest charged on inter-affiliate loans.

Several commentators have argued the case for an international agency to render assistance to low-income countries in gathering this type of information and supporting them in their negotiations. Bilateral technical assistance is bound to be suspect when companies are concerned that reside in the parent country, so that this is *par excellence* an area for multilateral technical assistance or for joint agencies run for and by less developed countries. The UN has established training centres for officials from developing countries in negotiating with the multi-nationals. The Andean Group (comprising Peru, Bolivia, Chile, Ecuador, Colombia and Venezuela) have agreed to lower tariff barriers, coordinate industrial development, and adopt common policies towards foreign companies, as well as to collect and pool relevant information from all members.

At present, the bulk of research is directed at problems of the rich countries and is either irrelevant or detrimental to the development efforts of poor countries. In addition, most channels of communication run from north to south and intra-Third World communications are weak or absent. An increase of relevant research and an improvement of communications between poor countries are important elements in a strategy of strengthening their bargaining power.

BARGAINING, SELF-INTEREST AND MORAL PRINCIPLES

It now remains to clarify the relation between appeals to the self-interest of rich countries, appeals to their conscience and the exercise of joint bargaining power. It is probable that, with some qualifications, a world in which each nation and group of nations exercises to the full its bargaining power to extract maximum concessions from others is a world in which most nations will be worse off. Bargaining must therefore appeal not only to self-interest but also to widely acceptable principles, rules, norms, on which tacit agreement can either be assumed or be assumed to be more readily reached than is possible about selfish concessions. If bargaining is seen and conducted in this light, its power to disintegrate the world community is greatly weakened. Properly used, it can strengthen world solidarity and cooperation through joint attempts to evolve a more acceptable system of rules and institutions.

INTEREST ALIGNMENTS

So far, we have discussed cartel-like agreements between poor countries and explored their potential bargaining power. But a map of interest alignments should not accept the nation state as the only relevant unit. Important interest groupings run across the boundaries of nation states. This fact gives rise to two sets of problems. First, nation states may act 'in their own interests', which are identified with those of the ruling group and are in conflict with those of the mass of poor people in their own countries. Second, particular groups in the nation may take action without enlisting the power of the state.

The first case, the governments and officials of nation states acting not in accordance with the interests of the poor of their countries, is an ever-present danger in commodity cartels (and, of course, all other negotiations in which they are involved). The producers who benefit from restrictions and price increases are often rich owners or managers of plantations or mines, sometimes allied to foreign interests, and there may not be much trickling down. Governments may form purchasing agencies or impose indirect taxes and attempt to cream off part of the monopoly gains for social benefits, but political will or administrative ability to ensure that the poor benefit may be absent.

Similarly, the beneficiaries of negotiations with multi-national enterprises may be groups of businessmen or managers in the public sector, whose interests conflict with those of the masses of the poor people. The 'host country' may benefit from certain arrangements, but the interests of the country are identified with those of a small rich and powerful group.

The second case is where alignments of interests can be exploited in the cause of development without the assistance of the state or by exercising countervailing influence on the state. Consumers are not as well organized as producers and are therefore victims of the powerful and articulate protectionist claims of producers in rich countries. Appeals to governments to give better access to the exports of poor countries are therefore not likely to succeed. But the retail chains that are independent of the large producers' or consumers' associations could be harnessed to side with the labour-intensive, low-cost producers of the poor countries. The Atlantic and Pacific Stores in the USA have a commercial interest in lowering the cost of processed coffee and other food items; Sainsbury's and Waitrose's in Britain are interested in low-cost fruit and vegetables. A department store like Marks & Spencer, interested in selling low-cost clothes, can subcontract the making of these to small manufacturers or craftsmen in less developed countries.

Multi-national and trans-national producing firms are important advocates and pressure groups of better market access in the industrial countries. To the extent to which some of their operations take place in developing countries, this pressure is a useful ally. Trade unions and competing firms form an opposition to this access. If interest pressures like the ones described above can be combined with adjustment assistance to those displaced by the low-cost imports, and with the assurance that the foreign exchange earned by better access will be spent on the products of the countries granting the access, they are likely to be more effective, as well as more humane.

The conclusion of this discussion is that there must be a shift from emphasis on gaining concessions from rich nation states to using interest alignments either among poor countries or between rich and poor countries or between common interest groups across national boundaries. It is not argued that each interest group should fully exploit its bargaining power, but that these latent sources of power should be used to devise a more equitable system of international rules and institutions. In particular, greater emphasis on the common interest of groups of developing countries is a source of strength, as long as the centrifugal, disintegrating forces can be restrained. National self-interest will have to be sacrificed for greater solidarity if the developing countries wish to match the power and skills of the trans-national companies, of the groupings of rich industrial countries and of the heavy bias of scientific and technical progress against the interests of the poor. There are untapped power reserves in the concerted action of developing countries if they are willing to unite. The *Communist Manifesto*, it will be remembered, ends with a call to the workers of the world to unite: they have nothing to lose but their chains; they can win a world. The exhortation, slightly adapted and allowing for the more complex network of domestic and international interest alignments, still applies.

NOTES

1. Reprinted from *Resources Policy* (June 1976). This chapter is an expanded version of one published in *A World Divided: The Less Developed Countries in the World Economy*, ed. G. K. Helleiner (Cambridge University Press (1975). I am grateful to Gerald Helleiner, Jeffrey James and Hans Singer for helpful comments.
2. For a more positive view of the achievements of UNCTAD, see Dell, S. 'An appraisal of UNCTAD III', *World Development*, vol. 1, no. 5 (May 1973).
3. Sen, Amartya K., 'Isolation, Assurance and the Social Rate of Discount', *Quarterly J. Econ*, vol. 81 (February 1967), pp. 112–13.
4. J. S. Mill saw clearly the need for state intervention 'not to overrule the judgement of individuals respecting their own interest, but to give effect to that judgement; they being unable to give effect to it except by concert, which concert again cannot be effectual unless it receives validity and sanction from the law'. He illustrates this by workers' restriction of their working hours. Mill, J. S. *Principles of Political Economy*, Longmans, Green & Co., London (1902) Book 5, Ch. 11, p. 581. A. K. Sen suggests that the difference between the non-cooperative equilibrium and the enforced solution corresponds to Rousseau's distinction between the 'will of all' and the 'general will'.
5. There are, of course, conflicts of interest between the rich oil-importing countries even without any action by OPEC. Even before the October War of 1973 *The Economist* suspected that if 'the Americans gave in to OPEC so readily', it was because 'they saw increased oil prices as a quick and easy way of slowing down the Japanese economy', Since then, Michael Tanzer has pointed out that 'one key effect' of the oil crisis has been 'a drastic shift in the economic power from Western Europe and Japan to the United States'. Tanzer, M., 'The Energy Crisis', pp. 124, 130, 133, 135, quoted in Barraclough, G. 'Wealth and Power: the Politics of Food and Oil', *The New York Review of Books*, vol. 22, (7 August 1975), p. 24.
6. Patel, I.G., 'Some reflection on trade and development', in *Trade Strategies for Development*, paper of the Ninth Cambridge Conference on Development, ed. Paul Streeten, Macmillan, London (1973) p. 45.
7. See also Bergsten, C. Fred, 'The threat from the Third World', *Foreign Policy*, vol. 11, (summer 1973).

10 Self-Reliant Industrialization[1]

INTRODUCTION

This paper surveys the role of industrialization in developing countries in the light of certain objectives (efficient growth, reduced inequality, diversified jobs, integrated development) and certain constraints (environmental damage, scarcity of resources, protectionist policies by industrialized countries). It is argued that the basic objective of development provides a key to the solution of a number of problems that appear to be separate but on inspection are related: urbanization, protection of the environment, equality, a better international division of labour. This approach throws a new light on the demand for sources of energy and for sophisticated products, the transfer of inappropriate technologies, the role of the trans-national enterprise, the relation between rural development and industrialization and the relation of domination and dependence.

Self-reliant development is a complex process in which many variables act upon one another and in which policies must act upon several objectives either simultaneously or in an appropriate sequence. Industrialization is clearly only a part of a unified, self-reliant development strategy. A unified, self-reliant strategy provides an opportunity to overcome the fragmentation that some critics have discerned in national policy-making and also in the organization of the United Nations specialized agencies. It is a challenge to organize and integrate all development efforts aimed at improving the lot of the poor people of the world.

In a concerted and unified strategy, industrialization has a special role to play. The poorer the country, the larger the proportion of the population that is engaged in producing food. To rise above poverty, industrialization is necessary, for industrialization means the application of power to production and transport. Output and consumption per head can rise towards desired levels only with the help of mechanical aids. In this sense, development, including rural development, is industrialization.

In addition, manufacturing industry is subject to increasing returns, to learning effects, and to cumulative processes. The exceptionally high growth potential of manufacturing industry (reflected in the annual average growth target of manufacturing output of 8 per cent) has been demonstrated in several countries in recent years.

Rapid economic growth, and especially industrial growth, has come under attack from several directions. It has been argued that social objectives, such as income distribution and jobs, are more important than the rise in some abstract index number to which industrial growth contributes substantially. It has been said that the drive for industrial growth has destroyed the environment and has rapaciously used up exhaustible natural resources, particularly sources of energy. It has been claimed that rapid growth, spurred by industry, increases inequalities and proceeds without regard to the damage inflicted upon its victims. Perhaps most convincingly, it has been argued that in countries where cultivable land and capital are scarce and where the labour force grows rapidly and mass emigration is ruled out, development must aim at raising the yield of the land; that food output can grow only if markets exist in which the food can be sold; and that, exports apart, these markets must be found in the countryside, amongst the mass of the rural population. Rural development, the argument goes, combined with income redistribution, is a necessary condition of economic growth.

In the face of all these charges against and criticisms of industrialization, it must be emphasized that to achieve the social objectives rightly advocated and to fight the evils of pollution, premature exhaustion of raw materials, unemployment, inequality, and market limitations, industrial growth is an absolutely essential condition. It must, of course, be growth that benefits the right groups. It must be correctly composed and measured so that social costs are fully accounted for and proper relative weights are given to different components, to the working conditions and to the human relations in which production is carried out.

Statistically there is no evidence of an inevitable conflict between high rates of industrial growth and the achievement of other development objectives; if anything, there is evidence to the contrary. In many—though not in all cases, the achievement of social objectives has been consistent with high rates of industrial growth and, indeed, has depended on them. The causal links between these variables are complex, controversial, and still partly unknown, but the promotion of industrial growth is one of the strategic variables in the complex set of related national and international development policies.

The current combination of a worldwide energy crisis and worldwide cost inflation has called into question the whole inherited framework of economic analysis and policy. If it needed underlining, the crisis has certainly underlined the fact that economic and political forces cannot be treated separately and in isolation, for the demands of the trade unions and the demands of the oil producers (and possibly of other producers of scarce raw materials and food) are economic exercises in political power. The role of industrialization in this new framework of thought and action also requires a thorough reappraisal.

INDUSTRIALIZATION FOR WHAT?

Many confusing and complex issues become clearer and simpler if we remind ourselves of the purpose of development and the place of industrialization in a development strategy. In particular, questions about energy, the environment, pollution, appropriate technology, appropriate products and consumption patterns, markets, international trade and integration, and the trans-national corporation can be answered more easily if we know where we want to go. Many apparently technical and separate problems are seen to be connected and become amenable to a solution if we bear the basic objective in mind.

Development is not about index numbers of national income, it is not about savings ratios and capital coefficients: it is about and for people. Development must therefore begin by identifying human needs. The objective of development is to raise the level of living of the masses of the people and to provide all human beings with the opportunity to develop their potential. This objective implies meeting such needs as adequate nutrition and safe water, continuing employment, secure and adequate livelihoods, more and better schooling, better medical services, shelter, cheap transport, and a higher and increasing level of measured income. It also includes meeting non-material needs, such as the desire for self-determination, self-reliance, political freedom and security, participation in making the decisions that affect workers and citizens, access to power, national and cultural identity, and a sense of purpose in life and work. Much of this can be achieved in ways that do not increase the measured output of commodities, while a high and growing index for national income growth can leave these basic needs unsatisfied.

If we approach development in these terms, the place of the private motor car, of heavy demand on sources of energy, of highly sophisticated luxury goods, of the transfer of inappropriate products and technologies, of the role of the trans-national enterprise, of urbanization, of the relation between industrial and agricultural policies, and of domination and dependency, all appear in a different light.

The disenchantment with industrialization in recent writings and speeches has been based on confusion; it is a disenchantment with the form that economic growth has taken in some developing countries and with the distribution of its benefits. Certain types of modern products and modern technology have reinforced an income distribution and a style of development that is out of tune with the basic goals sketched out above. After a reorientation of goals, industrialization as the servant of development regains its proper place in the strategy. Industry should produce the simple goods required by the people, the majority of whom live in the countryside—hoes, simple power tillers, and bicycles, not air conditioners, expensive cars, and equipment for luxury flats.

An industrialization strategy guided by the goal of meeting the needs of the poor not only leads to a different composition of products and of techniques but also reduces the demand that rapid urbanization makes on scarce capital, scarce skills, and scarce natural resources. By raising the level of living of the poor people in the countryside, it may reduce the pressure to leave the farms and to expand expensive urban services.[2]

In subsequent sections, I shall survey several problem areas and reexamine the appropriate policy in the light of the basic objective. The conclusions depend on countries opting for a style of development that gives priority to satisfying the simple, basic needs of the large number of poor people. Industries producing clothing, food, furniture, simple household goods, electronics, buses, and electric fans would thrive without the need for heavy protection in a society that had adopted this style of industrialization and development. Much of the recent criticism of inefficient, high-cost industrialization behind high walls of protection and quantitative restrictions should be directed at the types of product and of technique that cater for highly unequal income distribution and reflect entrenched vested interests. It is in no way a criticism of industrialization for the needs of the people.

This does not mean that opting for such a style is an easy matter. Among the enormously difficult tasks are the required changes in the thrust of research and development expenditure and of science policy; the attack on the living standards and power of those profiting from the present pattern of trade, technology, and products; the more complex system of decentralized administration of rural development; and the required coordination and changes in trade and investment policy. The point, however, is that no solution is possible unless the fundamental objective is borne in mind.

INDUSTRY AND AGRICULTURE

The dispute about whether to give priority to industry or agriculture is a sham dispute. The answer is not either/or, but both/and. Industry needs agriculture and agriculture needs industry, and for some purposes the very division into the two categories is wrong. Thus, when we are concerned with evaluating an agro-industrial project, the relevant project appraisal criteria cut across the demarcation line between industry and agriculture.

Still, some people might object by saying that the speed of progress of an economy in which the scope for substitution between sectors is limited is controlled by the speed of its slowest-moving sector. For this reason in the last 15 years attention has been focused on agriculture. Although it is true that agriculture is the slowest-moving sector, how do we identify it as such in the first instance? How do we unmask it as the laggard, so that we can bring pressure to bear on it to improve its performance? It has been a platitude for many years now to say that non-export agriculture, especially in dry zones, has been the lagging sector in many developing countries. But today's platitudes are yesterday's startling discoveries. In the 1930s, when all the talk was of agricultural surpluses, nobody would have believed what we find so obvious today. It is the very success of rapidly moving, dynamic industry combined with high growth rates of agricultural productivity in the advanced countries, and especially in the United States, that has shown up agriculture in the developing countries as the slow coach: an instance of the uses of unbalanced growth.

In spite of the Green Revolution and substantial, though patchy, progress in agriculture, we have not yet turned industry into the lagging sector. We need continuing advances in industry to provide agriculture with the inputs and with the markets; we need progress in agriculture to provide industry with food, raw materials and, again, markets (and in some cases, exports). If several things done together are essential for success, it does not make sense to ask which should have priority. There is less scope for substitution, even at the margin, than is sometimes thought.

Even at the margin, the choice is not between industry and agriculture. The choice is between projects and complexes of projects, many of which, like processing local raw materials (see below, p. 200), cut across the line between industry and agriculture. Priority must be given to a form of industrialization consistent with a strategy of rural transformation. Some plead for a type of agriculture that supports urban industrialization; others for industrialization that serves agriculture. The argument here is that mutual support and consistency are required.

URBAN AND RURAL LOCATION OF INDUSTRY

The concern with growing inequality has a regional dimension. There are both economies and diseconomies in the rapidly growing cities of the developing world. Urban centres offer businesses advantages of location; economies of scale; low costs of information; availability of a suitable labour force; access to administrators, policy-makers, and sources of learning; and opportunities to exchange information and coordinate actions. On the other hand, the inability of the rural sector to hold the growing working population has led to migration to the towns with the resulting shanty towns and slums and the growing burden of constructing urban public services for the rapidly expanding number of town dwellers. The more that is done to meet the needs of the urban immigrants through creation of jobs, clearance of slums, building of houses, and provision of public services, the more people flood in from the countryside. The social costs of urban industrialization diverge from its private costs. Even with the best policies, urban industry is incapable of providing anything like an adequate number of jobs or a satisfactory level of living for all those wishing to leave the country for the promises of the city.

This proposition is sometimes criticized by those who say migration to the towns is an improvement for the migrants and that economic progress consists in reducing the number of those in agriculture. But this view neglects the fact that the absolute number of people in agriculture and industry depends not only upon the rate of growth of the labour force and the rate of growth of employment opportunities in industry but also on the initial, relative size of the industrial sector. For the same growth rates in the labour force and in employment opportunities, the existence of an initially relatively small industrial sector implies that the absolute number (though not the proportion) of people in agriculture (or at any rate, in the rural sector and in the urban "informal sector") must increase. The belief that the absolute number of people in the rural work force and the "informal sector" can decline in the early stages of industrialization is false.

The creation of rural industries and rural public works could contribute to the absorption of some of the large and rapidly growing under-utilized labour force. The purpose of these industries would be to use agricultural labour when it can be spared from seasonal peak demands, to use local materials, and to mobilize the underemployed labour force for the construction of rural public works, such as feeder roads, houses, and schools, which would support rural indus-tries.

EXPORTS OF MANUFACTURED PRODUCTS: PROSPECTS OF GROWTH AND THE INTERNATIONAL DISTRIBUTION OF GAINS

The spectacular export performances of a few, but growing number of, countries (and by no means only those with high GNP growth records) have shown that breakthroughs into the markets of developed countries are possible in spite of existing tariff and non-tariff barriers. However, there is evidence of growing restrictions against these exports whenever they begin to be seriously felt by the protected and local industry of an importing country. Annual growth rates in the 1960s of 10 to 15 per cent of exports of manufactured products from the developing countries are liable to run into obstacles put up by importing countries. These would become more serious if the lesson were to be generalized and more developing countries were to engage in massive export drives, particularly if these exports were concentrated on a few "sensitive" products.

Policy restrictions are liable to be supported by a form of "adjustment assistance" that directs research and development and compensation expenditure at defensive investment to re-equip the industry hit by the low-cost imports or simply to subsidize it to remain competitive.

Apart from restrictions by importing countries, there are also institutional limitations to increasing exports, limitations that cannot easily be classified under "supply and demand". Such limitations include absence of export credits, absence of marketing and sales organization, and lack of knowledge of required designs. Calling in a trans-national corporation to overcome these obstacles may solve some of the problems while raising others (see below, pp. 206–9).

There are also supply limitations. These may lie in the lack of entrepreneurial ability to spot the type of products for which world demand is expanding and which can be produced at low costs; in weak organizational and administrative ability (in both the private and public sectors); in the inability of the economy to supply enough food for the workers engaged in manufacturing to keep industrial wages low and prices competitive; and in the inability to resist the power of the urban trade unions to extract ever higher money wages.

While organizational and other supply obstacles clearly account for part of the export failure of some countries, this failure contributed to the success of the successful exporters. If all developing countries had adopted the strategy of Taiwan and Korea, their exports and the exports of some other countries would have fared less well in the 1960s than they did.

There is also the question of the distribution of the gains from the rising volume and value of manufactured exports. When trans-national corporations are engaged in producing and selling exports, part of the gain accrues to countries other than the exporting country. In conditions of oligopoly, low costs are not automatically passed on either to buyers, in the form of lower prices, or to workers, in the form of higher wages, but may only swell profits.

What is often considered to be the peculiar virtue of private foreign enterprise—that it brings a "package" of capital, enterprise, management, and know-how—is also its peculiar defect: it means that monopoly rents and profits accruing to these factors go abroad and that only the reward for unskilled or semi-skilled labour, in highly elastic supply and with little bargaining power, goes to the host country. If, on top of this, the country gives tax concessions to the foreign firm and subsidizes it through trading estates or import privileges, the division of the gains is very uneven, and export figures give a misleading picture of the host country's gain.[3] Alternatives might be subcontracting, the encouragement of indigenous firms with management contracts, national export sales corporations, or various forms of joint venture.

If we are interested in the limits to the growth of exports of manufactured products and the likely international and internal distribution of gains, a typology by product will be useful. We may then distinguish between the following products.

1 PROCESSED LOCAL PRIMARY PRODUCTS

These include products such as vegetable oils, foodstuffs, plywood and veneer, pulp and paper products, and fabricated metal. The processing may be into semi-processed, refined, or completely manufactured products. When these products are less expensive to transport in a processed form rather than in a raw state, countries processing them enjoy an advantage over the countries in which they are sold. Cascading tariffs (rising with the stage of processing) in developed countries discriminate against this type of export. Yet processing is clearly not appropriate in all cases where a developing country has the raw material. But, where appropriate, countries with highly sought-after raw materials can insist that the materials be processed locally. This is another instance of a strategy directed at exploiting the scarcities of raw materials and food in combination with industrialization.

2 TRADITIONAL LABOUR-INTENSIVE GOODS

These include garments, textiles, footwear, and simple engineering goods. While low labour costs make the exports of developing countries competitive in these products, they face particular obstacles in importing countries where the competing industries are often concentrated and politically well organized. Successful exporting may have to be combined with the mobilization of interests in importing countries. Independent retail chains, mail-order firms, trading houses, or consumers' associations are useful allies in organizing pressures against the producers' organizations and their lobbies. A better system of international monetary adjustments would also give wider scope to increased exports of these products.

3 NEWER LABOUR-INTENSIVE GOODS

Goods such as plastic and wooden items, rattan furniture, glassware, pottery, and wigs have appeared in recent years. The fact that their impact on importing countries is more dispersed and less noticeable makes them better export prospects as long as not too many countries compete in selling them.

4 PROCESSES, COMPONENTS, AND ASSEMBLY IN A VERTICALLY INTEGRATED INTERNATIONAL FIRM

A comparatively recent phenomenon is the location of a wide range of activities in a vertically integrated trans-national corporation in developing countries. Semi-conductors, tubes, and other electronic components are assembled in developing countries for the parent firm in developed countries. Garments, gloves, leather luggage, and baseballs are sewn together in Taiwan, South Korea, Thailand, and India; automobile parts, such as radio antennas, piston rings, cylinder linings, headlights, brakes, batteries, and springs are made in many countries. Data are flown to South-East Asia and the West Indies for punching on tape by low-wage key-punch operators; watchmakers fly jewels to Mauritius for precision drilling. These industries are footloose, attracted by low wages, tax concessions, docile trade unions, relative absence of corruption, and political stability. They also represent an organized interest in the importing country opposing import-competing interests and sometimes enjoy tariff advantages.

5 IMPORT SUBSTITUTES OR LOCAL PRODUCTS TURNED EXPORTS

These products, often goods such as automobiles (Brazilian Volkswagen is an outstanding example), car parts, steel pipes and tubes, electric wires and cables, bicycles, electric motors, and diesel engines, were set up initially to replace imports; having become established, they have entered the export market. They represent the last stage in the product cycle. Marginal-cost pricing for exports is common (i.e., export prices are lower than domestic prices), and exports may be subject to anti-dumping measures.

This classification is useful for identifying problems of adjustment and pressure groups in the importing countries, and hence for identifying the possible limits to growth in the exporting country and the division of gains between different factors of production and different countries. The classification also indicates that it would be rash to conclude that promotion of exports of manufactured goods through price incentives is necessarily the best strategy for all developing countries. A good deal has recently been written about negative value added in import-substituting manufacturing as a result of excessive protection. We should not forget that negative value added can also occur in exports and that a recipe of universal export promotion, extrapolated from the experience of the 1960s, supported by trans-national enterprises with concessions, privileges, and incentives, can be as detrimental to the developing host country as high-cost import substitution.

The next ten years will be a more difficult period, especially as more and more countries adopt export-promoting strategies. Over-expansion may turn the income terms of trade against the exporting countries (though this would improve the terms of trade of developing primary producers); import capacity and import willingness are not likely to keep in step with accelerated export expansion; and even when exports are successful, the gains to the developing countries may be small or, in extreme cases, negative. This does not mean that developing countries should not devote considerable efforts to promoting exports, or that export-oriented strategies do not have advantages over import-substituting ones. It does mean that institutional, political, and technological constraints will have to be investigated and overcome and that some coordination and cooperation between developing countries is essential if they are not to erode the benefits through excessive competition.

COLLECTIVE SELF-RELIANCE AND INTERNATIONAL TRADE

An industrialization strategy guided by the goal of meeting the needs of the poor also introduces different incentives and opportunities into international and intra-regional trade: it implies a reorientation toward more trade between developing countries. Starting with similar factor supplies and similar levels of demand, developing countries can more appropriately produce for one another what they consume and consume what they produce.[4] This can be the basis of mutually beneficial trade. In simple goods for mass consumption, often produced in a labour-intensive, capital-saving way, the developing countries have a comparative advantage and could expand trade among themselves.

I have argued that even if the developed countries were to resume high rates of economic growth, their ability and willingness to absorb large increases of manufactured products from developing countries is limited. There are good arguments on grounds of comparative advantage for increasing trade among developing countries. Some developing countries, such as Brazil and Mexico, have been registering high rates of growth, and it might well be in the high-growth countries of the Third World, rather than in the OECD countries, that the future of the international division of labour lies. To interpret "collective self-reliance" in this sense is entirely compatible with the most conventional economic doctrine. Sir Arthur Lewis drew a historical parallel.

Besides competing in the OECD markets, the tropics can also compete in their own markets. In 1965 they imported manufactures, excluding metals, valued at $14.1 billion; to wit $2.3 billion of chemicals, $4.7 billion of light manufactures and $7.2 billion of machinery and transport equipment. At least $12.5 billion of this came from outside the region. It follows that the tropics do not have to depend on competing with OECD countries in OECD markets. They can just as well compete with OECD in their own tropical markets.

This point sometimes comes as a surprise to policy-makers in the tropics. We have got so accustomed to the idea that the tropics trades with the temperate world that we tend to assume that the chief way to expand tropical trade is to sell more to the temperate countries. Actually, as Germany industrialized in the second half of the nineteenth century, she did not concentrate primarily on breaking into the British and French markets, though she did this too. She looked rather to the countries around her in Eastern and Central Europe, who were even more impoverished than she, and made big gains there. Similarly Japan's trade drive in the 1930s was directed not at the industrial nations but at Asia and Africa and Latin America. This is where the rising new exporters should surely be looking, rather than to European and North

American markets, since it is surely easier to beat your competitors in third markets than it is to beat them at home, once you have established the machinery for making customer contacts.

The continuous discussion of the possibility of creating new customs unions or common markets in Africa and Asia and Latin America indicates that many people have seen the light, though the paucity of actual results also indicates how difficult the problem is. The basic difficulty centres in the fact that only a handful of tropical countries are currently in a position to benefit from expanded opportunities for exporting manufactures. Twelve of these accounted for 85 per cent of the trade.[5] The problem stands out clearly if one asks the following question: Since among themselves the tropical countries now import over \$14 billion of manufactures, why do they have to wait for preferences for their exports in OECD markets? Why do they not just accord preferences to each other in their own markets, in line with the already agreed principle that discrimination against developed countries is acceptable? The answer is because this would benefit the leading 12 at the expense of the remaining 70, who might now have to pay higher prices to these 12 than they would have had to pay to OECD countries. The problem differs only in scale when one shifts from global tropical preferences to more limited regional preferences, customs unions or free trade areas. In each region one or two countries stand out as the ones most likely to benefit at the expense of their regional partners, who are therefore not anxious to rush in without some clearer indication of what the balance sheet of profits and losses is likely to be.[6]

But there is another type of argument for increased trade between developing countries that does not rest on comparative advantage and a combination of protection in advanced countries and demand expansion in developing countries. It embraces variables not normally included in a narrowly economic analysis.

Orthodox arguments for protection are based on the principle that to protect one industry one has to *pull* resources *into* this type of activity. If there is full employment, so that no spare resources are available for this absorption, this implies that resources must be *pulled out of* some other type of activity. It would be nonsense to wish to protect *all* industries. Protection, according to this argument, always favours one type of production at the expense of some other type. Conventional arguments for protection based on increasing returns or external economies imply pulling resources out of agriculture or services into manufacturing industry.

The new argument that we are now considering requires some protection (though not autarky), at least in principle, for nearly *all* activities. By opening up a society indiscriminately and too widely, incentives and opportunities for the development of indigenous processes and products, appropriate for the low-income groups in developing countries, are reduced. The educational, psychological, and institutional arguments against a move towards world free trade, free capital flows and general openness, point to the need to protect *all* activities from the eroding influences of the advanced world economy. More important, they point to the need for constructive, indigenous efforts, which may be hampered by an *excessively* outward-looking strategy and by emulation of the style of the rich.

Something like this also underlies the distinction between self-reliance and dependence, between autonomy and domination. Countries and groups of countries that generate their own technological capability and their own social institutions and organizations (not only in technology and industry but also in land tenure and rural institutions) will be able to mobilize their efforts more effectively than those that look at how these things are ordered in the metropolis.

There are alternative styles of development, and one type of society may prefer to develop by adapting technologies and products from abroad, while another will find its identity by raising a curtain around its frontiers or around the frontiers of a group of like-minded countries with similar factor availabilities and similar income levels. A judicious selection of features of an outward- and inward-looking strategy is likely to give the best results (drawing on foreign research and developing indigenous research or drawing on and adapting foreign technology and products, for example). The lessons of industrializing Germany, France, Japan, and Soviet Russia, which used and adapted the foreign ways of blending new institutions with old traditions, are not directly applicable because international income gaps were narrower then and the dimensions of the demographic problem, which determine the scale of the need for jobs, were quite different. Yet, as the Lewis quotation shows, even these countries did not look at the established markets of England but at new opportunities and the growing markets of the future. The main point is that there may be a choice of styles of development that can be understood only if institutional and educational variables are included in the model and if a narrowly defined static economic model is transcended.

Some authors prefer to put the contrast more starkly and simply in terms of planning versus laissez-faire. According to them, it is the need for stronger, more effective, centralized planning according to social priorities and the search for independence from the vagaries of the world market that distinguishes the advocates of different trade policies.[7] Others, while in sympathy with the planning approach, see the differences in the areas of learning, education, and institutions. A third group sees them in the political power structure. Planning and controls in an inegalitarian society reinforce inequalities and encourage corruption; the use of prices in an egalitarian society will contribute to the eradication of poverty and increasing equality.

THE TRANS-NATIONAL CORPORATION: ITS POTENTIAL ROLE IN INDUSTRIALIZATION

The role of the trans-national corporation in industrialization is of growing importance. Policies must be evolved that enable governments, willing to admit the corporation, to harness its potential for the benefit of the development effort. It has been argued above that the basic objective of development (that is, meeting the needs of the hundreds of millions of poor) provides one rallying point around which many development issues can be grouped. The trans-national corporation is not a goal but an instrument of achieving certain goals. It, too, provides a focus for a number of different issues.

1 REGIONAL INTEGRATION

Two distinct sets of problems arise here. One is an anxiety shared by many countries. When several developing countries form a customs union, a free trade area, or a closer region of cooperation, new profit opportunities arise for the already operating and newly entering foreign companies. Polices have to be devised to ensure a fair sharing of these profits between the union and the foreign companies.

A second set of problems concerns the sharing of the gains from integration between different members of the union. The creation of a new form of international company, the shares of which are held by the member countries of the union, might be one way of solving this problem, though so far it has not been successful. The proposal would be for the company to combine low cost and efficient location and operation with sharing of the gains between member countries.

Alternatively, there can be agreement on other forms of compensation, such as agreeing to pay higher prices for the exports of the less industrialized member countries, or to permit their citizens to migrate within the region or to locate universities and research institutes in the less-developed partner countries.

2 ENVIRONMENT

In the new international division of labour that would be guided by differential pollution costs in different countries, the location of certain "dirty" processes in developing countries could be one of the functions of the trans-national corporation. This function could be carried out either by locating "dirty" processes within the firm's vertically integrated system of operations in a developing country, where the social costs of pollution would be lower and the benefits from industrialization higher, or by transferring the whole operation to such a country. The argument would be analogous to that of locating unskilled- or semi-skilled labour-intensive processes using unskilled and semi-skilled workers in developing countries. The comparative advantage consists in one case in an unpolluted environment, in the other in inexpensive labour. One important point to be investigated here is whether the trans-national corporation could be used as a pressure group to ensure access for the products to the markets of the developed countries.

3 TECHNOLOGY

In terms of technology, the objective would be to devote more research and development expenditure to the invention and dissemination of appropriate technologies and products either in the developed or in the developing countries. The potential, but as yet unrealized, contribution of the trans-national corporation to transferring and adapting existing technology and to inventing new and appropriate technology may be substantial. It would raise the problem of the ability of the developing countries to absorb existing or new technologies and of the contribution that the trans-national corporation could make, preferably through joint ventures, to training people, encouraging research, and fostering attitudes favourable to such absorption.

4 BARGAINING

Since the transnational corporation has become one of the main vehicles for transferring technology from developed to developing countries, an important aspect of policy is the terms on which the technology is transferred. In settling the bargain and in drawing up the contract, a large number of items may be up for negotiation. Some may involve incentives, such as protecting the market for the product or improving the quality of input (public utilities, a disciplined labour force); others may lay down conditions for sharing the benefits with the host country, such as tax provisions, use of local materials, local participation in management, training workers, creating jobs, raising exports, and so on; others will relate to such policies as conditions for repatriation of capital and profits, raising local capital, and so forth.

Hitherto, multilateral technical assistance in negotiations of this type and in training negotiators has been given on a very small scale. International organizations could render vital technical assistance in strengthening the bargaining power of LDCs in negotiating such contracts and could contribute to an informed dialogue between managers of companies and public officials through training courses, in an area at present obscured by emotional and ideological fumes. What is needed is both direct technical assistance in drawing up contracts, possibly with the aid of model contracts, and indirect aid through training and the provision of information.

5 INSTITUTIONS

Another important area of policy is the imaginative exploration of new legal and business institutions that combine the considerable merits of the trans-national corporation with the maximum beneficial impact on development. This area comprises joint ventures—that is, joint both between private and public capital and between domestic and foreign capital. Such ventures would give developing countries access to information and a role in decision-making; they would also include provisions for divestment and gradual transfer of ownership and management from foreigners to the host country. Thus countries wishing to curb the power of large groups in their manufacturing sector might find investment reduced. This might make it advisable to institute a "joint sector" in which public capital is combined with private national management with or without an equity stake, or in which public capital is combined with private international capital. Another possibility would be a management contract with a national or international investor.

Thought and action in this area have suffered from poverty of the institutional imagination, which has lagged behind the scientific and technological imagination. Discussions have turned partly on the ideological dispute between private and public enterprise. Yet, the real issues have little to do with this type of ideology. Mixed companies can be devised that simultaneously harness private energy and initiative, yet are accountable to the public and carry out a social mandate. Equally arid has been the dispute over the virtues and vices of private foreign investment. Here again, the task should be to identify the positive contributions of foreign firms and the social costs, to see how the former can be maximized or the latter minimized, and to provide for gradual, agreed transfer to national or regional ownership and management. There is a need for a legal and institutional framework in which the social objectives that are not part of the firm's objectives can be achieved, while giving the firm an opportunity to contribute efficient management and technology.

COSTS AND BENEFITS OF ALTERNATIVE POLICIES OF INDUSTRIALIZATION

Since the last world war, many developing countries have attempted to promote their manufactures by a large number of direct interventions, such as physical controls, licences, and so on. These were accompanied by a host of other incentives and deterrents, such as multiple exchange rates, import entitlements, export bonus vouchers, and subsidies. In some cases, there have been periodic reversions to more simplified and uniform policies, often under pressure from the World Bank and the International Monetary Fund, and the government of the United States. The theoretical pros and cons of both approaches are by now well known. At the same time, quantitative estimates of their practical significance are scarce, unsystematic, and usually out of date.

It would be useful to compare high levels of intervention and the incidence of decline in efficiency, not only in a narrowly allocative sense, but also through blunting of incentives and divergence between social and private productivity; between the pursuit of static comparative advantage and the mobilization and generation of new resources; between the costs of and returns to a sizable bureaucratic control of industry; and between unified and multiple exchange rates. Such comparisons might be made in the light of certain social and economic objectives over time.

The debate is sometimes confused by an identification of the interventionist approach with protectionism and of the "market" approach with free trade. These distinctions, in turn, are occasionally confused with that between "inward-looking" and "outward-looking" policies. The issue here is *not* the well-rehearsed dispute between protectionists and free traders, nor the less understood dispute between those who advocate looking inward and those who advocate looking outward. The issue is *instruments,* and comparing the effects of a battery of direct controls and intervention with operation through prices and the market. Export-orientation and looking outward have been and can be pursued through intervention and directives, just as import substitution and looking inward have been so pursued. An objective, quantitative appraisal would contribute to taking some of the ideological wind out of the sails of the better-known disputes between "freedom and planning" and similar choices presented to developing countries.

TECHNOLOGY AND ENTREPRENEURSHIP

Technologies both determine and are determined by the objectives of development strategy: growth, distribution, savings, employment. Capital-intensive, labour-saving methods will generate large profits and high salaries for a small labour aristocracy. Unless ownership of capital assets is widely shared or is public, these incomes will accrue to a small group of owners of physical assets and people with the required skills and access to education. Their consumption—often influenced by advertising, open communications, and foreign imitation—will reinforce the demand for capital-intensive, foreign-exchange-using luxury goods, the production of which will reinforce unequal distribution of income. It is often maintained, though not enough hard evidence has been produced as yet, that a more equal income distribution would give rise to a consumption pattern that is more capital-saving and labour-using. More capital-saving, labour-intensive techniques may distribute a larger *share* of income to the unskilled and semi-skilled and are likely to lead to a different consumption pattern. But the causal nexus in either direction is not yet established with any certainty.

These connections between choice of industrial technology, both in core processes and in ancillary activities, choice of industrial products, income distribution, wealth distribution, access to education and training, and consumption patterns are vital for policy decisions.

Inward-looking policies of import substitution have been blamed for distorting the price and incentive system; these distortions have been said to cause growing inequalities. At the same time, it has been argued that reliance on the price mechanism and outward-looking, freer trade policies also increase inequalities, though these have a different cause and take on a different form. Is it true that both inward-looking and outward-looking industrialization and trade policies increase inequalities? Are there forces inherent in rapid industrial growth that make for greater inequality? If so, institutional, structural, and technological changes are required to distribute the fruits of growth more evenly.

It is in the nature of modern technology that it reduces the scarcity value and hence the rewards of unskilled labour and traditional know-how, while modern medical science, by reducing mortality rates, increases the supply of unskilled labour. An important question arises here about strategies that proceed on "both legs" by simultaneously promoting the modern, capital-intensive, high-technology sector, and the non-organized, self-employed, "informal", labour-intensive sector. Can rapid, modern industrialization proceed in a manner that will not destroy, but encourage, the non-organized, low-income, low-productivity sector? Can the surplus from modern industry be used to create jobs, to raise productivity, and to generate incomes in that part of of the economy that has not yet been absorbed in it?

Income distribution and employment are only two aspects of an entire cluster of social objectives. Different forms of industrial organization are accompanied by different degrees of workers' participation and different power structures.

The test of a successful self-reliant strategy of industrialization is the extent to which it reduces the gap between the high incomes in the high-productivity, high-technology sector and the low incomes in the low-productivity, low-technology sector, by raising the performance of the latter, without impeding progress in the former.

NOTES

1. This article was written for The *Political Economy of Development and Underdevelopment* ed. Charles K. Wilber, 2nd edn., New York (1979). It draws on Paul Streeten's contribution to *Employment, Income Distribution and Development Strategy: Problems of the Developing Countries—Essays in Honour of H. W. Singer*, ed. Alec Cairncross and Mohinder Puri, Macmillan (1976) and a paper for UNIDO written in 1972.
2. On the other hand, the turmoil, turbulence and disruption caused by rural modernization, with better roads, easier transport, better primary schools, the introduction of radios, cinemas, and other media of communication bring about more migration to the cities than if the villages had continued in their traditional ways. Nevertheless, sufficiently attractive rural opportunities, combined with limited opportunities in the towns, is bound to reduce the flow of migrants.
3. Paul Streeten, "Policies Towards Multinationals", *World Development*, vol. 3, no. 6, (June 1975) and Ch. 16 in this volume.
4. It might be thought that having similar factor supplies and demand patterns there would be less scope for trade. Even without calling on Stefan Burenstam Linder's trade theory, according to which most trade takes place between countries with similar income levels, conventional trade theory would lead us to

expect scope for trade where countries start off, under protection, with similar production and demand patterns but, as trade is opened, become complementary. Trade within the European Economic Community has confirmed that unions between similar but potentially complementary patterns are most promising.

5. The leading exporters of manufactures in 1965 were as follows (figures in $m.): India, 799; Singapore, 295; Pakistan, 190; Mexico, 170; Brazil, 124; UAR, 123; Rhodesia, 116; Philippines, 66; Malaya, 64; Colombia, 34; El Salvador, 32; Trinidad, 28. Kenya is also a substantial exporter if her trade with Uganda and Tanzania is counted as foreign trade.

6. W. Arthur Lewis, *Aspects of Tropical Trade*, Wicksell Lectures, Stockholm (1969), pp. 42–43.

7. Ignacy Sachs, *Trade Strategies for Development*, ed. Paul Streeten, Macmillan (1973), Ch. 3.

11 World Trade in Agricultural Commodities and the Terms of Trade with Industrial Goods[1]

1 TERMS-OF-TRADE PESSIMISM

It is now more than 20 years since Prebisch, Singer and Myrdal announced the thesis that the poverty of the poor countries is largely the result of bad and worsening terms of trade between their primary exports and their manufactured imports. The remedy recommended by these authors was liberation from dependence on primary and especially agricultural exports through import-substituting industrialization behind protective barriers. The idea appealed to the newly independent governments, whose ideology inspired them to do the opposite to what the colonial powers had done. Colonialism meant *primary* production (mines and plantations) and *exports*: so independence came to stand for *secondary* or *manufacturing* production and *import substitution*. Table 11.1 shows the four options.

Whether it was the power of this idea that persuaded the authorities to adopt policies that created the vested interests, or whether it was the

TABLE 11.1 Trade strategies

	Outward-looking: export-oriented	Inward-looking: import-substitution-oriented
Primary production: agricultural and mining	Colonial enterprise (plantations, mines)	Common Agricultural Policy (CAP)
Secondary production: manufacturing	For LDCs: the 'new' recipe – Korea, Taiwan	Post-independence reaction: Prebisch–Singer–Myrdal

interests of the politicians and the vested interests of the budding, high-cost industrialists that seized the idea as a convenient ideology, many countries have in fact adopted the recommended policies and now find it difficult to change course in the direction of a strategy of encouraging agriculture and exports. The trade pessimism that underlay the import-substituting industrialization policy has turned out to be a self-fulfilling prophecy: neglect of exports has led to poor export performance.

2 SHOULD PROTECTION IN INDUSTRIALIZED COUNTRIES BE ABOLISHED?

The deterioration of the terms of trade of the primary producers has been attributed to (a) protection of primary production by the rich countries and (b) a biased distribution of productivity gains. But with respect to (a), it seems inconsistent to argue *both* that the rich countries condemn the poor to remain hewers of wood and drawers of water *and* that the rich countries do not buy enough "wood and water" because they protect their own hewers and drawers.

Reduced agricultural protection in advanced countries might hurt developing countries for two reasons. First, if reduced home production and freer access to markets raises the world price of food—as it is intended to do—poor food-importing countries lose. (Some rich food exporters gain and liberal rich food importers shoulder a heavier burden.) Second, the accelerated shift of resources into manufacturing industry subject to increasing returns, in the advanced countries, which would result from reduced protection, would make the manufactured exports from the developing countries less competitive and industrialization more difficult. If the terms-of-trade pessimists thought that the long-term comparative advantage of the poor agricultural countries lay in industrialization, they should have recommended agricultural protection in the rich industrial countries. This would have reduced the comparative advantage that the rich countries had in industry and would have helped to establish the superiority in manufacturing in the poor countries, which had been the aim of policy.

It could be replied that, though this would have given the poor countries the *incentive* to industrialize, it would have deprived them of the *means* (whereas free access would have given them the *means* without the *incentive*). But the means could have been provided through aid, commercial loans or direct private foreign investment.

Those pleading simultaneously for industrialization in developing countries and for abandoning protection in developed countries might also argue that there is still scope for specialization within the industrial sector (*vide* the large and rapidly growing trade between industrial countries); and that the favourable repercussions of accelerated growth resulting from abandoning protection would more than outweigh the unfavourable effects of greater competitiveness in industrial products. But such arguments do not dispel some doubts about the consequences of abandoning protection.

It is possible to question the three assumptions on which the case here argued rests: that agricultural resources in the advanced countries would flow into "industry"; that "industry" is subject to increasing returns to scale; and that "industry" is directly competitive with "industry" in developing countries. But as long as the argument is conducted in terms of "industry" versus "agriculture", the abolition of agricultural protection in the rich countries is bound to perpetuate the comparative advantage of the poor countries in (increasing-cost) "agriculture" and to delay the shift to (decreasing-cost) "industry".

3 THE UNEVEN DISTRIBUTION OF PRODUCTIVITY GAINS

More important than protection is said to be the uneven distribution of productivity gains between primary and secondary producers. The disparity between the industrial centre, where productivity increases are reflected in higher money wages, and the agricultural periphery, where productivity growth lowers prices, was said to be one of the reasons for the tendency of the terms of trade to deteriorate. This kind of monetary mechanism requires a number of assumptions which were never clearly stated. If the demand and supply elasticities are such that the periphery suffers balance-of-payments deficits, the movement of the terms of trade will depend upon how these deficits are corrected or financed. If the trouble is simply the movement in relative prices, why can it not be remedied by more inflation or an appreciation of the exchange rate in the periphery? There may, of course, be asymmetrical responses. But if the demand curves or the supply curves are kinky, it is not the different mechanism by which productivity increases are passed on that accounts for the bad terms of trade. Nor is it clear why the *commodity* terms of trade rather than the single or double *factoral* terms of trade are considered the index appropriate for measuring the distribution of gains from trade. Worsening commodity terms of trade may, after all, give a country a competitive edge that enables it to export more and to reap larger gains from trade, whereas improving commodity terms of trade may simply be a symptom of rising costs and inefficiency.

4 EMPIRICAL EVIDENCE

The doctrine is vulnerable not only *a priori* but also *a posteriori*. There is no evidence of a secular deterioration of the terms of trade of primary products in relation to manufactured products, unless one chooses base years arbitrarily in order to prove the thesis. Measuring changes in the terms of trade presents certain problems.

There are at least three reasons why the measured terms of trade between agricultural and industrial products tend to overstate the deterioration or understate the improvement.

(1) Product innovation and quality improvements occur mainly in industrial products. As a result, the benefits derived from industrial products are understated and the rises in their prices are overstated. What appears as a worsening of the terms of trade reflects in many cases new and better industrial products. This is, of course, a general problem and applies also to measured rates of inflation in industrial countries.
(2) New industrial products subject to increasing returns often have initially high prices and become cheaper as they become more plentiful. To use the initial small quantities as weights for the price reductions understates the fall in prices in a price index of all manufactured products. (The use of current-period quantity weights would overstate the reductions.)
(3) Export price statistics of agricultural products of developing countries are often based on commodity markets in London or New York. As a result, lower freight costs combined with constant f.o.b. prices will show up, misleadingly, as lower prices of agricultural products.

There are, however, factors working in the opposite direction. If agricultural prices include an element of profit earned by foreign companies (net of taxes accruing to the exporting country), this should be excluded from an index. Above all, it must be remembered that the terms of trade of agricultural producers must not be identified with those of developing countries. Many of them import individually, and even all of them import as a group, agricultural products and they export increasingly manufactured products. The share of agricultural products in total exports of developing countries dropped from 53 per cent in 1955 to 37 per cent in 1968.

Bearing these points in mind, it appears that the terms of trade for most primary producers, and therefore for most developing countries were unusually favourable in the early 1950s; that they were worse before and have declined since. But it is difficult to show any long-term trend. Tables 11.2–11.7 show indices for the 1960s. Table 11.8 shows the prices of coffee and cocoa.

5 WHAT IS LEFT OF TERMS-OF-TRADE PESSIMISM?

While many of the criticisms of the doctrine that the terms of trade of primary producers steadily deteriorate appear to be damaging, the core of the doctrine may well survive the onslaughts. This core is that in the world economy there are forces at work that make for an uneven distribution of the gains from trade and economic progress generally, so that the lion's share goes to the lions, while the poor lambs are themselves swallowed up in the process.

Already in the late 1950s, C. P. Kindleberger pointed out that, while it was not proven that the terms of trade of primary *products* deteriorated, it

TABLE 11.2 Exports 1 Quantum index (1963 = 100)

	1959	1962	1965	1968	1970
DCs	75	93	120	155	189
LDCs (excluding oil)	83	95	108	125	144
2 Price index					
DCs	97	99	103	104	114
LDCs (excluding oil)	101	96	105	105	116

Source: *UN Monthly Bulletin of Statistics* (April 1972).

TABLE 11.3 Primary commodity export price indices (1963 = 100)

	1964	1966	1968	1970	1971
All food	105	105	102	111	116
Coffee/tea/cocoa	121	113	111	138	123
All agricultural non-food	102	104	96	100	104
Fats/oils/oilseeds	104	111	100	109	118
All minerals	102	104	102	109	126
Metal ores	108	105	108	122	125
Fuel	100	101	100	105	126

TABLE 11.4 Commodity price indices for developed and less developed countries (1963 = 100)

	1966	1968	1970	1971
Primaries				
DC exports	107	100	107	116
LDC exports	102	100	107	112
Food				
DC exports	108	102	108	118
LDC exports	102	102	116	114
Agricultural non-food				
DC exports	106	96	100	104
LDC exports	100	94	98	101
Minerals				
DC exports	107	104	122	142
LDC exports	103	102	104	119
Non-ferrous base metals	*			
DC exports	144	142	167	155
LDC exports	177	165	191	168

Source: *UN Monthly Bulletin of Statistics* (March 1972).

TABLE 11.5 World export prices (1963 = 100)

	1938	1948	1953	1963	1969
Food/raw materials	35	112	109	100	105
Manufacturers	47	95	94	100	108

Food = SITC 0 + 1. Raw materials = SITC 2 + 4.

Source: *UN Statistical Yearbook (1970)*.

TABLE 11.6 Price trends in primary products from DCs and LDCs (1963 = 100)

	Exports to market economies			
	1953	*1958*	*1963*	*1969*
Food				
From DCs	103	96	100	108
From LDCs	115	108	100	103
Raw materials				
From DCs	113	102	100	106
From LDCs	105	98	100	98

Source:UN Statistical Yearbook (1970).

TABLE 11.7 Indices of prices of main exports and imports of developing countries (1963 = 100)

	Main exports of developing countries			Main imports of developing countries	
	Tropical beverages[a]	Non-food agricultural raw materials[b]	Total[c]	Cereals[d]	Manufactured products
1961	99	102	101	94	99
1962	96	97	97	99	99
1963	100	100	100	100	100
1964	121	102	106	103	101
1965	111	103	105	99	103
1966	113	104	106	104	106
1967	111	96	99	106	107
1968	111	96	99	102	106
1969	120	101	105	102	110
1970	138	100	108	99	117

Note: based on UN export price indices.

[a] Coffee, cocoa and tea.

[b] Fats, oils and oilseeds, textile fibres, wood and wood pulp, rubber, tobacco hides and skins.

[c] Calculated by FAO, using UN index-number weights for tropical beverages and agricultural non-food raw materials.

[d] Wheat, maize, barley and rice.

Source: *FAO Commodity Review and Outlook, 1970–71*, Table 2.

TABLE 11.8 Data on Coffee[a] and cocoa,[b] deflated by the US general wholesale price index (1947–9 as base for US price levels)

	Deflated Price	
Coffee		
	$28/lb	$37/lb
1921–48	Above in only six years	Never a year above this
1949–70	Never a year below this	Above in eleven years
	Deflated Price	
Cocoa		
	$17/lb	
1921–46	Above this in only three years	
1947–70	Below this in only one year	

[a] Santos 4. New York.

[b] Spot Accra: New York.

was then true that the terms of trade of underdeveloped *countries* tended to deteriorate if the exceptionally good years 1950–1 are taken as the base (see Tables 11.9–11.10).

TABLE 11.9 Terms of trade,[a] 1938, 1948, 1950–69 (1950 = 100)

Year	Developed countries	Developing countries
1938	109	71
1948	103	85
1950	100	100
1951	96	105
1952	98	95
1953	102	94
1954	100	100
1955	100	98
1956	101	96
1957	100	93
1958	104	93
1959	105	94
1960	107	93
1961	108	89
1962	109	88
1963	109	89
1964	109	91
1965	109	89
1966	109	91
1967	110	90
1968	110	91
1969	111	93

[a] Terms of trade means unit value index of exports divided by unit value index of imports.

Sources: UN Monthly Bulletin of Statistics (April issues).

TABLE 11.10 Terms of trade (1963 = 100)

	1959	*1962*	*1965*	*1968*	*1970*
DCs	97	100	100	101	102
LDCs (excluding oil)	103	96	102	103	106

Source: UN Monthly Bulletin of Statistics (April 1972).

This led him to turn the doctrine upside down: it is not bad terms of trade that cause poverty, but poverty that causes bad terms of trade. It is their inflexibility and their lack of adaptability that prevent underdeveloped countries from seizing new trade opportunities, that condemn them to remaining stuck in dead-ends. The sooner they drop the "terms-of-trade hypochondria" (it was then argued) and get on with producing and marketing what the world wants, the sooner their terms of trade, and in any case, and more relevantly, their gain from trade, will improve. While accepting the shift from commodity to country, one may emphasize that the causal process can operate both ways: poverty and underdevelopment causing poor terms of trade, but poor terms of trade preventing the earnings that could lift the economy out of poverty.

But the evidence that the commodity terms of trade of LDCs tend to deteriorate is not stronger than that those of agricultural producers tend to deteriorate. It is true if 1951 is taken as a base; but 1969 is substantially better than 1938 and the improvement since 1963 has been greater for LDCs than for DCs.

6 TRADE VOLUME AND VALUE PESSIMISM

Rather than focusing on the terms of trade, one could argue that developing countries are unfortunate in having slow-growing exports, though this leaves open the question whether slow growth is the result of supply or demand limitations or an interaction of the two.

Between 1962 and 1969 the value of world exports of agricultural products grew at 3 per cent per annum, far less than total growth of world trade, which was 10 per cent. The different performance of DCs and LDCs within the total agricultural trade is shown in Tables 11.11–11.12.

The following tables (11.13–11.17) show (a) that trade in agricultural products has grown much more slowly than trade in manufactured products, and (b) that LDC trade in agricultural products has grown more slowly than DC trade in these products.

LDC exports grew more slowly than those of DCs because of their higher primary product content, but also because of poorer performance in each category.

A partial explanation of the differential growth rates of DC and LDC exports of agricultural products is that DCs specialize more in agricultural commodities for which world demand has grown rapidly (protein-rich food, animal feedstuffs). But to the extent that LDCs and DCs competed in the same agricultural product markets, LDCs also often did less well: thus,

TABLE 11.11 Growth in the value of exports of principal agricultural commodities

| | Estimated value in 1970 | | | Average annual change 1962[a] | | |
	Developing countries	Developed countries	World[b]	Developing countries	Developed countries	World
	(US $ million)			(%)		
Basic foods and feeds						
Wheat and wheat flour	133	2845	2,978[c]	+3	+1	–[c]
Coarse grains	734	2,026	2,760[c]	+8	+5	+6[c]
Rice	386	455	917	–1	+13	+5
Fats and oils[d]	1175	2029	3578[c]		+3	+3[a]
Oilcakes and meals[f]	861	1713	2648	+5	+12	+9
Butter	6	686	659	–6	+5	+4
Beef and voal	455	1147	1677[g]	+11	+10	+11[g]
Mutton and lamb	24	306	336[g]	+8	+7	+8[g]
Pork	11	438	468[g]	+10	+16	+14[g]
Bacon	3	331	367[g]	+6	+2	+2[g]
Poultry	3	271	337[g]		+5	+6
Canned meat	161	449	700[g]	+4	+7	+6[g]
Sugar	1838	479	2525	+1	+1	–
Total above	5790	13075	19950	+3	+5	+5
Tropical crops						
Bananas	461	78	539	+4	+14	+5
Coffee	2918	–	2918	+4	–	+4
Cocoa and cocoa products	990	–	990	+10	–	+10
Tea	532	1	533	–2	–	–2
Total above	4901	79	4980	+3	+13	+4

Agricultural raw materials

Cotton	1 734	442	2 577	+2	−11	—
Wool	176	1 099	1 336	−6	−1	−2
Jute[h]	150	—	150	—	—	—
Hard fibres	83	—	88	−10	—	−10
Rubber	1 059	—	1 059	+2	—	+2
Hides and skins	172	493	674	—	+6	+4
Total above	3 380	2 034	5 884	+2	+4	+3
GRAND TOTAL	14 070	15 188	30 814	+2	+4	+3

Note: Percentage changes are computed from rounded data.
[a] Compound rate, 1961–3 average to 1969.
[b] Including centrally planned countries.
[c] Excluding centrally planned countries.
[d] Including oilseeds, excluding butter, excluding the value of the cake content of oilseed exports.
[e] Including Antarctic.
[f] Including the estimated value of the cake contents of oilseed exports.
[g] Excluding USSR and the Asian centrally planned countries.
[h] Including kenaf and allied fibres.

Source: FAO Commodity Review and Outlook, 1970–1, Table 1.

TABLE 11.12   Export Growth (1955–67) (% p.a.)

	LDCs	DCs
Value of agricultural exports	2.1	6.1
Value of total exports	4.5	7.8
Per capita agricultural exports	−0.4·	4.9
Per capita total exports	2.0	6.6

Source: *FAO Commodity Review and Outlook*, *1969–70*, originally UNCTAD, Table 52.

TABLE 11.13   Volume of trade (at 1963 prices)

World exports (US $m)				
	1938	*1953*	*1963*	*1969*
Food and raw materials	26 500	27 100	44 150	55 870
Manufactures	21 000	37 000	75 550	146 500

Source: *UN Statistical Yearbook*, *1970*, pp. 71 ff.

TABLE 11.14   Relative growth of trade in primary products exports to market economies developed or developing (current value, US $ billion)

	1953	*1958*	*1963*	*1969*
Food				
From DCs	8.57	10.33	14.27	20.51
From LDCs	7.53	8.01	8.77	11.00
Raw materials				
From DCs	6.84	8.05	11.40	16.25
From LDCs	5.69	5.58	6.67	8.68

Source: *UN Statistical Yearbook*, *1970*, pp. 71 ff.

TABLE 11.15   Value of exports (f.o.b., $ million)

	1938	1953	1963	1969
At 1963 prices				
All commodities	54 000	74 600	135 400	228 400
Food and raw materials	26 500	27 100	44 150	55 870
Manufactured goods	21 000	37 700	75 550	146 500
At current prices				
All commodities	21 000	74 800	135 400	242 300
Food and raw materials	9 200	29 500	44 150	58 760
Manufactured goods	9 800	35 300	75 550	158 500

Sources: UN Statistical Yearbook, 1970, Table 14, p. 71.

TABLE 11.16   Relative volume trends in food and raw materials
(1963 = 100)

	Exports to market economies			
	1953	1958	1963	1969
Food				
From DCs	58	76	100	133
From LDCs	75	85	100	122
Raw materials				
From DCs	53	70	100	134
From LDCs	84	85	100	133

Source: UN Statistical Yearbook, 1970. See p. 401 of this source for detailed breakdown.

TABLE 11.17   Growth of exports, 1953–65
(index numbers of value in 1965, 1953 = 100)

	Primary products	*Manufactures*	*Total exports*
LDCs	165	283	174
World	168	291	220

Source: Little, Scitovsky and Scott, Industry and Trade in Some Developing Countries, Table 7.5.

1961–3 average to 1968, DC exports grew more/declined less for rice, fats and oils, oilcakes and meals, butter, beef and veal, wool, and hides and skins. The reverse was true only for coarse grains, sugar, wheat and cotton.[2] For rice, concessional sales by Japan affected market shares, but for fats and oils, and oilcakes and meals, shortfalls in supplies by LDCs were a major factor.

Those LDCs whose agricultural exports grew fastest between 1955 and 1967 were particularly likely to export products with fast-growing demand. On the other hand, these countries often included products with slow-growing demand among their major exports, and achieved well above average growth rates in exports of such commodities. Thus, of 19 cases where countries with $5\frac{1}{2}$ per cent plus annual growth of agricultural exports had major exports of commodities with world export growth of 0·3 per cent per annum or less, *they* achieved export growth rates above $4\frac{1}{2}$ per cent per annum in nine cases, *for these commodities.*[3]

These results emphasize that many factors other than the commodity composition of agricultural exports influence the export performance in these products. Adequate production at competitive prices, accompanied by good marketing, enables successful countries to raise their shares in exports of slowly growing commodities. On the other hand, the 'right' commodity composition may not do any good if efficiency of production and marketing are low.

The impression that the slow growth in agricultural exports is partly the result of supply limitations and supply deficiencies is confirmed if we consider individual commodities. Thus trade in oilseeds suffered a decline only in developing countries, while developed countries continued to expand their exports in the 1960s.[4]

7 DIVERSIFICATION

A common prescription for poor agricultural export performance is diversification or 'export substitution'. The principal objectives of diversification are:

(1) to reduce fluctuations in export earnings;
(2) to reduce fluctuations in expenditure on imports, resulting from fluctuations in the supply of domestic crops;
(3) to increase total export earnings above what they would otherwise have been: (a) this may be aggressive as in the case of monopoly pricing where diversification is used to back up a cartel; (b) or it may be defensive, where diversification is an escape from the losses threatened by a shrinking market;
(4) to reduce outlays on imports below what they would otherwise have been through domestic import substitution.

Each of these objectives requires different policies and imposes different costs. Some of them may conflict with one another. Quite distinct principles apply to achieving the different objectives. Portfolio investment theory and the theory of insurance are applicable to objectives (1) and (2), whereas the theory of monopoly and cartels and the general theory of development are applicable to (3) and (4). The *FAO Commodity Review and Outlook, 1969– 70,* found a tendency for countries whose agricultural exports were more diversified to have higher rates of growth of export earnings, though this tendency was not strong.[5]

Diversification in practice can be of four distinct types:

(a) Diversification as part of general economic development; alertness to new profit opportunities is here the *cause* and diversification is the response.

(b) Diversification because a commodity is facing a deteriorating position in world trade and defensive action is indicated.

(c) Diversification to back up an international monopoly pricing agreement that involves restricting supply.

(d) Diversification to reduce fluctuations in export earnings or import outlays, without raising the average above what it would otherwise have been.

(a) is not a major development problem for agricultural diversification policy. Countries which diversify from strength need, to that extent, less help. It might, however, be interesting to study cases of successful diversification (e.g. Taiwan, Malaysia, Ivory Coast) and to compare these with countries continuing to produce the same commodity in a shrinking market. One of the chief lessons may well be that it is a set of factors *other* than diversification which accelerates development and also leads to diversification, rather than *diversification* that leads to accelerated development. Indeed, diversification without these 'other factors' might be worse than no diversification.

(b) is probably the main development problem. Taking the list in TD/B/348 (see Table 11.18), six countries showed annual growth of export earnings of the specified commodities above 6 per cent, even though they were in 'problem' commodities (Uganda, Chad, Rwanda, Nicaragua, Guatemala and Kenya). Brazil and Colombia, being members of the International Coffee Agreement, fall into category (c) Cuba had special problems because of the break with the United States, and Burma and Haiti had internal difficulties. This leaves about 15 other countries on the list, to which might be added countries with slow export growth but in

TABLE 11.18 Dependence of developing countries on exports of commodities facing significant competition from synthetics and/or in persistent surplus on the world market

Country	Value of exports of specified commodities		Value of total exports	GDP in 1967[a]
	As proportion of total exports 1966–8	Average annual rate of growth 1959–61 to 1966–8		
	(%)	(%)	(%)	($ billion)
Mauritius	90	2.9	3.2	0.17
Burundi	88	−8.3[b]	−5.9[b]	0.17
Fiji	87	5.9	5.5	0.15
Ceylon	85	−1.4	−0.9	1.71
Cuba	84[d]	−1.0[e]	0.6	..
Uganda	83	7.1	6.6	0.70
Chad	82	6.4	6.4	0.24
Cambodia	69	2.9	3.1	0.96
Ethiopia	68	5.4	5.3	1.40
Rwanda	67	11.4[b]	3.9[b]	0.15[a]
Colombia	66	0.5	2.0	5.78
Dominican Republic	64	1.9	0.3	0.98
Haiti	64	0.9	1.8	0.39
Egypt	62	0.5	2.4	4.99
Madagascar	61	4.9	4.8	0.65
Burma	61	−9.1	−6.5	1.61
El Salvador	60	3.6	8.3	0.82
Nicaragua	58	11.0	1.35	0.62
Guatemala	58	6.6	9.8	1.35
Sudan	57	2.5	2.3	1.43
Brazil	53	1.7	4.2	24.88
Tanzania	52	4.3	7.1	0.79
Kenya	51	6.1	6.3	1.14

[a] In current prices at factor cost, converted to dollars at current exchange rates.

[b] 1964 to 1966–8.

[c] GNP

[d] 1966–7.

[e] 1959–61 to 1966–7.

Source: FAO, *Trade Yearbook*; IMF, *International Financial Statistics*: U.N., *Yearbook of International Trade Statistics* and *Yearbook of National Accounts*; OECD, *National Accounts of less Developed Countries*.

which the value of exports of the specified commodities was less than 50 per cent.

(c) presents special problems. Typical countries in this category are Brazil and Colombia with long histories of efforts to diversify.

(d) is probably of least interest, though most amenable to theoretical treatment. But in analysing the other categories, attention should be paid to the impact of diversification on fluctuations in earnings or import requirements. Thus it is possible for certain types of diversification to increase, rather than reduce, fluctuations in export earnings. Vertical diversification into finished products which substitute for imports would deprive a country of benefits derived from the lower price of finished imports when the price of the raw material falls. Even where the prices of manufactured goods show greater stability than those of raw materials, dependence on the same markets, which may characterize vertical diversification, may be reflected in unemployment instead of price reductions when demand recedes. Cordage and sisal or rubber tyres and rubber may serve as illustrations.

8 PROJECTIONS OF INTERNATIONAL TRADE IN AGRICULTURAL PRODUCTS

International trade projections are derived from projections of national production, national consumption and the differences between the two. This paper draws on FAO's *Agricultural Commodity Projections, 1970– 1980*, and Eric M. Ojala's paper for the Stanford Conference (1971).[6] The assumptions on which these projections are made include unchanged national policies, constant 1970 prices, continuing improvement in technology and its application and continuing trends in income and population growth. The projections are not forecasts but hypothetical extrapolations of past trends.

On these assumptions, 1980 would witness surpluses in the main groups of cereals. For wheat, annual world export availabilities would exceed import requirements by 15 million tons, for coarse grains by 40 million tons and for rice by $2\frac{1}{2}$ million tons. The effects of the green revolution are apparent in the disappearance of India and Pakistan as wheat importers; in coarse grains the green revolution plays only a minor part in changing the international trade prospects, with India disappearing as an importer and Argentina, Thailand, Mexico, Brazil and Morocco expanding production faster than domestic demand. The main increase is assumed to come from developed countries like the United States, France and South Africa. While international trade in rice is much smaller than in wheat and coarse grains, developing countries predominate in its production and trade. But since world trade in rice is a small difference between the large totals of home production and consumption, this projection is even less certain than the other two. Burma, Thailand and Egypt would have larger surpluses for export in a contracting world market. This small aggregate change may, however, hide a very serious loss for some developing countries. Projections by the US Department of Agriculture indicate that the developed countries may become net importers of rice, the communist countries may become self-sufficient, while the developing countries will change from being importers to being exporters. This will be largely the result of greater self-sufficiency in some previously rice-importing countries. There is a serious danger that the price of rice will drop substantially and that the rice-exporting countries will earn less foreign exchange from a large volume of sales. This will have been largely the result of import substitution and greater self-sufficiency in some Asian countries.

If import requirements of the United Kingdom from LDCs were to be substantially reduced as a result of her joining the EEC and continuing the Common Agricultural Policy, the surpluses would be even greater. Equally, countries that have in the past imported cereals and, as a result of the green revolution, have become self-sufficient, may later decide to enter the export market. An example of this is Malaysia. Events will depend as much on political decisions as on technology. The adjustments to imbalances between world demand and supply will either become the result of the play of power, or an international framework will have to be set up with rules of behaviour that will constrain nationalistic competition.

NOTES

1. This chapter is reprinted from Nurul Islam, (ed.), *Agricultural Policy in Developing Countries* (1974). I am indebted to Michael Sharpston for help with the statistical tables and for valuable comments.
2. FAO, *Commodity Review and Outlook, 1970–1*, Table 1.
3. FAO, *Commodity Review and Outlook, 1969–70*, Ch. 3.
4. Trade pessimism with respect to total volume and value was given a hard knock by the successful export records of the developing countries in the 1960s and the quite fantastic rates of growth by historical standards of exports of some of them. Exports of LDCs grew by 7 per cent annually in the 1960s and in 1969 by 9 per cent. Some countries achieved 30 per cent and 40 per cent. It is true that the *share* of developing countries in world trade has shrunk (from 30 per cent in 1948 to 17.2 per cent in 1970) and that the exports of developed countries grew even faster. But this is surely beside the point. The mere fact that trade between industrialized countries grew even faster is irrelevant. More to the point is the argument that the import requirements of the developing countries, on average, have risen even faster than exports.
5. FAO, *Commodity Review and Outlook, 1969–70*, p. 154.

6. FAO, *Agricultural Commodity Projections, 1970–80*; Eric M. Ojala. 'Impact of the New Production Possibilities on the Structure of International Trade in Agricultural Products', Conference on Strategies for Agricultural Development in the 1970s, Stanford University, 13–16 Dec 1971 (mimeo).

12 It *is* a Moral Issue[1]

Governments of wealthy states frequently explain their contribution to development assistance in terms of long-term self-interest. Is this the only stance appropriate to international relations; in what sense do nations have a moral responsibility towards each other transcending national gain?

Many arguments have been advanced for international cooperation in development, for rich countries to help poor countries in their efforts to improve the lot of their people. They range from Machiavellian arguments, through arguments of economic, political or strategic national self-interest and self-respect, to purely moral arguments of altruism. It has been said that cooperation for development produces the future markets for British exports, that it creates a "world safe for democracy", that it wins us friends or at least votes in the United Nations, that it advances world peace.

Of course, it would be nice if moral duty and national self-interest pointed in the same direction. This identity of moral duty and self-interest is particularly congenial to the Anglo-Saxon temperament, and was expressed by Bishop Joseph Butler in the eighteenth century when he said, "when we sit down in a cool hour, we can neither justify to ourselves this or any other pursuit [i.e. the pursuit of what is right and good], till we are convinced that it will be for our happiness" (Sermon 11, para. 20). He also observed that "Conscience and self-love, if we understand our true happiness, always lead us the same way. Duty and interest are perfectly coincident" (Sermon 3, para. 9).

Echoing the heading of a famous *Times* leader on the Profumo affair("It *is* a moral issue"), a reviewer of a hard-headed, if not hard-boiled, book on aid entitled his dissenting review: "It *is* a moral gesture." The fear of being cast in the role of a woolly do-gooder should not obscure the economic sacrifice that development aid and certain types of concessions in trade of manufactured goods and raw materials involve (semantically as well as morally), even if there may be military, political or economic compensations, and even if the conventional way of counting the cost of aid overstates the sacrifice. If donor countries were determined to use overseas development policy only as a measure of sales promotion for exports or for

232

democracy, or as a bribe to win or strengthen military allies or to get votes in the United Nations, the geographical pattern, the form, the terms and the amount of aid and other measures would be quite different from what they actually are.

It is odd that a moral, disinterested concern by rich countries for the development of the poor is hardly ever conceded (though Sweden, the Netherlands and perhaps Canada are notable exceptions). As hypocrisy is the tribute that vice pays to virtue so professions of national self-interest (however qualified by "long-term" and "enlightened") in the development of poor countries may be the tribute that virtue has to pay to vice.

What is needed, but hardly ever offered, is a clear distinction between: (a) what donor countries do and why they do it; (b) what they would do if they acted correctly in their national interest; and (c) what a theory, based on international welfare as the objective, would say that they ought to do. And actions springing from national motivation should be subjected to the double test: are such policies effective? Are they morally defensible?

THE BASIS OF THE MORAL ARGUMENT

In my view, the most fundamental argument for international cooperation in development is that human beings, wherever born, should be able to develop to the fullest extent their capacities, both in order to fulfil themselves and in order to contribute to the common heritage of civilization. The simple argument for making sacrifices in order to assist development is this: we, the rich, are partly (though only partly and arguably) responsible for the poverty of the poor; we can do something about it: it follows that we ought to. The argument rests only partly (and controversially) on our responsibility. Even if we had no share at all in the responsibility, the Christian and humanist belief in the brotherhood of man imposes certain obligations to alleviate misery and to aid in the full development of others where we can. Nor does the argument depend upon development aid or other forms of assistance having in fact been used productively, effectively or non-corruptly in the past. If there have been faults in the use of aid, it is our duty to eliminate the faults, not the aid.

This is not the place to discuss our responsibility. It does not, in my view, rest on colonial or imperialist exploitation (though colonial neglect is more to the point) but on the fact that the international distribution of income is arbitrarily determined by the division of the world into states, and that those nations that are skilled or lucky enough to be rich, pursue policies with respect to immigration, international trade, international money and international capital movements which prevent others from sharing in their wealth and in their opportunities. A purist might wish to draw a distinction between differential national wealth that is due to initiative, efforts and skills, which might be regarded as deserved, and differentials due to mere luck, like the existence of natural resources, the exploitation of which should be guided by considerations of world solidarity. International development policies may also be regarded as one way in which we can make some compensation for the selfishness of the affluent welfare state and for the biases and injustices of the international economic system.

"Injustice" means the unequal treatment of equal people in equal situations. The standard classical reference is Book 5 of Aristotle's *Nicomachean Ethics*, where Aristotle distinguishes between a general and several specific senses of the word "just". "Unjust" does not exclusively mean wrong deliberately done in contravention of law and custom. It can refer to the effects of institutions, organizations and arrangements, whether intended or unintended. I shall show that the poverty of the Third World is partly the result of our arrangements—the political arrangements of the rich nations. But even if no deliberate wrong-doing were involved, the law and the customs themselves can be said to be unjust. Left-handed people and non-smokers have argued on similar grounds that our arrangements are unjust to them. It was we, the citizens of rich countries, who introduced lowered death rates (through malaria control and modern medical and public health services), into societies with primitive birth rates, while keeping our frontiers shut against the resulting population increase. Possibly no deliberate wrong-doing there, but the results are part of a system of arrangements which, in their effects, are unjust. The eighteenth-century adherents of laissez-faire were more consistent in advocating also laissez-passer.

THE RESPONSIBILITY OF WEALTH

I shall return to the question of the responsibility of the rich. An international arrangement, by which human beings are organized in nation states which can enjoy the resources within their boundaries, and an international distribution of wealth, power and opportunity, determined by the ratio of people to resources within the boundaries of each nation state is, by Christian and humanist standards, an unjust arrangement. A *really* free market, including the free movement of men, might be more consistent with international justice.

There is a sense of the word injustice which is more specific: "wrong deliberately done by members of a society to others in contravention or disregard of law and custom". It is important to bear this sense in mind and to distinguish it from the more general sense. The injustice of exploitation is not the same as the injustice caused by neglect and this again is not the same as the injustice that springs from the fact that we are organized as nation states. But the former is not the only legitimate sense. And again, a just arrangement derived from human needs may conflict with a just arrangement derived from desert. Some might think that our present arrangements are just because the citizens of the rich countries have earned their wealth by hard work, initiative and thrift. Our idea of justice is highly complex. The argument based on desert may prevent the logical conclusion to be drawn from the argument that world incomes should be completely equalized. But the case for *some* aid and concessions remain.

CAN INTERNATIONAL COMMERCE BE ORGANIZED JUSTLY?

In its *Declaration on World Poverty* the Churches' Action for World Development said: "to obtain justice among men the international financial and trading system can and must be changed". This statement has been criticized as being meaningless and/or mischievous and it has been said that the wish to change the system of fixed exchange rates or the price of gold or to create more international liquidity or to cooperate more with Europe cannot be justified by Christian principles or any moral principles. But the statement is not primarily about exchange rates or the price of gold or Europe. It is about a set of rules of a game which at present gives the lion's share to the lion. Personally, I should have included in the statement rules regulating the movement of men, as well as of capital, goods and services. We deprive the poor countries of their scarce doctors, nurses and engineers but bar entry to the masses of unskilled workers whose survival our medical knowledge has brought about, and whose employment and poverty is aggravated by our draining off many of their skilled men. We impose low tariffs on raw materials and high tariffs on processed industrial goods, penalizing the poor countries' attempts to set up their own processing industries. We restrict the export of long-term, direct private investment but do everything to encourage short-term trade credits to finance the sale of junk to poor countries. Unless we start from the thoroughly un-Christian notion that only citizens of our own nation count and foreigners count for nothing, these arrangements are clearly unjust.

It is often said that the terms of international trade have discriminated in favour of the rich and that a new international economic order must correct this bias. Many economists and politicians in industrialized, advanced countries have difficulty with such statements. They believe that the terms of trade should be left to the forces of the market and that discrimination, bias and injustice can exist only between persons, not between products. Yet, purchasing power and therefore prices are determined by the distribution of power, income and wealth between rich and poor. If world distribution is extremely unequal, and if inequality is unjust, the resulting barter terms of trade will reflect this injustice. If we had an ideal system of income distribution, a perfectly competitive market in which all prices are determined by free and atomistic competition, the growers of cotton, the cane sugar cutters, the cocoa peasants and the landless labourers would exchange their products and their services for fertilizers, petrol, farm equipment, radios and bicycles on better terms than under the present system. As things are now, the prices of the products of the poor tend to fall to their lowest competitive level, while the prices of the products of the rich are administered by large, powerful companies. A drive through an African country at night brings out this contrast starkly. There are the dark shacks of the poor coffee or cocoa farmers, large families crowded into miserable hovels. And there is the glitter and splendour of the beautifully laid out petrol stations of the large oil companies, with clean, concrete bases, brightly lit and uninhabited. I often wish that an economist, propounding the virtues and neutrality of market forces, should drive through this scene and, as he considers the terms of exchange between coffee growers (not the governments which benefit from the restrictive coffee agreements) and oil producers, say to himself: "Each party exchanges what he values less for what he values more and the terms of exahange are neutral."

NOTES

1. Reprinted from *Crucible* (July–September 1976).

13 The New International Economic Order

THE LAG OF INSTITUTIONS BEHIND TECHNOLOGY

The international dissemination of cultural influences has enormously increased. Its ultimate cause is the advance of technologies in transport and electronic communications. Popular songs, styles in dress and hair styles, attitudes to divorce, abortion, homosexuality, drugs, even crimes, are spreading rapidly across the globe. While in previous ages the common culture was confined to a thin layer of the upper class, today it has reached the mass culture in many countries. In the huge underdeveloped regions of the south, however, the masses of people live in extreme poverty and cultural isolation, though a small upper class has become part of the international culture. Even among the élite, there are now moves to assert indigenous cultural values and to establish national and ethnic identities. It is partly a reaction against the rapid spread of the mass culture of the West.

International relations have grown not only in the cultural but also in the economic sphere. This growth is usually measured by the rapid growth of world trade in the last two or three decades, a growth that was substantially faster than the growth of GNP, so that the ratio of exports to GNP has also grown. World trade has increased from over $100 billion in 1960 to over $1 trillion in 1977, and the ratio of exports to GNP has risen from 13·7 per cent in 1960 to 21·8 per cent in 1976.

Taking a longer historical perspective, the ratio of trade to GNP for the main industrial countries is not much higher now than it was in 1913.[1] But there has been a large increase in the trade share of the private sector. The aggregate ratio conceals this because of the large increase in the public sector and the relative rise in prices of those services that are not internationally traded.

It is useful to draw a distinction between integration and interdependence.[2] International integration was probably greater in the nineteenth century, when national governments adhered to the gold standard, fixed exchange rates, and balanced budgets, than today, when domestic policy has set up targets for employment, growth, price stability, income distribution, and regional policy, among other objectives, while at the same time rejecting the constraints which integrated the world internationally. Greater economic interdependence consists in greater international mobility and substitutability of goods, services, and capital, and greater mobility across frontiers of management and technology.

But in trade, as in culture, the poorest countries did not share in this expansion. The share of the low-income countries, excluding the petroleum-exporting countries, fell from 3·6 per cent in 1960 to 2·2 per cent in 1970, and to 1·5 per cent in 1977. Of the total exports of the industrial countries 17·3 per cent went to the non-oil-exporting developing countries in 1970, but only 15·8 per cent in 1977.[3]

While cultural dissemination and economic interdependence between countries have grown, international cooperation between governments has lagged and in some cases grossly failed. The gap of our times is not so much, as is often said, that between science and morality as that between our soaring technological imagination and our inert institutional imagination. Technologically, we know no boundaries. Institutionally, we are stuck where we were hundreds of years ago. The most flagrant failure of international cooperation is the arms race and the $400 billion annually devoted to military expenditure, which has increased violence in the world.

International cooperation for meeting the impending energy crisis has also failed. There is a need for a global energy programme for conservation and exploration of alternative sources of energy.

National policies to fight the evils of pollution have been successfully designed, but the solution of problems of global pollution (like that of the oceans or air across national boundaries) have been much less effective. The same is true of policies to prevent excessive depletion of non-renewable resources.

There has been almost no international cooperation in fighting the world-wide crisis of unemployment, accompanied by inflation and sagging growth. National policies are being pursued in isolation, the balance of payments surpluses of a few countries are kicked around from country to country, Japan and Germany are exporting their unemployment, and what each country does often increases the difficulties of others. There is no exchange of information on investment plans, hence we lurch from excess capacity to shortages in steel, fertilizers and shipbuilding.

International cooperation for development—our main concern here—has also lagged behind the challenge to eradicate world poverty. Insufficient attention has been paid by analysts to this discordance between the success of interdependence and our failure to cooperate and use it for our joint benefits.

The failure in cooperation has been accompanied by a growth of inter-governmental organizations, fora and conferences charged with tackling these issues. Even though practical solutions are proposed, the resistance, often on some minor point, by one or two governments, prevents joint action. This resistance to global action on the part of governments is in stark contrast to the successful coordination of international action by big business—by the trans-national corporations and by the banks in the Euro-currency market. We have the framework for inter-governmental action, but it is largely unused.

There are two opposite forces at work. National integration has contributed to international disintegration. The rejection of the gold standard, of fixed exchange rates and of balanced budgets has liberated national policy to pursue a growing range of national objectives, but has contributed to international disintegration. The rejection of irrational constraints by each state has produced worldwide irrationality. At the same time, the integration of the upper classes of developing countries into the international system has contributed to national dualism, national division and national disintegration in some developing countries. Hence the call for "delinking" and the assertion of a national identity, based on indigenous values.

There are, however, some instances of successful inter-governmental cooperation, usually in specialized, technical fields: The International Postal Union (more than a hundred years old), the International Telecommunication Union, the International Civil Aviation Organization and the World Meteorological Organization are examples of outstanding successes in international cooperation. The World Health Organization and UNICEF have also been successful. Stressing the technical, non-political aspects of cooperation helps to remove issues from becoming politicized. I shall return to this theme and the lessons to be learned at the end of the paper.

ORIGINS OF THE CALL FOR A NIEO

The developing countries' call for a New International Economic Order has many diverse sources, some going far back in history. At the root of this call lies the dissatisfaction with the old order which, it is felt, contains systematic biases perpetuating inequalities in power, wealth and incomes and impeding the development efforts of the developing countries. Three recent phenomena can be singled out that gave the demand for a New International Economic Order special impetus: the disappointment with aid, the disappointment with political independence, and the success of OPEC.

Development aid, on which so many hopes had been pinned in the 1950s and early 1960s, after a vigorous beginning, partly inspired by the Cold War, was regarded as inadequate in amount and poor in quality. A target for official development assistance to the developing countries of 0·7 per cent of the gross national product of the developed countries had been set up. But the net official development assistance given by the DAC members fell from 0·42 in 1964–6 to 0·30 in 1976. Inter-governmental aid negotiations led to pressures, frictions, and acrimony. Although it was correctly seen that for aid contributions to be effective a country's whole development programme had to be scrutinized, developing countries found it intolerable that donors who contributed only 1 to 2 per cent of their national income should meddle in their economic and political affairs. Performance criteria and political, as well as economic, strings produced tensions and recriminations, which led to a plea for a "quiet style in aid". By this was meant a transfer of resources that would be automatic or semi-automatic, hidden, or at least unconditional. The inefficiencies and inequities (as a result of the capricious impact) of commodity agreements, trade preferences, debt relief, SDR links, etc., were regarded as a price worth paying for a hoped-for larger volume of transfers and a defusing of diplomatic tensions.

The second source of the call for the automatic, concealed, unconditional transfers of the NIEO is the disappointment with political independence that has not produced the hoped-for economic independence. True, most Latin American countries have been independent for a long time, but it is precisely from there that the doctrine of *dependencia* has emerged. It explains the demand for "sovereignty over resources" and the hostility to some features of the trans-national corporations and, more generally, to the international rules of the game as they had evolved after the war.

The third cause is the success of OPEC (and a few other mineral exporters), which appeared to offer an alternative to the appeal to the conscience of the rich. This success was accompanied by a change to a sellers' market and to world shortages of food and raw materials. These events encouraged developing countries to explore the scope for similar action on other fronts, to emphasize joint bargaining, the use of "commodity power", and the exercise of power in other areas, such as the treatment of trans-nationals.

INTERPRETATIONS OF THE NIEO

The NIEO means different things to different people. Under its banner, a great variety of interpretations have been gathered. Three distinctions are useful in clarifying some of the ambiguities.

Some have interpreted the NIEO as a demand for exemptions from established rules. Non-reciprocal preferences for manufactured exports, debt relief, more concessionary aid fall under this heading. Others have interpreted the NIEO as a radical change in the rules.

A second distinction is between those who seek a few more concessions from the developed countries, more aid, more trade preferences, contributions to commodity agreements, better access to capital markets, cheaper technology transfer, debt relief, etc., and those who want fundamental structural change, in the form of new institutions and a shift in power relations.

A third distinction is that between those who interpret the NIEO as being essentially about rules and restraints, like those laid down at Bretton Woods and the GATT, whether the demand is for exemptions from old or for new rules, and those who interpret the restructuring to refer to the totality of economic, political and even cultural relations. This second interpretation sees in the post-colonial power structure the continuation of domination and dependence, caused not only by rules, procedures and institutions designed by the powerful, rich countries, but also by numerous other factors, such as the thrust of science and technology, the priorities in research and development, the cumulative nature of gains, the structure of markets, the influence emanating from the mass media, the educational systems and the values they impart, etc.

The discussion about appropriate rules for international economic relations has suffered from a long-standing confusion. It is the confusion between *uniform* (sometimes also called *general*) principles or rules (the opposite of specific ones, and therefore necessarily simple) and *universal* principles or rules (which may be highly specific and complicated, provided that they contain no uneliminable reference to individual cases). Further confusion is caused if a third characteristic of rules is added: *inflexibility* over time, and confused with either uniformity or universality. A rule is capable of being *altered*, though it remains either uniform, i.e. simple, or universal, i.e. may have a lot of "exceptions" written into it. The "equal" treatment of unequals is not a principle of justice, and a general rule commanding it is an unjust rule. In order to prevent partiality and partisanship, rules have to be universal, i.e. not contain references to individual cases. They may, and indeed should not be uniform. They should pay attention to the varying characteristics and circumstances of different countries.

Those who charge the developing countries with asking for exemptions from rules are guilty of this confusion between *uniform* and *universal* rules. Thus a differentiated system of multi-tier preferences, according to the level of development of the exporting countries, may be best and most just for a group of trading countries at different stages of development. A fair system of rules also points to the differentiation in responsibilities and rights according to circumstances. Middle-income countries would not have the responsibility to give aid, but neither would they receive it. They would not have to give trade preferences, but neither would they receive them. Even finer differentiation would be possible. A country like Saudi Arabia might be asked to contribute to loans because of its foreign exchange earnings, and to aid because of its income per head, but might receive trade preferences, because of its low level of industrialization. The 0·7 per cent aid target would be replaced by a system in which those below a certain income per head are exempted, and the percentage target rises with income per head.

There is, of course, a practical and tactical case for *simple* rules, which might overrule the case in fairness for universal (though complex) rules: they are less open to abuse and easier to police. And there my be a tactical case for uniform rules; they may be easier to negotiate. It is for such pragmatic reasons rather than on theoretical grounds that one may advocate that rules should not be too complex, and should not be changed too often.[4]

Any specific proposals, like non-reciprocity in trade concessions, or trade preferences would, of course, have to be examined on their merits. But the distinction between "exemption from rules" and "drawing up new rules" is logically untenable, to the extent to which the call for exemption is really a call for a set of *universal* rules that pays attention to the different characteristics and circumstances of different countries, just as income tax allowances for dependants or lower rates on earned than on unearned income, are not "exceptions" but reflect our notions of fairness.

Those who are concerned with changing the rules of international relations are aiming partly at removing biases in the present rules, partly at the exercise of countervailing power where at present the distribution of power is felt to be unequal, and partly at counteracting biases that arise not from rules but from the nature of economic processes, such as the cumulative nature of gains accruing to those who already have more resources, and the cumulative damage inflicted on those who have initially relatively little (polarization or backwash effects).

In so far as the NIEO is about strictly economic relations, there is scope for positive-sum games. But in so far as it is about national power relations between sovereign states with different aims, power is by its very nature a *relative* concept, and what is at stake are zero-sum games. The demand for greater participation in the councils of the world and for corrections in the biases of the international power distribution are bound to diminish the power of the industrialized countries.

It is part of the weakness of the poor countries and of the syndrome of underdevelopment that they have not succeeded in articulating these pleas altogether convincingly. An unsympathetic approach can always find faults and criticize specific proposals and the manner in which they are presented. A more imaginative approach would attempt to understand the underlying grievances, even though often badly expressed and poorly translated into concrete proposals. An entirely adequate approach would require a well-staffed, highly qualified secretariat of the Third World, which would muster the evidence, prepare the case for international negotiations, and propose feasible reforms, worked out in detail.

HETEROGENEITY OR HOMOGENEITY OF THE THIRD WORLD?

The NIEO has been acclaimed by *all* developing countries, but the diversity of their interests is reflected in the long list of the UNCTAD agenda, by the strains caused by specific proposals, such as debt relief, by the inconsistency of some of the targets, and by the OPEC oil price rise. Concern with reforming the international system has, at least in the rhetoric, been closely linked with concern for the world's poor. But the poor are largely in what is sometimes called the Fourth World: south India, sub-Saharan Africa and a few islands. Their need is mainly for additional financial and technical assistance. The more advanced countries of the Third World need better access to capital markets, to markets for their manufactured exports and to modern technology.

The cohesion between these two groups of countries has been maintained largely because OPEC has used its petro-power to press for other reforms on the agenda, such as the inclusion of non-energy issues in the Paris Conference on International Economic Cooperation (CIEC) discussions, initially intended to be devoted solely to energy. It has succeeded in the liberalization of IMF credits, and the liberalization of the compensatory finance facility. OPEC has also given substantial aid.

The cohesion of the Third World may also be threatened by the formation of north–south blocs, Europe forging special ties with Africa through Lomé, Japan (and Australia and New Zealand) with East Asia through ASEAN, and some non-oil Arab countries with the Arab members of OPEC. It would not be surprising if, in default of global progress, developing countries were to attempt to strike bargains with specific developed countries, or groups of them. Some of the weaker and poorer countries are bound to suffer, inequalities to be increased, and the cry of neocolonialism to be raised again. Such fragmentation of the world into regional blocs is not in the interest of development or of the developed countries.

In spite of heterogeneity and diversity of interests, there are strong common interests in the Third World, which can provide a basis for collective action. These countries are, by and large, poorer than the developed countries (the existence of borderline cases with small populations does not destroy the distinction), many have been colonies and they benefit and suffer from the impulses propagated by the advanced, industrial countries in similar ways.[5]

In answering the question whether homogeneity or heterogeneity is stronger among the countries of the so-called Third World, we would have to begin by listing criteria for a typology of countries, relevant to the dimensions of what might constitute the "Third World". These might include income per head, growth rates, inflation rates, indicators of economic structure (such as proportion of the labour force in agriculture, trade ratios), human and social indicators (life expectancy, infant mortality, literacy), water supply, indicators of inequality, population growth, indicators of dependence such as concentration of exports by commodities and by destination, statistics of brain drain, political indicators, etc. If we find that on the whole the same countries cluster round each end of these scales, the division will be found to make sense. If, on the other hand, groupings cut across the conventional north–south division, we may have to revise our typology and the notion of a homogeneous "Third World".

But it may be both tactically wiser and in the service of truth to acknowledge that many problems of the developing countries are not just the problems of a block, but are common to us all: there are rich and poor among the OECD countries, there are relations of dominance and dependence between developed countries, and even between regions within one country, there are biases and imperfections in the system of international relations that discriminate against members of the First World and there are important interest alignments that cut across national frontiers. On the other hand, many of the objectionable features of the relations between the industrial and the developing countries are replicated in those among the stronger and weaker developing countries.

Moreover, there is another danger for the fate of the poor within what has been called the "trade union of the Third World". This danger is that, as in the original trade union movement, the benefits from joint action may be reaped by the stronger members, who wield the power, and the weakest and poorest get left out.

For reasons such as these, emphasis on the homogeneity of the Third World may be both mistaken and misguided, and appeal to universal principles and globally shared problem may be wiser.

CRITICISMS OF THE NIEO

There has been no shortage of criticisms of the proposals under the NIEO. Very often these have taken the form of evaluations by professional economists, in the light of the objectives of efficiency and equity commonly accepted in the profession. Yet a proper evaluation ought to start from the objectives of the developing countries themselves (or specified groups within them) and distinguish between criticisms of the objectives and criticisms of the proposed means of achieving these objectives. There is also the danger that we may impute objectives to the developing countries that they do not share with us. One difficulty is that in the discussions ends and means have been confused, so that greater self-reliance, larger shares in income, wealth, or power, larger shares in industrial production, or trade, earnings stabilization, price stabilization of particular commodities and price stabilization of all exported commodities, have been debated at the same level. An appraisal of the NIEO is likely to come to different conclusions according to whose objectives are chosen, according to the degree of generality at which the instruments for these objectives are discussed, and according to whether we are discussing ends or the appropriateness of instruments.

Another source of confusion is the fact that criticisms often compare the proposals with some "ideal" solution, when in fact they should be compared with the most likely alternative. Thus transfers through commodity agreements may, by some criteria, be thought to be worse than direct transfers through unconditional, untied, grants, which can be related to the needs of the recipients and the capacity to pay of the donors. SDR creation that should be guided by the world's liquidity requirements should, ideally, be separated from increases in development aid, not fused together in a "link", etc. But the NIEO proposals have to be seen in the context of a world which is not "ideal" but very imperfect. The alternative to doing things badly is often not doing them at all.

Another question is whether NIEO proposals should be assessed individually or collectively. It is possible to raise criticisms against each individual item on the agenda, some at least of which would be answered by accepting certain packages. The Common Fund has been criticized for its inequitable impact on distribution between countries; debt relief, on the other hand, which benefits the poorest countries, has been criticized for its impact on capital markets, of concern mainly to middle-income countries. A package of the Common Fund, debt relief to the poorest and soft ODA might meet the needs of both middle- and low-income countries.

Criticisms have also been directed at the objectives and motivations of the NIEO. It has been easy to disprove the argument that reparations are due for the exploitation in the colonial era. But the disproval is irrelevant, because the case for progressive redistribution of income and wealth and for international contributions to poverty eradication does not depend on the infliction of past damage. Few believe that colonial rule was necessarily harmful, though it would be difficult to prove that it was necessarily beneficial. It should be plain that internal measures are crucial for both growth and equity, but that the international environment can facilitate or impede domestic advance.

A more fundamental criticism of the NIEO has been along the following lines. Moral imperatives apply only to individuals, not to governments. If international transfers are to be justified on moral grounds, donors must ensure that the moral objectives are attained. This implies highly conditional, targeted transfers for basic human needs, poverty alleviation, reduction of unemployment, etc. The proposals of the NIEO do not meet this condition, since the distribution of benefits between countries and within countries is capricious. Only strict control and monitoring by donor countries can ensure that the target groups are reached.

The first point to be made in reply to this criticism is that, in a complex, interdependent world, institutions have to be used as vehicles for achieving moral objectives, even if it were agreed that only individuals are the appropriate ultimate targets of moral action. Up to a point, these institutions have to be trusted to concern themselves with the intended beneficiaries. The risk of some leakage has to be accepted. Family allowances intended to benefit children are paid to mothers and fathers who might spend them on gambling and drink. Local governments receive grants, intended for their citizens, from central governments, or states and provinces in a federation from the federal government. It is therefore perfectly legitimate to apply moral rules to states, the necessary conduits for channelling funds to individuals in the world order as it exists. (That this principle is accepted even by the advocates of the view that only individuals are appropriate moral targets can be seen when these same advocates demand debt service from countries whose governments have changed since the debts were incurred, or when they demand that multi-national companies should be treated as "moral persons".) Of course, funds accruing to governments through commodity agreements and debt relief can be spent on the wrong purposes and may benefit the rich in poor countries, but so may aid funds. The best method to make it probable that donor objectives of poverty alleviation are achieved is not to rule out institutional intermediaries, nor to attach strict performance criteria to all transfers and monitor meticulously expenditure, but to select governments committed to anti-poverty policies and support them. Such selection is, to some extent, consistent with the proposals of the NIEO.

But a dilemma remains. Developing countries insist on national sovereignty in the use of resources, while the supporters of larger transfers in the developed countries through overseas development assistance, the special drawing rights link, debt relief, the integrated commodity pro-gramme or any other vehicle, stress the need for monitoring performance and internal reforms to benefit the poor. The resolution of this dilemma can be found in moves towards the "global compact", or the "planetary bargain" which Mr McNamara, the Aspen Institute, Mahbub ul Haq and others have advocated. But as the positions of the north and south are at present defined, we are still some way from such a global compact. The north is not prepared to transfer the additional resources, the south is not prepared to give the necessary undertakings.

It is unfortunate that the developing countries have chosen a set of ill-designed measures to translate worthy objectives into reality. Generalized debt relief (now dropped) and commodity schemes, in so far as they are concerned with more than price stabilization, are regarded by many professional economists as inefficient and inadequate ways of achieving the objective of significant transfers of income, wealth and power, and of achieving a radical restructuring of the international system. In addition, the conflict over the demand by the developing countries for sovereignty over the use of resources, and by the developed countries for careful targeting and internal reforms, adds a serious obstacle in the way of reaching agreement. On the other hand, it is at least equally unfortunate that the developed countries have not responded more constructively and imaginatively to the pleas of the developing countries.

ALTERNATIVE RESPONSES BY THE THIRD WORLD TO THE CURRENT IMPASSE

The responses of the Third World to the current impasse in the dialogue can be discussed under the following headings:

(1) self-reliance, in the sense of doing desirable things for themselves and for each other, whether on an individual country, group of countries or collective Third World basis;

(2) exercise of joint bargaining power to counter biased income, wealth and power distributions;

(3) exploration of areas of common and mutual interests between the south and north;

(4) evolution of rules, procedures and institutions to avoid mutually damaging confrontations and conflict.

The first area overlaps with the subsequent two. Greater self-reliance will increase bargaining power and make it more likely that adjustments in imperfections and inequities will be brought about. If self-reliance raises incomes and purchasing power, it will give rise to new common interests. But self-reliance is not in need of these secondary justifications. In the longer term, most of the things developing countries need they can produce for themselves, and most of the things they can produce they themselves need.

Reduced dualism and a more poverty-oriented approach will tend to create greater intra-Third World trade opportunities. Various forms of joint multi-national enterprises will give rise to opportunities of investment coordination. Monetary cooperation can encourage trade expansion, and growing trade, e.g. through Third World preferences, can be financed by intra-Third World financial cooperation, such as clearing or payments unions. Mutual aid and technical assistance in rural development, family planning, technology, is often more effective between countries that are not at too dissimilar levels of development than when inappropriate methods are transferred from highly advanced countries. Joint activities could be developed in professional associations, in research, in the exchange of information, in education and training, in transport and communications, in food and energy policy. In these ways, the developing countries could make themselves less dependent on concessions from the rich countries and, at the same time, evolve their own styles of development.

Such a strategy calls for new types of institutions. A strong Third World secretariat, with a first-class staff and Third World loyalties has been proposed. Institutions in other fields, like a bank capable of creating monetary assets for Third World trade, or a board coordinating investment decisions, or a community of developing country governments monitoring each other's basic-needs policies,[6] are possibilities.

In addition to such actions of self-reliance, the developing countries could use (2) joint action in certain spheres to strengthen their power in bargaining with the developed countries. The debate over the course of the terms of trade has been shunted on to the wrong track by disputing the question as to whether they had deteriorated historically. The relevant question is not what are the terms of trade compared with what they were, but what are they compared with what they should and could be. Producers' associations in some instances might take the place of commodity agreements on which consuming countries are represented. The fact that current price rises might speed up the process of inventing substitutes is not necessarily an argument against them, for the greater short-term receipts could be used for diversification funds. The question is complicated not only by the difficulty of estimating short-term and long-term elasticities of demand and their interdependence, but also by the possibility of the developed countries retaliating by raising their export prices. But it might be easier to get agreement of purchasing countries on non-retaliation than on commodity agreements.

Joint action vis à vis multi-national corporations could replace or reinforce a generally agreed on code. Developing countries could agree not to erode each other's tax base by giving competitive tax concessions and to apply similar rules and guidelines. Bargaining power can be used also in other spheres, such as overflying rights for airlines, narcotics control, patent law, etc. The main obstacle is that some differences among developing countries are as great as those between them and the developed countries, and joint action is difficult to achieve without a much stronger system of incentives to form and adhere to these agreements. Producers' associations are notorious for their instability, for the more successful the agreement is in raising the price, the stronger the incentive for individual members to defect. And the fear that others may operate outside the agreement, or that all may have to operate without the agreement, is itself a powerful destabilizing force. More thought should be devoted to mechanisms to create incentives to penalize outsiders and defectors, and to reward adherents, as well as to strengthen solidarity, in order to increase the stability of joint action.[7]

Successful cooperation among developing countries may not be possible in all areas but may be feasible in some, e.g. in improving the terms of technology transfer, in bargaining with multi-nationals, in controlling migration of professionals, in reaching joint action on taxation of foreign investment. Much has been written recently on the importance of exploring mutual interests (3) and (4). Clearly this is a promising area because it provides a firmer basis for action than unilateral, unrequited concessions. Since reform in this area is in the interest of both the developing and developed countries, it will be discussed in the next section that deals with the response of the developed countries.

A CONSTRUCTIVE RESPONSE BY THE DEVELOPED COUNTRIES

Although some of the proposals for a NIEO of the developing countries have not been well designed, the response of the developed countries has not been constructive or imaginative. If the package proposed at present were to be the only one on which developing countries could agree, this would be an argument for supporting it, in spite of its deficiencies. It is, however, worth considering modifications of this package (it has already been modified by the abandonment of the demand for general debt relief and the scaling-down of the Common Fund) and alternative packages. It would require a separate paper to map out such alternatives but it is possible to lay down certain principles on the basis of which progress may be made.

There are three areas in which more thought should be devoted to the design of appropriate policies.

(1) First, there is the area where developed and developing countries have common or mutual interests. This covers the exploration of positive-sum games.

(2) Second, there is the area of the avoidance of negative-sum games. Other countries can be not only sources of positive benefits, but also of threats that we must try to avert. Co-existence in an interdependent world can give rise to the production of goods; but it can also give rise to the production of "bads", which have to be combatted by "anti-bads". The exploration of areas of joint action for "anti-bads" may be even more important than the search for goods.

(3) Third, there are areas where existing biases, discriminations and imperfections in the international economic order work against the interests of the developing countries and where we have to explore joint methods of correcting them. This looks like an area of zero-sum games, although long-term benefits to all may accrue. Under this heading would

also fall more "voice" for the developing countries and concessional, gratuitous transfers.

Clearly, the three areas overlap, and each overlaps with self-reliance on the part of the developing countries. Where there is common interest and harmony, so that reforms yield joint gains, there remains the division of these gains between rich and poor countries which can give rise to conflict. Self-reliance by the poor may be in the short-term and long-term interest of the rich countries. They may prefer Korea to sell its shoes in Lahore, and Taiwan its textiles in Indonesia, to having their own markets swamped. And the correction may impose short-term losses on rich countries but benefit them in the long run.

Following on from the work in these areas is the question of the links between restructuring the international system as it affects relations between governments, and the consequential domestic measures required in both developing and developed countries to ensure that the benefits accrue to the poor, and that the costs are borne fairly.

Trade liberalization involves both restructuring in developed countries, so that the whole burden is not borne by the dismissed workers in depressed areas, and in developing countries, so that the gains from liberalization do not wholly accrue to big exporting firms, possibly even multi-nationals. In reaching commodity agreements, there should be some safeguards that the higher prices do not fall exclusively on poor consumers in rich countries, and that the restrictions that quota schemes involve are not largely borne by small farmers in poor countries, so that the big plantations benefit from both higher prices and unrestricted sales. And when we agree on debt relief, we want to be sure that it is more than relief for bankers in rich countries, whose loans are serviced out of aid funds. Such consequential domestic measures are necessary both inside developed and inside developing countries, if the ultimate impact of the reforms of the New International Economic Order is to be on improving the lot of the poor.

COMMON AND MUTUAL INTERESTS

Until 1973, issues of economic interdependence and development belonged to largely separate areas. Development was dealt with by development assistance and trade preferences of varying generosity. Interdependence was dealt with in the OECD.

The validity of this dichotomy has been questioned in the last five years. The developing countries' shares in world population, in world trade and in world production have increased. Some developing countries have now large international reserves, others large international debts.[8] They supply raw materials, especially metals, on which the developed countries increasingly depend. The one-way dependence of the south on the north has now become a two-way interdependence.

International inter*dependence* should be distinguished from international *relations*. The test of the difference is this: if relations were cut off, ready substitutes could be found so that not much damage would be done. Inter*dependence* means that if relations were cut off, substantial damage would result. To illustrate: much trade between industrial countries is conducted in similar finished consumer goods and caters for slight differentiation in tastes. A smaller volume of trade (and a less rapidly growing one) with the developing countries consists of vital food and raw materials. In technical language, it is consumers' (and producers') surpluses that count, not trade volumes (values) and their growth.

Trade is not an end in itself, but a means to a more efficient allocation of resources and to greater consumers' satisfaction. The long-term importance of trade is, therefore, measured not by its total value or its rate of growth, but by (a) the difficulty in *production* of substituting domestic goods for imports by shifting resources employed in exports; and (b) the sacrifice in *consumption* of shifting from imports to domestic import substitutes, if the products are not identical, or of doing without them altogether.[9] A vast and ever-growing exchange of Volkswagen for Morris Minors reflects small importance; a small exchange of coffee or copper (not to speak of oil) for engineering goods reflects vital dependence (or interdependence). Americans would not suffer much hardship if they had to drive Fairmonts instead of Volvos, but might if they had to drink Almadén instead of Château Margaux, and certainly would if they had to do entirely without manganese, tin or chromium imports. Total trade figures are, of course, relevant to other issues, such as changes in the balance of payments, which in turn may affect consumption and welfare. But these sequences would have to be spelt out.

The most generally accepted area of mutual interest is trade liberalization and liberalization of the flow of the factors of production, capital and labour. On trade, it could be argued that already fairly rich developed countries should weigh the costs of adjustment, probably repeated and painful adjustments, against the gains from further additions to income. Countries, or at any rate their governments, might decide that it is in their national interest to forgo at the margin further income rises for the sake of a quieter life, and greater industrial peace.

The difficulty with this position is that the security of employment is not necessarily guaranteed by protection, for jobs in export trades are endangered, and that the costs of such a form of a quiet life can be very high indeed, particularly for a country dependent on foreign trade. Moreover, if several countries adopted such a position, the mutual impoverishment could be substantial.

There are also gains from the flow of capital. Here, special attention should be paid to measures which, without being identified with aid, could have a leverage effect on aid, such as guarantees, co-financing, improved access to capital markets and markets for manufactured exports, etc. Freer movement of goods and of capital and labour would not only register all the mutual benefits expounded by the theory of comparative advantage, but would also accelerate growth, reduce inflation, generate employment, expand choice and support the international system of trade and debt service.

Two specific issues under the heading of international trade are worth exploring. The first is the reform of tariff structures which now tend to cascade with successive stages of processing. Such de-escalation would improve the international location of industries and would permit developing countries to benefit from the external economies of learning effects from a primary-product-based form of industrialization. They might also be able to make better use of waste products, now discarded by the richer countries.

The second area is that of stabilization of commodity prices.The large fluctuations that occur now benefit neither producers, who are discouraged from investing, not consumers, who find it difficult to plan production.

On present evidence and theoretical consideration, there is not much in the argument that *general* flows of ODA to developing countries — what is sometimes called a Marshall Plan for the Third World — can regenerate growth in the developed countries. For the Third World to be an "engine of growth" for the industrialized countries, the quantities are too small (though they can make a contribution), and domestic measures (tax reductions and public-expenditure increases) can do the same with higher political and economic returns, if the narrowly interpreted national interest were the only guide. Some of the demand created in the north is from arms sales. If these were to be reduced, another source would have to replace them. Moreover, the greatest need for ODA is in the poorest countries, the trade share of which is small and only slowly growing, whereas the best "investment" of such aid would be in the middle-income developing countries, which are already earning much foreign exchange through their exports.

The argument that *specific* exports can be supplied from under-utilized capacity at low, zero, or negative costs, and that *specific* imports can contribute to bottleneck busting, and hence to the resumption of orderly growth without premature inflation, deserves closer examination.

Aid from surplus capacity has certain draw-backs. If, in the long run, the surplus capacity should be scrapped and the workers retrained, this process is delayed and an inefficient production structure is perpetuated. This can be particularly damaging if the surplus capacity competes with imports from the developing countries. If the production could have been used at home, or could have been exported at a commercial value, the costs of the aid are correspondingly higher. Nor is it always the case that recipients need or want the surplus production, when it is available.

There remain, however, sectors and industries, especially those where indivisibilities are important, in which the temporary (cyclical) emergence of surplus capacity could be harnessed to the aid effort. Steel-plant manufacturing capacity, shipbuilding capacity, or other heavy-capital-goods sectors are for technical reasons subject to fluctuations in utilization, and periods of under-utilized capacity might be used for aid-financed exports to developing countries in need of steel plants, ships, or other capital goods.

As far as *imports* are concerned, in resuming growth developed countries are liable to run into *bottlenecks* before full employment for the economy as a whole is achieved. Imports from developing countries can help to break these bottlenecks and thereby enable developed countries to resume higher levels of activity with less inflation.

The removal of certain world-wide scarcities, which now prevent countries from resuming non-inflationary, full-employment growth, may be against the interests of small groups benefiting from these scarcities, but is clearly in the interest of all countries and humanity at large. More specifically, food, energy and certain minerals fall into this category. Investment that raises the world supply of food and of energy is bound to benefit all people in the long run.

These bottlenecks can be either of a short-term nature, or they can represent long-term scarcities. In the latter case, investment by the north in the south, in order to overcome these global scarcities, can make a contribution to the resumption of long-term orderly growth without inflation. But in the long-term interdependence is likely to be less than in the short-term, because substitutes for and economies in the use of the scarce materials are possible. With technological advance, it is doubtful whether, in the long run, any country or group of countries can be said to be wholly dependent on some other countries. This is true both for the north and for the south.

An area of positive-sum games is policies towards trans-national corporations and direct private foreign investment. In the past, fears of expropriations, restrictions on repatriation or remittances, price controls and other policies reducing profitability or leading to losses have caused uncertainty and have raised the required rate of return on foreign investment. This high rate of return has, however, often led to the very measures that the investor feared, for host governments felt that companies were taking out of the country more than they were putting in.

There is a specific dilemma for developing countries. If the rate of reinvestment of foreign profits is lower than the rate of return on the capital invested, remission of profits presents a drain on foreign exchange. If, on the other hand, the rate of reinvestment of foreign profits exceeds the rate of return, on plausible assumptions about the rate of growth of national income and the capital-output ratio, a growing proportion of the stock of capital is going to be owned by foreigners. This dilemma between foreign exchange losses and alienation of assets has led some countries to expropriate foreign enterprises. A reduction in the uncertainty about such measures would reduce both the rates of return required by the companies and incentives to take measures by host governments that raise risks for companies. Well-designed measures to reduce uncertainty can increase the flow of foreign investment, induce companies to take a longer-term view, alleviate fears of host governments, and thus benefit both firms and host countries.

Among such measures would be investment guarantees, agreements on arbitration procedures, sell-out and buy-out options after agreed periods at prices to be determined by agreed procedures, model contracts, investment codes, joint ventures, and new public–private hybrid institutions, combining the virtues of private initiative and enterprise with those of a commitment to development.

Another area of mutual interest for policies towards multi-national firms is the application of anti-trust action to the international behaviour of these companies. It is just as much in any industrial country's interest that its companies should not act like cartels or monopolies internationally, as it is that foreign companies should not monopolize its domestic market. There is now an asymmetry in that anti-trust action and restrictive practices tend to be outlawed for domestic activity but permitted (or even encouraged) for international ones.

Common interests can also be established in cooperation in the management of the global commons: ocean fisheries, air and sea pollution, radio frequencies, civil air and merchant shipping routes and world monetary conditions. The already mentioned success of some institutions devoted to technical aspects of international cooperation, like the International Postal Union or the International Telecommunication Union or the World Meteorological Organization bear witness to the possibility of successful international cooperation if strictly defined technical areas are at stake. As a by-product of this global management, revenues might be raised from some of these activities, such as ocean fisheries or international travel.

AVOIDING NEGATIVE-SUM GAMES

The essence of interdependence is that members of the world community are capable, by unilateral action, to inflict harm on others. The fear that others may take such action can be a sufficient condition for defensive, detrimental action of this kind.

The prime example in this field is the arms race which absorbs scarce resources and, beyond a certain critical point, which we have long ago exceeded, breeds violence. Between 1946 and 1976 120 wars were fought, 114 of them in the Third World. The number of people killed is somewhere between those killed in the First and Second World Wars. It has often been noted that economic growth has not abolished poverty. It is less often noticed that large defence expenditure has actually bred violence. The Laffer curve, whatever may be true for taxation, seems to apply to expenditure on arms. Three per cent of the total annual expenditure of $400 billion now devoted to armaments would be doubling the annual resources devoted to official development assistance. But such arguments do not cut any ice until it can be established that the expenditure at present levels is counterproductive and that we would get better security from a reduced volume of expenditure.

In the economic area protectionism and deflation to protect the balance of payments are instances of negative-sum games. In the area of private foreign investment, actions by both parent and host governments to tilt the advantages from private foreign investment in their direction have similarly destructive effects. Large incentives are offered to bid for these investments in "investment wars", like the trade wars of the 1930s. Over-fishing, the pollution of the sea and the global atmosphere and the excessive exhaustion of non-renewable resources are other examples. Coordination of policies and international institutions for cooperation are needed to avoid such mutually destructive actions.

The institutional responses might be illustrated by internationally coordinated action.[10] In order to avoid the self-defeating and mutually destructive actions arising from attempts to correct balance of payments deficits imposed by a few persistent surplus countries, an international central bank, with power to create liquid assets, is necessary. It has been argued that the system of flexible exchange rates has restored full autonomy for national monetary policies. But this is by no means as obvious as is often thought. Hardly any government would permit completely "clean" floating; and "dirty" floating may well require larger rather than smaller reserves to counter speculative attacks.

A second institutional reform would be a mechanism for some form of coordination of investment decisions, so as to avoid the swings between over-capacity and shortages of capacity from which we have suffered in the past. Opponents of such coordination fear lest this is the entry of market-sharing agreements and cartels, but in many national plans coordination of investment decisions has proved entirely compatible with maintaining competition.

Other illustrations would be agreements to refrain from trade and investment wars and the already mentioned establishment of international firms that would combine the virtues of private enterprise and freedom from bureaucratic controls with the objective of promoting development. Another area would be taxes on activities where independent national actions now lead to the deterioration of the world environment: a tax on over-fishing, on polluting the sea and atmosphere, or on mining non-renewable natural resources.

ZERO-SUM GAMES

Exploration of areas of zero-sum games, that is to say actions where a sacrifice is required on the part of the developed countries in order to benefit the developing countries, comprise three fields. First, the correction of imperfections and biases in the existing world order which work against the developing countries. Second, transfers of resources from the rich to the poor. And third, more "voice" for them in the councils of the world.

EXISTING BIASES, IMPERFECTIONS AND DISCRIMINATIONS IN THE INTERNATIONAL SYSTEM AND HOW TO CORRECT THEM[11]

An international economic order that discriminates systematically against one group of countries can give rise to confrontations and conflicts and to negative-sum games in which all lose. But the appeal to correcting inequities need not be wholly to national self-interest. There is an independent moral case for a just world order.

Countries should be willing to cooperate in correcting biases in market structures and government policies that are damaging to the developing countries. Such corrections would contribute to a more equitable and therefore acceptable world order and, by reducing frictions and conflicts, can be seen to be also in the long-term interest of the developed countries.

A response along such lines would meet the demands of both efficiency and distributive justice. Not only are the specific proposals more in line with the canons of economic efficiency, but, by accommodating the developing countries' call for a fairer international order, they would prevent the recriminations and conflicts that are bound to cause international disorder, one of the greatest sources of inefficiency.

At the national level, governments attempt to provide macro-economic stability through monetary and fiscal policies, to redistribute income through progressive taxes and social services, to guarantee farmers an adequate income, to correct for the worst features of free competitive markets, and to cushion victims against the damage of change. All these government actions are in the nature of public goods. There is no international government to do any of these things on a global scale. In the nineteenth century Great Britain, and for about 25 years after 1945, the USA provided a power centre that fulfilled some of the functions of an international government, such as providing compensating capital movements and being a lender of last resort. Since about 1970 such a centre has been lacking. The international organizations have been too weak to fulfil the required functions. International institutions are needed to provide internationally the "public goods" of stability and equity that civilized national governments provide as a matter of course for their citizens. The implementation of such reforms would be a contribution to the foundation of a stable, equitable and prosperous world order.

Whatever our motivation for correcting imperfections or biases in the present international economic order, such biases occur in various fields. The division of the gains from trade may be very unequal because a few large buying companies from rich countries confront many weak sellers from developing countries, and the demand for the final product is fairly inelastic. Or the bulk of the processing of raw materials from developing countries may be done in the developed countries, who reap the large value added, not because they enjoy a comparative advantage but because of market power and policies, such as cascading tariffs, or discrimination in shipping or credit. Or the distribution of the gains from productivity growth between exporters and importers may be uneven, so that improving commodity terms of trade are consistent with deteriorating double factoral terms of trade. It has already been argued that the crucial issue here is not what has happened to the terms of trade now compared with the past, but what the terms of trade are now compared with what they should (and could) be.

In this context, thought should be given to what reforms are needed, by creating new or changing old institutions, rules, policies and other measures to change the location of economic activities and to improve the developing countries' bargaining power, so as to reduce the bias in the distribution of gains from trade.

There are imperfections in the export markets of developing countries. There are also imperfections in the supply of imports. Developing countries are not normally faced with uniformly priced imports and often suffer from price discrimination, restrictive trade practices, export cartels, inter-firm arrangements for the allocation of markets, etc. There exists evidence that small countries pay higher prices for imported machinery, chemicals, iron and steel than large countries. The USA prohibits cartels internally, but specifically exempts export cartels. Should there not be an anti-trust law internationally, just as there is one to protect US citizens?

There are imperfections in access to market information. The ability to buy cheap and sell dear depends upon full market information. The large trans-national firms possess this but poor developing countries do not. The disadvantage is cumulative: ignorance about how to acquire information about production processes reinforces the absence of information about these products or processes themselves. There are imperfections in access to knowledge and technology. Several measures have been proposed to correct this bias. They involve reforms of the patent law, in the market for technology and in the thrust of research and development expenditure. There is a bias in the developing countries' access to capital markets. There may be no shortage of finance in Euro-currency markets, suppliers' credits or through the World Bank, but there may be a bias in the issues and bond markets. What needs to be done in order to reduce imperfections and other obstacles in the way of access to the world's capital markets?

Imperfections in labour markets are reflected in the present bias in the admission and encouragement of certain types of professional manpower, often trained by the developing countries (Brain Drain), and the severe restrictions on the movement of unskilled labour. The world's division into nation states, each monopolizing the physical and technical assets within its boundaries for its own benefit, is not consistent with a rational or moral or acceptable world order.

Does the international monetary system discriminate against developing countries? Monetary restrictions have an important impact on unemployment. The SDR-aid link is probably dormant for a while, but there should be a gold aid link. As central banks sell gold to the IMF for SDRs, the IMF can sell the gold and use the receipts for contributions to IDA.

Trans-national corporations also introduce imperfections. How can we strengthen the bargaining position of developing countries in drawing up contracts with TNCs; how enlarge the scope for "unbundling" the package of capital, management, know-how and marketing; what is the role of public-sector enterprises in negotiating with private TNCs?

An analysis of the distribution of gains arising from much-touted "outward-looking" foreign investment, where the quasi-rents and mono- poly profits accruing to capital, management and know-how go to the rich countries, while the near-subsistence wages for semi-skilled labour go to the developing countries would be useful. The world in which we live corresponds to neither of two popular models: it is neither a truly "liberal" world in which all factors are completely mobile across frontiers, so that they can seek their highest rewards; nor is it the world of the textbooks in which all factors are completely immobile internationally and trade is a substitute for factor movements. Some factors of production, such as capital, management and know-how, are fairly mobile internationally, and earn high rewards, whereas unskilled and semi-skilled labour are immobile internationally and earn low rewards. This has important implications for the distribution of gains from trade, technology and investment, and for the attitudes towards multi-national firms.

There are biases in information on political news coverage. Are the media biased in the scope and content of their news coverage? Is there a need for additional press agencies representing the point of view of developing countries?

Should reforms in all these areas take the form of restoring genuine competition, to reduce market power concentrations in rich countries, or should they take the form of mobilizing countervailing power, like organizing numerous poor producers (as the trade unions did in the nineteenth century), or should they take the form of changes in rules, institutions or legislation? Should there be reforms in the accumulation, selection and dissemination of information and knowledge? Many current recommendations are based on the false premise that existing markets are competitive and efficient, and spread the benefits of economic progress widely. This assumption is quite unrealistic for the world as a whole.

RESOURCE TRANSFER

A new international economic order calls for a substantial increase in the amount of resources to be transferred to the developing countries, with the primary objective of eliminating the worst aspects of poverty within the lifetime of a generation. The specific forms this transfer takes is a secondary question. It has been proposed that developed countries should commit themselves to a total, but that each country should be free to decide in what form it wishes to make its stipulated contribution, whether through commodity agreements, preferences, debt relief, additional ODA, etc. Such an approach would prevent differences among developed countries over specific instruments blocking the achievement of an agreed objective.

The rational way would be an international, progressive income tax, with a lower exemption limit and a rising aid/GNP ratio as income per head rises. Other tax proposals have been made, such as a tax on over-fishing, on global pollution, on seabed resources, on international travel, etc. But an international income tax would be the most rational way towards automaticity and fair sharing.

Monitoring of the objective, poverty eradication, can be done in a way that would avoid the intrusion of donor-country performance criteria, with all the suspicions to which this would give rise, and without the abuse of funds received by developing countries. Harlan Cleveland has proposed a system like that under the Marshall Plan, in which the developing countries themselves would examine and monitor each other's performance in reducing poverty. Accepted extra-national secretariats are another possibility.

"VOICE"

The demand of the developing countries for greater participation in the international decision-making process calls for a reform in the membership and voting system of international institutions. More "voice" for the developing countries is likely to remove some of the frustrations that spring from the perception of powerlessness. But greater participation by the developing countries would be pointless if it were accompanied by reduced contributions from the industrial countries.

The demand for "more voice" is, of course, ultimately a demand for a different power distribution. Power to achieve common objectives can be a positive-sum game, in the sense that joining others can strengthen this power. But where objectives conflict, power is a zero-sum game. If there were a harmony of interests, more voice would not be needed. The demand for "more voice" implies that certain objectives of the claimants have not been met. What is ultimately at stake is a restructuring of power relations.

THE RELATION BETWEEN NARROW AND "HIGHER" NATIONAL SELF-INTEREST

We can build on areas of common national interests, emphasizing mutual benefits to be derived from, e.g. resumption of orderly and equitable growth in the world economy, forswearing self-defeating protectionism, exploring ways of increasing the resources in globally scarce supply, etc. But while there is considerable scope for positive-sum games in exploring areas of common and mutual interests, and of avoiding self-defeating, mutually destructive policies, there is also a "higher" interest in a world order that both is, and is seen to be, equitable, that is acceptable and therefore accepted, and that reduces conflict and confrontation.

All societies need for their self-regulation and for social control a basis of moral principles. Individuals are ready to make sacrifices for the communities they live in. Can this principle stop at the nation state? A belief in the harmony between self-interest and altruism is deep-seated in Anglo-Saxon thought and action. Holland, Sweden and Norway, which have put international cooperation squarely on a moral basis, have hit the 0·7 aid target. It is the countries in which aid has been sold to the public as in the national self-interest where the effort is sadly lagging.

The common interests must also be defined in terms of different time horizons: the next year, the next 5 years, the next 20 years. There may be conflicts and trade-offs between these different time spans. For example, concessionary aid to the poorest may involve economic sacrifices in the near future but, by laying the foundations for a world in which all human beings born can fully develop their potential, it contributes to the long-term interest of mankind.

One difficulty is that in democracies adults have votes, but children and the unborn have no votes. The fight is not only against powerfully organized vested interests, but also against all our own short-term interests, that neglect the interests of future generations.

The "higher" interest in an acceptable world order can be defined either in moral terms or in terms of the desire to avoid negative-sum games, to avoid break down and chaos. Whatever the definition and justification, its aim is to transform adversary relationships into cooperation. When interests diverge or conflict, the task of statesmanship is to reconcile them. This is a task quite distinct from, and more important than, that of exploring areas of common or mutual interest. It is in this light that cooperative actions to eradicate world poverty and to restructure the international economic order have to be seen.

NOTES

1. The ratio of exports to GNP was for the UK 19.3 per cent in 1913 and 20.7 per cent in 1976; for the USA 6.5 per cent in 1913 and 6.8 per cent in 1976; and for Germany 20.5 per cent in 1913 and 22.3 per cent in 1976.
2. For another distinction, that between interdependence and international relations, see below, p. 252.
3. In the low-income developing countries exports were 13.8 per cent of GNP in 1960 and 15.7 per cent in 1976. Low-income countries are those with an income per head of less than $300 in 1975.
4. Of this long-standing confusion between universal and uniform, or general rules even such a clear-headed thinker as David Hume is guilty. Hume contrasts the highly specific reactions when we are seeking our own self-interest with the "universal and perfectly inflexible" laws of justice. He seems, like many others (including GATT), not to make a necessary distinction between general principles (the opposite of specific ones and therefore necessarily simple) and universal principles (which may be highly specific and highly complicated, provided that they contain no uneliminable reference to individual cases). Thus, Hume says, in one place "universal and perfectly inflexible" but lower down "general and inflexible". And the use of the world "inflexible" conceals a confusion between a principle being able to be altered (which has nothing to do with its universality or generality) and its having a lot of exceptions written into it (which is consistent with universality but not with generality). Hume evidently thinks that the rules of justice have to be simple, general ones. He argues that unless the rules are general, people will be partial in their application of them and "would take into consideration the characters and circumstances of the persons, as well as the general nature of the question . . . the avidity and partiality of men would quickly bring disorder into the world, if not restrained by some general and inflexible principles." But this is fallacious. In order to prevent people from being partial, the principles have to be universal, i.e., not contain references to individuals; they may, and indeed should, not be general; surely our judgements based on them ought to "take into consideration the characters and circumstances of the persons, as well as the general nature of the question".
5. For a valiant attempt to demonstrate common factors in the Third World, see Ismail-Sabri Abdalla, "Heterogeneity and Differentiation – The End of the Third World?", *Development Dialogue* (1978) p. 2.
6. See Harland Cleveland, *The Third Try at World Order*, New York (1976).
7. See Ch. 9.
8. The share in total world trade of all developing countries has increased from 21·4 per cent in 1960 to 24·6 per cent in 1976 (though excluding major oil exporters the share declined from 14·8 to 10·2); their share in international reserves has increased from 17·8 per cent in 1960 to 45·9 per cent in 1976 (excluding OPEC from 13·8 to 20·2); their share in population from 72 per cent in 1960 to 76 per cent in 1976; and their share in production from 18·2 in 1960 to 22·6 in 1976, measured to constant 1975 dollars.
9. Irma Adelman, in private correspondence, has suggested that the major influence of international trade on development is that it enables a country to decouple production from consumption, and thereby presents more options for development policy.

10. The first two items have been proposed by Mahbub ul Haq.
11. The subject is well treated in Gerald K. Helleiner *World Market Imperfections and the Developing Countries*, Overseas Development Council, occasional paper no. 11, (1978).

Part III Trans-National Companies

14 The Multi-National Enterprise and the Theory of Development Policy[1]

I INTRODUCTION

In the early phase of the theory of development policy in the 1950s it was capital that was stressed as the strategic factor in development. Foreign investment by the multi-national enterprise (MNE) was therefore regarded mainly as a source of foreign funds which supplemented domestic savings efforts. Nurkse's thesis that countries are poor because they are poor and needed large injections of foreign capital became widely accepted.[2] According to this view, a poor country could not raise its low ratio of savings to national income very quickly or very easily. A low savings and investment rate led to a low rate of capital accumulation. This, in turn, implied that workers were endowed with relatively little capital: this kept their productivity low. Low productivity per worker perpetuated low income per head. The low investment ratio was both cause and effect of poverty. In order to break out of this vicious circle of poverty, massive injections of capital from abroad would be necessary. Foreign investment could contribute to pulling poor countries out of this low equilibrium trap.

The experience of the last twenty years has shown that capital was considerably less scarce, and that capital/output ratios were lower, than this doctrine has postulated. Capital was more abundant, partly because more foreign aid and private foreign capital were available, and partly because, in spite of their low incomes, many countries achieved quite high domestic savings ratios. During the 1960s, the share of gross investment in the GNP of developing countries was nearly 20 per cent and the share of savings in GNP over 15 per cent, substantially higher than either the early writers had anticipated or countries industrializing earlier had achieved at a corresponding stage. W. W. Rostow had reasoned that the ratio of investment to income would have to rise from 5 per cent to 10 per cent in order to achieve 'take-off'. England had a savings ratio of only 5 per cent in the eighteenth century, during her industrial revolution, and achieved 10 per cent not until the 1840s.[3] It is, of course, true that the savings ratio of 16·6 per cent in 1970 for all developing countries is lower than the 22·9 per cent achieved by the industrialized countries in the same year. But by historical standards domestic savings ratios were unprecedentedly high and by the standards of the early writers they were unexpectedly high.

In addition, there is now much evidence that the capital in existence was underutilized. The under-utilization of labour had, of course, been a common theme from the beginning of the study of development policy, but the emphasis on capital under-utilization, often substantially greater than in developed countries, is relatively recent.[4]

The absence of a severe bottleneck in capital was confirmed by certain *a priori* considerations. It was found that there was no reason why the savings ratio out of low incomes should be smaller than that out of high incomes. It was also argued that savings and capital are not so much a factor of production with which countries are 'endowed' and which causes development to proceed, as the *result* of the adoption of new technologies and of development. The identification of investment opportunities tends to generate the necessary savings.

High growth rates were associated with relatively high savings ratios and low capital/output ratios. Capital/output ratios were low, partly because the adoption of existing Western techniques of production economized in the use of capital to invent new techniques, thus avoiding the waste of trials and errors, partly because some countries spent relatively little on capital-intensive overhead facilities, and partly because in countries where land was abundant a high rate of growth of the labour force yielded considerable extra agricultural output with relatively little extra capital, even if non-monetary investment, such as land-clearing, is properly accounted for. For these reasons capital turned out to be not such a severe constraint as had been thought.[5]

Another strand of thinking stressed the contribution that foreign capital could make to scarce foreign exchange. Foreign exchange scarcity was derived from the trade pessimism that prevailed in the 1950s and from doctrines of structural imbalance. While foreign exchange clearly was a serious bottleneck in the progress of many countries, others achieved remarkably high growth rates of exports in the 1960s.

The contribution of private overseas investment tended to be seen in the framework of a Harrod – Domar model, linking growth rates with either savings or foreign exchange receipts. But it soon became evident that many activities of the MNE brought with them relatively little capital or foreign exchange, but a good many other things instead.[6] Direct foreign investment in developing countries, including re-invested earnings, rose to $4,000 million annually at the end of the 1960s; compared with total capital formation in the developing countries of about $40,000 million and the total external flow of financial resources of nearly $16,000 million.

Later writers stressed training and the transfer and local creation of skills (investment in human capital), management, entrepreneurship (i.e., innovative rather than administrative management), science and technology, and research and development (R & D). As it became increasingly clear that development involves also social, cultural and political change, interacting in a complex manner with economic factors, and as the definition and objectives of development shifted from accelerated aggregate economic growth to social objectives such as equality and, above all, jobs, livelihoods and generally meeting the needs of the masses of poor people, the contribution of the MNE came to be judged in the framework of a more general theory of capital comprising physical and human capital, as well as knowledge, by its effects upon these objectives rather than by the contribution of savings or foreign exchange to economic growth.

The relation between the MNE and these social objectives will, to a large extent, depend upon the ability and willingness of the host government to pursue the 'right' policies. A view focusing only on the contribution of the MNE to resources generally available for development is justified if the government pursues appropriate policies with respect to distribution and employment, through science policy, land reform, foreign exchange rates, etc. If, on the other hand, such policies are absent or defective, or are themselves the result of the pressures of the MNE, the MNE may be judged by its impact on variables normally regarded as proper direct objectives of government policies.

Thus, with an efficient fiscal system and an honest administrative service, the MNE can be encouraged to pursue efficiency and high profits. Through tax collection, these profits will then make a contribution to the attainment of the social objectives. But if the fiscal and administrative system is defective, the direct contribution of the MNE towards the social objectives will have to be taken into account. Efficiency and profit criteria will then have to be supplemented by criteria of social justice, regional development, employment creation, environmental protection, etc.

The change in thinking reflected earlier changes in the nature of private overseas investment. The most important of these is the shift from nineteenth-century portfolio to direct foreign investment, often accompanied by the MNE's efforts to raise capital locally. There was also the growing importance of new technologies, some of them embodied in capital equipment, others independent of specific pieces of equipment but related to organization, marketing and the commercial use of scientific knowledge. The growing size of the multi-national firm and the tendency to horizontal, vertical and, much more rarely, lateral integration of the operations of the firm meant that monopoly or oligopoly power played an increasing role. The shift of analytical emphasis from capital goods and financial flows to technology, advertising and bargaining reflects these changes in the system of international production.

2 THE OPERATIONS OF THE MNE AND THEIR IMPLICATIONS FOR POLICY OBJECTIVES

The difference between targets, needs or requirements and domestically mobilizable resources has been identified or measured by a variety of 'gaps'—gaps in savings, foreign exchange, skills. While such aggregation has serious weaknesses and has recently been replaced by much greater emphasis on detailed project-by-project appraisal, it can serve as a very rough first approximation. The impact of MNEs on national development policies can then be listed under their contribution to filling these various gaps and by their effects on other variables relevant to the development objectives.

(1) First, there is the contribution to filling the resource gap between desired investment and locally mobilized savings.
(2) Second, there is the contribution to filling the foreign exchange or trade gap between foreign exchange requirements and foreign exchange earnings plus official net aid. While this gap is *ex post* always identical with the savings gap, requirements or targets for foreign exchange are not identical with those for savings if there is a structural balance-of-payments problem.
(3) Third, there is the contribution to filling the budgetary gap between target revenue and locally raised taxes.
(4) Fourth, there is the contribution to filling the management and skill gap by providing foreign management and training local managers and workers.

The analytical value of looking at the contribution in terms of one or more of these gaps is that the value to the economy may exceed the value accruing from a particular project. Gap analysis brings out the multiplier effect of the foreign contribution. If domestic resources are under-utilized because some crucial component is missing (e.g., foreign exchange or a particular kind of skill), the breaking of this bottleneck has a magnifying effect upon resource mobilization in the rest of the economy. Unless such externalities are properly allowed for in project appraisal, they will get left out.

In addition, the contribution of the MNE may be judged by the following criteria.

(5) Technology is very poorly developed in many developing countries. The MNE may either transfer foreign and often inappropriate technology or, by adaptation or new invention, generate a more appropriate technology. It is in the market for knowledge that some of the most interesting problems arise.

(6) Entrepreneurship is something different from a skill that can be taught and learned. The MNE may contribute to the growth of indigenous entrepreneurs by subcontracting to ancillary industries, repair shops, component makers, etc. It may be in its interest to stimulate such growth among its suppliers or buyers or those performing intermediate tasks between inputs and outputs of the firms.

(7) The MNE may, through its own actions, shift the balance of bargaining power in negotiating and renegotiating contracts. Most obviously, the balance of power will be quite different at the time before an investment is made and after money has been sunk. Less obviously, negotiation will itself improve the skills in negotiation and will contribute to the stock of useful knowledge for later negotiations.

(8) An important contribution often quoted is the ability of the MNE to establish contact with overseas banks, market outlets, sources of supply and other institutions, which would otherwise remain unknown to the indigenous firms.

Finally, there are the contributions to macro-economic policy objectives. Among these the following may be singled out.

(9) The MNE may make a contribution to creating jobs and thereby raising employment.

(10) It may improve a country's income terms of trade either by lowering costs more than export prices or by reducing dependence on foreign products.

(11) It may contribute to a more efficient market structure or reduce the type of monopoly profits that are enjoyed in the form of inefficiency and a quiet life.

A major difficulty in assessing these contributions is that far from being able to quantify precisely these effects, we do not even know, in general, their direction. MNEs provide capital, but also may reduce domestic savings (e.g., if saving is limited by investment opportunities and these themselves are limited, or if foreign investment leads to a shift to wages with a lower savings propensity) and impose capital servicing costs upon the host country. They may improve its foreign exchange position but equally may reduce foreign exchange earnings and may impose a primary and secondary foreign exchange burden, depending on the relation between retained profits and new investment on the one hand and remittances on the other.[7] They may contribute to public revenue, but frequently tax concessions, investment grants, the provision of factory sites and tariff policy erode this contribution. They may transfer and adapt technology, but it may be inappropriate for the available factors or social and physical conditions of the country, not just in some abstract, irrelevant sense but inappropriate in relation to the cost that the country has to pay for it. They may provide foreign management and train local managers, but, like engineering technology, the management techniques may be inappropriate, because they economize in the use of uneducated, diseased, ill-nourished and undisciplined labour, the employment of which would yield social but not equivalent private benefits. They may encourage local entrepreneurs, but again they may stifle the growth of indigenous entrepreneurship in weak and rudimentary markets. They may provide training in the skills of negotiation by producing managers and officials who put their experience to work in negotiating for their countries, but they may also reinforce the uneven initial balance of power.

They open up a society to world influences and thereby enable it to draw on resources and skills on a worldwide scale, but they also destroy local activities by exposing them to these influences. They may reduce unemployment or they may raise it by increasing wage costs and destroying traditional crafts. They may improve or worsen the terms of trade according to the direction of their activities and their foreign trade bias. They may make local industry more competitive or more monopolistic. Politically, they may introduce benefits by wider contacts, but may also create unrest and, by buying up politicians and officials who should be controlling them, spread corruption. Socially and culturally, they may increase inequalities between income groups, sectors and regions, may Westernize attitudes, on the one hand imposing a sophisticated, high-income, consumption pattern, on the other, possibly leading to high turnover, low-mark-up methods of business. They often use capital-intensive techniques to produce capital-intensive products for a small, relatively well-off élite, including the aristocracy of workers fortunate enough to hold jobs. On the other hand, they may identify processes or components in a set of vertically integrated operations which are labour-intensive and locate these in low-income countries, exporting the semi-finished products and then re-importing them to the parent country. They may bring traditional societies into the twentieth century or they may reduce them to 'dependence', imposing technical, managerial and cultural subservience on the host country.

Another theoretical difficulty in analysing the contribution to development of the MNE is the problem of attribution. The MNE may, in particular circumstances, do things that (a) are not essential attributes of the MNE but might be peculiar to particular individuals responsible for its affairs, or to the policies of host governments,[8] or to a specific locality or to history; or (b) could have been done equally well or better in other ways than through the MNE. Ideally one would wish to identify those features that are peculiar to *all* MNEs and *only* to MNEs. Both vices and virtues must be peculiar to the MNE, so that the vices must not be attributable to other factors and the virtues cannot be attained by other means.

Amongst the most common charges raised by developing host countries against the MNE are the following. Some of them raise the problem of attribution, especially to government policy. Some of them were mentioned as the reverse side of the positive effects but it is worth bringing them together.

(1) Its impact on development is very uneven and it therefore creates or reinforces dualism and inequality. This inequality may apply to income by size (employed workers *versus* the rest), by sector (manufacturing, mining, plantation versus food for domestic consumption) and by region (urban, industrial versus rural).

(2) It introduces inappropriate products, which are normally closely linked to the technology and inappropriate consumption patterns. This point is related to the previous one, for inequality of income distribution gives rise to a fragmented consumption pattern and to a small market for sophisticated consumer goods.[9] These are the goods produced by the sophisticated technology in the rich industrial countries for their high-income markets, in which the monopolistic advantage of the MNE lies.

(3) A consequence of the previous two points is that the *local* investment funds on which the MNE draws and which have an opportunity cost are wrongly allocated and not in accordance with the social priorities of the country.

(4) The MNE is also charged with influencing government policy in directions unfavourable to development. It may secure excessive

protection, tax concessions, subsidies to inputs or provision of factory sites or other services of infrastructure. As a result substantial private profits may be consistent with low or negative social returns.

(5) It is said to stifle private enterprise, because its superior know-how and management prevent indigenous entrepreneurs from initiating enterprises.

(6) Finally it is accused of causing political friction by the suspicion that foreign interests control assets and jobs.

The above approach of listing under various headings the merits and drawbacks of the MNE (which might be described as the laundry list approach) is common but unsatisfactory. What would be more satisfactory is an analytical framework in which these various possibilities are accommodated, possibly classified according to relevant criteria, and then filled with empirical, quantitative content.

In the first place, one would seek criteria by which the importance of the different headings can be distinguished. These might be found in the nature of the MNE's operations: are they conducting vertically-integrated activities, beginning with extraction and ending with the final processed product? Or are they market-oriented manufacturing subsidiaries drawing on the brand name or the research of the parent company? Distinctions by type of product or by type of process may be useful here.

Next, it is important to identify the causes leading to the various possible outcomes: are they government policies and, if so, are these themselves autonomous or exogenous variables, or are they the result of the firms' pressure, persuasion or bribery? Are they the result of the transfer of existing but inappropriate technologies? Are they the result of the use of bargaining power by large, well-informed companies confronting small, weak, ignorant, fragmented and competing governments?

3 RESEARCH ON MNEs

Much of the research on the MNE has been in the neo-classical tradition. Sir Donald MacDougall analysed foreign investment as a flow of additional capital into a country, while everything else is held constant. The static effects of marginal investments can be analysed according to marginal productivity theory.[10] This approach can then be enlarged by gradually relaxing the restrictive assumptions and tracing the implications of increasing returns, indivisibilities, imperfect competition, learning by doing, etc. Much of this was done by Sir Donald MacDougall. It is also possible to assume that the foreign firms shift or twist the production function in various ways with varying results on marginal returns, intra-marginal returns and the distribution of profits between domestic and foreign capitalists and workers. As restrictive assumptions are relaxed, the range of possible conclusions is enlarged and it is then quite possible to construct cases in which the introduction or enlargement of privately profitable foreign investment detracts from the host country's real income. MacDougall concluded that the most important direct gains from more rather than less foreign private investment 'seem likely to come through higher tax revenue from foreign profits (at least if the higher investment is not induced by lower tax rates), through economies of scale and through external economies generally, especially where . . . firms acquire 'know-how' or are forced by foreign competition to adopt more efficient methods.'[11]

Some of the limitations of this approach were pointed out by T. Balogh and P. P. Streeten,[12] although not with specific reference to developing countries. MacDougall himself had reasoned that the host country might lose if the foreign investment used strongly labour-saving techniques or if the foreign firms used their monopoly power to exploit local buyers.[13] These objections were elaborated by subsequent writers.

Most of the writings on the MNE had, of course, to abandon the assumption of perfect competition on which much of MacDougall's analysis was based. Charles P. Kindleberger, Richard E. Caves and Carlos Diaz-Alejandro[14] specifically build their analysis on the assumptions of imperfect competition, oligopoly with interdependence recognized or monopoly power.

Even in the case of developed countries, where markets are less imperfect, the widely observed fact of two-way investment in the same industry is inconsistent with the assumption of perfect competition. In developing countries competition is notoriously imperfect or absent in sectors and industries in which the MNE operates.

Awareness that oligopoly is in the nature of the MNE has led to an approach that has combined the theory of industrial organization as applied to the relations between oligopolies and the theory of international trade and investment.[15] This approach identifies a special advantage of the firm (economies of scale or superior knowledge or goodwill acquired by the use of a brand name) that enables it to produce abroad in spite of the inferiority of local knowledge and connections, combined with an advantage in producing near the place of sales or the source of supply. In this way the superiority of producing abroad over exporting from a home base or licensing the right to make use of the special advantage, are explained.

Tariffs and other protectionist devices, often cited as the main cause of the establishment of local subsidiaries, will tend to raise profits of the subsidiary but are neither a necessary nor a sufficient condition; not necessary, because even without protection the special advantage may be exploited; not sufficient, because where the special advantage is absent, no amount of protection will lead to the establishment of a subsidiary.[16] The exploration expenditure or the proprietary knowledge or the goodwill possessed by the firm is an indivisibility, so that its use abroad involves low costs to the firm, and it tries, through patents or advertising, to prevent others from appropriating this advantage. The local knowledge acquired in the process, also, is indivisible and this will tend to make for a few large firms carrying out investment and setting up an oligopolistic structure.

A related approach, without, however, the rigorous framework of a theory, has become known as the doctrine of the product cycle. This doctrine[17] has emphasized *monopolistic* elements in investment, *technological innovation* with special rights in new discoveries and *uncertainty* about costs, demand and rival behaviour. The new theory (or 'model' or 'concept' or 'hypothesis', as Raymond Vernon perfers to call it) also emphasizes the need for experiment and reconnaissance, the economies of scale to be reaped from research, marketing and management and the ability to routinize novel processes after a time. It is essentially a model of a succession of temporary monopolistic advantages, which are gradually eroded through diffusion and imitation. It is a model of a know-how treadmill.

According to this model, new products are first introduced by large firms with extensive research programmes in their established, wealthy domestic markets. Consumers' tastes are better known there, incomes are high and demand for the new product is price inelastic. If the product proves successful, output expands, costs per unit fall and the firm begins to export. In markets where exports are successful, they are backed at first by small foreign investments aimed at marketing and servicing the product. These are followed by assembly and local purchase of some components. If conditions are favourable or if exports are threatened by rivals, more processes are located abroad and foreign subsidiaries are established to make use of lower labour costs and proximity to the market. Ultimately, the product may be exported from the foreign subsidiary to the parent home market or to other markets abroad. This particular product cycle is closed, though new ones will meanwhile have started. On this view, exports serve as a feeler, a form of reconnaissance. They establish whether a market exists and whether it should be backed by investment. Diffusion may, however, take other forms than foreign investment. There may be licensing or imitation.

The model of the product cycle does not, however, account fully for a recent trend in foreign investment to which attention has now turned, namely the location in low-income countries of low-skill, labour-intensive processes or the production or assembly of components or spare parts in a vertically integrated multi-national firm. Above all in electronics and electrical components, but also in the making of gloves, leather goods, luggage, baseballs, watches, motor-car parts and other consumer goods, and in electrical machinery, machine tools, accounting machines, typewriters, cameras, etc., processes that require much labour and limited capital and skills (sewing, boring holes, assembling) have been located in South Korea, Taiwan, Mexico, Hong Kong, Singapore and the West Indian islands.[18]

In one sense, the doctrine of comparative advantage seems to be vindicated, though in a manner quite different from that normally envisaged. It is foreign, not domestic, capital, know-how and management that are highly mobile internationally and that are combined with plentiful, internationally immobile, domestic, semi-skilled labour. Specialization between countries is not by commodities according to relative factor endowments, but by factors of production: the poor countries specializing in low-skilled labour, leaving the rewards for capital, management and know-how to the foreign owners of these scarce but internationally mobile factors. The situation is equivalent to one in which *labour itself* rather than the *product of labour* is exported. For the surplus of the product of labour over the wage, resulting from the cooperation of other factors in less elastic supply, accrues abroad. The differential international and internal elasticities of supply in response to differential rewards and the differences in monopoly rents entering the rewards of these factors have important implications for the international distribution of gains from investment and trade.

Since the firms operate in oligopolistic and oligopsonistic markets, cost advantages are not necessarily passed on to consumers in lower prices or to workers in higher wages, and the profits then accrue to the parent firms. The continued operation of this type of international specialization depends on the continuation of substantial wage differentials (hence there must be weakness of trade union action to push up wages and a docile labour force, sometimes disciplined by forces less liberal than the trade policies), continuing access to the markets of the parent companies (hence stronger pressure from importing interests than from domestic producers displaced by the low-cost processes and components, including trade unions in the rich importing countries) and continuing permission or encouragement by host countries to operate with minimum taxes, tariffs, bureaucratic regulations and labour troubles.

The packaged nature of the contribution of the MNE, usually claimed as its characteristic blessing, is in this context the cause of the unequal international distribution of the gains from trade and investment. If the package broke or leaked, some of the rents and monopoly rewards would spill over into the host country. But if it is secured tightly, only the least scare and weakest factor in the host country derives an income from the operations of the MNE, unless bargaining power is used to extract a share of these other incomes.[19]

The situation is aggravated if there is technical progress, so that the labour-intensive activity in the underdeveloped host country might be knocked out by an innovation using capital or technology in the parent country. Other processes or components will still be left to which the labour force could be switched. But such switching has its costs. Skills acquired are wasted and the bargaining power of the host country and its labour force is further reduced, unless retraining is short and its costs are carried by the MNE.

The bargaining power of host countries and of the plentiful factor— semi-skilled labour—in such a situation is likely to be weak and the question is whether such a division of gains between parent and host, between the foreign investment 'package' and domestic labour, remains acceptable. The gains to the host country are confined to the wages of those employed if the alternative is unemployment. The fact that these earnings are in foreign exchange may put them at a premium. There may, in addition, be linkages, but these may be positive or negative. While such investment has attractions for some countries faced with labour surpluses and foreign exchange shortages and poorly endowed with natural resources, the potential gains may not be considered worth the social risks and social costs, including a form of dependence and dualistic development of a new kind, different from that of the colonial mines or plantations economy, but similar in its distributional impact.

4 TRANSFER PRICING

One important reason why the MNE does not fit easily into the theory of comparative advantage and its normative conclusions is the phenomenon of transfer pricing. A large and growing volume of international trade today is conducted within the firm—between affiliates, subsidiaries, branches located in different countries—and not between independent firms. It has been estimated that one-quarter to one-third of world trade in manufactures (and possibly more) is intra-firm trade and therefore not at arm's length. This proportion is likely to be even larger for LDCs. This fact has very important implications of which existing trade and investment theory has hardly begun to take note.

The reason why intra-firm trade raises entirely different issues from inter-firm trade is that the items entering such trade will be valued according to other considerations than those determining competitive market prices. The chief considerations relevant to the pricing of intra-firm transactions will be taxation (including allowances and loss-offset provisions), tariffs, exchange rates (expected changes, multiple rates, restrictions on remissions), political and social pressures (trade unions, fear of potential competitors, price controls related to costs, requests for protection) and joint ventures with local shareholders.[20] The phenomenon goes much deeper than 'fiddling' prices to evade tax payments. The allocation of the large overhead and joint costs (exploration, R & D or advertising), that give the MNE its special advantage, between firms, products and components is bound to be arbitrary within wide limits and a policy of maximizing global post-tax profits from the world wide system of operations of the firm will greatly reduce the significance of declared prices, capital values and rates of return for purposes of national policy.

It may, of course, remain true that the actual quantities traded will obey the principle of comparative advantage. Firms will presumably be guided by money costs, and, to the extent that these reflect comparative costs, the principle will remain applicable. Those looking for the appropriate competitive prices would find them in the hypothetical or real second set of books kept by the companies for their accounting purposes. Indeed, the theory of transfer pricing presupposes that the firm has some idea of what it would charge in a competitive market. Other forces, such as oligopolistic market structures, bilateral monopoly and subjective risk premia will, of course, qualify or suspend the application of the doctrine of comparative advantage, but the transfer pricing mechanism by itself need not interfere with it as far as quantities traded are concerned.

But this is of little use to ignorant and weak host governments with *national* horizons, concerned with framing policies with respect to taxation, tariffs, foreign exchange rates, foreign exchange restrictions and local participation in shareholding for companies taking a *global* view. Neither existing theory nor practice is equipped to deal with this new phenomenon and it presents an important agenda for future research.[21]

The implications for the theory of economic policy will become clearer only after considerably more work has been done on the range, scope and limits of transfer pricing. But it is plain that there are important implications for tax policy, tariff policy and setting other incentives for MNEs. The incentive and opportunity to overprice inputs in order to reduce declared profits can be mitigated, for example, by a state trading corporation trading in all imports or by local participation and control (though participation without control based on full information creates an incentive to over-invoice inputs and may lead, instead of to the nationalization of foreign interests, to the externalization of domestic). These corrective measures, however, may create new difficulties.

Ultimately, the only proper response to an organization that takes a global view will be global control. Thus, if companies had to be incorporated internationally and pay uniform internationally determined tax rates, one important incentive for transfer pricing would be removed. But until such denationalization and internationalization, national governments will have to find ways of counteracting some of the potential damage done to them by transfer pricing.

5 PROBLEMS OF BARGAINING

The oligopolistic structure and certain other features peculiar to the market for advanced technology limit the use of analysis in terms of smooth and continuous marginal productivity and demand functions and of project evaluation by means of shadow prices. The location of subsidiaries in developing countries normally draws on the R & D expenditure of the parent firm and on its technical know-how generally, or on exploration costs or on heavy advertising expenditure or on other overhead or joint costs. These expenditures precede and do not enter into the operating costs of the enterprise but they bestow a 'special advantage' on the enterprise. (Whether the advantage is real, because based on scientific knowledge, or imagined and 'artificial', because based on the exploitation of created fears and wants, is not relevant here, except in so far as the 'advantage' cannot be used to justify the activity.) The 'special advantage' of the MNE is an indivisibility of this type. Since the activities in low-income countries do not enter into the calculations when R & D expenditure (the Philips research center at Eindhoven is an exception), exploration costs or administrative costs are decided at headquarters, the cost of using the results of these expenditures in LDCs is small, not only *ex post*, when only variable costs count, but also *ex ante* in relation to expected returns. In the extreme case, this cost is zero or even negative. Normally, there will be positive costs of administration and adaptation. There may also be opportunity costs of using the technology in low-income countries. Operations there may reduce profits on established lines in other countries. Asking for favourable terms in one country may also set a precedent for quotations in other countries, where the opportunity costs may be higher.

On the other hand, such opportunity costs may be negative. Operation by the subsidiary may raise profits, or may prevent a fall in profits, elsewhere. The possibility of such 'organic' interaction makes the bargaining process even more difficult for the host country, for it implies that entirely properly calculated local profits may be low, yet be of greater value to the company than is reflected in these profits, because of their contribution to the profits, or to the reduction of losses, of the whole system of the company's worldwide operations. The use of bargaining power in this situation would require knowledge of the worldwide operations, including the threats from competitors, not just of those in the country. So much for the cost to the MNE.

To the host country desiring to acquire the technology (or any other of the 'special advantages'), on the other hand, the cost can be high. It is the cost of embarking itself on the research and independently evolving the know-how or of duplicating exploration. The existence of such large fixed and joint costs means that there is a large gap between the minimum "returns" a MNE will accept and still find it worthwhile investing, and the maximum 'returns' the enterprise can enjoy and make it still worthwhile for the host to permit operations. In principle, it would be possible to determine this range for different acts of investment both by different firms and for different sizes of investment and different contracts of the same firm.

This large gap between marginal and average costs of the technology is only one of several factors making for monopoly power. Another arises from the fact that knowledge to buy knowledge is often the knowledge to be bought itself and from the fact that tie-in agreements make it possible to make the transfer of technical knowledge conditional on the purchase of certain pieces of equipment or other inputs. In these ways the MNE can extract a yield substantially above the marginal costs incurred by the transfer.[22] The only mitigating factor is the competition between several oligopolies in possession of competing know-how.

One source of monopoly power of the MNE therefore derives from the technological dependence of the developing host country. Not only knowledge is power: know-how is power. But there is a second quite distinct source, which also leads to a divergence between private profits and social benefits and establishes a range within which bargaining can take place. The source is the policy pursued by the government of the host country. Tariffs and non-tariff barriers on competing imports, taxes on the exports of necessary inputs, subsidies to inputs, overvaluation of exchange rates and tax concessions can lead to social losses. If imported inputs are overvalued, costs overstated and profits understated, an appearance of greater need for protection is created than is warranted.[23] While apparently no or low real profits are repatriated, repatriation takes place through transfer pricing or charges such as management fees, royalties or interest which accrue to the parent firm. The point is well made by Carlos F. Diaz-Alejandro: 'If foreign investors can borrow from host country's credit resources at interest rates which are often negative in real terms, make profits sheltered behind effective rates of protection which reach 100 per cent and above, benefit from holidays and exemptions from import duties on their raw materials, and remit profits abroad at overvalued exchange rates, there may be doubts as to the net benefits which the host country receives from such an activity.'[24]

It is often argued that governments have the remedy in their own hands. Let them reduce protection, liberalize trade, establish 'realistic' exchange rates, raise the price of capital, lower the cost of labour and thus align private costs to social costs. There is some evidence that, where the incentives are right (e.g. the relative price of capital is high), the MNE *does* adapt its techniques of production to local factor availabilities, using more capital-saving methods of production than domestic enterprises.[25] But assuming the government believes that the investment is useful for the country, it is often the MNE that uses pressure on the government to introduce the 'distortions'. Ignorance about the value of the technology and the accounting methods induce the country to accept the terms of the MNE.

Policies themselves are influenced by the MNEs, both when negotiations are conducted about their establishment and, later, by their operations. The link between unequal distribution of income and wealth and the tendency of the MNE to cater for the needs of a relatively rich élite illustrates the point. While it is true that the MNE caters for the needs of an unequal income distribution, the profits and wages it generates reinforce this distribution. The more sophisticated the product, the greater the oligopoly advantage, the higher the quasi-rents. Simple, mass-produced goods are too easy to imitate. It is just as true to say that the income distribution elicits the product range and the processes employed by the MNE, as it is to say that product range and the processes reinforce the income distribution.[26]

Similarly, protection is often treated as if it were autonomously determined by government policy. In fact, governments yield to the pressures of foreign companies and associated domestic interest groups. This is not to say that foreign companies welcome the complicated system of import controls, delays, red tape and corruption. But such a system is partly the result of the pressures of interest groups, including those of foreign companies.

I have argued that continous, smooth, marginal productivity curves are inappropriate in analysing the relations between host government and MNE. For the transfer of a certain 'package' of know-how, capital, management and inputs there is a range of values which would be acceptable to both sides but which both sides have an interest in concealing. The ability to conceal the relevant values is however much greater for the MNE than for the host country.

In settling the bargain and in drawing up the contract, a large number of items may be for negotiation, in addition to income and sales tax concessions and tariff and non-tariff protection of the product.[27] Among these are:

(a) specific allowances against tax liabilities, such as initial or investment allowances, depletion allowances, tax reporting techniques, loss offset provisions, etc.;
(b) royalty payments, management fees and other fees;
(c) duty drawbacks on imported inputs for exports;
(d) content of local inputs;
(e) profit and capital repatriation;
(f) structure of ownership and degree and timing of local participation;
(g) local participation in management at board level;
(h) obligations to train local labour;
(i) transfer pricing;
(j) rules and requirements relating to exporting,
(k) degree of competition and forms of competition; price control and price fixing;
(l) credit policies (e.g. subsidized interest rates);
(m) extent of capitalization of intangibles;
(n) revalorization of assets due to currency devaluation;
(o) subsidies, e.g., to energy, rent, transport; or export expenses such as insurance, freight, promotion;
(p) place and party of jurisdiction and arbitration;
(q) time and right of termination or renegotiation.

A contract between the MNE and the host government will contain provisions under some of these headings.[28] Such possible contracts can be ranked in an order of preference by the MNE and by the government. If both the MNE and the government prefer a certain contract to another, the latter can be eliminated. The only complication here is that either party has an interest in concealing the fact that its interest coincides with that of the other party. For by appearing to make a concession, when in fact no concession is made, it may be spared having to make a concession on another front where interests conflict.

But leaving this complication aside, amongst the contracts that remain when those dominated by others have been eliminated, the order of preference for the MNE will be the reverse of that for the government. If the least attractive contract from the point of view of the MNE is outside the range of contracts acceptable to the government, no contract will be concluded. But if there is some overlap, there is scope for bargaining. The precise contract on which the two partners will settle will be determined by relative bargaining strength.

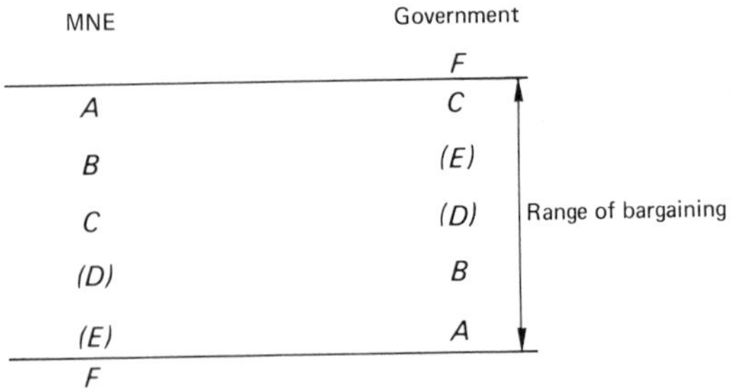

MNE	Government	
	F	
A	*C*	
B	*(E)*	
C	*(D)*	Range of bargaining
(D)	*B*	
(E)	*A*	
F		

FIGURE 14.1   Ranking of contracts in order of preference

E and *D* are ruled out because both the MNE and the government prefer *C*; *F* is ruled out because it is unacceptable to the MNE.

At the same time, in determining the relative value of the different contracts, the host government will find cost–benefit analysis useful. By comparing the present value of the stream of benefits with that of the costs the disparate components in the bargain can, at least in principle, be made commensurable. Cost–benefit analysis and bargaining-power analysis are not alternative methods of approach but are complementary. Cost–benefit analysis will not tell a government whether a particular project is acceptable or not, i.e., whether it falls within the acceptable bargaining range, but it will help it to rank those that are acceptable.

It has sometimes been argued that host countries are well advised to accept any project and contract that shows a rate of "return"[29] to the foreign firm lower than the maximum that the country would find acceptable.(In terms of the figure: the government should accept *A*.) But this is clearly one-sided pleading. Vaitsos has compared this with advice given to workers to settle for a subsistence wage. It could equally well be said that the foreign company should be content with any returns higher than the minimum acceptable to it (i.e., *C*).

A particular form of this argument is the often repeated attack on those who compare the inflow of new investment and retained profits with the profits remitted abroad and use the difference as an index of the gain to the host country. The attack usually takes the form that the effects of the foreign investment on real incomes in the economy and on exports and import substitution must be taken into account. The fault of this argument is that it neglects to compare the impact of the foreign investment with the best feasible alternative, such as domestic investment or borrowing and hiring the necessary factors. If the social opportunity costs of foreign investment were to include the benefits to be derived from the forgone next best alternative , there would, for any specific project, be only one way of doing it that shows positive returns. The maximum returns forgone by choosing the foreign investment project must appear as a cost of this project. The appropriate shadow price is the benefit lost as a result of not adopting the best of the alternative projects rejected.

In cases where good, other foreign, non-foreign or less-foreign feasible alternatives exist, the analysis should compare profit outflows with the opportunity cost of providing the same package from alternative sources. Only in cases where no alternative exists is the analysis that takes full credit for the foreign investment for all its indirect effects correct.[30]

The main forces determining where within this bargaining range a settlement is made are information, skill in negotiation and competition from other countries that have similar attractions for the MNE, and from other firms wishing to enter a particular country. Information about some important aspects of cost and price determination is secret. Information about other aspects is hard to get. The market price of some imported component produced by the vertically integrated firm and not normally bought and sold is not easy to verify. As Vaitsos puts it, "there is no price for Volkswagen doors." Such transactions are essentially different from market transactions.

Another aspect of bargaining power arises from the threat that the firm will go to some other developing country if the terms of the contract are too hard. This raises the possibility of joint action by several LDCs, such as that displayed by OPEC. Such agreements suffer from the drawbacks of all cartel agreements: they face the prisoners' dilemma. The more successful the ring, the stronger the incentive for any member to break away and to underbid the ring. On the other hand, if others were to break away, the losses to those who adhere might be greater than if they had never joined an agreement. The situation is therefore highly unstable unless solidarity is strong or effective deterrents are applied. Cartel-like agreements on taxation also encourage the search for substitutes that reduce dependence on the host country.

There is almost universal evidence that foreign investors say that tax concessions and pioneer status play no or only an insignificant part in bringing them to the country.[31] This is entirely consistent with the rejection of a continuously downward-sloping marginal revenue function and the presence of a vertical range of outcomes (a substantial element of rent or quasi-rent), all acceptable to the firm, which would induce the specific investment.

Since there are possibilities of trade-off between various items on the list on p. 283, a proper evaluation would have to consider the whole set of conditions. Thus it might be possible to recoup some of the taxes lost by an understatement of profits resulting from transfer pricing by putting a tariff on intermediate inputs or capital goods. Or, for the firm, the removal of protection may be compensated for by the provision of public services such as transport, power or training.

From the point of view of the host country, it is important to evolve a strategy that maximizes the impact on domestic policy objectives subject to not deterring the company, assuming that at least one contract has positive benefits. There may be a number of items on which negotiation will benefit both sides. There will be others, where changes in conditions will alter the types of MNEs attracted but not the total of foreign investment.

A specific choice arises as to whether to make *markets* more attractive by tariff and non-tariff barriers against competing products or whether to improve *resources* and *inputs* by providing better physical and social overhead facilities. The firms attracted will be those catering for import substitutes for the domestic market in the first case and those producing exports and re-exports in the second.

The second strategy of making resources and inputs more attractive implies:

(1) fewer controls and greater administrative efficiency;
(2) greater security and less political uncertainty;
(3) more investment in education, training, transport facilities and utilities.

6 PECULIARITIES IN THE TRANSFER OF TECHNOLOGY

If, then, the specific contribution of the MNE is technological knowledge and if this knowledge bestows bargaining power, why has competition in the market not eroded this power? Why has the market system not provided incentives for the appropriate direction and utilization of science and technology? Though underdeveloped countries are poor, they are potentially large and growing markets. Why have there been so few inventions of low-cost, simple, agricultural or industrial machinery? Why has there not been more progress in low-cost construction or transport? Why do those industrial countries that have a comparative advantage in manufacturing industry protect, often at high cost to themselves, their agriculture, instead of exchanging low-cost machinery and durable consumer goods (say a £10 refrigerator) for the agricultural exports of underdeveloped countries? Henry Ford announced in 1909 that his aim was to produce and sell a cheap, reliable model "for the great multitude" so that every man "making a good salary" could "enjoy with his family the blessing of hours of pleasure in God's great open space". The mass production of the Model T Ford ushered in a major industrial and social revolution, the products of which have, incidentally, destroyed the "great open space". Why has no one initiated a corresponding revolution to raise and tap the purchasing power of the world's teeming millions? Insufficient foresight in the face of still small markets (small in terms of purchasing power) and overestimating of risks or a divergence between private (including political) and social risks may be part of the explanation. Another part follows from the concept of the product cycle. The multinational enterprise is aware of its vulnerability. Concentration on sophisticated, high-income, high-technology products rather than simpler products is the result of wishing to maintain its monopoly advantages in technology. Simplicity is easier to imitate than complexity and the profits of the MNE derive from maintaining superiority in technology.

It is easier to see why the market in complex, specialized, often secret or patented, modern technology is different from the market for turnips or even for land. Technical and managerial knowledge and its commercial and industrial application cannot readily be assimilated to the treatment of the conventional factors of production: land, labour, and capital, for at least five reasons.

In the first place, knowledge, although clearly not available in superabundance, is not scarce in the sense that the more we use of it in one direction, the less is left over for use in another, or the more I use it, the less is left for you. The stock of knowledge is like an indivisible investment and average costs diverge widely from marginal costs. The result of this is that it is much cheaper for the MNE to use what it already has—the existing but "inappropriate" technology developed in high-income, labour-scarce countries—than to spend money on developing a new technology, more appropriate for the conditions of the developing countries, particularly if quasi-rents on the latter are more quickly eroded.

Second, there is the well-known difficulty of appropriating the fruits of efforts devoted to increasing knowledge and the need either to treat it as a public good or to erect legal barriers to appropriation by others, in order to create and maintain incentives for research and invention. This leads to the divergence of social from private benefits and costs.

Third, knowledge is, in a sense, substitutable for other productive factors, so that an improvement in technical knowledge makes it possible to produce the same product with less land, labour or capital, or with more capital but a more than proportionate decrease of labour or land, or a better product with the same amount of other factors. But its costs fall. under those of either labour (especially trained employees) or capital (purchase of patents or research laboratories or equipment or intermediate products or other assets embodying the knowledge). As a result, the market for knowledge is normally part of the market for these inputs. If the owners of the inputs that embody knowledge command monopoly power, they can exercise this power over the sale of the knowledge component of the whole package.

Fourth, the accumulation of knowledge is only tenuously related to expenditure on its acquisition. Indeed, useful knowledge can be accumulated without any identifiable allocation of resources for this purpose and, conversely and more obviously, large resources can be devoted to research without any productive results. There is, in the nature of discovery, uncertainty about the outcome of efforts devoted to inventions. This uncertainty cannot be removed by insurance, for insurance would also remove the incentive for research. A common way of reducing it is through diversification of research activities. Only large corporations are capable of this. In a private enterprise system the large MNE has an enormous advantage in reducing the risks attached to research.[32]

A fifth and even more fundamental difference lies in the absence of the justification of the common assumption about the 'informed' buyer. Where technology is bought and sold, as it often is, through the purchase of an asset (or through admitting direct private foreign investment), the underdeveloped recipient country as 'buyer' of the technology is, in the nature of things, very imperfectly informed about many features of the product that it buys. The common assumption about an informed buyer choosing what suits him best is even less justified here than is usual. In some cases, if the country knew precisely what it was buying, there would be no need – or considerably less need – to buy it. Knowledge about knowledge is often the knowledge itself.[33] Part of what it buys is the information on which an informed purchase would be based. As a result, the recipient government will be in a weak position vis-à-vis the investing firm when it comes to laying down terms and conditions. Excessive 'prices' paid by recipient governments for capital equipment or imported components and technologies inappropriate from the country's point of view, or acceptance of excessively onerous conditions, must therefore be the rule rather than the exception in a market where information embodied in equipment is bought by ignorant buyers.

The five features characteristic of the market for technical knowledge— (i) indivisibility, (ii) inappropriability, (iii) embodiment in other factors, (iv) uncertainty and (v) impossibility to know the value until the purchase is made—go some way towards explaining the absence of a free market in which the low-income countries could buy knowledge.

The situation is quite different from that of an 'equilibrium price' reached in a competitive market. It is more like that of a bilateral monopoly or oligopoly where bargaining theory applies. There is a gap between the incremental cost of the owner of the technology of parting with it and the value to the country or firm wishing to acquire it. The cost to the seller is either zero, since the investment has already taken place, or the small amount required to adapt it to the circumstances of the developing country. The value to the buyer is the large amount that he would have to spend to start inventing and developing from scratch and to 'go it alone'. The final figure in the range between these two limits is determined by bargaining strength, which is unequally distributed.

International inequality and internal inequality in the poor countries reinforce one another. Unequal income distribution is both effect and cause of inappropriate technologies and products. It is an effect because capital-intensive methods and products raise the share of profits and of rewards for skills and reduce that of unskilled labour; and markets for sophisticated, differentiated products require a small élite with high income. And it is a cause, because the existence of a market for differentiated luxuries deprives enterprises of any incentive to produce for a mass market of low-cost, more appropriate products.[34] Henry Ford had the advantage not only of imagination but also of relatively high real wages.

7 REGIONAL INTEGRATION AND THE MNE

Many developing countries are eager to promote regional integration and one of the questions they ask is what contribution the MNE can make to this. According to traditional theory, tariff reductions between a group of countries which maintain a common external tariff afford higher protection to investment within the protected area. The export opportunities of foreign firms to the region are reduced and therefore, if they wish to continue selling, their incentive to invest in the region is raised. We have seen that such tariff protection is neither a sufficient nor a necessary condition for the establishment of local subsidiaries by the MNE. It is not sufficient because, without the special advantage over indigenous enterprises discussed on p. 276, investment cannot take place; and it is not necessary because with that advantage investment may take place even without tariff protection, though protection may lead to the establishment of a local subsidiary instead of exports to the country. But given the necessary and sufficient conditions, regional protection will raise the returns and strengthen the incentive to invest.

This incentive is further reinforced if, as a result of tariff reductions, the market is enlarged or its rate of growth accelerated, and if some firms, wishing to maintain market shares, fear that unless they invest others will anticipate them, or if some firms see themselves forced to follow those that have gone ahead, in order to maintain their shares of the market.

It is, of course, true that such regional arrangements will tend to reduce profits and hence investment incentives for industries which are now prevented from purchasing lower-cost outside supplies required for their inputs and those hampered in selling to outside markets.

In addition, the risks of investment inside the region will be reduced and hence the incentive to invest strengthened. If each nation pursues its own commercial and monetary policy, markets may be suddenly cut off or precipitously reduced as a result of import or foreign exchange restrictions, exchange rate changes or other measures. Regional integration provides a degree of security of selling within the region, which will stimulate investment by the MNE. At the same time, the risks of trading with and investing in other regions many be raised.

Against these forces must be set the fact that real wages will tend to be raised as a result of integration. To that extent, the incentive to invest that resulted from low wage costs is reduced. While integration will tend to lead to greater efficiency, stronger competition and economies of scale, these same forces will tend to raise labour costs and to that extent reduce the otherwise stronger incentive of the MNE to operate.

Here again, the question of the distribution of the gains from integration arises: distribution between the MNE and integrated countries as a group, and distribution between different participating countries. In oligopolistic conditions, there are no forces making automatically for lower prices of products or higher rewards to indigenous factors. If the gains are wholly absorbed by higher profits, whether open or concealed, the host countries, which created the opportunities for these gains, will not find the arrangement acceptable. But even if the countries as a group benefit, difficult problems of the distribution of these gains between the more advanced countries, which will attract the firms, and the less advanced, will have to be resolved.

In analysing the effects upon the MNE, it is important to distinguish between the incentives of a larger and securer market and those of a more rapidly growing market. The former enables investing firms to exploit economies of scale and to set up larger plants; the latter makes for the more rapid introduction of up-to-date equipment, incorporating the latest technical knowledge. Both make for unit cost reductions, but the reasons are different in the two cases.

An important difference between regional integration between advanced industrial countries and that between developing countries is the emphasis on improved *trade* patterns for the former, and on improved *investment* planning for the latter. Obviously, both trade and investment are important for both groups of countries, and equally obviously there are causal links between international trade and investment. But when developing countries seek closer regional integration, trade between them is initially relatively small and, more important, it is neither always desirable nor politically feasible to permit the mechanism of 'trade creation' to work, according to which the established high-cost industries in the region have to contract or die to make room for lower-cost industries in normally already more industrialized member countries. Resources are not as shiftable as this doctrine supposes. Moreover, countries joining a union are not concerned with maximizing intra-union production, but, at the cost of some union inefficiency, in securing for themselves some of the new industries, jobs and accompanying technology that cater for the whole market. The criterion of comparative advantage may be politically unacceptable where the location of new firms is concerned just as much as in guiding trade from existing firms.

Another important difference between regional integration among advanced countries and developing countries is that in the former case the domestic economies are already integrated. Economic opportunities are open to all, factors of production are relatively mobile, agents respond to incentives and income differentials are not too large. This is not true of most developing countries. The domestic economies of these countries are 'dualistic'. A modern sector confronts a traditional one. While it is impossible to draw a sharp line between the two and while movements and transactions between them take place, they are not as fully integrated as the market in a rich economy. If such dualistic economies pursue regional integration with reliance on the MNE, there is a danger that only the small, modern sectors of the joining countries are integrated, while the rest remains in isolated poverty. One cannot rely on the automatic effects of market forces to spread the benefits widely. It is therefore important to bear in mind the need to promote measures of greater *national* integration, side by side with a move towards *regional* integration, if the dualistic division is not to be aggravated by the operations of MNEs.

NOTES

1. Reprinted from *World Development*, vol. 1, no. 10 (October 1973). I am grateful to G. Helleiner, S. Lall, M. Sharpston and Frances Stewart for comments on an earlier draft. This article forms a chapter in a book, ed. Professor John H. Dunning, entitled *Economic Analysis and the Multinational Enterprise*, Allen & Unwin (1974). Acknowledgement is made to the editor and publisher for giving permission to reprint.
2. Nurkse (1953).
3. Cameron (1967), Deane (1961), Deane and Cole (1962), Deane (1965).
4. Cf. Baer and Hervé (1966), Bruton (1965), Islam (1967), Kabaj (1969), Lewis and Soligo (1965), Meier (1969), National Council of Applied Economic Research, New Delhi (1966), Power (1963 and 1966), Schydlowsky (1971), Steel (1971), Thomas (1966), United States Department of Commerce (1968), Williamson (1969), Winston (1968, 1970 and 1971d).
5. Lewis (1965).
6. Behrman (1969).
7. See p. 285.
8. For the problem as to what consequences are to be attributed to government policy and which to the MNE, see p. 282.
9. See pp. 281 and 288.
10. MacDougall (1960).
11. MacDougall (1960), p. 210. MacDougall wrote with special reference to Australia and assumed, *inter alia*, perfect competition.
12. Balogh and Streeten (1960).
13. MacDougall (1960), pp. 199 and 203.
14. Kindleberger (1969), Caves (1971b), Diaz-Alejandro (1971).
15. Caves (1971).
16. See p. 290.
17. Among the contributors to this discussion are Hirsch (1967), Hufbauer (1965), Posner (1961), Linder (1961), Vernon (1966 and 1971) and Wells (1969).
18. Helleiner (1973).
19. Pazos (1967) writes: 'The main weakness of direct investment as a development agent is the consequence of the complete character of its contribution' (p. 196). Cf. also Hirschman (1969). But Pazos and Hirschman emphasize the detrimental effect on the growth of indigenous factors, whereas the question treated here is the distribution of gains. See Ch. 16.

20. The argument is developed and documented in an interesting paper by Lall, (1973) and by Vaitsos, mimeo (1970; 1972).
21. The literature on this subject is still somewhat thin. The main work has been done by Vaitsos, mimeo (1970a and 1972), Vernon (1971) and UNCTAD (1972). C. Tugendhat discusses the problem (1971) and refers to a Ph.D thesis by J. Shulman. The firms have defended their policies in J. Greene and M. Duerr (1968). The US tax authorities have done a good deal of work on the subject.
22. See below, p. 289.
23. But understatement of profits will not normally occur if the country grants generous tax concessions or if there are double taxation agreements, making the difference between the tax rates small compared with the tariff rate. Although higher tax rates than in other countries are not the only reason for underdeclaration of profits, they, together with the desire to remit profits in the face of foreign exchange restrictions, are among the most important ones.
24. Diaz-Alejandro (1971).
25. See Pack (1972). For inconclusive evidence, see Mason (1973) and Cohen (1973).
26. Stewart (1973).
27. See Constantine Vaitsos (1974).
28. The treatment of the government as the guardian of the interests of the whole nation is, however, misleading. See Streeten (1971). A third force in the bargain may be the government of the parent company.
29. 'Returns' are in quotation marks because they do not refer to the irrelevant ratio of declared profits to arbitrarily valued capital, but to the whole range of benefits over costs, some of which cannot readily be quantified.
30. As we have seen in the discussion of attribution, just as certain faults have to be attributed to government policies rather than the MNE, so certain virtues may be the result of combining capital, management and know-how but not necessarily through the MNE. A host country has to ask itself the following questions: (i) is the MNE wanted at all? (ii) if so, should the particular product that it produces be available? (iii) if so, should it be imported or produced at home? (iv) if produced at home, how is the package most effectively assembled? (v) if through a MNE, how can the best bargain be struck?
31. Hughes and Seng (1969) and UNCTAD Study (1969). There are several reasons for this, e.g., firms tend to regard special incentives as liable to be soon removed.
32. Cf. Arrow (1962).
33. Vaitsos (1970b). Arrow (1962) writes:' . . . there is a fundamental paradox in the determination of demand for information: its value for the purchaser is not known until he has the information, but then he has in effect acquired it without cost.'
34. Stewart (1973).

REFERENCES

Arrow, K. J. (1962), 'Economic Welfare and the Allocation of Resources to Invention', in *The Rate and Direction of Inventive Activity: Economic and Social Factors*, National Bureau of Economic Research,

Princeton University Press, pp. 609–26, reprinted in D. M. Lamberton (ed.), *Economics of Information and Knowledge*, Penguin Modern Economics Readings.

Baer, W. and Hervé, M. (1966), 'Employment and Industrialization in Developing Countries', *Quarterly Journal of Economics*, vol. 8, no. 1 (February), pp. 88–107.

Balogh, T. and Streeten, P. P. (1960), 'Domestic versus Foreign Investment', *Bulletin of the Oxford University Institute of Statistics*, vol. 22, no. 3 (August), pp. 213–24.

Behrman, J. N. (1960), 'Promoting Free World Economic Development through Direct Investment', *American Economic Review*, Papers and Proceedings, vol. 50, no. 2 (May), pp. 271–81.

Bruton, H. J. (1965), 'On the Role of Import Substitution in Development Planning', *Philippine Economic Journal*, 1st Semester.

Cameron, R. (1967), 'Some Lessons of History for Developing Nations', *American Economic Review*, Papers and Proceedings, vol. 57, no. 2 (May), p. 313.

Caves, R. E. (1971a), 'International Corporations: the Industrial Economics of Foreign Investment', *Economica*, vol. 38, no. 149 (February), pp. 1–27.

—— (1971b), 'Industrial Economics of Foreign Investment: the Case of the International Corporation', *Journal of World Trade Law*, vol. 5, no. 3 (May–June), pp. 303–14.

Cohen, B. I. (1973), 'Comparative Behavior of Foreign and Domestic Export Firms in a Developing Economy', *Review of Economics and Statistics*, vol. 55, no. 2 (May), pp. 190–7.

Deane, P. (1961), 'Capital Formation in Britain before the Railway Age', *Economic Development and Cultural Change*, vol. 9, no. 3 (April), pp. 352–68.

—— (1965), *The First Industrial Revolution*, Cambridge University Press, Cambridge.

—— and Cole, W. A. (1962), *British Economic Growth, 1688–1959: Trends and Structure*, Cambridge University Press, Cambridge.

Diaz-Alejandro, Carlos (1971), 'The Future of Direct Foreign Investment in Latin America', Yale Economic Growth Center Discussion Paper, no. 131.

Greene, J. and Duerr, M. G. (1968), *Intercompany Transfers in Multinational Firms*, The Conference Board, New York.

Helleiner, Gerald K. (1973), 'Manufactured Exports from Less Developed Countries and Multinational Firms', *Economic Journal*, vol. 83, no. 329 (March), pp. 21–47.

Hirsch, S. (1967), *Location of Industry and International Competitiveness*, Oxford University Press, London.

Hirschman, A. O. (1969), *How to Divest in Latin America and Why*, Princeton Essays in International Finance, no. 76.

Hufbauer, G. C. (1965), *Synthetic Materials and the Theory of International Trade*, Duckworth, London.

Hughes, H. and Seng, Y. P. (1969), *Foreign Investment and Industrialization in Singapore*, USA, p. 183.

Islam, N. (1967), 'Comparative Costs, Factor Proportions, and Industrial Efficiency in Pakistan', *Pakistan Development Review*, vol. 7, no. 2 (summer), pp. 213–46.

Kabaj, M. (1969), 'Problems of Shift Work as a Means of Improving Capacity Utilization', United Nations Industrial Development Organization, Vienna.

Kindleberger, C. P. (1969), *American Business Abroad*, Yale University Press, New Haven.

—— (ed.) (1970), *The International Corporation*, MIT Press, Cambridge, Mass.

Lall, S. (1973), 'Transfer- Pricing by Multinational Manufacturing Firms', *Oxford Bulletin of Economics and Statistics*, 35: 3, 6.

Lewis, S. and Soligo, R. (1965), 'Growth and Structural Change in Pakistan Manufacturing Industry, 1954 to 1964', *Pakistan Development Review*, vol. 5, no. 1 (spring), pp. 94–139.

Lewis, W. Arthur (1965), 'A Review of Economic Development', The Richard T. Ely Lecture, *American Economic Review*, Papers and Proceedings, vol. 55, no. 2 (May), pp. 1–16.

MacDougall, G. D. A. (1960), 'The Benefits and Costs of Private Investment from Abroad: a Theoretical Approach', *Bulletin of the Oxford University Institute of Statistics*, vol. 22, no. 3 (August), pp. 189–211 reprinted in R. E. Caves and H. G. Johnson (eds), *Readings in International Economics*, George Allen & Unwin, London, Ch. 10, pp. 172–94.

Mason, R. H. (1973), 'Some Observations on the Choice of Technology by Multinational Firms in Developing Countries', *Review of Economics and Statistics*, vol. 55, no. 3 (August), pp. 349–55.

Meier, G. (1969), 'Development without Employment', *Banca Nazionale del Lavoro Quarterly Review*, vol. 22, no. 90 (September), pp. 309–19.

Linder, S. B. (1961), *An Essay on Trade and Transformation*, Almqvist & Wiksell, Stockholm.

National Council of Applied Economic Research (1966), *Underutilisation of Industrial Capacity, 1955–64*, New Delhi.

Nurkse, R. (1953), *Problems of Capital Formation in Underdeveloped Countries*, Blackwell, Oxford.

Pack, H. (1972), 'Employment in Kenyan Manufacturing', mimeo.

Pazos, F. (1967), 'The Role of International Movements of Private Capital in Promoting Development', in J. H. Adler (ed.), *Capital Movements and Economic Development*, Macmillan, London.

Posner, M. V. (1961), 'International Trade and Technical Change', *Oxford Economic Papers*, vol. 13, no. 3 (October), pp. 323–41.

Power, J. H. (1963), 'Industrialization in Pakistan: a case of Frustrated Take-off?', *Pakistan Development Review*, vol. 3, no. 2 (summer), pp. 191–207.

——(1966), 'Import Substitution as an Industrialisation Strategy', *Philippine Economic Journal*, 2nd semester.

Schydlowsky, D. (1971), 'Fiscal Policy for Full Capacity Industrial Growth in Latin America', Development Advisory Service, Centre for International Relations, Harvard University, Economic Development Report, no. 201 (fall). Published in *Fiscal Policy for Industrialization and Development in Latin America*, ch. 10, ed. by David T. Geithman.

Steel, W. (1971), 'Import Substitution and Excess Capacity in Ghana', Development Advisory Service, Centre for International Relations, Harvard University, Economic Development Report, no. 198 (October).

Stewart, F. (1973), 'Trade and Technology', in P. P. Streeten (ed.), *Trade Strategies for Development*, Macmillan, London.

Streeten, P. P. (1971), 'Costs and Benefits of Multinational Enterprises in Less Developed Countries', in John H. Dunning (ed.), *The Multinational Enterprise*, Macmillan, London, reprinted in *Frontiers of Development Studies*.

Thomas, P. (1966), 'Import Licensing and Import Liberalization in Pakistan', *Pakistan Development Review*, vol. 6, no. 4 (winter), pp. 500–44.

Tugendhat, C. (1971), *The Multinationals*, Eyre & Spottiswoode, London.

UNCTAD (1969), Queen Elizabeth House Study on Private Foreign Investment.

——(1972), *Policies Relating to Technology in the Countries of the Andean Pact: Their Foundations*, Santiago, TD/107.

US Department of Commerce (May 1966, April 1968), *Overseas Business Reports*.

Vaitsos, C. V. (1970a), 'Transfer of Resources and Preservation of Monopoly Rents', Harvard Development Advisory Service, mimeo.

——(1970b), 'Bargaining and the Distribution of Returns in the Purchase of

Technology by Developing Countries', *Bulletin of the Institute of Development Studies*, vol. 3, no. 1 (October), pp. 16–23.

—— (1972), 'Inter-Country Income Distribution and Transnational Corporations', mimeo.

—— (1974), 'Income Distribution, Welfare Considerations and Transnational Enterprises', in John H. Dunning (ed.), *Economic Analysis and the Multinational Enterprise*, Allen & Unwin, London.

Vernon, R. (1966), 'International Investment and International Trade in the Product Cycle', *Quarterly Journal of Economics*, vol. 80, no. 2 (May), pp. 190–207.

—— (1971), *Sovereignty at Bay: The Multinational Spread of US Enterprise*, Longman, London (and further references on pp. 290–7).

Wells, Jr, L. T. (1969), 'Test of a Product Cycle Model of International Trade: US Exports of Consumer Durables', *Quarterly Journal of Economics*, vol. 83, no. 1 (February), pp. 152–62.

Williamson, J. (1969), 'Capital Accumulation, Labour-Saving and Labour-Absorption: a New Look at Some Contemporary Asian Experience', SSRI Workshop Series EDIE 6932, University of Wisconsin.

Winston, G. C. (1968), *Excess Capacity in Underdeveloped Countries: The Pakistan Case*, Centre for Development Economics, Williams College.

—— (1970), 'Overinvoicing, Underutilisation, and Distorted Industrial Growth', *Pakistan Development Review*, vol. 10, no. 4 (winter), pp. 405–21.

—— (1971a), 'The Four Reasons for Idle Capital', Oxford, mimeo.

—— (1971b), 'Capital Utilisation in Economic Development', *Economic Journal*, vol. 81, no. 321 (March), pp. 36–60.

—— (1971c), 'Capital Utilisation and Development: Physiological Costs and Preferences for Shift Work', Centre for Development Economics, Williams College (February), mimeo.

—— (1971d), 'A Comparison of Capital Utilisation in Pakistan and the United States', Karachi (February), mimeo.

15 Bargaining with Multi-Nationals[1]

It is not uncommon in the literature on private foreign investment to assume a downward-sloping marginal productivity of investment curve, relating different amounts of investment by the multinational company (MNC) to expected rates of return (Fig. 15.1). It then follows that any action by the host government that reduces the expected rate of return is bound to lead to reduced investment. The host government will have to balance, at the margin, more or less foreign investment (*OA* against *OB*) against less or more tax receipts or other benefits to it that reduce the attractions to the foreign investor (e.g. the use of higher-cost inputs such as local materials, or restrictions on repatriation of profits). This model has dominated thought and, to some extent, action in this area.

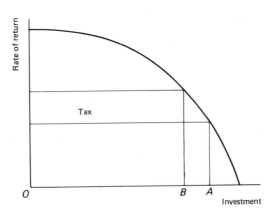

FIGURE 15.1

Reality is different. Instead of a smooth, continuous, downward-sloping marginal productivity of investment curve, there is a step-like function (Fig. 15.2). The vertical sections of the steps (*ST = PQ*) are the bargaining

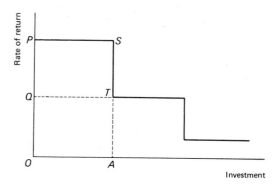

FIGURE 15.2

range. The lower limit of this range is determined by the special monopolistic or oligopolistic 'advantage' enjoyed by the MNC, the upper limit by the costs to the host government of alternative access to this advantage or the cost of doing without it. The limits of the range *P* and *Q* are set by the maximum 'returns' the company may earn, while the country is still willing to admit the investment, and the minimum 'returns' the company is prepared to accept and still invest (the amount *OA*). The company will have spent money on R & D, or on advertising or other marketing costs, or it will have incurred other fixed or joint costs. Operation with investment *OA* in the host country will be possible at relatively low incremental costs. As long as receipts from these operations cover avoidable local costs and make some contribution towards central overheads (R & D, technology, management, administration, etc.), the operation is profitable, though clearly the firm prefers higher contributions to lower ones. Charging what the market will bear is the firm's optimum policy. Charging just above incremental costs is its least preferred policy that will still bring about the investment.

It may be argued that this may be so *ex post*, after the expenditure at headquarters has been incurred. But if each host country squeezes returns to the MNC to the minimum, the source for R & D or other HQ expenditure will dry up. Or, put another way, in deciding on the fixed expenditure, the firm will have expectations that the local contribution will exceed local operating costs and that it will be able to recoup its fixed expenditure.

While this is clearly true of the major markets in the developed countries, less developed countries (LDCs) are normally too small a component to play an important role in this type of decision (e.g. all LDCs account for about 14 per cent of world pharmaceutical consumption; Wortzel, 1971,

p. 40). Therefore even *ex ante* LDC 'rates of return' play no, or only a minor, role in decisions to embark on R & D or marketing expenditures.

The upper limit of the bargaining range (*P*) is set *either* by the expenditure that the host country would have to incur in order to do for itself what the MNC has been doing for its global operations. Where an infrastructure of research is absent, and where the scale of operations is small, this cost may be very high. *Or* the upper limit may be set by alternative sources of buying the 'special advantage', either from rival MNCs or through acquiring the knowledge more cheaply, refusing to sign patent conventions, etc. *Or*, finally, the upper limit may be set by the cost to the country of doing without the 'special advantage'.

I have used the word 'returns'. It does not accurately describe what I have in mind. In view of the arbitrariness (within a range) with which the capital equipment is valued, the costs of intra-firm imported inputs and the prices of intra-firm exported outputs are fixed and fees for intra-firm services are set, nominal rates of return are of little relevance. What matters is the net ratio of benefits over costs, as seen by the MNC from the point of view of its global operations, and the ratio of benefits over costs for the host country. From the point of view of the firm, not only the costs of capital and other inputs have to be set at their true opportunity costs to the firm, but the operations in a particular country have to be viewed in relation to their effects on profits earned in other countries. From the point of view of the country, the whole range of economic and social objectives, not all readily quantifiable, enter into the assessment.

The concept 'returns' may well be inappropriate in an even more fundamental sense. By 'returns' we normally refer to profits earned as a ratio of capital owned, or fixed interest received as a proportion of a sum of money lent. But the sums at issue in the negotiation are a return for a package of services that includes technical knowledge, managerial services, marketing services, goodwill created by advertising, as well as returns on the services of capital. With the growing desire of LDCs to participate in ownership or to acquire full ownership, and the increasing tendency for MNCs to raise local capital, returns on capital owned by the foreign company have been and will be increasingly replaced by returns on other services and skills. The expression may then refer to the terms of a management contract or consultancy contract rather than the returns on equity investments, and has only a tenuous connection with any planned capital expenditure, however broadly we interpret the term 'capital'.

There will be certain elements in the bargain in which the interests of the MNC and of the host country coincide. Higher wages to local labour may increase the productivity of that labour and will, to that extent, be both in the interest of the country and that of the firm. The use of lower-cost local materials, the training of skilled manpower, the provision of infrastructure may also fall into this category. The exploration of these areas of non-zero-sum games is an important task both for the negotiators and for international agencies rendering technical assistance. A complication is, of course, that both sides have an interest in presenting self-interested actions as concessions to the other side, in order to gain counter-concessions on items where interests do conflict. But apart from this real complication, the separation of areas of interest conflicts, where concessions have to be met by counter-concessions, from areas of interest harmony, where progress can be made jointly, is a useful exercise.

An important corollary of the above analysis is that the MNC has an interest in shifting upwards the upper limit of the bargaining range. The higher the cost to the host country of losing the proposed investment, the better the chances of settling the bargain nearer the maximum point.

It is this tendency that accounts partly for the excessive sophistication and over-elaboration of many products and processes and their in-appropriateness for LDCs. True, part of the explanation must be found in the fact that these products have been developed in high-income, high-savings, high-investment-per-worker countries, where consumer demand is sophisticated and capital per worker plentiful. But this is not the whole story. Companies in search of profits should not find it difficult to invent and develop cheap, mass-produced products, appropriate for the lower incomes of the masses in the poor countries. But if imitation is easy, as it is in the case of simple products and processes, and the advantage soon lost, the incentive is lacking. It is therefore in the nature of the MNC that its products and processes should be excessively sophisticated in relation to the needs of the LDCs and in relation to the chances of a favourable bargain.

The bargaining position radically changes once capital has been sunk locally. While before the contract is signed the MNC will tend to be stronger, after factors of production have been committed locally, the strength shifts to the host government. How much will depend upon whether it wishes the MNC to continue operations, to enlarge operations and other MNCs to come in.

If the MNC has an interest to push up the upper limit of the bargaining range, the host country has an interest to push down the lower limit.[2]

NOTES

1. Reprinted from *World Development*, vol. 4, no. 3 (March 1976), pp. 225–9.
2. The sources of bargaining power are discussed in Ch. 9.

REFERENCE

Lawrence H. Wortzel, *Technology Transfer in the Pharmaceutical Industry*, UNITAR Research Report No. 14 (UNITAR, 1971).

16 Policies towards Multi-Nationals[1]

SUMMARY.

The 'complete package' of private foreign investment presented by the multinational enterprise has not only the advantages frequently claimed for it, but has also serious weaknesses, particularly for international income distribution. High international mobility of scarce rent and quasi-rent earning factors (technical know-how, management, marketing), combined with no international mobility of unskilled and semi-skilled labour in highly elastic supply domestically implies an uneven division of gains. To prevent the lion's share going to the lion, bargaining strategies are suggested that enable the developing host country to share in some of the rents and quasi-rents.

THE WEAKNESS OF COMPLETENESS

In a chapter on 'The role of international movements of private capital in promoting development' in a volume entitled *Capital Movements and Economic Development*, edited by John H. Adler (Macmillan, 1967), Felipe Pazos wrote: 'The main weakness of direct investment as a development agent is the consequence of the complete character of its contribution' (p. 196). This remark has always seemed to me provocative and stimulating, not only because of its attractively paradoxical character, inverting what is usually claimed to be the great *strength* of direct private foreign investment, but also because it invited us to reconsider the contribution of the investment 'package' to development. It contains a whole agenda for research.

What Felipe Pazos meant in the context in which he was writing was that private foreign investment might inhibit the creation and mobilization of indigenous enterprise, management, technology and savings. It is now generally recognized that resource transfer often amounts not to a net addition to, but only to a displacement of, domestic efforts. Indeed, in certain conditions, when effects on private and public incentives and opportunities are taken into account, preventing or reducing the 'transfer', closing the developing society off from foreign flows and influences, erecting a 'bamboo' or 'poverty' curtain, contributes more to development than opening up, widening and smoothing channels of communication, trade and investment flows.

The same problem is discussed by Albert Hirschman in his essay 'How to divest in Latin America and why?' Referring to Felipe Pazos as one of the few exceptions, he says that capital has normally been considered as complementary to indigenous factors, but that it, or some other components of the investment 'package', 'will no longer be purely complementary to local factors, but will be competitive with them and could cause them to wither or retard or even prevent their growth'.[2]

I am not here concerned primarily with this aspect of Pazos's pregnant comment. The question I wish to ask is how, in the light of 'the complete nature' of the investment, should we analyse a recent trend in foreign investment to which attention has turned—the location in low-income countries of low-skill, labour-intensive processes or the production or assembly of components or spare parts in a vertically integrated multi-national firm. Above all in electronics and electrical components, but also in the making of gloves, leather goods, luggage, baseballs, watches, motor-car parts and other consumer goods, and in electrical machinery, machine tools, accounting machines, typewriters, cameras, etc., processes that require much labour and limited capital and skills (sewing, boring holes, assembling wires) have been located in South Korea, Taiwan, Mexico, Hongkong, Singapore and the West Indian islands.[3]

How does this phenomenon fit into the theory of comparative advantage and its recommendations? Superficially, it might be thought to confirm the Heckscher-Ohlin version of the doctrine. Factors of production are allocated so as to produce products that make more use of the relatively abundant factor in countries where this factor is abundant. These countries then trade these products for those which use more of the relatively scarce factor. In this manner, international trade augments the resources available to the country. But on reflection, it is seen that the facts and the implications are vastly different from those of the accepted doctrine. It is foreign, not domestic, capital, know-how, enterprise, management and marketing that are highly mobile internationally, and that are combined with the plentiful, but internationally immobile, domestic, semi-skilled labour. One set of factors (enterprise, management, knowledge and capital) are in relatively *inelastic* supply *in total*, but easily moved around the world and therefore in *highly elastic* supply *to any particular country*. The other factor, labour, is in *highly elastic* supply domestically, but *immobile* across frontiers.

Specialization between countries follows not different commodity groups but different factors of production: the poor countries specializing in low-skilled labour, leaving the rewards of enterprise, capital, management and know-how to the foreign owners of these scarce, but internationally mobile, factors. The situation is equivalent to one in which plentiful unskilled or semi-skilled labour itself, rather than the product of labour, is exported. For the surplus of the product of labour over the wage, resulting from the the co-operation of other factors in less elastic supply, accrues to foreigners. The differential international and internal elasticities of supply in response to differential rewards and the differences in monopoly rents entering the rewards of these factors have important implications for the internal and international distribution of gains from investment and trade.

Since the firms operate in oligopolistic and oligopsonistic markets, cost advantages are not necessarily passed on to consumers in lower prices or to workers in higher wages, and the profits then accrue to the parent firms. The operation of this type of international specialization depends upon the continuation of substantial wage differentials (hence trade unions must be weak in the host country so that low wage costs are maintained), continuing access to the markets of the parent companies (hence stronger pressure from importing interests than from domestic producers displaced by the low-cost processes and components, including trade unions in the rich importing countries) and continuing permission by host countries to operate with minimum taxes, tariffs and bureaucratic regulations.

The packaged or complete nature of the contribution of the multi-national enterprise, usually claimed as its characteristic blessing, is then, as Felipe Pazos remarked, the cause of the unequal international distribution of the gains from trade and investment. If the package broke, or leaked, some of the rents and monopoly rewards would spill over into the host country. But if it is secured tightly, only the least scarce and weakest factor in the host country derives an income from the operations of the multinational enterprise, unless bargaining power is used to extract a share of these other incomes.

The situation is aggravated if there is technical progress, so that the labour-intensive activity in the underdeveloped host country might be knocked out by an innovation using capital or technology in the parent country. Other processes or components will still be left to which the labour force could be switched. But such switching has its costs. Skills acquired are wasted and the bargaining power of the host country and its labour force is further reduced, unless retraining can be done quickly and its costs are carried by the multinational enterprise.

The bargaining power of host countries and of the plentiful factor – semi-skilled labour – in such a situation is likely to be weak and the question is whether such a division of gains between parent enterprise and host country, between the foreign investment 'package' and domestic labour, remains acceptable. The gains to the host country are confined to the wages of those employed if the alternative is unemployment. The fact that these earnings are in foreign exchange may put them at a premium, if the country suffers from a foreign exchange shortage. There may, in addition, be linkages, but these may be positive or negative. While such investment has attractions for some countries faced with labour surpluses and foreign exchange shortages and poorly endowed with natural resources, the potential gains may not be considered worth the social risks and social costs, including a form of dependence and dualistic development of a new kind, different from that of the colonial mines or plantations economy, but similar in its distributional impact.

What are the lessons for policy? The most obvious conclusion is that developing host countries should share in the monopoly rents by appropriate tax policies. But this requires *joint* action of countries with similar attractions for the foreign enterprise in order to reduce the elasticity of supply with which any one country is faced. Such joint action is difficult to achieve. The more successful the agreement on not giving tax concessions promises to be, the more attractive it is to any one country to break it. And the fear of someone breaking it may be a deterrent for the others to reach, or, once reached, to adhere to, the agreement.

Apart from sharing in the gains through tax collection, the host country may attempt to impose conditions so as to turn the foreign factors from being competitive to becoming complementary to indigenous factors: joint ventures, local participation in board membership, requirement of training for higher skills, etc. The aim would be to use the foreign investment as an instrument for the mobilization of local resources. The question is whether without protection of the markets, without tax concessions and without heavy subsidies to inputs, such conditions remain within the bargaining range that satisfies the objectives of both the foreign firm and the host country.

Other important lessons can be learned in the area of differential treatment of foreign and domestic enterprises, tariff policies, restrictive business practices, and the selection of products and their indirect taxation.

HOW TO PREVENT THE LION'S SHARE GOING TO THE LION

In this section we turn to the operation of the multi-national enterprise in general, and do not confine ourselves to the form discussed in the previous section. The policy-maker in a developing country will have to decide, in the first place, whether he wants private foreign investment at all. If his country does not raise objections in principle to admitting private foreign firms, the next question is whether, for a particular project, foreign investment is the most effective method of promoting development. The package, whose merits and drawbacks were discussed in the previous section, might be taken apart and its components bought more cheaply separately. Too little attention has been paid to the possibility of 'shopping around' and assembling capital, management and technology from separate sources.

The answer to the question of the best way of assembling the package will depend partly on the sophistication of the technique, partly on access to markets and partly on the interdependence of the different operations of the firm. Very few countries would today invite foreign companies to construct or manage railways or public utilities, as was done in the nineteenth century, when techniques in these enterprises were still new. Foreign or domestic borrowing, combined with hiring or training engineers and managers, is usually a cheaper way of assembling the package. On the other hand, petrochemicals or pharmaceuticals, if they are considered at all as appropriate products to be manufactured in the country, could probably not be produced in any other way than through a multi-national enterprise.

Having decided that the country wants to produce the product, rather than do without it (a question too often neglected), or import it, and having found that private foreign investment is the best way of assembling capital, management and technology, the policy-maker will have to draw up a contract with the foreign firm. The terms of this contract may include a wide range of items.[4]

On many items solutions can be found that are in the common interest of the foreign firm and the host country. But clearly on others interests conflict. Thus, the more tax the government collects, the less profits are left over for distribution or retention. In the area where there is conflict, relative bargaining power will determine the outcome.

The multi-national enterprise derives its strength from the fact that it enjoys a special advantage, which makes its operation superior to anything the host country might try to do by itself. This advantage or superiority frequently is derived from a large central expenditure which, however, is not closely related to the operation in any particular place. This expenditure may take the form of heavy exploration costs for oil or other minerals; or it may take the form of outlays on research and development, as in the case of a new drug; or it may be a heavy investment in advertising and marketing, creating good will for the product, as for a soft drink. The local operating costs of a particular oil well, or of producing a particular tranquillizer or a soft drink, are then quite small, compared with the costs that lie behind this operation and that took the form of exploration or research or advertising. Variable costs are small compared with fixed or sunk costs, or, in the jargon, marginal costs diverge widely from average costs.

Long before the Report of the British Monopolies Commission on the Swiss firm Hoffmann – La Roche, and its British subsidiary, La Roche Products, comparative figures were available for the prices charged by the large multi-national and by other companies (cashing in on the R & D expenditure of the big brother) for the two drugs Chlordiazepoxide and Diazepam, also called Librium and Valium. The price charged by the large multi-national was $1,250 per kilo for Librium, compared with $18.90–$20 charged by other (mainly Italian) firms and $2,500 for Valium, compared with $30–$45. This range gives a broad indication of the bargaining range if the country cannot, or does not wish to, import the cheaper product.

Having incurred the high costs for exploration, research or advertising, the firm could afford to operate at quite low profits. As long as its operating costs are covered and some contribution is made to the central costs, the operation is profitable.

Of course, it would never have undertaken the heavy central expenditure, had it not hoped to recoup its total costs and make a profit. To that extent, the large, apparently excessive, profits from the 'lucky strike' (whether for a mineral or for a new discovery) are no indication of what is required to induce the production, for it neglects the losses on the unlucky strikes. But, apart from some extractive industries, developing countries do not figure very importantly in these initial decisions, because their markets are so small. They therefore need not worry that using their bargaining power will discourage the multi-national companies from carrying out their research expenditure.

On the other hand, the benefit to the developing host country of producing the product might be quite large. If it were not for the multi-national, it would itself have to spend large sums on exploration or research, which it could ill afford.

There is, then, a range, between the minimum returns, after tax and when all conditions and terms of the contract are met, which the firm would just accept and still operate in the host country, and the maximum returns to the foreign firm that the host country would just find tolerable and still permit it to operate. Within this range the bargain will be struck. 'Returns' must be interpreted broadly, to cover all items such as those included in the list on p. 283.

Where, within this range, will the bargain be struck? The answer obviously depends on the relative power of the negotiators. As for the developing country, this power will depend upon mainly three things: information; solidarity with other developing countries that might offer rival attractions, such as tax concessions or docile workers; and competition between rival foreign firms. What is therefore needed is access to better information, joint action by several developing countries and competition between foreign companies.

It must be emphasized that, while improved bargaining strength is in the interest of the developing host country, the multi-national enterprise also has an interest in well-informed, hard-headed negotiators. Ill-informed, weak bargaining tends to lead to regrets and regrets may cause reactions. Expropriations or prohibitions on remittances often follow contracts based on ignorance, weakness or corruption. An open-eyed, firm bargain has a longer life and improves stability. By reducing political and economic risks, it reduces the required rate of return; and by reducing the rate of return, it reduces the risks for which these higher returns are a compensation.

A particularly important area for negotiation is the underexplored area of transfer pricing. A large and growing proportion of world trade now consists of intra-firm transactions. Prices of these are not determined at arm's length but are guided by a host of considerations, including taxes, tariffs, foreign exchange regulations, joint ventures, trade union action, price controls, anti-monopoly policies and others. It is through such transfer pricing that profits can be concealed and shifted between countries so as to attain the global objectives of the multi-national firm. Nothing illegal is here involved. I am not talking of tax fiddles. It is in the nature of the fixed or joint headquarter costs that attribution of these costs to particular operations is arbitrary within a wide range, and companies naturally use this to achieve their global aims.

The problems of transfer pricing arise because one institution, the multi-national enterprise, operates on a world scale, whereas political institutions, including fiscal and monetary authorities, still operate on a national scale. Ideally, an international political authority should legislate for the multi-national firm. This is not practical. But it may be possible to evolve institutions that bridge the gap between the global vision and operations of the multi-national firm and the national limitations and concerns of governments. Multilateral technical assistance in negotiating with the firms should be expanded and strengthened. Bilateral agencies would be suspected of promoting the interests of the firms based in their countries. The technical assistance would take the form of gathering and conveying information and of a careful analysis of the bargaining range. It might also attempt to coordinate the efforts of several host governments that would otherwise compete with one another. If such an agency can grow into an embryonic international tax and law authority, asserting itself on so far unexplored territory such as the sea and the sea-bed, this would be another step forward.

NOTES

1. Reprinted from *World Development*, vol. 3, no. 6 (June 1975). This paper appeared in Spanish in a volume of Essays in Honour of Felipe Pazos, ed. Carlos Díaz-Alejandro. I am grateful to the Economic Development Institute of the World Bank and its director, Andrew Kamarck, who provided the facilites, the encouragement and the agreeable atmosphere in which this paper was written. I am also grateful to Constantine Vaitsos for helpful comments.
2. Albert O. Hirschman, *A Bias for Hope*, Yale University Press, New Haven and London (1971) Ch. 2, p. 228.
3. Gerald K. Helleiner, 'Manufactured Exports from Less Developed Countries and Multinational Firms', *Economic Journal* (March 1973).
4. See Constantine Vaitsos, 'Income distribution, welfare considerations and transnational enterprises', in John H. Dunning (ed.), *Economic Analysis and the Multinational Enterprise* (London: Allen and Unwin, 1974). See Ch. 14, p. 283.

17 Multi-Nationals Revisited[1]

The multi-national is no longer so multi-fashionable. It is true that much is still being written about it, and this reviewer of some recent books and articles on the subject succumbs to the Swiftian thought that he who can make one word grow where there were two before is a true benefactor of mankind. Yet, in spite of the continuing controversy, some of the steam has gone out of the debate. There is no longer the sharp separation between those who think that what is good for General Motors is good for humanity and those who see in the multi-national corporations the devil incorporated.

The reasons for this lowering of the temperature are to be found in five recent trends that suggest that the role of multi-national corporations in development has to be reassessed.

First, there has been a shift in bargaining power between multi-nationals and their host countries, greater restrictions on the inflow of packaged technology, a change in emphasis from production to research and development and marketing, among other factors, that have increased the uncertainties of direct foreign investment. As a result, there is some evidence that it has become the policy of multi-national companies to shift from equity investment, ownership of capital, and managerial control of overseas facilities to the sale of technology, management services, and marketing as a means to earn returns on corporate assets, at least in those countries that have policies against inflows of packaged technology (Baranson, 1978).

Second, many more nations are now competing with US multi-nationals in setting up foreign activities, which means that the controversy is no longer dominated by nationalistic considerations. Japanese and European firms figure prominently among the new multi-nationals. The number of US companies among the world's top 12 multi-nationals declined in all of the 13 major industry groups except aerospace between 1959 and 1976, whereas continental European companies increased their representatives among the top 12 multi-nationals in 9 of the 13 industries, and the Japanese scored gains in 8 (Lawrence Franko, *Harvard Business Review,* Nov.–Dec. 1978). The reasons for this are to be found in the decline of US predominance in technology transfer; in the fact that foreign production follows exports, and exports from these countries steadily rose; in the steady growth of European and Japanese capacity to innovate; and in the greater adaptability—both politically and economically—of these companies to the needs of host countries. For example, Michelin's radial tires, Bosch's fuel injection equipment, and French, German, and Japanese locomotives, aircraft, and automobiles are more energy-saving than their American counterparts.

Third, developing countries themselves are now establishing multinationals. In addition to companies from the Organization of Petroleum Exporting Countries (OPEC), and firms established in tax-haven countries, the leading countries where multi-nationals are being established are Argentina, Brazil, Colombia, Hong Kong, India, the Republic of Korea, Peru, the Philippines, Singapore, and Taiwan. According to Louis Wells, in Indonesia "Asian LDC investors together account for more investment than either Japanese, North American, or European investors, omitting mining and petroleum." It may well be that these firms use more appropriate technology and are better adapted and more adaptable to local conditions. Wells notes that there is a strong preference in the developing countries for multi-national corporations from similar countries. Korean companies put up buildings in Kuwait, pave roads in Ecuador, and have applied to Portugal for permission to set up an electronics plant; Taiwanese companies build steel mills in Nigeria; and Filipino companies restore shrines in Indonesia. Hindustan Machine Tools (India) is helping Algeria to develop a machine tool industry; Tata (India) is beating Mercedes trucks in Malaysia; and Stelux, a Hong Kong-based company with interests in manufacturing, banking, and real estate, bought into the Bulova Watch Company in the United States. C. P. Wong of Stelux improved the performance of the US company. There are other instances of Third World multi-nationals that have aimed at acquiring shares in firms in developed countries (Heenan and Keegan, 1979).

The data on the extent of developing countries' foreign investment are inadequate and the evidence is anecdotal. A partial listing of major Third World multi-nationals in *Fortune* (14 August 1978) contains 33 corporations with estimated sales in 1977 ranging from $500 million to over $22,000 million, totalling $80,000 million.

If there is a challenge, it is no longer uniquely American; and if multinationals are instruments of neo-colonialism, the instrument has been adopted by some ex-colonies, and at least one colony (Hong Kong), and is used against others. (Excluding mining and petroleum, Hong Kong is, for example, the second largest investor in Indonesia.) Neither developed nor developing countries are any longer predominantly recipients of multi-nationals from a single home country.

Fourth, not only do host countries deal with a greater variety of foreign companies, comparing their political and economic attractions, weighing them against their costs, and playing them off against one another, but also the large multi-nationals are being replaced by smaller and more flexible firms. And increasingly alternative organizations to the traditional form of multi-national enterprise are becoming available: banks, retailers, consulting firms, and trading companies are acting as instruments of technology transfer.

Fifth, some multi-nationals from developed countries have accommodated themselves more to the needs of the developing countries, although IBM and Coca-Cola left India rather than permit joint ownership. Centrally planned economies increasingly welcome the multi-nationals, which in turn like investing there, partly because "you cannot be nationalized".

Several distinguished authors, former US Under Secretary of State George Ball, Professor Raymond Vernon, and Harry Johnson among them, had predicted that sovereignty would be at bay and some of these authors even suggested that the nation state, confronted with large and ever more powerful multi-nationals, would wither away.

> Competition among nation-states for the economic favours of the corporation and the xenophobic character of the nation state itself will prevent the formation of a conspiracy or cartel of nation-states to exploit the economic potentialities of the international business in the service of national power. Therefore, the long-run trend will be toward the dwindling of the power of the national state relative to the corporation.

Such was Harry Johnson's vision of the future. The nation state has shown considerable resilience in the face of multi-nationals; its demise, as with reports of Mark Twain's death, have been somewhat exaggerated. The Colombians succeeded in extracting substantial sums from their multi-nationals. The Indians dealt successfully with firms that introduced inappropriate technologies and products. The Andean Group and OPEC showed that solidarity among groups of developing countries in dealing with multi-nationals is possible and can pay.

STILL IMPORTANT FORCE

This is not to say that multi-nationals are no longer an important force. It has been estimated that the foreign production of multi-nationals accounts for as much as 20 per cent of world output, and that intra-firm trade of these companies (defined narrowly as trade between firms linked through majority ownership) constitutes 25 per cent of international trade in manufacturing. There has been an increase in the proportion of US technology receipts, which are intra-firm. The share of total US imports accounted for by intra-firm transactions of multi-nationals based in the United States rose from 25 per cent in 1966 to 32 per cent in 1975. The share of these transactions from developing countries showed a rise from 30 per cent in 1966 to 35 per cent in 1975; however, this rise can be accounted for by the rise in the price of petroleum imports, which constitute the largest category of imports from developing countries. The share of US intra-firm trade in manufactures from developing countries declined from 16 per cent in 1966 to 10 per cent in 1976. But control can take many forms other than majority ownership in subsidiaries. And multi-nationals are adept in assuming these other forms (UNCTAD, 1978).

An essential feature of the multi-national enterprise is a special advantage over the local rival, who knows the local conditions and the local language better than the foreigner. This advantage must be sufficiently large to permit rents to be collected that exceed the extra costs of geographical and cultural distance. It may consist in a natural monopoly, in size, in risk-spreading, in goodwill, or in proprietary knowledge acquired through research and development expenditure. It may be bestowed upon a firm by what Veblen called "business methods", such as advertising, or by "production methods", such as superior knowledge or larger scale.

It was recognized quite early that it is wrong for multi-nationals to benefit from a natural monopoly in which know-how is widespread, such as that enjoyed by public utilities. As a result, these enterprises were nationalized early. Host countries also learned to appropriate for themselves a larger share of the monopoly rents in minerals. In manufacturing, monopoly profits for multi-nationals were generated partly as a result of high levels of protection, on which the companies often insisted, and excessive subsidies and tax concessions, and partly as a result of trade names, market-sharing agreements, and other monopolistic practices.

Expenditure on the creation of this advantage does not vary with the unit operating costs in a particular country, which may be quite low compared with the prices charged. The large fixed costs that arise from research and development, exploration, scale, or advertising make the allocation of these costs between operations in different countries arbitrary within wide limits. But while one school of thought has used this to justify companies charging prices substantially in excess of the incremental costs of operating in a particular country, as a way of recouping what are regarded as necessary overhead expenditures, another school has emphasized the element of monopoly profit in these pricing policies. The existence of such profits or rents (which may be concealed, for example, through transfer pricing of imported inputs, management or licence fees, interest rates on intra-firm loans, and royalties) implies that the "marginal productivity of investment curve", which relates returns to amounts invested, has vertical branches, within the limits of which the division of gains between the host country and firm is a matter for bargaining. Higher shares going to host countries would not be accompanied by reduced investment or lower operating efficiency, as the conventional theory has maintained.

This theory states that any policy that raises costs to the multi-national is bound to lead to reduced capital or technology inflow. Policy-makers have to "trade off" their desire for raising taxes, imposing conditions about local participation or training, or limiting remittances abroad against the advantages of more foreign capital and know-how. Though their relationship to the foreign exterprise may be a love–hate relationship, at the margin they have to make up their minds whether they love or hate the investment of the foreign company.

But the correct analysis must start from the monopolistic advantage of the firm and the monopoly rent that it yields. There will, therefore, be a range between a high "rate of return" to the company that will make the operation just acceptable to the host country and a low rate that will make it just worthwhile for the company. The maximum point of this range is determined by the host country's ability to acquire the advantage in an alternative way, or to do without it; the minimum point being set by the operating costs to the company of conducting the activity in the country.

It might be objected that if governments were to beat down returns to such low levels that they barely covered their local operating costs and did not permit firms to recoup a contribution to their overhead expenditures (such as those on research and development), they would kill the goose that lays the golden eggs. Pharmaceutical companies, for example, would have to go out of business if they were allowed to charge only the direct costs of producing drugs, for the sources of their research funds would dry up.

But this is not a valid objection as far as developing countries are concerned. The argument may hold for advanced, industrial countries. In deciding upon its research expenditure the company usually has the large markets of the advanced countries in mind. Anything it gets from the small, relatively poor markets of the developing countries over and above operating expenses is frequently a bonus. To forgo that bonus would not reduce its research expenditure. The potential bargaining strength of the developing countries (where they have the ability, solidarity, and knowledge) lies precisely in their small size: an instance of the importance of being unimportant.

TOWARDS A POLICY

Any developing country has to ask itself four questions in evolving a policy towards multi-nationals—a positive answer to each giving rise to the next question: (1) Are foreign enterprises wanted at all? Some countries, though their number is declining, may reject outright the idea of foreigners making profits in their country. (2) Is the particular product or product range wanted? Many products of multi-nationals are overspecified, overprocessed, overpackaged, oversophisticated, developed for high-income, high-saving markets, produced by capital-intensive techniques and, while catering for the masses in richer countries, can cater for only a small upper crust in poorer countries. (3) Should the product be imported or produced at home? Home production could be for the domestic market or for export. (4) Is direct foreign investment the best way to assemble the package of management, capital, and know-how? The host country has a variety of choices. It can borrow the capital, hire managers, and acquire a licence; use domestic inputs for some components of the "package"; or use consultancy services, management contracts, importing houses, or banks. If it is decided that direct foreign investment in the form of a multi-national subsidiary is the best way of assembling the package, the terms of the negotiation will have to be settled, so that the host country strikes the best bargain, consistent with efficient operation of the multi-national. This is an area in which international organizations, like the World Bank, could give technical assistance to host countries. (Bilateral technical assistance would be suspected of taking the side of the companies.)

The correct approach is therefore a combination of cost–benefit analysis and a bargaining framework. In one sense, though not a very significant one, the two approaches amount to the same thing. It is always possible, formally, to regard forgoing the second-best bargain to any given bargain as an element in the "opportunity cost" (the cost of forgoing the alternative) of the bargain in question. If, then, all bargains are ranked in order of preference, only the best bargain will show an excess of benefit over cost. But this is a purely formal way of getting round the difficulty of distinguishing between cost–benefit and bargaining issues. It would be more illuminating to say that cost–benefit analysis is useful in ranking the bargains, so that the host country knows what it should go for and what it will sacrifice with any concession, whereas the bargaining framework is necessary to strike the best bargain within the numerous items for negotiation. Here a number of issues may arise; do elements in the bargain in one country affect bargains in other countries? Can concession on one front be traded for counter-concessions on another? Are there clear areas of common interests that can be delineated from areas of conflicting interests? More fundamentally: can the government negotiators take a truly independent position that reflects the interests of their country, or do they not represent partial group interests within their own countries, that are aligned with the interests of the foreign company?

Bergsten, Horst, and Moran in their book *American Multinationals and American Interests* distinguish between four conventional schools of thought. The imperialist and mercantilist school argues that there is a joint effort by US multi-nationals and the US government to dominate the world both politically and economically. The sovereignty-at-bay thesis (Raymond Vernon, 1971) holds that multi-national firms have become dominant over all nation states, both host and home, with largely beneficial effects on all concerned. The global reach school (Barnet and Müller, 1974), while agreeing that the firms have become dominant, concludes that the effects can be detrimental for both home and host countries. There is also the view espoused by labour unions in the United States that multi-nationals hurt the United States and benefit foreign countries. Bergsten, Horst, and Moran find that none of these (somewhat oversimplified) models really fits and propose a policy to get the best out of these firms. They find that the main distortions to be corrected arise from competitive government policies, by both host and home governments (with respect to tax policies, for example), and from the structure and behaviour of the companies. The type of rules and procedures that we have evolved in the area of trade and money need also to be negotiated in the area of foreign investment and multi-national behaviour.

Can multi-nationals make a contribution to meeting basic human needs? Since it follows from the above argument, about the special advantage, that the multi-nationals from the developed countries are likely to produce and market rather sophisticated products on which oligopoly rents can be earned for some time, they are not likely to make a contribution to the simple producer and consumer goods that a basic-needs approach calls for. (They may, however, contribute to intermediate goods, capital goods, and exports.) Such products would be readily imitated by local competitors and the rents soon eroded. There can be a conflict between the basic goods the poor need and the advertised consumer goods of the multi-nationals.

The chairman of a multi-national food company writes in the *Columbia Business Journal* on the subject of marketing in developing countries:

> How often we see in developing countries that the poorer the economic outlook the more important the small luxury of a flavored soft drink or smoke . . . to the dismay of many would-be benefactors the poorer the malnourished are, the more likely they are to spend a disproportionate amount of whatever they have on some luxury rather than on what they need. . . . Observe, study, learn. We try to do it at [our company]. It seems to pay off for us. Perhaps it will for you too.

It is probable that the new multi-nationals from the developing countries will be more adapted to local needs. The costs to the host country are likely to be lower and the technology and product design more appropriate to local conditions. They often are of smaller scale, use more capital-saving techniques, create more jobs, are better adapted to the supply and social conditions in the host country, are more responsive to requests for exporting, local participation, joint ventures, or local training, and design products more adapted to the consumption and production needs of the poor—hoes, simple power tillers, and bicycles, rather than air conditioners, expensive cars, and equipment for luxury apartments. Their special advantage would consist not in the monopolistic package of capital, technology, and marketing, but in special skills. Their costs of overcoming geographical and cultural distance are often less than those of multi-nationals from industrial countries. Their relative bargaining power is weaker. The visible hand of these multi-nationals is less visible than that of US companies. Because of these characteristics, their ability to survive in a world in which developing countries become increasingly interdependent among themselves is increased.

NOTES

1. Reprinted from *Finance & Development (June 1979)*.

PUBLICATIONS REVIEWED

Jack Baranson, *Technology and the Multinationals*, Lexington, Lexington Books, (1978).

R. J. Barnet and R. Müller, *Global Reach: The Power of the Multinational Corporations*, Simon & Schuster, (New York) (1974).

C. Fred Bergsten, Thomas Horst, and Theodore M. Moran, *American Multinationals and American Interests*, Brookings Institution, Washington DC (1978).

Thomas J. Biersteker, *Distortion or Development? Contending Perspectives of the Multinational Corporation*, MIT Press, Cambridge (1978).

Peter Evans, *Dependent Development; the Alliance of State, Multinational, and Local Capital in Brazil*, Princeton University Press, Princeton (1979).

Lawrence G. Franko, "Multinationals: the End of US Dominance", *Harvard Business Review* (November–December 1978).

David A. Heenan and Warren J. Keegan, "The Rise of Third World Multinationals", *Harvard Business Review* (January–February 1979).

Harry G. Johnson, *Technology and Economic Interdependence*, Macmillan, London (1975).

Sanjaya Lall and Paul Streeten, *Foreign Investment, Transnationals, and Developing Countries*, Macmillan Press, London (1977).

Sanjaya Lall, "Developing Countries as Exporters of Industrial Technologies", *International Economic Development and Resource, Transfer*, Herbert Giersch, (ed.) Institut für Weltwirtschaft, Kiel (1979).

D. Lecraw, "Direct Investment by Firms from Less-Developed Countries", *Oxford Economic Papers* (November 1977).

UNCTAD Seminar Programme, *Intra-firm Transactions and Their Impact on Trade and Development*, (May 1978), Report Series no. 2, UNCTAD/OSG/174.

Paul Streeten, "Transnational Corporations and Basic Needs", in *Growth with Equity: Strategies for Meeting Human Needs*, Mary Evelyn Jegen and Charles K. Wilber, (eds), Paulist Press, (1979).

Raymond Vernon, *Sovereignty at Bay: The Multinational Spread of U.S. Enterprises*, Basic Books, New York (1971).

Louis T. Wells, Jr, "The Internationalization of Firms from Developing Countries", in *Multinationals from Small Countries*, Tamir Agmon and Charles P. Kindleberger (eds.) MIT Press, Cambridge, (1977).

Part IV   From Growth to
Basic Needs

18 From Growth to Basic Needs[1]

How is it that, in spite of growing hostility and misconceptions, the concept "basic human needs" has been widely accepted? In order to understand this, it is helpful to reflect on the internal logic of the development of the concept and on the way in which accumulating experience has called for successive responses. Otherwise we might be tempted to say that the international development community takes up, from time to time, new publicity slogans, new fads and fashions, or that we are acting out a comedy of errors. Basic needs is not just another fad. (Nor, of course, is it the revelation of ultimate truth.) It is no more, but also no less, than a stage in the development of thinking and responding to the challenges of development over the last 20 to 25 years. The following brief survey of the evolution of our thinking has to simplify, but I believe that the main features are correct.[2] If, in the following pages, the deficiencies of pre-basic-needs approaches are stressed and the virtues of the basic-needs approach overstressed, this is done in order to bring out sharply its distinctive features. It is not intended to imply either that the previous approaches have not taught us much that is still valuable, or that the basic-needs approach is not subject to some of the objections raised to the earlier approaches.

Basic needs is concerned with removing mass deprivation, which has always been at the heart of development. The discussion started strongly influenced by Sir Arthur Lewis[3] and others, who emphasized economic growth as the solution to poverty eradication. At this early stage we were quite clear (in spite of what is now often said in a caricature of past thinking) that growth is not an end in itself, but a performance test of development.

We had three types of justification for the emphasis on growth as the principal performance test:

(1) We thought that economic growth would, through market forces, such as the rising demand for labour, higher productivity, higher wages,

323

or lower prices, spread its benefits widely and speedily, and that these benefits can best be achieved through growth. There were, of course, even in the early days some sceptics who said that growth is not necessarily of this kind. In conditions of increasing returns, growth gives to those who already have; it tends to concentrate income and wealth.

(2) Alternatively, we assumed that governments are democratic or at any rate are concerned with the fate of the poor. Therefore, progressive taxation, social services and other government action would spread the benefits downwards. Poverty alleviation would not be automatic through market prices but governments would take corrective actions where market forces concentrate benefits.

(3) The third justification, more hard-headed than the previous two, said that we must not worry initially about the fate of the poor. In order to help them, it is necessary to build up the capital, infrastructure and productive capacity of an economy, so that it can improve the lot of the poor later. For a period of time—and it can be quite a long period—the poor have to tighten their belts and the rich must benefit. But if the rewards of the rich are used to provide incentives to innovate, save and accumulate capital which can eventually be used to benefit the poor, the early poverty will turn out to have been justified. It is interesting to note that some radical egalitarian philosophers like John Rawls[4] would sanction such a strategy. Inequalities in their view are justified if they are a necessary condition for improving the lot of the poor.

We were also strongly influenced by the so-called Kuznets curve.[5] This curve relates average income level to an index of equality and suggests that the early stages of growth are accompanied by growing inequality. Only at an income of around $600 per head is further growth associated with reduced inequality (measured by the share of the lowest 20 per cent). This association has been suggested by tracing the course of the same country over time and of different countries with different incomes at the same time. In the early stages of development, as income per head increases from, say, $100 to $600, inequality tends to grow and this may mean that absolute poverty for some groups also increases. But after a while we reach the turning point, the bottom of the "U" curve, after which we enter the stage in which growing income is accompanied by greater equality and reduced poverty.

Each of these three assumptions turned out to be wrong, or at least not true worldwide. It was not the case, except for a very few countries, with special initial conditions and policies, that there was an automatic tendency for income to trickle down. Nor did governments always take corrective action to reduce poverty because, after all, governments of many countries were themselves formed by people with mixed motives and mixed objectives, but who had close psychological, social and political links with the beneficiaries of the concentrated growth process. And it certainly was not the case that a period of increasing poverty or inequality was needed in order to accumulate capital. It was found that small farmers saved at least as high a proportion of their income as the big landlords and were more productive, in terms of yield per acre, and that entrepreneurial talent was widespread and not confined to large firms. So prolonged poverty or inequality were not needed in order to accumulate savings and capital, and stimulate entrepreneurship.

Judging by economic growth the development process of the last 25 years was a spectacular, unprecedented, and unexpected success. But at the same time there was increasing dualism. Despite high rates of growth of industrial production and continued general economic growth, not much employment was created. Nor were there many spread effects. Arthur Lewis had predicted[6] that subsistence farmers and landless labourers would move from the countryside to the higher-income, urban, modern industries. This would increase inequality in the early stages (as long as rural inequalities were not substantially greater than urban inequalities), but when all the rural poor had been absorbed in modern industry, the golden age would be ushered in, when growth is married to greater equality. It became evident, however, that the Lewis model, which strongly dominated not only academic thought but also political action, did not work. It did not work for three reasons:

(1) The rural–urban income differentials were much higher than Lewis had assumed, owing partly to trade union action on wages, partly to minimum wage legislation, partly to differentials inherited from colonial days, and for other reasons. This impeded rapid absorption of the rural labour force.

(2) The rate of growth of the population and the rate of growth of the labour force were much larger than expected.

(3) The technology transferred from the rich countries to the urban industrial sector was labour-saving and, while raising labour productivity, did not create many jobs.

It was not surprising, then, given all these problems, that attention turned away from economic growth and GNP. Some even called for "dethroning GNP". Since 1969 the International Labour Organization has attempted to put the focus on jobs not growth. It has organized employment missions to seven countries—Colombia, Kenya, the Philippines, Iran, Sri Lanka, the Dominican Republic, the Sudan—

charged with exploring how to create more jobs. While this was a useful learning stage, we soon came to see that unemployment is not really the main problem. In *Asian Drama*[7] Gunnar Myrdal devoted numerous pages to criticizing the concepts of employment, unemployment and underemployment in the context of underdeveloped Asia. Employment and unemployment only make sense in an industrialized society where there are employment exchanges, organized and informed labour markets, and social security benefits for the unemployed who are trained workers, willing and able to work, but temporarily without a job. None of this applies to many of the poorest developing countries, in which livelihoods are more important than wage employment. It is an instance of the transfer of an inappropriate intellectual technology from modern societies to the entirely different social and economic conditions of the developing countries.

Myrdal talked about "labour utilization", which has numerous dimensions when applied to small, self-employed, subsistence farmers, landless labourers, artisans, traders, educated young people, women, and others, in societies without organized labour markets. "Employment", as interpreted in industrial countries, is not the appropriate concept. The ILO employment missions discovered or rediscovered this, and they also discovered that, to be able to afford to be unemployed, one has to be fairly well off. For an unemployed to survive he must have an income from another source. The root problem of poverty is not unemployment, it is very hard work and long hours of work in unremunerative, unproductive forms of activity. This discovery has drawn attention to the informal sector in the towns: the blacksmiths, the carpenters, the sandal makers, the builders, the lamp makers. All those who often work extremely hard, are self-employed or employed by their family, and are very poor. And it has drawn attention to the women who, in some cultures, perform hard tasks without even being counted as members of the labour force, because their production is not sold for cash. The problem then was redefined as that of the "working poor".

The dimensions of labour utilization are more numerous than the demand for labour (lack of demand gives rise to Keynesian unemployment) and the need for cooperating factors of production such as machinery and raw materials. (Their lack may be called Marxian "non-employment".) There is a good deal of evidence that not only labour but also capital is grossly under-utilized in many developing countries, which suggests that other causes than surplus labour in relation to scarce capital are at work. More specifically, these causes of low labour utilization can be classified under the headings (a) consumption and levels of living, (b) attitudes and (c) institutions.

Nutrition, health and education, aspects of the *level of living*, are important for fuller labour utilization. But they have been neglected because in rich societies they count as consumption which has no effect on human productivity (or possibly a negative one, like four-martini lunches). The only exception that is admitted in the literature is some forms of education. In poor countries, better nutrition, health and education can be very productive. They constitute forms of human resource development. (This is one thread that goes into the fabric of basic needs.)

Attitudes also make a difference to what jobs people will accept. In Sri Lanka, a large part of unemployment is the result of the excess aspirations of the educated, who are no longer prepared to accept manual, "dirty" jobs. Caste attitudes in India also present obstacles to fuller labour utilization. In Africa, those with primary education wish to leave the land and become clerks in government offices. In many societies manual work or rural work is held in contempt.

The third dimension is the absence or weakness of such *institutions* as labour exchanges, or credit institutions, or an appropriate system of land ownership or tenancy laws. As a result, labour is under-utilized.

For reasons such as these, an approach to poverty which runs in terms of unemployment and underemployment as we understand these concepts in the north, in which levels of living, attitudes and institutions are assumed to be adapted to full labour utilization, has turned out to be largely a dead end. "Unemployment" can co-exist with considerable labour shortages and capital under-utilization.

There are other reasons why the employment concept is questioned. The creation of more employment opportunities, far from reducing unemployment, increases it. Those who come from the countryside to the towns compare the high expected earnings with the probability of getting a job.[8] As job opportunities are increased, more people are attracted. This has contributed to the problem of the high rate of urban drift and the shanty towns. The employed urban workers, though poor by Western standards, belong to the better off when measured against the distribution of income in their own countries.

All this forced the development debate to focus on the question of income distribution. One of the landmarks was the book published in 1974 by the World Bank and the Sussex Institute of Development Studies, entitled *Redistribution with Growth*.[9] There were two sets of questions:

(1) how can we make the small-scale, labour-intensive, informal sector, which was "discovered" by some of the ILO employment missions, more productive; how can we remove discrimination against

this sector and improve its access to credit, information and markets? The question here is how does redistribution affect efficiency and growth? Does helping the "working poor" mean sacrificing productivity, or is helping the small man an efficient way of promoting growth?

(2) Turning the question the other way round, how does economic growth affect distribution?

It was quite clearly seen that in poor countries growth is a necessary condition for eradicating poverty, but it also seemed that economic growth in some countries was of a kind which reinforced and entrenched existing inequalities in income, asset and power distributions. Therefore, not surprisingly, a certain type of growth, beginning with an unequal asset and power distribution, made it more difficult to redistribute income or eradicate poverty.

It was said that it would be difficult, if one began with an unequal asset and power distribution, to redistribute existing assets. This was called "static". The distinction drawn between "static" and "dynamic" is that "static" means redistribution of the *existing* stock of land and "dynamic" redistribution of *increments* of income. (It will be seen that this approach is an elaboration of the second assumption mentioned on p. 324). But the static solution is in reality much more dynamic, because static redistribution of assets (the "expropriation of the expropriators") involves a radical land reform and the introduction of workers' participation and self-management or nationalization into industry. "Dynamic" redistribution meant that out of incremental income—this was thought to be easier—a little would be taken away in the form of taxation and channelled into public services intended to benefit the poor. This is "redistribution with growth". But it was discovered that the results of so-called "dynamic" redistribution are very modest, at any rate for low-income countries. According to one simulation exercise[10] an annual transfer of 2 per cent of GNP over 25 years into public investment to build up the stock of capital available to the poor, which was upheld as a very "dynamic" policy, raises after 40 years the consumption of the bottom 40 per cent by only 23 per cent, that is to say their rate of consumption growth would accelerate by 1/2 per cent a year: $1 for a $200 income. The model excluded, however, the human capital aspects of some forms of consumption and the impact on labour utilization, which are stressed by the basic-needs approach.

Much of the redistribution literature measures inequality by the Gini coefficient. It runs through the whole range, from the richest income to the poorest. It focuses on somewhat meaningless deciles instead of socially, regionally or ethnically identifiable, deprived groups. It does not tell us who is in these decile groups, for how long and for what reasons. Nor does it tell us about the scope for mobility, the degree of equality of opportunity. What interests us is either redistribution from rich to poor or, even more, the reduction of absolute poverty. We are not particularly interested in redistribution to the middle, which would reduce inequality but leave poverty untouched. Nor in income deciles as such, for these are not sociologically or humanly, or politically interesting groups.

It is an empirical question to ask how economic growth affects inequality and poverty reduction, and how these reductions in turn affect economic growth. The answers to these questions will depend on such things as the initial distribution of assets, the policies pursued by the government, the available technologies, and the rate of population growth. It is also an empirical question how policies aiming at reducing inequality and meeting basic needs affect freedom. The concern here is not with these empirical questions but with the question which objective is more important: reduction in inequality or meeting basic needs, egalitarianism or humanitarianism?

In societies with very low levels of living (and perhaps elsewhere too) meeting basic needs is more important than reducing inequality for three reasons. First, equality *per se* is probably not an objective of great importance to most people other than utilitarian philosophers and ideologues. Second, this lack of concern is justified, because meeting basic human needs is morally a more important objective than reducing inequality. Third, reducing inequality is a highly complex, abstract objective, open to many different interpretations, and therefore operationally ambiguous.

(1) It has been argued that the fact that no group ever asks to be paid *less* in the interest of social justice demonstrates that people are not really concerned with equality *per se*. It could be said against this that in democracies people *do* vote for progressive taxes and a lack of clamour to be paid less may have something to do with the fear that the benefits might go to the fat-cats rather than the poor. Nevertheless, the rarity of perceptions by the members of certain groups that they are paid too much does suggest that equality as such does not figure importantly in people's objectives. And it is fairly plain that many claims for greater social justice are only thinly disguised claims for getting more for oneself.
(2) Meeting the basic human needs of deprived groups, like removing malnutrition in children, eradicating disease or educating girls, are concrete, specific achievements, whereas reducing inequality is abstract.

There is, of course, nothing wrong with an abstract moral objective, but if we judge policies by the evident reduction of suffering, basic needs scores better than inequality reduction.

(3) It is true that we do not have a production function for meeting adequate standards of nutrition, health and education. We do not know precisely what financial, fiscal and human resources and policies produce these desirable results. The causes are multiple and interact in a complex and still largely unknown manner in producing the results. But at least we have a fairly clear notion as to when we have attained our objective, and of the criteria by which we judge it. In the case of equality, we neither know how to achieve (and maintain) it, nor how precisely to define it, or by what criteria to judge it. To have no clear-cut criteria for defining the optimum degree of equality does not imply that we do not know whether inequality is too great or too small. We may be able to judge improvements in distribution, without a clear idea of the optimum distribution, as we may judge whether water in a well is higher or lower, without knowing its depth. But the uncertainties surrounding permitted differences in income and assets, because of differences in age, sex, location, needs, merit, etc., and how to resolve conflicts between, e.g., merit and need, make it difficult to give operational meaning to the objective of redistributive policies: they make "equality" conceptually elusive.

It might, however, be objected that poverty necessarily contains a relative component, that it is measured against a standard set by the norms of a society, and that it is therefore closely related to inequality. Without rejecting this view, it must be asserted that there is an irreducible core of absolute deprivation which can be determined by medical and physiological criteria, without having recourse to reference groups, averages, or other relative criteria. In addition to this core of absolute poverty, it has been recognized, at least since Adam Smith and Karl Marx, that poverty contains a relative component. In the first place, whatever doctors, nutritionists and other scientists may say about the objective conditions of deprivation what is also relevant is how the poor themselves perceive their deprivation. Second, this perception is a function of the reference group from which the poor take their standards of what comprises the necessities required for a decent minimum level of living. But we should not define poverty and deprivation in such a way that they can never be reduced, however much absolute income levels rise, if the measure of inequality remains unchanged. This would make poverty eradication rather like the electric hare used to spur on greyhounds at dog races.

After the dead end of "employment" and the limitation and irrelevance of egalitarianism, we have now reached the final step, basic human needs. It is a logical step in the path of development thinking. There are at least five fundamental advantages in zooming in on basic needs, compared with previous strategies, concepts or approaches to growth, employment, income redistribution and poverty eradication.

First, and most important, basic needs reminds us of the objective, of the end of the development effort, which is to provide all human beings with the opportunity for a fuller life. This cannot be done without first meeting basic needs. In the last two decades, we have sometimes got lost in the intricacies of means—production, productivity, savings ratios, export ratios, capital/output ratios, tax ratios, and so on—and lost sight of the end. We came near to being guilty, to borrow a term from Marx, of "commodity fetishism". Being clear about the end obviously does not mean that we can neglect the means: on the contrary, it directs our efforts to choosing the right means for the ultimate ends we wish to achieve. We have, in the past, moved away from one of the aims of development, which is meeting basic human needs, to the means, which is some type of conglomeration of commodities valued at market prices, irrespective of whether they are air conditioners or bicycles, luxury houses or rural shelters, whether they benefit the rich or the poor. The basic needs approach reminds us of the fundamental concern of development, which is human beings and their needs.

Second, basic needs spells out in considerable detail human needs in terms of health, food, education, water, shelter, transport, energy, simple household goods, as well as non-material needs such as participation, cultural identity and a sense of purpose, which interact with the material needs. Basic needs is a more positive concept than the double negatives of eliminating or reducing unemployment or alleviating poverty.

Third, it goes behind abstractions like money, income, employment. These are aggregates and have their place and function. They are important concepts and should not be abandoned; but they are useless if they conceal specific, concrete objectives toward which we want to move. It is a step from abstract to concrete, from aggregate to specific.

The evolution sketched above shows that our concepts have become decreasingly abstract and increasingly disaggregated, concrete and specific. We started with GNP and its growth, a highly abstract and unspecified conglomerate of goods and services, irrespective of what and for whom. We then turned to employment, which is a somewhat more specific goal. We increasingly narrowed down the discussion to particular groups of unemployed: the school leavers, the recent migrants to the city, the landless labourers, the small farmers without water supply, and so forth. But "employment" also was seen to have serious limitations. We narrowed down our ideas to identify deprived groups of individuals and families—women, children under five, the old, youths with specific needs, ethnic groups discriminated against, communities in distant and neglected regions.

Fourth, basic needs has an appeal to members of the national and international community, and is therefore capable of mobilizing resources, which vaguer (though important) objectives, such as raising growth rates or contributing 0.7 per cent of GNP, or redistributing for greater equality, have not. We do not normally share lottery prizes or stock exchange gains with our grown-up brothers and sisters, but we do help when they are ill, or their children need education, or some other basic need is to be met. Similarly with the wider human family.[11] Basic needs has something of the nature of a public good. The fact that I get satisfaction from knowing that a hungry child is fed does not detract from your satisfaction. Basic needs therefore has the power to mobilize support for policies that more abstract notions lack.

Fifth, basic needs has great organizing and integrating power intellectually, as well as politically. It provides a key to the solution of a number of apparently separate, but on inspection related problems. If basic needs is made the starting point, these otherwise recalcitrant problems fall into place and become amenable to solutions. Urbanization, the protection of the environment, equality, international and intra-Third World trade, appropriate technology, the role of the trans-national enterprise, the relation between rural development and industrialization, rural—urban migration, domination and dependence, all appear in a new light and are seen to be related.[12]

In one sense, this is a home-coming. For when we embarked on development 30 years ago, it was surely the needs of the poor of the world that we had in mind. In the process we got side-tracked, but we also discovered many important things about development. We learned about the importance of making small farmers and members of the informal urban sector more productive; we learned about the scope for "efficient" redistribution, that is redistribution that also contributes to economic growth of a more equitable kind; we learned about the numerous dimensions of labour markets and the importance of creating demand for certain types of product and the labour producing them.

We are now back to where we started in the 1950s, when pioneers like Pitambar Pant in India and Lauchlin Currie[13] who led the first World Bank mission to a developing country—Colombia—told us that development must be concerned with meeting basic human needs (though their strategies were quite different). But we are back with a deeper understanding of the issues, of many of the inhibitions, obstacles and constraints, but also with a clearer vision of the path.

NOTES

1. The views expressed are purely personal and not necessarily those of the World Bank. I am indebted for helpful comments to Shahid Javed Burki, Robert Cassen, Mahbub ul Haq, Richard Jolly, Akbar Noman, Frances Stewart and T. N. Srinivasan.
2. A good survey, to which I am indebted, is to be found in H. W. Singer, "Poverty, Income Distribution and Levels of Living: Thirty Years of Changing Thought on Development Problems", in *Reflections on Economic Development and Social Change. Essays in honor of Professor V. K. R. V. Rao*, C. H. Hanumantha Rao and P. C. Joshi (eds.), Allied Publishers Private Ltd., Bombay (1979); and Institute of Economic Growth, Delhi (1979).
3. W. A. Lewis, *The Theory of Economic Growth*, Allen & Unwin, London (1955).
4. John Rawls, *The Theory of Justice*, Harvard University Press, Cambridge, Mass. (1971).
5. Simon Kuznets, "Economic Growth and Income Inequality", *American Economic Review*, vol. 45, no. 1 (1955).
6. W. A. Lewis, "Economic Development with Unlimited Supplies of Labor", *Manchester School* (May 1954).
7. Gunnar Myrdal, *Asian Drama: An Inquiry into the Poverty of Nations*, Twentieth Century Fund (1968).
8. J. R. Harris and M. P. Todaro, "Migration, unemployment and development: a two-sector analysis", *American Economic Review* (March 1970).
9. Hollis Chenery, *et al.*, *Redistribution with Growth*, Oxford University Press, London (1974).
10. *Ibid.*, p. 228.
11. Arnold C. Harberger, "On the Use of Distributional Weights in Social Cost–Benefit Analysis". Paper presented at a conference on research in taxation sponsored by the National Science Foundation and the National Bureau of Economic Research, Stanford, California (January 1976). Supplement to April 1978 *Journal of Political Economy*.
12. See Ch. 10.
13. World Bank, *The Basis of a Development Program for Colombia*, Washington, DC (1950).

19 The Distinctive Features of a Basic-Needs Approach to Development

There are two ways of defining a basic-needs approach to development (BN). The first sees in BN the culmination of 25 years of development thought and experience. On this definition, BN embraces the components of previous strategies and approaches, such as rural development, urban poverty alleviation, employment creation through small-scale industries, "redistribution with growth", and other poverty, employment, and equity-oriented approaches. The merit of such a definition is that it rallies support under the appealing banner of "Basic Needs" from a wide variety of people and institutions. The new element is a shift of emphasis towards social services designed to help and mobilize the poor, and an extension of "new style" projects in nutrition, health and education. The fact that BN means many things to many people is, from this point of view, an advantage.

But there are also drawbacks in elevating BN to the all-embracing, almost exclusive, development strategy. It is intellectually clumsy, because it runs into difficulties of demarcation and of incorporating objectives other than basic needs; and in so far as its specific contribution is concerned, it suffers from political unreality. More generally, this type of definition tends to blur the features that distinguish BN from other strategies and therefore makes it more difficult to reach agreement by defining areas of disagreement.

The second way of defining a basic-needs approach is to bring out sharply the distinctive features of BN and to define the strategy as one supplementing or complementing existing strategies. This approach has the tactical defects of its intellectual merits: it will tend to evoke controversy, arouse opposition to those aspects that opponents dislike and may reduce the chances of reaching agreement on action. But it has intellectual and political appeal, because it cannot be accused of simply pouring old wine into new bottles, or of concealing behind a polemical slogan questions calling for serious analysis and experiment.

In this section an attempt will be made to define the differentiating features of a basic-needs approach. It then becomes not the development strategy but an adjunct to, and a modification of, existing development strategies.

A basic-needs approach to development starts from the objective of providing the opportunities for the full physical, mental and social development of the human personality and then derives the ways of achieving this objective. It focuses on the end of mobilizing *particular* resources for *particular* groups, identified as deficient in these resources (e.g., caloric adequacy by age, sex and activity). These groups, as we have seen, might be malnourished children under five, or they might be rural communities in distant regions where harvests are uncertain, or they might be women, or ethnic groups discriminated against, or the old. They are not deciles in an abstract scale of income distribution. The basic needs approach then concentrates on the nature of what is provided and its impact on needs, rather than on income alone. It does not replace the more aggregate and abstract concepts, which remain essential to measurement and analysis; it gives them content. Nor does it replace concepts that are means to broader ends, such as productivity, production and growth, but it derives from the end of meeting basic human needs the need for changing the composition of output, the rates of growth of its different components, the distribution of purchasing power, and the design of social services.

In addition to the *concrete* specification of human needs in contrast to (and supplementation of) *abstract* concepts, and the emphasis on *ends* in contrast to *means*, BN encompasses "non-material" needs. Unlike some material needs, the means to their satisfaction cannot be dispensed, but they are a vital component of a basic-needs appraoch, not only because they are valued in their own right, but also because they are important conditions for meeting "material" needs. They include the need for self-determination, self-reliance and security, participation in making the decisions that affect workers and citizens, national and cultural identity, and a sense of purpose in life and work. While some of these "non-material" needs are conditions for meeting the more "material" needs, there may be conflict between others. For other sets of needs, there may be neither complementarity nor conflict.[1]

INCOME APPROACH *VERSUS* BASIC NEEDS

The BN approach is contrasted with the income approach, which recommends measures that raise the real incomes of the poor by making them more productive, so that the purchasing power of their earnings (together with the yield of their subsistence production) is adequate to enable them to buy (and grow the produce of) the basic-needs basket. The basic-needs approach, in the narrow sense, then regards the income-orientation of earlier approaches as inefficient or partial, for seven reasons.

(1) There is some evidence that consumers are not always efficient optimizers, especially in nutrition and health; and especially when changing from subsistence farmers to cash-earners. Additional cash income is sometimes spent on food of lower nutritional value than that consumed at lower levels (e.g., polished rice for coarse grains or rice for wheat) or on items other than food.[2]

(2) The manner in which additional income is earned may affect nutrition adversely. Female employment may reduce breast-feeding and therefore the nutrition of babies, even though the mother's income has risen, or more profitable cash crops may replace "inferior" and "cheaper" crops grown and eaten at home, such as millets, or dairy farming, though employment-creating, may divert land from producing cheaper but more nutritious maize. Or the energy costs of producing a cash crop replacing subsistence agriculture may be so great in relation to wages that the dependent members of the family are systematically deprived of adequate nutrition. In such a situation more food would mean lower levels of nutrition.[3]

Both (1) and (2) raise difficult and controversial questions about free choice and society's right to intervene, and about effective methods of aiding choice and strengthening and reaching the weak.

(3) There is maldistribution within households, as well as between households; women and children tend to be neglected in favour of adult males. In some of these societies women also carry the heaviest work load, so that it cannot be argued that food is distributed according to marginal productivity.

(4) Perhaps 20 per cent of the destitute are sick, disabled, aged, or orphaned; they may be members of households or they may not; their needs have to be met through transfer payments or public services, since, by definition, they are incapable of earning. This group has been neglected by the income and productivity approach to poverty alleviation and employment creation. Of course, it raises particularly difficult problems of implementation, not only in poor societies.

(5) Some basic needs can be satisfied only, or more effectively,

through public services (education, health, water, sanitation), through subsidized goods and services, or through transfer payments; these services and those under (4) call for progressive taxation, indirect taxation of luxury goods, and for a system of checks against abuse. The provision of public services is, of course, not a distinct feature of BN. But the emphasis on investigating why these have so often failed to reach the groups for whom they were intended, or were claimed to be intended, and, by redesigning them, ensuring that they do, is.

(6) The income approach has paid a good deal of attention to the choice of technique, but has neglected the need to provide for appropriate products. In many developing societies, the import or domestic production of oversophisticated products, transferred from relatively high-income, high-saving economies, has frustrated the pursuit of a basic-needs approach, by catering for the demand of a small section of the population, or by pre-empting an excessive slice of the low incomes of the poor. The choice of appropriate products, produced by appropriate techniques, giving rise to more jobs and a more even income distribution, which in turn generates the demand for these products, is an essential, distinct feature of the BN approach, and not necessarily fully achieved by a redistribution of income.

(7) Finally, as already mentioned, the income approach neglects the importance of "non-material" needs, both in their own right and as instruments of meeting more effectively and at lower costs some of the material needs. This point becomes particularly relevant if the non-satisfaction of non-material needs (such as participation) increases the difficulty of meeting basic needs more than that of achieving income growth.

THE CASE FOR BASIC NEEDS

The selective approach makes it possible to satisfy the basic human needs of the whole population at levels of income per head substantially below those that would be required by a less discriminating strategy of all-round income growth, and therefore sooner.

This point is crucial. If a military but apt metaphor is permitted, the choice is between precision bombing and devastation bombing. By attacking the evils of hunger, malnutrition, disease and illiteracy with precision, their eradication (or at least amelioration) can be achieved with fewer resources (or sooner) than by choosing the round-about road of raising incomes.

We may think of a "gap" between available resources and resources required to meet basic needs, though this way of putting it is somewhat mechanical, because it neglects alternative methods of mobilizing these resources. The great merit of a BN approach is, then, that it can close this "gap" more successfully for two reasons: first, because it *requires* fewer resources for closing the "gap" in a given time (or the same resources can close it more quickly), and, second, because it makes more resources *available*.

Fewer resources are *required*, or the objective can be achieved sooner, because a direct attack on deprivation economizes in the resources on which income would be spent, which do not contribute to meeting basic needs. These include, in addition to improvements in the instruments of implementation, (i) the non-basic-needs items in the consumption expenditure of the poor; (ii) part of the non-incentive consumption expenditure of the better off; and (iii) investment expenditure to the extent that its reduction does not detract from constructing the sustainable base for meeting basic needs.[4]

In addition, these fewer resources needed show a higher "productivity" in meeting BN. A combined operation for meeting an appropriately selected package of basic needs (e.g., water, sewerage, nutrition and health) economizes in the use of resources and improves the impact, because of linkages, complementarities and interdependencies between different sectors.

Finally, a direct attack on infant mortality,[5] women's education and even the apparently purest "welfare" component, the provision for old age, illness and disability, is thought to reduce desired family size and fertility rates more speedily and àt lower costs than raising household incomes.[6] The causal nexus has not been established beyond controversy, but presents one of the hypotheses thrown up by the BN approach. (Alternatively, reduced population growth can be regarded as a factor increasing available resources.) Freedom from unwanted pregnancies is, moreover, itself a basic need. If met, it does not reduce desired family size but fertility rates by reducing the number of unwanted births. For these three reasons—saving resources on objectives with lower priority than BN, economizing on linkages and reducing fertility rates (and, on certain assumption about the relation between mortality and fertility rates, reducing population growth)—BN economizes in the use of resources and in the time needed to satisfy basic needs.

BN will also tend to make more resources *available*, both domestically and (possibly) internationally. More resources will be available *domestically* for three reasons. First, the composition of output needed to satisfy basic needs is likely to be produced more labour-intensively. In countries with underemployed labour, this will raise not only employment but also production. Second, an attack on malnutrition, disease and illiteracy not only lengthens life and improves its quality (desirable in their own right) but also improves the quality of the labour force. It is, however, an open question whether the returns to this form of human investment are higher at the margin, than those from more conventional investment in physical capital.Third, a BN approach that is based on participation will mobilize local resources and increase incentives for higher production.

More resources may be available *internationally*, because the pledge for meeting the basic needs of the world's poor as a first charge on our aid budgets has stronger moral and political appeal than most other schemes advanced for the promotion of international assistance. There can be no certainty about this, but it is already clear that the concept has international appeal and may help to overcome the present aid fatigue by defining new forms of international cooperation and commitments.[7] Since food is an important element in BN, and since, given the distribution of votes in Western democracies, food aid is politically easier than financial aid, properly channelled food aid can make an important international contribution to meeting basic needs.

It remains to be investigated how a BN approach is likely to affect specific resource constraints, like foreign exchange, administrative skills, etc. It might be thought that BN would reduce exports, but it would also tend to reduce import requirements. It would certainly call for more administrative skills, but if local energy can be harnessed, motivation for raising the supply of these skills would be strengthened; and they might not be of a particularly sophisticated kind and therefore speedily acquired.

In brief, therefore, a BN approach, because it saves resources, because it mobilizes resources, and because it makes these resources more productive, achieves an agreed priority objective sooner than a solely income-oriented approach, even if poverty-weighted. The BN "resource gap" is narrowed or closed from both ends.

But two crucial questions remain: one of value and one of fact. The *value* assumption underlying the above argument is that substantially lower weight is attached to the uses of all extra resources that do not meet basic needs. It may be objected that governments and people who do not accept this value judgement will reject the whole approach, and those that do, won't need it. But aid agencies might wish to adopt it and governments and people do not have monolithic value systems. By dialogue and selective support they might be induced to accept the value judgement.

The crucial *factual* assumption is that leakages, inefficiences and "trickle-up" in a selective system are smaller than in a general system. The "wastage" of the BN approach may be as large as, or even larger than, that of the income-oriented, non-selective approach. There is some evidence that this need not be so. But this is an important area for operational research and experimentation.

THE POLITICS OF BASIC NEEDS

It is sometimes argued that BN is an ideological (polemical, religious, emotive) concept that conceals a call to revolution. Such an interpretation can be justified neither historically nor analytically. (Even if justified, it would still require a "delivery system" for the revolution.) It is evident that a wide variety of political regimes, like those of Japan, Israel, Costa Rica, Taiwan, South Korea, the People's Republic of China, Yugoslavia, Sri Lanka and others have satisfied basic needs within a relatively short time. Options for the future are even wider than the limited experience of the past 25 years.

It is, of course, true that the success of these different political regimes in meeting basic needs cannot be attributed to their having written BN on their banner. But they share certain "initial conditions" (in the distribution of land, tenure systems, levels of education and health, etc.) and a set of policies that present important lessons to others attempting to meet basic needs. The fact that they started from a base at which some basic needs for health and education were already satisfied obviously reduced the time required for meeting basic needs, both directly, and through their indirect effect on the quality and motivation of the labour force.

If some political regimes have succeeded in satisfying basic needs within a short period without adopting the BN approach as an explicit policy, others have paid lip service to the objective, without succeeding in implementing it. The reasons for this gap between profession and practice are, ultimately, political. To some extent (it might be objected), governments lack the knowledge and administrative power to meet basic needs. Rural-development programmes are far more difficult to administer than those for the urban élite, though the same governments are often capable of administering complex programmes of import restrictions or investment licensing, where the protection of the privileged is in question. The neglect might also, partly, be explained by the system of incentives and the type of technologies considered to be essential to a development strategy. But neither administrative weakness nor incentives and technology can fully account for what must ultimately be attributed to absence of a political base. High marginal tax rates, paid by very few, and land reform legislation on paper that remains unimplemented, are the result not so much of administrative weakness, or belief in the need for incentives, as of the fact that the rich operate the machinery to what they regard as their advantage. The second assumption of the growth strategy, mentioned on p. 324, that governments in societies in which power is concentrated have no interest in eradicating poverty, applies with equal force to a basic-needs approach. It is not ignorance that has prevented the implementation of anti-poverty programmes, nor even lack of political will, but the absence of a political base.

If the failures of past strategies were caused by vested interests and the political obstruction of those who would lose from a basic-needs approach, it becomes essential to show how these forces can be kept in check. In many regimes the poor are weak bargainers and are not a political constituency. But measures to meet basic needs can be implemented by a reformist alliance, in a peaceful manner. Some of these measures are clearly in the narrow self-interest of the dominant groups, such as the eradication of communicable diseases or the preservation of social peace. Others are in the longer-term interest of some groups who would have to mobilize support for gradual reform. In nineteenth-century England, the rural rich campaigned against the urban rich for factory legislation, which improved the condition of the poor, while the urban rich campaigned against the rural rich for the repeal of the Corn Laws, which reduced the price of food for the poor. Urban industrialists and workers may support a land reform benefiting small farmers and landless labourers, if this promises more food.

It is, however, possible that the mobilization of the rural and urban masses, required for this approach could initiate a revolutionary process which the initiators of the mobilization process may regret. The conditions in which this is liable to happen, and the conditions in which a grass-roots democracy on a pluralist model would emerge, have received almost no attention so far.

Nor have the macro-economic implications of the *transition* from the present state to one in which basic needs are met been thoroughly investigated. Inflationary pressures, as demand is redirected towards basic-needs goods in inelastic supply, increased imports, capital flight, brain drain, strikes by disaffected groups and even coups d'état would present obstacles in the path of implementation.

Whatever the route, a BN approach, having identified the political, administrative and institutional obstacles to fulfilling basic needs, must specify how these constraints are to be removed.

SUPPLY MANAGEMENT

It has been argued that a distinguishing feature of the BN approach is that it is not sufficient to channel purchasing power into the hands of the poor, through employment creation, productivity-raising measures, improvements in access to productive factors for the self-employed, and appropriate policies for relative prices. The structure of production must be such that it responds speedily to the demand generated by a BN approach. The issue here is whether additional direct interventions in the productive system are then required.

There are merits in a system that relies on raising the productivity of the poor sufficiently to channel purchasing power to them, and then permits prices and market forces to allocate supplies. No objections in principle are commonly raised against using selective price policies (indirect taxes and subsidies) to steer consumer and producer choices in the direction of meeting basic needs. Experience in some countries has shown that attempts to interfere directly with supply by rationing, licensing, building permits and other direct controls have been open to abuse and have, at best, bred inefficiency, at worst strengthened monopoly power, increased inequality and encouraged corruption. Yet, it may be necessary to combine the generation of earning opportunities with some forms of direct supply management, in order to prevent the intentions of demand policy from being frustrated. The purpose of higher money incomes for the poor can be frustrated by rising prices of the goods and services on which they spend their income, if additional supply is not forthcoming, so that real incomes have not improved (e.g., when improved agricultural prices lead to higher prices of the industrial products bought by farmers). Or the higher money incomes of one group of poor may be met by extra supplies, but only at the expense of the supplies to another group who then suffer from deprivation.

The disadvantages of rationing and other direct controls have been examined largely in the light of the efficient allocation of resources for productivity and growth, though there has been some work on the impact on employment and income distribution. But there has been hardly any work on the scope and limits of these instruments for the purpose of meeting basic needs. A reassessment may well lead to the modification of some of the conclusions.

Changes in relative prices are useful instruments for marginal adjustments, but they are not always equally suitable for bringing about discrete changes.[8] And the transition from the present state to a basic-needs-oriented approach will call for large and fairly sudden changes. Total prohibition of the import and the domestic production of a non-basic-needs item is often a better way of controlling its consumption (and, indirectly, technology and income distribution) than a tariff combined with an excise tax, if policing to prevent smuggling and bootlegging is effective. Since controls can only prevent activities, not induce them, the positive counterpart to controls may be production in the public sector.

According to one interpretation of BN, the domestic structure of production must be adapted to BN requirements. If this were to imply forgoing the benefits from foreign trade, such an interpretation would, of course, be nonsense. "Supply management" must cover wholesale and retail distribution, transport and storage, and foreign trade. But a needs-oriented approach may raise previously neglected issues in interregional and international trade. Thus, if it were found that the poor in scattered rural communities cannot purchase the food grains imported from abroad (or produced in the most "efficient" areas domestically) because, in comparing costs, the costs of transport, distribution and storage were not fully taken into account, it may well turn out that the food should be locally produced, even at what appear to be somewhat higher costs.[9]

IMPLEMENTATION: DANGERS OF TRICKLE-UP

Some critics of the BN approach share the goal of meeting BN but object that, unless specific steps are spelt out that lead to their satisfaction, it cannot be called a strategy. This is an entirely valid invitation to think through the implications of a BN approach. No doubt, as yet there is nothing that could be described as a fully articulated BN strategy, even as an adjunct to other strategies. More emphasis on low-cost, mass public services, more emphasis on participation, and more emphasis on meeting the needs of small children and women in households does not amount to a strategy. For those who agree on the objective, the conclusion ought to be (a) further work in areas of ignorance (see below p. 361) and (b) experimentation with a wide variety of approaches in the initial stages, so that experience from pilot projects is gathered for replication.

Among the many areas in need of clarification is the question whether meeting basic needs directly is more promising than doing so indirectly. Certain types of indirect approach, such as "trickle-down" through concentration on sectors with high commercial returns and the resulting high income growth, irrespective of its composition and distribution, have been discredited. But others remain to be explored. Thus, if we are concerned with the bottom 40 per cent, would it be better to concentrate on those who are potentially viable farmers, and hope that out of their higher production welfare payments for the poorest 10 per cent will become possible, or employment opportunities will be generated, or should the needs of the poorest be met directly and immediately? The importance of channelling particular resources to particular groups does not imply that some indirect ways of channeling them may not be more effective than direct ways.

One of the inadequacies of past approaches is that they have not done full justice to the precise impact of public services on satisfying needs. The study of how public services can reach the poor and how the poor can moblize their own efforts to make these services effective is still in a rudimentary state. There is evidence that in countries where the distribution of incomes, assets and power is uneven, not only private but also public goods are distributed to the better off. The incidence of public services reinforces that unequal income distribution. The questions to be investigated are: how can we ensure that public revenues, devoted to public services to meet BN, actually reach the vulnerable groups? How is access to the bureaucracy secured, how appropriate priorities in the line of applicants, and how efficient ultimate benefits for those in need? What system of checks against abuse, and of monitoring to ensure success are required?

While social services for the poor and their biased impact have received a good deal of attention, the biased impact of many systems of taxation has received less attention. Either taxes do not exist, or nominal taxas are not collected, or, where they are collected, their ultimate incidence is shifted on to those least able to bear them. A thorough scrutiny of the system of collecting revenues and the incidence of taxation from the point of view of meeting basic needs is as important as the examination of the incidence of public services.

LINKAGES AND COMPLEMENTARITIES

The improvement of nutrition, or of water supply, or of sanitation, or of health services, each in isolation, has a smaller impact on the mortality or morbidity of a poverty group than a concerted attack. Without adequate nutrition, resistance to diseases will be lower and the cost of a health programme higher. Without the elimination of gastro-intestinal diseases, nutritional requirements are higher. Without safe water, control of communicable diseases and improvements in public health, nutritional programmes are unlikely to have permanent benefits. There is evidence that family-planning programmes are more effective if combined with nutrition and health measures. The benefits of education in raising the effective impact of all other services is obvious. And equally, improved nutrition and health enable children to benefit more from education.

Certain linkages between different public services reduce costs; others improve the impact. In addition, there are important and sometimes neglected linkages between private income and access to public services. Parents have to earn adequate incomes before they can afford to spare their children from work and send them to school; and they need money to equip them with books and transport and to provide them with properly lit rooms for their home work. The sick must be able to afford to travel to clinics.

While a concerted attack on several fronts or a "Big Push" is, therefore, more effective, resources are scarce and policies have to be selective. Alternatively, there may be trade-offs between say, eradicating malaria and some other operation, or between education and supplying safe water. In such cases a "vertical" or spearhead approach would be more appropriate than a "horizontal" approach. This implies that the quantification of the costs and the benefits of these services must be conducted in terms of selective packages and appropriate phasing. The implications for project appraisal are clear. Costs per unit of a given public service may be reduced if the service is combined with others, and the impact on health, education, nutrition or family planning may be raised by such a combination. For some purposes "balanced growth", for others an "unbalanced" attack may be more economical. Detailed investigation of these issues is an essential feature of the successful implementation of a BN approach.

TECHNOLOGIES AND ADMINISTRATION

The cost of providing for basic needs will vary over a wide range, depending on the technology. But the technology, in turn, will depend on the degree of local initiative, commitment and participation, the amount and quality of local factors of production and materials mobilized, and local cultural attitudes and social institutions. The managerial and administrative framework for implementing BN is crucial for its feasibility and costs. Much is talked about the need for participation and self-management. The important questions, however, relate to the precise combination of central leadership, central coordination and central resource contribution, with decentralized decision-making and mobilization of local resources (especially underemployed, low-cost labour) which would, in specific circumstances, be most effective.

There is also the question as to what forms the participation should take in a democracy. The fascist corporate state claimed that it drew on the participation of workers, employers and farmers. It has been said that Tito had got the idea of self-managed enterprises from Mussolini. Whether true or not, self-management has been practised more in socialist dictatorships than in democracies. There are forms of participation that bypass representative democratic institutions.

Democratic representatives, on the other hand, are for that very reason unrepresentative. They are more ambitious, more articulate, more capable and frequently better off than the people they "represent". It is, therefore, not at all clear who it is who should formulate the priority and content of basic needs, and how to avoid the twin dangers of élitist dictation or "consciousness-raising" from above, and non-articulated basic needs from below.

Past calculations of an independently determined range of needs have often started by counting those in need and estimating the cost of an independently determined range of needs eliminating the deficiency. The count ing was often wrong (in view of the poor data base), and the standards of what was supposed to be supplied often ill-chosen. The resulting bill for "needed services" was exorbitant, and in practice, the partial attempts to provide them that resulted rarely succeeded in reaching the poor. Planning for BN should set standards that are correct and allow for the wide interpersonal and intertemporal variations in human requirements; it should pay attention to what can be afforded by the use of appropriate technologies; it should pay attention to social and cultural factors, respect indigenous values, mobilize local resources and concentrate on processes and sequences that meet the needs of the poor. The "count, cost and carry" approach has little to contribute to this.

Allowing for individual variations in energy requirements, for example reduces the estimated shortfalls. As P. V. Skhatme has shown, the incidence of undernutrition for India comes to 25 per cent for the urban areas and 15 per cent for the rural area against the estimates of 50 and 40 per cent respectively made by Dandekar and Rath based on a poverty line corresponding to average requirements.[10]

There are at least six reasons why the technology and administration of projects intended to meet the basic needs of particular deprived groups present special difficulties, additional to those encountered with more conventional development projects.

(1) Technologically, the methods used (e.g. in water supply and waste disposal) may have to be adapted or especially designed to reach the group.

(2) Geographically, the vulnerable groups may be remote from the centres of economic activity, adding to transport, communication and administrative problems.

(3) Socially and linguistically, the groups may be distinct from those involved in the mainstream of economic activity.

(4) Politically, the groups may be weak and inarticulate and may therefore have little power, access to power, or influence upon the allocation of resources.

(5) Economically, the groups may be outside the cash economy and therefore not affected by the forces of economic progress.

(6) The valuations of these groups may be different from those of the planners and administrators, and the setting of objectives, as well as the appraisal of the results of the projects may have to follow criteria that are different from those adopted in the rest of the economy.

Although the call on administrative resources for implementing a basic-needs approach is likely to be heavy, economy and better results can be achieved by devolution or decentralization, by mobilizing those at whom improvements are aimed, and by a programme of appropriate phasing.

TIME DISCOUNT RATES AND POVERTY WEIGHTING

A distinct feature of the BN approach is the structure of time discount rates. Implicit in the BN approach is a high rate of time discount for the near future, reflecting the urgency of meeting basic needs soon, subject to maintaining achieved satisfactions of basic needs indefinitely.

Another distinct feature is the weighting of meeting the basic needs of those at different distances below the basic-needs standard. Previous approaches either simply count the heads of those below a defined poverty line, without distinguishing degrees of deprivation among them, or attach differential weights to income growth of different deciles. A. K. Sen has suggested a weighted measure of the income shortfalls below the basic needs line.[11] He takes the rank values of the poor in the income ranking as the weights to be put on the income shortfalls of the different persons in the category of the poor. If there are m people with incomes below the basic-needs line, the income shortfall of the richest among the poor gets a weight of 1, the second richest a weight of 2, and so on, ending up with a weight of m on the shortfall of the poorest poor. This measure has the virtue of being sensitive to the exact pattern of the income shortfalls of the poor from the basic-needs line.

But we have argued that income is an inadequate and only partial guide to basic needs. We need to supplement the above approach by taking explicit account of which goods and services are going to whom. Again, Sen has suggested that "commodity j going to person i may be thought to be a good ij in itself, not the same as the same commodity going to another person k, which is now taken to be a different good, kj. . . . The approach can, of course, be married also to that of dealing with characteristics such as calories as opposed to specific commodities such as rice of bajra."[12] In this manner, weights would be attached not to income but to specified goods and services or even to the impact on specified basic needs.

A pure BN approach would give zero weight to meeting the needs of those above the basic needs line, until the basic needs of all are met. But if the BN approach is regarded as an adjunct to other strategies, the relative weight to be attached to income growth of those above the basic-needs line remains to be determined by the policy-makers. To illustrate: a pure BN approach would sacrifice any amount of capital accumulation, if thereby the BN of all can be satisfied, on a sustainable basis, within a short period. A mixed strategy might prefer to leave the BN of 5 per cent unsatisfied, if thereby sustained growth of income above basic needs can be attained for the remaining 95 per cent.

BASIC NEEDS AND GROWTH: A TRADE-OFF?

Critics of the basic-needs approach to development often complain that such an approach would sacrifice savings and productive investment, and incentives to work, for the sake of current consumption and welfare; that poor countries can ill afford this and that, in any case, the advocates of basic needs should bring out the choice clearly, so that the costs in terms of forgone growth can be seen.

Basic needs and growth are not strictly comparable objectives. Growth emphasizes annual increments of production and income. Basic needs emphasizes the need to mobilize particular resources for particular groups, now, tomorrow, and later. All basic-needs approaches must also contain a time dimension. "Maximizing growth" is not a sensible objective. It would mean squeezing consumption to the bare productive minimum, investing the whole surplus over an infinite time period, and indulging in an infinite consumption orgy on doomsday. Accelerating growth makes sense, if the distribution of consumption over the time span of the planning period would be improved. The call for more growth reflects a concern for the future. A basic-needs approach proposes a set of policies that increasingly meet a dynamic range of basic needs, of a growing population. Just as no sensible person would advocate squeezing consumption to the bare minimum for ever, so no sensible person would wish to meet basic needs tomorrow and face collapse the week after.

If basic needs and growth are to be compared at all, the question should be: does meeting basic needs imply sacrificing current output and current incomes? Such a sacrifice then may reduce aggregate growth of income per head by raising the capital/output ratio and/or lowering the savings ratio, and/or raising population growth. And such reduced aggregate growth, in turn, may reduce *future* consumption.

Four types of trade-off can be envisaged:

(i) there may be a trade-off between benefits to higher income groups in favour of benefits to lower income groups (redistribution of consumption);

(ii) there may be a trade-off between non-basic-needs goods and services consumed by *all* income groups, including the poor, in favour of basic-needs goods and services consumed by the poor (reallocation of consumption pattern);

(iii) there may be a trade-off between activities that create incentives for larger savings and efforts to work (incentive goods, private savings, budget surplus) in favour of current consumption (lower savings ratio); and

(iv) there may be a trade-off between goods and services which make a larger contribution to future production in favour of those that make a smaller contribution or none (higher capital–output ratio).

Trade-offs (iii) and (iv) would mean sacrificing investment and future consumption in favour of current consumption.

All policies have certain distributional dimensions, in both space and time; they imply decisions about how goods and services are distributed between income groups, between regions, between occupations, and, of course, over time. The concern of those who suspect that basic needs involves a trade-off with growth is that the children and grandchildren of those whose basic needs are met now would have to accept lower levels of living than if the present generation were asked to tighten its belt more, and postponed meeting basic needs, for higher prosperity later.

As we have seen, basic needs draws attention to a principal objective of development, which is to eradicate poverty. This logical precedence of an end over the means of achieving this end in no way implies that means can be neglected. On the contrary, it focuses attention on the means required to achieve the end. Although there is a welfare component in basic needs, to meet basic needs on a sustainable basis in poor countries calls for considerable investment and growth of production, but this growth would be differently composed and distributed (and may be differently measured) from non-BN-oriented growth. Growth is also required to meet the rising standards of basic needs, as incomes rise and new needs replace those already satisfied, and to achieve objectives other than basic needs, like rising prosperity for the less poor, non-basic needs satisfaction for all, provision for the prosperity of future generations, for national defence, etc.

We have seen that meeting basic needs has itself production- and productivity-raising consequences, which have not yet been precisely quantified. First, a well-nourished, healthy, vigorous, educated, skilled labour force is a more efficient and better motivated labour force than one whose basic needs have not been met. This applies both to the present labour force and, through meeting the basic needs of children, to the next generation. Second, we have seen that basic needs contains thrusts which are important "correlates of fertility decline". Third, basic needs for the mass of the people can be met only by a large-scale mobilization of under-utilized local labour (and local materials).

Ignoring for the moment problems of measurement, the options can be illustrated by four paths. On the diagram we trace the log of consumption per head of the poor on the vertical axis and time on the horizontal axis (so that a straight line shows growth at a constant proportionate rate). Path 1 starts with depressing levels of consumption, but, as a result of better incentives and productive investment, overtakes path 2 at some point (T_1) and, forever after, the consumption of the poor is higher. Path 2 starts with higher consumption by the poor but, by neglecting incentives, private and public savings and productive investment, falls behind path 1 after a certain date, T_1. This is how the option is often presented and how it has also been implemented in a few countries.

It should be clear that sound policies should rule out path 3, which lies below path 2 and, after a period, also below path 1. This could be the result of inefficient ways of meeting the needs of the poor, in which both current consumption and future consumption are lower than on the alternative paths. (There clearly are also inefficient paths in the pursuit of investment and growth.)

The rationale behind basic needs, however, is path 4. High priority is given to some components of current consumption of the poor which may then, for a while, fall below the consumption level that could have been attained by a more growth-oriented strategy. But when the present generation of children are entering the labour force and human capital begins to yield returns, (T_2), the growth path is steeper than it would have been under 1, and overtakes first the welfare path 2 and later the growth path 1.

Stalinist forced industrialization and the Industrial Revolution in England followed path 1. Taiwan, Korea and perhaps Japan followed path 4, laying in earlier years the runway for future "take-off into self-sustained growth", by meeting certain basic needs through land reform and massive investment in human capital, especially education. Critics charge that Sri Lanka and Tanzania may be following path 2 and Burma path 3 though these experiences have not yet been fully analysed.

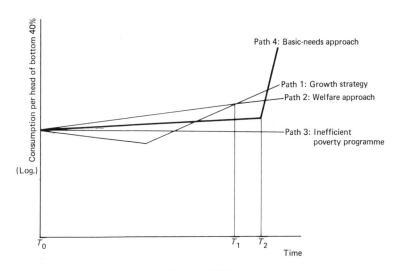

FIGURE 19.1

In comparing growth paths, it is important that growth and its components are correctly measured. Basic needs are measured, in the first place, in terms of physiological needs and physical inputs—so many primary school teachers, so many paramedical workers, so many calories—and financial costs are calculated from these. Growth, on the other hand, is an aggregate in which the existing, often very unequal, income distribution determines purchasing power, and with it the price weights. A 10 per cent increase in the income of a man who earns $10,000 is weighted a hundred times as much as a 10 per cent increase in the income of a man with $100.

Redistribution with Growth has suggested modifications of the conventional growth measure, which weights initial shares of each income group by their share in the national income, so that the weight of the poorest is the smallest and that of the richest the largest. One possibility is to weight each group equally, according to the number of people (or households, allowing for size and age distribution) in it, so that a 1 per cent growth of the poorest 25 per cent has the same weight as a 1 per cent growth of the richest 25 per cent. An even more radical system of weighting would attribute zero weights to the growth of income of all income groups above the poorest 25 or 40 per cent, and a weight of unity to those below the poverty line. Whatever method is chosen, any discussion of the "trade-off" between basic needs and growth ought to specify what weights it attaches to income growth of different income groups. This would bring out clearly the value judgements underlying the strategy.

The relative importance of different items in the consumption basket is normally determined by their relative prices. We register growth when the consumption of whisky has risen, even though the consumption of milk has declined. This is not because we regard whisky consumed by the rich as more important than milk consumed by the poor, but because the higher incomes of the rich determine the relatively high price of whisky, while lack of purchasing power of the poor is reflected in the low price of milk. In societies with unequal income distributions, the standard measure for GNP growth, therefore, gives excessive weight to the growth of non-basic-needs goods and deficient weight to basic needs goods.

There is, however, a complication that does not arise from problems of measurement. It may be thought necessary to neglect the welfare of the poor people in the short, and possibly even the medium run in order to permit the non-poor to make money, for this is what benefits the poor in the long run.

Certain forms of "trickle-down" approach have been discredited, but there are a number of mechanisms by which the wealth of the non-poor could benefit the poor: expanded demand for their labour, higher wages or lower prices resulting from productivity growth, upgrading of skills, tax revenues collected from the rich and spent on social services or transfers, etc. There is now firm evidence that as far as agriculture for food production is concerned, inequality of land holdings is not a necessary condition of raising yields per acre or even (above a critical minimum size) yields per unit of all inputs, but the same may not be true of the industrial sector. Where encouraging the better off to improve their position now is regarded as a necessary condition for improving the lot of the poor later, a genuine conflict between basic needs and growth arises.

We conclude that one difference between "growth" strategies and "basic-needs" strategies consists in the content and beneficiaries of "growth". Conventionally measured economic growth uses weights that show no concern for what is produced and consumed, and who benefits. A dollar's worth of purchasing power is counted the same, whether spent on whisky or milk, whether it is consumed by the affluent or by deprived children. Basic needs puts the needs of the poor into the centre. If this is reflected in a proper measure, what at first appears as a trade-off may turn out not to be one.

At the same time, since:

(i) permitting the better-off to accumulate may be a necessary condition for meeting basic needs;

(ii) not all basic needs can be satisfied at once, even by the most radical redistribution of income and restructuring of production, so that growth is needed to meet them;

(iii) needs represent a hierarchy in which the satisfaction of currently dominant ones brings new ones into the fore;

(iv) basic needs is a minimum programme, to which other objectives will normally be added; and

(v) with increasing populations more resources are needed in order to maintain present standards,

growth is the necessary inter-temporal component of a basic-needs approach. But having specified the particular resources needed for the particular target groups, and having defined a time profile for meeting the basic needs of a growing population on a sustainable basis, growth will turn out to be the *result* of a basic-needs policy, not its *objective*. Growth is not normally something that has to be sacrificed, "traded-off", in order to meet present needs. On the contrary, in the light of the above considerations, a "basic-needs" approach may well call for *higher* growth rates than a so-called "growth" strategy. But the composition and the beneficiaries (and the measure) of such growth will be different from those of a conventional high-growth strategy.

HEALTH SERVICES: AN ILLUSTRATION

The kind of evidence one would hope to gather from country, programme and sector studies can be illustrated by a comparison of the organization of health services. The "barefoot doctors" in *China* are the best-known example of an "appropriate medical technology". A village appoints one from among its members to go off for a period to be trained and then return and serve the community at a rate of pay that is calculated in points, as it is for all other members of the team. It is important that the health worker is not an outside bureaucrat, sent in by the government, but a full member of the commune. There is equal access to the health services, at least within the village, though better-off communes appear to be able to acquire better social services.

The collective farm is not the only organization capable of doing this. Villages with individual farming in other parts of the world have pooled resources and provided members of the village the means to acquire special training, but the collective farm has advantages in this form of pooling. Clearly, there must be a corresponding decision at the centre to provide the required training for the commune's candidate. In China, the central government had to make a conscious effort to reallocate a significant portion of its resources away from urban services towards activities that benefited rural areas.

This provision of rural health services was not delivered as a separable and isolated benefit. The impact and cost of these services is in many ways dependent on the provision of basic levels of food and income. Rural health services, for example, provide birth control information and contraceptives. The old and the sick, who were not helped much by land reform, could draw on the welfare funds of the commune. The availability of old age sickness benefits that do not depend on having several surviving sons provides villagers with the incentive to use these contraceptives. The provision of improved health services interacts with other rural efforts, such as the mobilization of labour for rural construction works.

In *India*, the proposal in the Draft Fifth Plan is to select from each village through the existing institutions of panchayats and gaonsabhas one literate individual for health training at the Primary Health Centres. But past experience shows that the training has been very poor, based on concepts borrowed from the West, unrelated to local practice and needs, with high costs and poor results. The training institutions were ill-equipped and under-utilized. There are problems of pay scales, and of frequent transfer of personnel after training. Trained health workers apparently work for a transfer from the day they are posted to a village. Dai (midwife) training suffered from the fact that the trainers (lady health visitors and auxiliary nurse midwives) competed rather than cooperated with the dais. The dais, moreover, having accepted kits and money from the government, were treated by the villagers as outside agents of the government. Neither the centre not the states provided adequate finance to support the scheme.

Social stratification in rural areas has created its own problems. Inadequate and deficient though the medical services were, they have tended to be monopolized by the rural rich. Planners, working with the myth of a "village community", have concluded that lack of medical care for the poor is the result of their indolence, inertia and servility. Basic decisions about leadership in health administration, resource distribution between urban, curative, and rural preventive services and the breaking of bottlenecks show strong urban bias.

Some states in India are exceptions to the above characterization. Kerala has attained the lowest mortality rates and the highest life expectancy among the states in India, at a level of income per head below the average. The higher levels of nutrition are probably connected with land reforms instituted in the nineteenth century. Improved calorie intake was largely the result of higher production of tapioca. But other states show both higher calorie intake and higher per capita incomes, and yet show higher mortality rates. This suggests that, in addition to other aspects of a better diet (e.g., more vegetables, fruits, fish and eggs), other factors than nutrition may have contributed to the remarkably good health record in Kerala. The main factor is the expansion and spread of appropriate health facilities. Figures for population numbers served by hospitals and dispensaries show a better coverage for West Bengal than for Kerala. But the proportion of persons who received treatment in hospitals and dispensaries in the two states show a utilization ratio for Kerala three and a half times that of West Bengal. Much of the trouble of the health services in the rest of India is gross under-utilization of existing facilities. Kerala has the highest utilization ratio. It thus achieves better results with a lower expenditure per person.

The factors responsible for the high utilization ratio have not been studied, but an important reason may be the spatial allocation of such facilities. Even if medical care is free, a person incurs direct and indirect costs in travelling to a hospital or dispensary. For those working on daily wages, a visit may mean sacrificing a day's pay. Only when the illness becomes serious enough to risk loss of employment will the journey become worthwhile. The objective of a good health-care system should be to enlarge the catchment area so that the utilization ratio rises, and discrimination by income and by location is reduced.

There is evidence that the high utilization ratio in Kerala is the result of a location matrix that has provided the widest catchment area for its health system. In different regions of the state, there is a clear correlation between, on the one hand, number of beds per 100,000 of population and area to be covered and, on the other, death and infant mortality rates. Accessibility to medical care (by income and residence) is one of the important variables determining the level of health in a region.

Like land reform, the policy goes back to the nineteenth century. The Maharajah announced the following state policy in 1865:

> "One of the main objects of my ambition is to see that good medical aid is placed within the reach of all classes of my subjects. It is a blessing which is not at present in the power of individuals generally to secure how much soever they may desire it. It is hence the obvious duty of the state to render its assistance in this direction."[13]

Again, it is clear that success was due to a multi-pronged attack. Side by side with medical institutions, the government of Travancore paid attention to preventive measures: improvement of public health and sanitation, eradication of contagious diseases, public health education, school health inspection, etc. More than anything else, the spread of education made the people accept the health programme of the government.

Kerala has also registered a sharp decline in birth rates. It is not clear how far this is the result of the extension of family planning facilities, of health services, of reduced mortality rates, of a rise in the age of marriage, of education, especially women's education, of provision for old age or a combination of these "correlates of fertility decline". (Birth rates in 1972 in India were 38·4; in Kerala 31·5 per 1,000 population.) It is also interesting to note that the rural–urban difference in birth rates in Kerala (where such differences are generally far less pronounced) was negligible in contrast to other states. The decline in the birth rate in Kerala began in the early 1960s (1951–60: 38·9 per 1,000), before the full-scale launching of the family planning programme, and may have had more to do with health and educational, than with family planning facilities.

It would be quite wrong to conclude that the success of Kerala is due primarily to measures by the communist elements in its state governments. The origins go back to a fairly radical land reform in the nineteenth century in the southern part of Kerala by a local monarchy interested in weakening the hold of feudal elements, another illustration of a reformist alliance. Moreover, Kerala succeeded in meeting basic needs as a state in a nation that was less successful with central measures. Other Indian states with substantially better economic performance have also been less successful in meeting basic needs. It is from comparisons such as these that one would hope to learn useful lessons for the implementation of a basic-needs approach.

THE INTERNATIONAL IMPLICATIONS OF BASIC NEEDS

BASIC NEEDS AND THE NEW INTERNATIONAL ECONOMIC ORDER

The developing countries are apprehensive lest a basic-needs approach adopted by donors implies sacrificing features of the New International Economic Order (NIEO). (And sceptics among the developed countries regard both the NIEO and BN as emotionally highly charged words without clear policy implications.)

It is true that on superficial inspection there appears to be a conflict. The NIEO aims at revising the rules of international economic relations so as to provide more equal opportunities to all *governments*, whereas basic needs is concerned with the needs of *individuals* and households. The NIEO deals with issues such as commodity price stabilization and support, indexation, the Common Fund, the Integrated Commodity Programme, debt relief, the SDR link, trade liberalization, trade preferences, technology transfer, etc., whereas BN deals with food, water, health, education and shelter. The NIEO aims at unconditional, automatic or semi-automatic, concealed transfers of resources (or at correcting past reverse transfers), whereas basic needs implies a highly targeted approach, aiming directly at the alleviation of deprivation of particular groups. The NIEO would eliminate conditions imposed on resource transfers, BN would wish to make transfers conditional upon their reaching the poor. The schemes proposed in the NIEO are likely to benefit the middle-income countries, and some very small (already relatively over-aided) countries, in whose economy foreign trade plays an important part, rather than the large, poor countries of Asia; and, within these countries, the proposed schemes are likely to benefit the higher income groups, such as exporting industrialists and large farmers, rather than the urban and rural poor.

But the conflict can be avoided. The differences between the two approaches point to the need to advance on both fronts simultaneously. The NIEO is concerned with formulating a framework of institutions, processes and rules that would correct what developing countries regard as the present bias of the system against them. This bias is thought to be evident in the structure of certain markets, where a few large and powerful buyers confront many weak, competing sellers; in discrimination in access to capital markets, and to knowledge, in the present patent law and patent conventions, in the thrust of research and development and the nature of modern technology, in the power of the trans-national corporations, in international monetary arrangements, etc. A correction in the direction of a more balanced distribution of power and access to power would enable developing countries to become less dependent and more self-reliant. But the NIEO by itself would be no guarantee that the governments of the developing countries would use their new power to meet the needs of their poor. The BN approach, by focusing on deprived individuals, households and communities, highlights the importance of the needs of individual human beings.

A BN programme that does not build on the self-reliance and self-help of governments and countries is in danger of degenerating into a global charity programme. A NIEO that is not committed to meeting basic needs is liable to transfer resources from the poor in rich countries to the rich in poor countries.

It is easy to envisage situations in which the benefits of international BN assistance are more than wiped out by the damage done by protectionist trade measures, or by an unequal distribution of the gains from trade and foreign investment, by transfer pricing practices of multi-nationals, by the unemployment generated by inappropriate technology, or by restrictive monetary policies. The global commitment to BN makes sense only in an international order in which the impact of all other international policies— trade, foreign investment, technology transfer, movement of professionals, money—is not detrimental to meeting basic needs.

The situation is similar in some respects to the rise of trade unions in nineteenth-century England. Concern with the fate of the poor remained relatively ineffective until the poor were permitted by law to organize themselves, bargain collectively, strike, and have their funds protected. On the other hand, there has always been the danger that trade unions would turn into another powerful estate, less concerned with the fate of the poor than with protecting the privileges of a labour aristocracy. And that the strong unions reap gains at the expense of the weaker ones and the unorganized workers.

The NIEO is a framework of rules and institutions, regulating the relations between sovereign nations, and BN is one important objective which this framework should serve. The way to make the institutions serve the objective is to strike a bargain: donors will accept features of the NIEO if, and only if, developing countries commit themselves to a BN approach.

There are those who maintain that integration into any international economic order in which advanced capitalist economies dominate is inconsistent with meeting the basic needs of the poor. Pointing to the People's Republic of China, until recently, they advocate "delinking," in order to insulate their society, or a group of like-minded societies, from the detrimental impulses propagated by the international system. Policies derived from such a view of the world order do not, of course, depend on wringing concessions from rich countries, but can be pursued by unilateral action.

Those, on the other hand, who think that the international system has benefits to offer if the rules are reformulated and the power relations recast, will not opt for complete delinking, but for restructuring.

A more specific question is how an international BN approach is to be implemented in a manner consistent with the spirit of the NIEO. The governments of developing countries are anxious to preserve their full sovereignty and autonomy and do not wish to have their priorities laid down for them by donors. They dislike strings attached to aid and close scrutiny of its use. Donors, on the other hand, wish to make sure that their contributions reach the people for whom they are intended. The solution is to be found in the strengthening of existing, and the evolution of new institutions that are acceptable to both donors and recipients, and that ensure that international aid reaches the vulnerable groups. Such buffer institutions and buffer processes would combine full national sovereignty with BN priority. They would be representative, independent and genuinely devoted to the goals of international cooperation.

It is clear that only multilateral or extra-national institutions can meet these conditions. But reform may be required on several issues. The distribution of votes must be such that the developing countries feel that they are fairly represented. The selection, recruitment and training of members of the international secretariat must be of a kind which transcends narrowly national loyalties, but is sensitive to the social and cultural issues in developing countries. Both narrow technocracy and an excessive politicization of issues must be avoided. It may be thought that this amounts to a prescription for perfection. But international institutions and their secretariats have in some instances approximated these ideal canons. Unless they do, there is little hope of implementing BN in the framework of the NIEO.[14]

THE CASE FOR ADDITIONAL OFFICIAL DEVELOPMENT ASSISTANCE (ODA) TO FINANCE BASIC NEEDS

Provisional and very rough estimates indicate that a basic needs programme aiming at providing minimum acceptable diets, safe water, sewerage facilities, public health measures, basic education and upgrading existing shelter would call for an annual investment of $20 billion over a 20-year period (1980–2000) at 1976 prices. If recurrent expenditures are added, the annual total costs would amount to $45–60 billion. If programmes are implemented only in the poorest countries, annual investment and recurrent costs are estimated to be $30–40 billion. This would be 12–16 per cent of these countries' projected GNP, and 80–100 per cent of their projected gross investment. Assuming the OECD countries concentrate their effort on the poorest countries and contribute about 50 per cent of the additional costs of these programmes, this would call for $15–20 billion ODA flows per year over 20 years.

At present, ODA flows from OECD countries amount to about $14 billion a year. Of this, the poorest countries receive only about $6 billion. The question arises why some part or the whole of this flow should not be devoted to BN, and why the flow to middle-income countries should not be devoted to the poor countries.

Only a part of this assistance is at present devoted to meeting BN, and the resource calculations are based on *additional* requirements. Nevertheless, it might be asked why the whole of the assistance should not be switched to what is agreed to be a priority objective, so that additional requirements could be greatly reduced. If, moreover, some ODA now going to middle-income countries could be redirected to the poorest countries, requirements could be further reduced.

Such redirection would, however, be neither desirable nor possible. Middle-income countries have a higher absorptive capacity and tend to show higher returns on resource transfers. They, too, have serious problems of poverty. Moreover, a reallocation of ODA flows is politically much easier if it is done out of incremental flows than if existing flows to some countries have to be cut. The legacy of past commitments and the expectations that they have generated cannot be discarded in a few years.

There are three reasons why additional resources of about $20 billion per year (on average over the period 1980–2000) are needed in order to make a convincing international contribution to BN programmes in the poorest countries. First, 20 years is a very short time for a serious anti-poverty programme. It calls for extra efforts both on the part of developed and developing countries. The domestic effort, economic, administrative and political, required from the developing countries is formidable. At the same time, while the figures for ODA seem large, total ODA flows that would rise annually by $2 billion between 1980 and 2000 (averaging $20 billion per year for the whole 20 years) would still be only 0.43 per cent of the GNP of the OECD countries in 2000, substantially below the target of 0.7 per cent. The acceleration (from the present 0.34 per cent) is certainly within the power of the developed countries and if the task is to be taken seriously by both sides, an increase of the percentage of GNP by 26 per cent over 20 years appears to be a reasonable basis for mutual reassurance.

The second reason for additionality is the fact that the transition from present policies to a basic-needs approach creates formidable problems (see p. 341). Investment projects that have been started cannot suddenly be terminated. An attempt to switch to basic needs programmes while the structure of demand and production has not yet been adapted to them is bound to create inflationary and balance of payments pressures. Unless a government has some reserves to overcome these transitional difficulties, the attempt to embark on a BN programme might be nipped in the bud.

The third reason for additionality is tactical and political. It is well known that the developing countries are suspicious of the BN approach. One reason for their suspicion is that they believe that pious words conceal a desire to opt out of development assistance. And there is no doubt that some people in the developed world see BN as a cheap option. If the international commitment to meet basic needs within a short period is to be taken seriously by the developing countries, the contribution by the developed countries must be additional and substantial. The essence of the Global Compact, announced by Mr McNamara in Manila in 1976, is that both developed and developing countries should reach a basic understanding to meet human needs of the absolute poor within a reasonable period of time. Such a compact would be a sham if it did not involve substantial additional capital transfers.

TOWARDS A COUNTRY TYPOLOGY

An important conclusion from having identified the distinct features of a BN approach is the redirection of research and policy. It is in the areas of the technology of public services, development administration and development politics discussed on pp. 342–7 that future work is likely to yield promising results. The work should start from an appropriate country typology that distinguishes:

(a) between countries with relatively high average incomes per head, in which an emphasis on redistribution of a relatively small percentage of national income and a redirection and redesign of social services can make a substantial contribution to meeting basic needs, and those with very low incomes, in which growth is an essential condition for meeting basic needs;

(b) between countries whose political system encourages self-reliance and local mobilization and those that will depend heavily on external assistance;

(c) between countries with high population density and little cultivable land, in which land redistribution holds out limited scope, and those with abundant cultivable land in relation to their population;

(d) between smaller countries that can hope for growth in employment opportunities from labour-intensive exports and larger countries, in which labour-intensive exports play a relatively smaller role and which, therefore, have to improve domestic technology;

(e) between countries in which a large proportion of the population live in the countryside and where rural development has greater importance and those with a large proportion of urban population.

Different political regimes and different administrative, technological and ecological conditions are also relevant.

THE ROLE OF GLOBAL MODELS

Attempts have been made not only to estimate national resource requirements for meeting basic needs, but also to design global models. Perhaps the best known one is *Catastrophe or New Society*, the report of a multidisciplinary group based on Bariloche, Argentina, under the direction of Amílcar Herrera. The Bariloche model contains certain novel and attractive features, relevant to a BN approach.

First, it is explicitly normative and rests on the premise that the satisfaction of basic human needs is the main objective of development. These needs are defined as nutrition, housing, education and health. They are defined not in consumerist terms, but as prerequisites for the ability of every individual to take a full and active part in his or her social and cultural environment.

Second, the maximand in the model is life expectancy, a healthy counterweight to GNP per head and the first approximation to a system of social and demographic accounts which, in principle, can be enriched in a sensible way by adding periods of time within the average life expectancy spent in primary and secondary school, at university, in employment, in retirement, in hospital, or vacation, in prison, on an analyst's couch, in a single, married, divorced or widowed state, etc. (Clearly, the system would fail to capture some of the choices and trade-offs that GNP per head does, but it would serve as a useful complement.)

Third, population is endogenously determined by the degree of satisfaction of basic needs. And, fourth, like a number of other global studies, it is a protest against the implicit recommendation of the *Limits to Growth* that developing countries must stop developing, in order to prevent (or delay) pollution, raw material exhaustion and the end of the world.

Apart from the explicitly normative nature of the model, its most interesting feature is its attempt to correct excessive emphasis on "maximizing" GNP or growth (nonsense objectives) by maximizing life expectancy. Since life expectancy has, unlike income distribution, an upper limit shared by all, just over 70 years, a rise in the average does say something significant about meeting certain basic needs of the whole population, though the improvement may be confined to certain groups and though we can clearly live longer and more miserable lives. Life can be nasty, brutish and long. Dispersions remain relevant but extreme skewness does not occur.

One trouble with the Bariloche model is that the "production function" by which life expectancy is maximized is somewhat odd. The terms of the equations, unlike land, labour and capital in, say, a Cobb-Douglas production function, cannot meaningfully be substituted for each other at the margin. Thus, in the model, by increasing the urbanization rate we reduce the birth rate and raise life expectancy. Presumably there is, therefore, according to the model, some rate of substitution at which we can reduce protein and calories per person and substitute increased urbanization and reach the same life expectancy; or reduce the population in the primary sector, while reducing education. Such a "production function" for maximizing life expectancy does not make sense. The authors say, rightly, "care must be taken not to confuse functional relationships with causal relationships. This is an empirical model that shows that there is a high correlation between demographic variables and certain socioeconomic variables, but in no way does it attempt to define the mechanisms that cause these links" (p. 51). But, in the light of this caveat, it is not clear how optimization can be achieved.

The conclusions of the Bariloche team are optimistic. The proposed world society is one in which basic human needs are satisfied. It is egalitarian, both at the national and international level, so that growth rates in developed countries are reduced to 1 to 2 per cent, once GNP per head has reached $4,500 (in 1960 dollars), although this would reduce net transfers (which are not an important contribution) and the terms of trade of the developing countries, via reduced demand for imports. Satisfying the needs of humanity along egalitarian and environmentally sound lines will then be possible in the 1990s in Latin America with a GNP per head of $809 (at 1960 prices), in 2008 in Africa with a GNP per head of $559, and in Asia in 2020, with a GNP per head of $506. There are, however, food limits in Asia which can be overcome by raising yields per acre, resorting to non-conventional food and importing food.

It is the political assumption of the study, that income is radically redistributed, that leads to the relatively low required growth rates, low investment ratios, and speedy satisfaction of basic needs. Population growth is treated endogenously as a function of the level of living, and more specifically of meeting basic needs, and not as an exogenous variable. Technical progress is also incorporated. The utopian character of the political assumptions, far from detracting from the value of the exercise, is its principal attraction. The combination of detailed, scholarly scrutiny with utopian vision is all too rare and yet essential for progress. We need, as the sociologist Peter Berger has pleaded, more informed fantasy, or pedantic utopianism, partly because political constraints can change quite suddenly and we should be technically prepared, and partly because these changes can occur only if the kind of work that the Bariloche team has done is being carried out.

NOTES

1. It may be thought that the notion "basic" precludes possibilities of conflict and trade-offs. But, since not all needs can be met at once, their hierarchy manifests itself as a succession in time. In the words of the Dreigroschenoper: "*Erst kommt das Fressen, dann kommt die Moral.*"
2. Even in much richer societies people delegate decision-making to their doctors and to the teachers of their children. Everywhere there are numerous exceptions to the principle that everyone knows best what is in his interest.
3. See Daniel R. Gross and Barbara Underwood "Technological Change and Caloric Costs: Sisal Agriculture in Northeastern Brazil", *American Anthropologist*, vol. 73, no. 3 (June 1971).
4. To the extent that meeting basic needs covers provision for the victims of disasters (floods, earthquakes, droughts) special arrangements are required and the argument of the text applies with less force.
5. Very low birth rates are registered in countries with low infant mortality rates and high life expectancy: Sri Lanka, China, Taiwan, South Korea.
6. Robert H. Cassen, "Population and Development: A Survey", *World Development* (October–November 1976). Cassen emphasizes the complex processes connecting these "correlates of fertility decline", other aspects of development, including income and fertility. David Morawetz confirms statistically the link between BN and fertility decline. See "Basic Needs Policies and Population Growth", *World Development*, vol. 6, no. 11/12 (November–December 1978).
7. A public opinion survey found that the majority of people do not support general "welfare" programmes, but at the same time do support specific measures, like helping poor families with deprived children. Similarly, "aid for development" is less appealing than help in meeting basic needs.
8. Total prohibition of the import and the domestic production of a non-basic-needs item is often a better way of controlling its consumptions than a tariff combined with an excise tax. There are arguments additional to those about greater quantitative certainty of quantitative controls. The theoretical assump-

tion that the consumer should be allowed to choose freely according to market prices requires qualifications if (i) he can enjoy the product more economically through joint consumption with others; (ii) his satisfaction depends on other people's consumption; (iii) present satisfaction depends partly on what he and others have consumed in the past; and (iv) he does not know what he wants or what is good for him. Some of these often go together. Thus if each consumer wanted coca cola because others drank it, because he had always drunk it (and would not miss it once he got used to do without it) and because he overestimated the difficulty of getting the same nutritional value from a local fruit drink, there would be a case for eliminating coca cola altogether rather than reducing the production of all fruit drinks at the margin, or putting a non-prohibitive tax on coca cola. Analogous assumptions apply to producers.

9. For evidence on this from Kerala, see *Poverty, Unemployment and Development Policy*, United Nations, New York (1975).

10. P. V. Sukhatme, *Malnutrition and Poverty*, Ninth Lal Bahadur Shastri Memorial Lecture (29 January 1977), Indian Agricultural Research Institute, New Delhi, p. 16.

11. A. K. Sen, "The Welfare Basis of Real Income Comparisons: A Survey", *Journal of Economic Literature*, vol. 17, no. 1, (March 1979) pp. 21–3 and "Poverty: An Ordinal Approach to Measurement", *Econometrica*, vol. 44, no. (March 1976) pp. 219–31.

12. A. K. Sen, *op. cit.*

13. V. Nagam Aiya, *The Travancore State Manual*, vol. 11, Trivandrum (1966) p. 537, quoted in *Poverty, Unemployment and Development Policy*, UN, New York (1975), p. 142.

14. For some imaginative ideas on how to combine basic needs with respect for national sovereignty, see Harlan Cleveland, *A Third Try at World Order*, New York (1976).

20 Human Rights and Basic Needs

Is the satisfaction of basic needs a human right? Are minimum levels of nutrition, health and education among the most fundamental human rights? Is there a human right not to be hungry? Or are human rights themselves basic needs? Are there basic needs other than material needs which embrace human rights? Does the respect for rights and the satisfaction of needs go together or can there be conflict?

Whatever the relation between needs and rights, they clearly are two different things. Meeting basic needs, at least physical basic needs, involves the use of scarce resources: land, labour, capital, foreign exchange, skills. Respect for human rights, in so far as they are negative rights, does not involve scarce resources. The right not to be assaulted, or not to be arbitrarily arrested, or to be permitted free expression does not absorb scarce resources. We can omit to do wrong to many people, and omit to do many wrongs to one person at the same time. The right to police protection against assault can be seen as a positive right to personal security. The negative right not to be assaulted is violated not by the government, but by the assailant.[1]

While it is congenial to some political ideologies and implicit in some versions of American liberalism to assume that "all good things go together", and that rights and needs are part of the same package, or even identical, there can be conflict between rights and needs, at least on some reasonable interpretations of these concepts. Narrowly interpreted material needs can be met in ways which conflict with rights. If society were organized, benevolently, like a zoo, or, less benevolently, like a well-run prison, physical needs would be met at a high level, but human rights would be denied. On the other hand, the civil rights principle of one man, one vote might easily conflict with the satisfaction of basic needs. In a democracy in which everyone votes in his narrow, material self-interest, and there are no cross-percentile alliances, the poor will never have enough votes to get redistribution to them enacted and, if redistribution is a condition for meeting their basic needs, will not have their needs met. The top 49 per cent

366

of the population will always be able to overcompensate the middle swinging vote of 2 per cent for not joining the bottom 49 per cent in anti-poverty measures, and have more left over for themselves than had there been redistribution to the bottom 51 per cent. Redistribution towards the middle, but not towards the poor, will be the result. Peacetime experience from democratic countries confirms the *a priori* reasoning, though the assumptions are unrealistic.[2] Thus basic needs can be met in ways which deny human rights, and human rights can be practised in ways which reject basic needs.

The psychologist Abraham Maslow, who explored the hierarchy of basic needs and who stands firmly in the American liberal tradition, had the following to say: "It is legitimate and fruitful to regard instinctoid basic needs and the metaneeds as rights as well as needs. This follows immediately upon granting that human beings have a right to be human in the sense that cats have a right to be cats. In order to be fully human, these needs and metaneed gratifications are necessary, and may therefore be considered to be natural rights."[3] This is not a very fortunate way of making the point that "all good things go together". If being human is a fact, no rights can be inferred from it. It may, of course, be necessary that certain conditions must be met before we can fully *function* as human beings. But again, no question of rights would arise. The function of a lawn-mower is to mow lawns, but a broken-down lawn-mower cannot be said to have a right to be repaired in order to become, fully and truly, a lawn-mower. If, on the other hand, to be human is to aspire to an ideal (it makes sense to say "Be a man!", while it does not make sense to say "Be a cat!" and even less "Be a lawn-mower!" and Nietzsche said "Become what you are!") the provision of the conditions for fulfilling this aspiration may be regarded as a right.

There is also an ambiguity between interpreting basic needs as "material preconditions" and "actual fulfilment". " I give you the toast of the Royal Economic Society, of economics and economists, who are the trustees not of civilization but of the possibility of civilization." So Keynes toasted the RES at the dinner in 1945. Substitute basic needs for civilization, and we must ask: can or should the state actually satisfy basic needs, or should it provide only for the possibility of their satisfaction? This question is, of course, closely related to the previous one about needs and rights, for some forms of satisfaction are possible only at the expense of rights (in the zoo or the prison), and some rights are inconsistent with *actual* need fulfilment by the state, though not with the *possibility* of need fulfilment.

In the Middle Ages scholars enunciated a system of natural law and natural rights. Both law and rights were thought to have religious sanction and moral certitude outside the realm of purely human thought and activities. More recently, the use of the term *rights* has come to imply a peculiar moral authority for the objective delineated. By calling some human aspiration a *right*, the objective in question has been given a moral and categorical supremacy, irrespective of the nature of the right, its appropriateness to the circumstances in which it is proclaimed or the possibilities or costs of achieving it. The violation of a right is *always* wrong, though conflicts between rights can arise.

The American Declaration of Independence says: "We hold these truths to be self-evident, that all men are created equal, that they are endowed by their Creator with certain unalienable rights, that among these are Life, Liberty, and the Pursuit of Happiness."

The use of the term "rights" in the Declaration and in many other places (including the quotation from Maslow) appears to attempt to achieve what since Hume many have thought to be impossible—to derive an *ought* from an *is*; and more than this, to derive from the derived ought a *will*. Man *is* human or *is* born equal; therefore he has the *right* to basic needs, life, liberty, etc.; therefore we *will* give it to him. The drafters of the Declaration were not, of course, so foolish as to believe that all babies were in all respects the same. Implicit in their descriptive *is* was a mystical *ought*. In spite of the fact that some were born larger than others, some heavier than others, some more intelligent than others, some more beautiful than others and some richer than others, "in the sight of God" they were all equal. The distinction between literal equality (which in the last resort reduces to the identity of indiscernibles) and mystical equality is well known.

Of concern to us here is the second derivation: from *ought* to *will*. Some rights at least are just objectives like other objectives with independent and instrumental values. Like other objectives, their achievement confers benefits but also incurs costs. Like these objectives, they may therefore be subject to economic analysis.

In order to clarify these issues, it is necessary to draw some distinctions. Human rights cover at least four distinct areas. Human rights in the narrow sense include the right not to be tortured or murdered. These rights apply to all governments, irrespective of their political colour.

A second group of rights are civil rights, or what in Anglo-Saxon countries is described as the "rule of law", in German as the *Rechtsstaat*. This group comprises the rights of citizens against their government. The rulers themselves are subject to the law. It is possible to have authoritarian states, without votes and other political rights, and yet an independent judiciary capable of acquitting people arrested by the executive. Civil rights are not consistent with totalitarian governments, which claim authority over the whole human being, but are consistent with authoritarian governments and dictatorships.

A third group are political rights. These enable citizens to participate in government by voting for their representatives. Representation can take many forms, of which one man, one vote is only one. Most people would regard political rights on the pattern of Western democracies as less important than human rights in the narrow sense, or civil rights. Some of these human rights are negative, others positive.

The most controversial area is that of economic and social rights, embodied in the UN Universal Declaration of Human Rights and the international covenants of economic, social and cultural rights. These are positive rights to resources and therefore distinct from the negative rights not to have certain things done to one. The right to universal primary education, to adequate health standards, to employment, to minimum wages and collective bargaining, are completely different kinds of rights from the negative rights. What the UN Declaration asserts is that everyone has a right to benefit from the services of a full-fledged welfare state, however poor the society. We often hear nowadays that the "negative", "abstract", "legalistic", or "passive" rights, such as equality before the law, must be accompanied, or even preceded by the "positive" rights to education, health and food. It is in this context that it is said that the satisfaction of basic human needs should be an integral part of positively, constructively and concretely defined "human rights". In Africa there is a saying: "Human rights begin with breakfast", and a song in Bert Brecht's *The Threepenny Opera* goes: "*Erst kommt das Fressen, dann kommt die Moral.*" (Grub first, then morality.) The formulation of civil and political rights occurred in the days when the duties of the state were regarded as minimal, and the rights were intended to protect the citizen against the state. The formulation of economic and social rights has occurred in a period when the duties of the state were much more positively interpreted.

The essential difference between the first three groups of rights—rights in the narrow sense, civil rights and political rights—in so far as they are negative rights (and they all have large negative components) and the fourth group—economic and social rights—is that negative rights require no resources (to refrain from certain actions does not call on resources though opportunity costs may be involved), whereas the latter require substantial resources. The latter can be assimilated to the former by permitting the acquisition and exercise of these rights without a financial charge. We can establish a right to education, health, fire fighting or parking by providing these services free, just as we can establish the right to freedom of speech and religion. But the rights to vote, to free speech, and free assembly are not only acquired and exercised without financial charges, they also do not cost the community any substantial sums. Not so with social and economic"rights". It follows that while there are duties corresponding to all rights, the debit item on the balance sheet of providing social and economic "rights" implies depriving someone else, or the same people later, of some resources.

It is, of course, true that negative rights can involve "opportunity costs"; by respecting these rights, courses of action may be precluded which would have had benefits for others, and forgoing these benefits is a cost that must be attributed to the rights. The construction of a dam or a highway may be ruled out if we respect the right not to be removed of those who would have to leave the area. But the existence of such opportunity costs does not detract from the categorical character of the negative rights.

Is there then a "right to survival", to a decent existence, to basic needs? Has every human being born into this world, irrespective of merit, ability, or available resources, the right to adequate food, education, and medical attention? Few would assert such a right even in such rich societies as the USA, which would be able to provide for such rights. A formal commitment to provide everyone with a decent existence would not only be very expensive, but would blunt incentives for work and saving. In poor, developing societies such "rights" have to be even more carefully examined.

The objection to assimilating positive social and economic rights to negative human rights is twofold. First, one may object on analytical grounds by pointing to the different logical justification of the two sets of rights. One may respect any number of negative rights to any number of people, without running into contradictions. Not so with positive rights. Second, one may object on practical and political grounds, for the assimilation may give rise, and has in fact given rise, to an interpretation which under the banner of implementing human rights, entrenches privilege and aggravates deprivation, by meeting the "right" of some at the expense of others.

Consider "the right to universal, free, elementary education" (Article 26 of the Declaration). First, the implementation of such a "right" in poor countries would be enormously expensive. Poor countries have, typically, perhaps one-tenth of the national income per head of rich countries. On the other hand, the proportion of the population aged 5 to 15 and to be educated (primary and secondary levels and therefore a larger group than that covered by the Declaration) is perhaps twice as large as in rich countries (25–30 per cent compared with 15 per cent) and teachers' salaries, which are near or below the national average in rich countries, are four or five times (or in Africa seven times) the average in poor countries. This means that a vastly greater share (typically eight to ten times as much) of a much smaller national cake (and budget) would have to be devoted to education, with the inevitable result that less would be left over for the implementation of other objectives, including other social and economic "rights".

Quite apart from the constraints set by available resources, one has to consider the social and economic results of implementing such a "right". In Africa and Asia the experience has been that a very high proportion, sometimes as many as four-fifths, of those educated in primary schools drop out or forget what they learn soon after, so that educational efforts on them are wasted. Even those who remember what they are taught seek to escape their miserable rural existence and hope to find employment as clerks in the towns. Since administration cannot offer jobs to all of them, far from becoming a source of productive activity, they are liable to become a source of disruptive activity. Far from being fulfilled, they are frustrated. If not sufficient jobs are available, the educated add to the ranks of the unemployed, the disaffected or the brain drain. The premature drive to universal literacy can result in a denial of basic needs and opportunities to the mass of the people. A carefully selective and phased education programme, including adult education, family education for parents and children, and non-formal education, can be much more cost-effective and do more for basic needs.

Another illustration is the attempt to implement social security (Article 22) and the right to health and medical care (Article 25). Here the interpretation (or misinterpretation) of human rights has reinforced urban bias. It has led to a concentration of medical training on producing highly qualified doctors in towns, at the expense of medical ancillary personnel, less expensively educated but more useful, which is desperately needed in the villages to teach hygiene and birth control and to cure or prevent communicable diseases. But whatever the interpretation of the right to health and medical care, the fact that its implementation involves costs must make it non-categorical, and therefore not a right.

A third area is labour rights. Labour standards applying to safety, hours, minimum wages, collective bargaining and anti-forced-labour conventions (Article 23) have often transferred inappropriate standards (for safety or minimum wages) and institutions (such as trade unions and collective bargaining) to societies in which they were damaging to meeting basic needs. Present union aspirations were formulated *after* industrial revolutions had occurred and when labour had become scarce. Collective bargaining, in such conditions, benefits both the workers and the community, by giving an impetus to mechanization. In pre-industrial societies, with populations and labour forces increasing at 2–3 per cent per year and a large proportion of the population of working age without hope for jobs, collective bargaining and minimum wages can aggravate social inequality, unemployment and poverty. While parading as an implementation of a human right, they are a flagrant denial of the needs of those outside the fortunate labour aristocracy who happen to have found a job.

The correct way to look at a strategy of implementing social and economic human "rights" is to construct a time profile, showing *who* achieves *what* needs, *how* effectively, at *what* time and at *what sacrifices* and *costs*. Premature attempts to aim at the best now may lead to sacrifices later and, in some cases, to sacrifices by others now. A more modest, partial attack on illiteracy, ill-health and unsatisfactory work standards is likely to lead to a fuller meeting of needs than an attempt to transfer at once alleged universal principles from rich countries to poor.

This can be illustrated by Article 23(1), the "right" to employment. It is plain that there is no prospect, for a long time to come, of full employment in most developing countries. The strategic questions that arise are:

(a) To what extent does the employment objective conflict with other goals of policy e.g. free choice of employment, more production now or later, higher living standards, greater independence from foreign assistance, etc?

(b) To what extent can more employment *now* be achieved only by sacrificing employment *later* and *vice versa*? What is the preference of policy-makers or of the people with respect to the time profile of employment growth?

(c) What social and institutional reforms are necessary to achieve higher employment? Are there serious social objections to multiple shift working? Are trade union objectives compatible with higher employment? What incomes policy is required to absorb additional labour and reduce the gross imbalance between urban and rural incomes?

We have reached the conclusion that negative human rights have a different status from the "positive" social and economic rights. But to conclude that therefore negative rights are the only human rights may strike many as too narrow an interpretation. We may wish to speak of violations of human rights even where all the "negative" rights are fully guaranteed. And we may think that these "negative" rights amount to little unless respect is paid to the integrity of the human personality in a more positive way. We cannot accept a positive right to the full paraphernalia of a modern welfare state. But is there not a right to a minimum share in a community's scarce resources, so as to avoid extreme deprivation? Do not all members of a community, especially an organized community like the state, but also all members of the human race, have a right, certainly not to an equal share, nor, in a poor society, to adequate food, education, health and employment, but to a fair share of the community's resources?[4]

If it is accepted that our common humanity and our membership of specific societies like the state, imposes some obligations on us, the right to a fair share of the available resources would appear to be a human right, complementing the negative human rights. But it cannot be the right to the satisfaction of any needs, however basic, for such a right would not take into account the scarcity of available resources and the necessity of choice. Nor can it be the right to an equal share, for that would ignore all other titles, such as merit, work, needs, etc. The precise meaning of "fair" cannot be determined here, but it is clearly a function of basic needs and available resources.

NOTES

1. See Charles Fried, *Right and Wrong*, Harvard University Press (1978), pp. 111–12.
2. Robert Nozick, *Anarchy, State and Utopia*, Basic Books, New York (1974).
3. *Motivation and Personality*, 2nd ed., (1970), p. xiii.
4. See Charles Fried, *Right and Wrong*, Ch. 5.

21 The Search for a Basic-Needs Yardstick

Norman Hicks and Paul Streeten

INTRODUCTION

In order to implement a basic-needs approach, a system of monitoring the satisfaction of basic human needs is needed. The development of economic indicators has reached a high degree of sophistication, but that of the human and social indicators required for a basic-needs approach is still primitive.

Ever since economists have attempted to tackle development problems, the principal yardsticks for measurements of economic development have been GNP, its components, and their growth. Despite the many problems with national accounting in developing countries, the national accounts have continued to be the main focus of discussions of growth, the allocations between investment, consumption and saving, and the relative influence of various sectors in total value added. GNP per head is widely accepted as the best single indicator of development, both historically and for international comparisons, despite well-known difficulties.

The use of national accounting was inspired by the attention of Western economists to the broad aggregates of Keynesian economics, which was itself of major influence on economic thought at the time (1950s) when attention was being increasingly paid to the less-developed countries. National accounting served to integrate, through a weighting system based on market prices or factor costs, such disparate items as agriculture and industrial production, investment, consumption and government services. In fact, national income accounting was a tool of analysis that other social scientists sometimes viewed with considerable envy.

The heavy emphasis on GNP, or GNP per head, and their growth rates, as the principal performance tests (not normally as the "objective") of development came under fire for the reasons given on pp. 324 ff.

The concern has shifted to eradication of absolute poverty, particularly by concentrating on basic human needs. Meeting these needs in nutrition, education, health and shelter may be achieved by various combinations of growth, redistribution of assets and income, and restructuring of production. It is the composition of production and its beneficiaries, rather than indexes of total production or of income distribution that have become the principal concern. This new focus on meeting basic human needs requires an indicator or a set of indicators, therefore, by which deprivation can be judged and measured, and policies directed at its alleviation and eradication can be initiated and monitored. The problems inherent in using GNP as a measure of social welfare have been recognized almost since the inception of national income accounting. This paper identifies and reviews four different approaches to the measurement problem:

(i) *adjustments to GNP*, through which modifications of standard national income accounting concepts are undertaken in order to capture some of the welfare aspects of development and to improve international comparability;

(ii) *social indicators* which attempt to define non-monetary measures of social progress;

(iii) the related *social accounting systems* which attempt to provide an organizing framework for some of these indicators; and

(iv) the development of *composite indices* which combine various social indicators into a single index of human and social development or the "quality of life".

In addition to these four broad areas, considerable effort has been expended in defining an adequate measure of income distribution, and the numbers living below a poverty line. We discuss this briefly under "adjustments to the GNP measure". The extensive literature on this subject could, however, warrant a separate review.[1]

ADJUSTMENTS TO THE GNP MEASURE

Despite the overwhelming attention to growth, the deficiencies of GNP per head as an indicator of *economic* development became apparent to many even during the early years. Pigou (1920) already had pointed out that economic welfare comprises not only national income per head, but also its distribution and the degree of steadiness or fluctuation over time.

Measurement problems became apparent when attempts were made to make inter-country comparisons of GNP per head. Part of the problem arises from the fact that official exchange rates do not measure relative domestic purchasing power, since a large portion of marketed GNP does not enter into world trade. In addition, trade policies often create distortions in nominal exchange rates, so that they fail to reflect the true value of even that proportion of GNP which is traded.

Colin Clark (1940, 1951) was one of the first to attempt to convert national accounts using purchasing power parities, which means measuring the output of each country at some common price level, usually international prices. The most recent and complete work on purchasing power parities has been undertaken by Kravis *et al.* (1976, 1978). The results of this research suggest that the GNP of India, for instance, should be adjusted upward by a factor of 3·5, while most other countries would be adjusted by a somewhat smaller margin. Even these kinds of adjustment, however, cannot eliminate all the problems of comparing GNP across countries. For instance, because of climatic conditions greater expenditures may be required for clothing and shelter in the more temperate parts of the world in order to survive, while dry tropical zones require more expenditure on irrigation and disease control. Evaluations of non-tradables, particularly public and other services, are difficult and subject to conceptual problems. In addition, a great deal of work is necessary, covering hundreds of goods and services, in order to estimate accurately purchasing power parities. Unless a "short cut" or reduced information approach is developed, it will be difficult to make wide use of this approach.

Nordhaus and Tobin (1972) attempted to adjust GNP so that it would be a better "Measure of Economic Welfare" (MEW). This approach entails subtracting from GNP an allowance for defence expenditures and other "regrettable necessities", such as the "disamenities" of urbanization (pollution, congestion, crime, etc.), while adding an estimate of the value of leisure and the services of consumer durables. At the same time, Nordhaus and Tobin reclassified health and education expenditures as investment, rather than consumption. The final result produced a MEW for the USA that was substantially larger than GNP (about twice), largely because of the high value imputed to leisure (the measure of which raises great difficulties) and other non-market activities. The growth rate of MEW for the USA between 1929 and 1965 was somewhat lower than that for GNP, mainly because of the larger value of leisure and non-market activities in the base year (1929), reducing the *proportionate* rate of growth, and partly because of the growth of defence expenditure and urban "disamenities". Denison (1971) and others have criticized this approach on the ground that

GNP was never meant to measure welfare, and attempts to adjust it only confuse the concept.

It might be possible to incorporate some of the items captured by social indicators by GNP adjustments. Thus life expectancy could be allowed for by using expected lifetime earnings instead of annual income per head or, more crudely, the product of average income per head and life expectancy. The consumption benefits of literacy could be allowed for by imputing the value of services from education as a durable consumer good, etc. (The benefits of literacy as a durable investment good already show in the form of higher productivity.) Distribution could be allowed for by taking the median or the mode rather than the mean income, or by multiplying the mean income by 1 minus the Gini coefficient, etc.

From the point of view of indicating the satisfaction of basic needs, the Nordhaus–Tobin corrections raise certain difficulties. "Regrettable necessities" are subtracted from GNP, because "we see no direct effect of defense expenditures on household economic welfare. No reasonable country (or household) buys 'national defense' for its own sake. If there were no war or risk of war, there would be no need for defense expenditures and no one would be the worse without them." But similar reasoning could be applied to the components of basic needs. We do not want medical services from nurses, doctors and hospitals for their own sake. If it were not for disease and accidents, we would not need to incur this expenditure. The same goes for shelter against the cold, for sewerage and, perhaps, for literacy. Even food for under- or malnourished people is a necessity to prevent hunger, disease or death. A logically consistent application of the Nordhaus–Tobin principle would lead to an *inclusion* in the national income only of those items that we do not really need, the inessentials and frills, which would be a paradoxical conclusion, contrary to the judgement of those who wish to *exclude* all frivolous luxuries from our national income accounts.

If it were possible to distinguish precisely between "goods", "bads", and "anti-bads", we could deduct from national income all "anti-bads": those that combat the "bads" generated by potential enemies (defence), those that offset the "bads" generated by nature (heating, shelter, medicines)— the narrowest definition of basic needs—and those that offset the "bads" generated by the domestic economic system itself ("artificially" created wants through advertising, emulation and social pressures). In fact, it is not possible to distinguish between good and bad "artificially" created wants without introducing value judgements (the desire for books, art and music is also "artificially" created), and it is not possible to distinguish between "anti-bads" (the need for deodorants or anti-dandruff shampoo created by the fear of social ostracism) and goods (the need for literature created by the desire to participate in the cultural life of society).

Adjustments to GNP for *distributional* value judgements can be made by weighting different components of the national income according to who receives them. Such a redefinition would, however, eliminate the distinction between the national income and its distribution. Kuznets (1972) and Ahluwalia and Chenery (1974) have suggested that the growth rate of GNP in itself is a misleading indicator of development, since it is heavily weighted by the income shares of the rich. A growth of 10 per cent in incomes of the upper 20 per cent will have more impact on the aggregate growth rate than a 10 per cent growth in incomes of the lower 20 per cent. They suggest two alternatives: either the equal weighting of each decile of income recipients, or the introduction of "poverty weights" which would place more weight on the growth of incomes for the lower 40 per cent. The result is a revised aggregate growth rate which makes an allowance for differences and changes in income distribution.

Another approach would be to use simply the absolute income level of the lower 40 per cent as the appropriate indicator to which development policies should be related. This has the advantage of shifting the focus away from the distribution of income, a politically sensitive subject in many countries, to the level of living of the poor. Progress in reducing poverty can be judged, however, only if the income level of the poor can be compared with some standard minimum which reflects a "poverty line". The general approach adopted by many is to calculate that level of income at which the average family consumes a nutritionally adequate diet, usually defined in terms of calories. Those families (or individuals) not having this income are therefore judged to be below the poverty line, and comprise the poverty target group.

The shortcomings of this approach are many, and will be discussed here only briefly. First, examination of family income and food consumption ignores the important problem of distribution of food and other amenities within the family. It seems clear that in many countries women (who, in some societies work harder than men) and children receive less than an "adequate" amount of food despite the fact that the family's total consumption is judged to be "adequate". Poverty line measures do not consider how far below the poverty line families find themselves. They do not show improvements that take place below this line and suggest a "solution" for those brought barely above the line. They pay no attention to the distribution of food between different families below the line. They therefore conceal the efforts required to reduce poverty. Sen (1973, 1975) has proposed a weighting of individuals on the basis of how far they fall below the poverty line, thus combining poverty line and income distribution approaches.

In addition, the concept of "nutritionally adequate" is difficult to define since caloric needs vary widely with climate, body weight, activity, and height, age and other factors, and even for the same conditions between persons and for the same person in the same conditions, from day to day. Household income surveys generally show that many families below the poverty line could consume an adequate diet by purchasing a different, and more efficient, basket of foods which are available but rejected on grounds of taste, variety, etc. Families living below the "poverty line" are often found to undertake certain non-food expenditures which many would judge to be non-basic, such as on drink and entertainment. Even with an income above the poverty line, a family may not be able to purchase essential goods and services which are controlled and in inadequate supply or supplied by the public sector (such as health, education, water supply), or they may have to rely on less efficient and more costly alternatives in the private sector (traditional healers, private water deliveries, private schools). The importance of the public sector in these areas derives from the view of these goods and services being "merit goods", as well as from the external economies present in both consumption and production. The main basis of the basic-needs approach, in fact, stems both from the view that raising incomes alone is insufficient in view of the inefficiencies in the consumption patterns of the poor and the lack of availability of essential goods and services. Thus any measure of poverty income, no matter how carefully derived, will be inadequate for measuring basic needs.

SOCIAL INDICATORS

An alternative approach is to develop better indicators of human, social and economic development which cover areas and aspects that cannot be reflected in most income-based measures. These so-called "social indicators" attempt to measure the development of health, nutrition, housing, income distribution, as well as other aspects of cultural and social development. A great deal of work has been undertaken by various agencies to compile a set of social indicators, including the UN (1975), OECD (1976), AID (1976), UNESCO (1977), to mention a few.

In theory, social indicators should be more useful in cross-country comparisons, since they avoid the exchange and valuation problem. In fact, the statistical basis for comparing these indicators between countries or over time remains very frail. The figures are often unreliable and not comparable, particularly because of different definitions used in collecting data. In addition, many data are based on limited sample surveys or other, highly inaccurate data collection methods. Differences observed in social indicators between countries often reflect these statistical and definitional variations in the indicators rather than real differences in social development. But this constitutes a challenge to collect better, more comparable data.

Unlike the national accounts which use the pricing mechanism to combine heterogeneous items, there is no obvious way to combine different social indicators. Consequently problems arise in absorbing the content of a large number of socio-economic indicators and in any attempt to draw general conclusions. The movement to develop social indicators, furthermore, has suffered from a lack of clear perception of purpose. The term "social indicators" has itself been used very loosely to encompass a whole range of human, economic, social, cultural and political indicators. The need to supplement the GNP as an indicator of *economic* development has become confused with a search for indicators of other aspects of development as well as for an indicator of the "quality of life". The latter concept has generally been taken to cover concepts such as security, peace, equality of opportunity, participation, and personal satisfaction, all of which present difficult measurement problems. It has never been clear whether the search was for an *alternative* to GNP, or a *complement* or a *supplement*.

Although we do not as yet have a unifying conceptual framework for these indicators, and despite the problems mentioned above, social indicators do have certain advantages over GNP per head. First, they are concerned with ends as well as means, or at least with intermediate ends nearer to the ultimate end of a full and healthy life, than aggregate average production measures. Even those social indicators that measure inputs (e.g. hospital beds per 1,000 population or school enrollment rates) rather than results (life expectancy, morbidity, literacy) attempt to capture inputs that are nearer to the desirable results than GNP per head.

Secondly, many social indicators say something about the distribution as well as the average, because skewness at the upper end is more limited than it is for income per head. (The mode or the median for income per head can, however, eliminate skewness and reflect some aspects of distribution in the average.) There is practically no limit to how much income a man can receive, but the maximum life span is limited. Any increase in literacy reflects also a distributional improvement, because the *proportion* of beneficiaries has risen.

Some indicators are better than others for showing also the distribution of basic-needs deficiencies since they are constructed on an either /or, have/have not basis. Thus measures such as literacy, access to clean water, and primary school enrollment can be used to indicate the percentage of the population having basic-needs deficiencies in each of these important sectors. Measures such as life expectancy, infant mortality, and average calorie consumption are less informative since they average the statistics of rich and poor alike. There seems to be a clear need to develop more specific measures related to the poor, such as life expectancy or calorie consumption indicators for those in the lower quintile of the income distribution, for women, for rural dwellers, etc.

Third, while GNP per head follows an ascending order from the poorest to the richest countries, some social indicators are capable of catching something of the human, social, and cultural costs of opulence (the diseases of affluence like heart disease, stomach ulcers or deaths in automobile accidents), as well as poverty. They can, in principle, register some of the shared global problems, such as pollution, cultural dependence or interdependence, etc., and reduce the false hierarchical and paternalistic impression that may be created by purely economic indicators. As a result, a different meaning can be attached to the "gap" between the so-called developed and developing countries. The GNP measure points to "catching up" and suggests a race. Social indicators can point to common and shared values and problems, to alternative styles of development, to the opportunities for learning from one another. Reducing or closing the international "gap" in life expectancy, literacy, infant mortality, or morbidity would appear to be a more sensible objective, and can be achieved at much lower levels of GNP per head and therefore much sooner, than reducing the "income gap", though we are even more ignorant about how to achieve the former than the latter.

INPUTS V RESULTS

Whether social and basic-needs indicators should reflect inputs or results depends upon their purpose. For performance testing there is something to be said for the approach of choosing indices that measure results or outputs, since these are closer to what we are trying to achieve. Furthermore, measures of inputs can introduce biases toward certain patterns of meeting needs which may not be universal. For instance, a country with fairly acceptable health standards should not be encouraged to acquire the same number of doctors as one with serious health problems. We are back with the problem of "regrettable necessities", which should not be counted as final goods or as social achievements. Moreover, the number of doctors does not measure the distribution of these doctors and medical services, or the degree of their specialization. Resources may be deployed in inefficient ways, failing to benefit the poor. Measures such as infant mortality and life expectancy, however, indicate the degree to which basic needs have been fulfilled, rather than the resources expended. Likewise, literacy measures the effectiveness of the educational system, and is a better indicator than the number of students enrolled or the student/teacher ratio. In general, output measures are better indicators of the level of welfare and basic-needs achievement. Moreover, most outputs are also inputs. Health, education and even nutrition are valued not only in their own right, but also because they raise the productivity of present and future workers, though higher productivity is valued because it contributes to a better life.

Input measures, such as doctors or hospital beds per thousand or enrollment rates in schools, on the other hand, also have their uses. They may reflect government intention, commitment and efforts to provide public services. For purposes of assessing policies and monitoring performance, both sets of indicators are necessary. Input measures are useful indicators of resources devoted to certain objectives (though these can be misdirected). To the extent to which we know how to link inputs to results, i.e. have a "production function", we can trace the connections between means and ends. Even when we do not have knowledge of a "production function" (e.g. linking expenditure on family planning to a decline in the fertility rate), the combination of input and output measures presents the raw material for research into the causal links between the two, particularly since, in a social system of interdependent variables, so many outputs are also inputs. In addition, where output measures cannot be readily found, it might be necessary to fall back on measures of inputs as useful proxies.

GNP SOCIAL INDICES

Several studies (McGranahan *et. al.*, 1970; United Nations, 1975) have indicated a high correlation between economic indicators, including GNP, and social indicators. This might suggest that GNP can be used as a proxy measure of social development. Morawetz (1977) found that there was a weak correlation between the level of GNP and indicators of basic-needs fulfilment, and even less correlation between the *growth* of GNP and *improvements* in basic-needs indicators. Sheehan and Hopkins (1978) concluded, however, that "the most important variable explaining the average level of basic needs satisfaction is per capita gross national product" (p. 95). These contradictory results appear to arise from the use of differing selections of indicators, sources of data, and country samples, as well as differing interpretations of results. Many scholars include in "social" indicators non-monetary measures of economic performance, such as newsprint or energy consumption or the ownership of automobiles and radios. These economic indicators are almost always highly correlated with GNP, and at times, have been suggested as a shortcut to estimating internationally comparable income levels (see Beckerman, 1966). Some researchers exclude the developed countries, whose high levels of both GNP and social development might dominate the sample. Likewise, different results can be obtained based on the inclusion or exclusion of the centrally planned economies, the OPEC countries, and the very small LDCs.

Correlations based on 1970 data from the World Bank's Social Data Bank are shown in Table 21.1.[2] The results for seven social indicators show a modest correlation with GNP (average $r^2 = \cdot50$), while a sample of five economic indicators shows somewhat higher correlation ($r^2 = \cdot71$). However, when the social indicator data are disaggregated into samples of developing and developed countries, the correlation coefficients for both groups drop significantly ($r^2 = \cdot25$ for developing countries, $\cdot18$ for developed). Similar declines in the correlation coefficients are also found when the economic indicators are disaggregated. Consequently, it would appear that studies which examine only social variables for developing countries are apt to discover a poor relationship, while those that consider economic and social variables for all countries are likely to find better relationships.

One reason why social indicators are not more highly correlated with GNP per head is that the relationships are often distinctly non-linear. Indicators such as life expectancy, literacy, and school enrollment have asymptotic limits which reflect biological and physical maxima. It is impossible, for instance, to have more than 100 per cent literacy. Furthermore, these limits are often reached by middle-income countries, so that further increases in income show little gains in social indicators. For instance, life expectancy reaches 70 years of age for countries with income per head (1970) of $2,000, and does not increase even as incomes increase to $5,000. Most countries have attained close to 100 per cent literacy by the time their income reaches the $2,500 level. Conversely, countries below $500 GNP per head demonstrate a wide variety of social development which is largely unrelated to the level of GNP. This can be seen more clearly from the two graphs on the following pages for GNP with life expectancy and literacy (other social indicators show similar patterns). The cluster of

TABLE 21.1　Correlation of indicators with GNP per capita (1970)

	Coefficients of determination (r^2)			Sample size
	All Countries	*Developing*	*Developed*	
Social indicators				
Expectation of life at birth	0·53	0·28	0·13	102
Calorie consumption (as % of required)	0·44	0·22	0·02	103
Infant mortality	0·42	0·34	0·25	64
Primary enrollment	0·28	0·24	0·05	101
Literacy	0·54	0·47	0·16	70
Average persons per room (urban)	0·58	0·08	0·29	34
Housing units without piped water (%)	0·74	0·13	0·36	36
Average[a]	0·50	0·25	0·18	
Economic indicators[b]				
Newsprint consumption	0·79	0·20	0·46	85
Automobiles	0·85	0·59	0·46	102
Radio receivers	0·43	0·14	0·07	97
Electricity consumption	0·67	0·30	0·24	102
Energy consumption	0·82	0·28	0·49	99
Average	0·71	0·30	0·34	

Source: based on data taken from the World Bank's Social Data Bank. Excludes centrally planned economies and countries with a population less than one million.

[a] Simple unweighted arithmetic mean of the r^2

[b] All economic indicators are on a per capita basis.

points along either axis indicates the lack of correlation at both the high and low income levels. It seems clear that a much better correlation could be developed using some sort of non-linear relationship.[3] A non-linear function would obscure the fact that the correlation exists, however, only among the middle-income countries. GNP per head is likely to be a

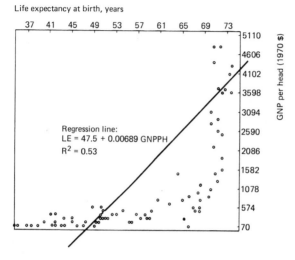

FIGURE 21.1   GNP and life expectancy (1970)

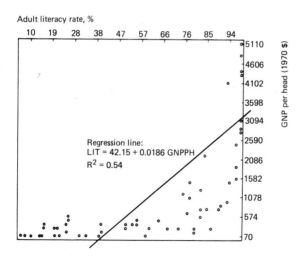

FIGURE 21.2   GNP and literacy (1970)

misleading indicator of social development and progress in meeting basic needs, particularly when used in some linear fashion. Yet rankings of countries by social indicators and GNP are likely to be very similar, because the ranking process obscures these non-linearities.

SOCIAL ACCOUNTING SYSTEMS

Some work has been done on developing a system of social accounts to provide a kind of national accounting framework for social indicators. Stone (1975) and Seers (1977) have proposed the use of lifetime activity sequences calculated by dividing total life expectancy into segments. Such tables would show the average time a person could expect to spend in various mutually exclusive states. One such matrix could divide lifetime activity between school, work, leisure, retirement, etc., while another might be built on a marital sequence (single, married, divorced, widowed). Such tables would combine various important social statistics from different fields, and would be used to indicate changes over time, either actual or planned. The system presents many problems, however, not the least of which is its inability to incorporate fully all aspects of social development. Some indicators (income distribution, security, police protection, pollution) cannot readily be transformed into life expectancies. Furthermore, the system goes far beyond the data available in most countries, and is thus more suited for the industrialized countries. Nevertheless, it is a concept which has some future potential for integrating a large variety of social variables, and providing the basis for a theory linking policies to results in the area of social planning. Other ideas have been developed for a more limited social accounting approach. The *Social Accounting Matrix* (SAM) of Pyatt and Round (1977) does not utilize social indicators, but expands the traditional input–output table into a matrix which details payments made by productive sectors to different income recipients. Recipients can be disaggregated in various ways so as to indicate the distribution of income between factors, urban/rural households, or income classes. The power of the SAM approach is that it integrates production and income distribution data in a way that gives a better view of the economy, and the flows between sectors. It still relies, however, on the use of GNP as a measure of welfare and is limited in its application by the absence of good income distribution data. Terleckyj (1975) has developed a matrix framework for analysing the impact of government programmes on various social goals, as indicated by the appropriate social indicators. Since programmes affect more than one social goal, the approach develops a matrix of inputs and outputs, and suggests the possibility of defining the most efficient set of programmes for achieving a particular set of goals. While this approach provides a useful rationale for using different indicators, it does not provide a better measure of growth or development.

COMPOSITE INDICES OF DEVELOPMENT

Relatively more work has gone into developing composite indices that could be used to replace or supplement GNP as an indicator of social, economic or general development. A large amount of work was undertaken by the UN Research Institute for Social Development (UNRISD) during the 1960s to develop better social indicators, including composite indicators. For instance, Drewnowski and Scott (UNRISD, 1966) developed the "Level of Living" index, which was defined as "the level of satisfaction of the needs of the population as measured by the flow of goods and services enjoyed in a unit of time" (p. 1). The Level of Living index itself, however, goes beyond the provision of goods and services, and considers "basic needs", subdivided between physical needs (nutrition, shelter, health), and cultural needs (education, leisure, security). "Higher needs" or "surplus over basic needs" is taken as the surplus income over some minimum level. The "basic needs" part of the index includes items which are very difficult to obtain for many countries, such as the amount of leisure time available, the number of people in possession of private saving, and the quality of housing. This makes the application of the index very difficult, and Drewnowski and Scott were forced to use short-cut approximations even for their limited sample of 20 countries. Furthermore, the work, once begun, was not continued after 1966 in the same form.

McGranahan *et. al* (UNRISD, 1970) examined 73 indicators which covered economic and social characteristics, and found that there was fairly high inter-correlation between these indicators. Through a process of elimination, he constructed a "Development Index" based on 18 "core indicators" which included 9 social and 9 economic indicators. The resulting index was highly correlated with GNP per head ($r = \cdot89$), although there were some countries (Venezuela, Chile, Japan) whose ranking was substantially different under the index. In general, the correlation of the index and GNP per head was somewhat lower for developing than developed countries. McGranahan concluded that social development occurred at a more rapid pace than economic development up to a level of about $500 per capita (1960 prices). Some of these results are themselves, however, a product of the method employed, whereby the selection of the 18 "core indicators" was based, in part, on their having a high inter-correlation with the other indicators. As a result of the high inter-correlation, the composite index was relatively insensitive to the choice of component variables. The UNRISD team found, for instance, that the country rankings remained virtually unchanged when the number of indicators was reduced from 18 to 10.

A study by the United Nations – ECOSOC (1975) sought to analyse development by ranking 140 countries by seven indicators other than GNP. These included two "social" indicators (literacy, life expectancy) and five "economic" indicators (energy, manufacturing share of GDP, manufacturing share of exports, employment outside agriculture, number of telephones). An overall rank for each country was calculated by giving equal weight to the ranks under each separate indicator. Arranging the results by quintiles, and comparing with GNP, the UN indicated that the overall index was closely associated with the ranking by GNP. It should be noted, however, that the UN index was heavily weighted by economic, rather than purely social, indicators and thus tends to replicate the findings of Beckerman (1966) and others that show that non-monetary indicators are highly correlated with GNP. A similar study by the OECD secretariat (1973) used regression techniques for six variables to establish a predicted GNP per head index for 82 developing countries. A more recent paper by the OECD/DAC (1977), however, concluded that "per capita GNP still appears to be the best measure" of the level of development.

A more recent study of the use of a composite index has been undertaken by the Overseas Development Council (ODC), under the guidance of Morris D. Morris. Morris's "Physical Quality of Life Index" (PQLI) uses three simple indicators with equal weights to attempt to measure the fulfilment of "minimum human needs"; life expectancy at age one, infant mortality and literacy. Morris argues that the use of indicators for judging performance under basic-needs criteria should concentrate on indicators of outputs or results, rather than inputs. Input measures, he feels, do not measure success in meeting the desired goals, and may lend an ethnocentric bias to the means employed. The use of only three indicators permits the calculation of the PQLI for a wide range of countries and facilitates the examination of changes in the index over time. The term "quality of life" is perhaps a misnomer, since what is really being measured is effectiveness in reducing mortality and raising literacy. Life expectancy measures the *quantity*, not the quality of life. (These aims also have an ethnocentric bias.) Most important, the weighting system of the PQLI is arbitrary and there is no rationale for giving equal weights to literacy, infant mortality and life expectancy at age one. It is not possible to prove that the PQLI gives a "correct" index of progress on human needs, as opposed to some alternative index having different weights or a different selection of component indices. It is not clear what is gained by combining the component indices with a weighting system that cannot be defended. Analytical work can be undertaken using the component indices almost as easily as with the composite index, without introducing the biases of the PQLI. While Morris's index has received much attention in the popular press, most serious scholars find it difficult to accept the results of a composite index without a stronger theoretical foundation.

Despite the potential attractiveness of having a single index of socio-economic development, there is little theoretical guidance to govern the choice of indicators, the correct scaling of component indices, or the appropriate weights. Moreover, an index that relies only on ranking neglects the distance between ranks.

Scaling problems arise when raw data on social indicators are converted into component indices ranging from 0 to 100. For instance, reasonable values for life expectancy could be either 40 to 75 years, or 40 to 100 years. A country with a life expectancy of 60 years will obviously have a different "score" depending on the scaling chosen (57 v 33), and this will materially change the composite index. Furthermore, the scaling system need not be linear. Drewnowski used "expert opinion" to derive a linear scale system reflecting set levels of basic-needs satisfaction. McGranahan developed an elaborate system of "correspondence points" to determine the appropriate scale range, and utilized non-linear (logarithmic) scaling for many indicators. Morris simply took the range of the data for each indicator with the "worst" country being defined as zero and the "best" as 100.

In addition, there is the even more difficult problem of the proper weights to be used in combining the component indices into the composite. Drewnowski tried both equal fixed weights and a system of sliding weights under which deviations from the normal were given more weight than indices close to the normal. The rankings of countries by sliding or equal weights were highly correlated with the rankings of countries by GNP per head or consumption per head, and the shift in the weighting system did not materially affect the rankings. McGranahan's weighting system gave greater weight to the component indicators that had the highest degree of inter-correlation with the other indicators, a somewhat dubious method. One would think that the absence of correlation would be an equally valid criterion, though one might then wish to know why there is no correlation, rather than integrate them. He also found that moderate changes in the weighting system did not affect the level of each country's index, or its ranking. The insensitivity of the general index to the choice of weights is a logical result of having high inter-correlation among the components, since the high correlation implies that any one component is a good substitute for any other. The UN – ECOSOC study gives equal weight to the country *ranks* of the social indicators, thus avoiding, in a certain sense, the scaling problem. As mentioned above, the PQLI gives equal weight to each of the three components without ascertaining if this implies the correct "trade-off" between the various components. None of these studies indicates that much effort was devoted to developing a theoretically sound rationale for the weighting system.

Because of these problems, it might well be argued that a composite index is either unnecessary, or undesirable or impossible to construct. It is unnecessary if the components are highly correlated with one another, because then any one of the component indicators by itself will serve as an adequate index. If, on the other hand, the components move in different directions in cross-country comparisons and time series, averaging would conceal the important issues and would be undesirable. To have the same index for a situation in which mortality is high and literacy low, as for one in which literacy is high and mortality low, implies evaluating the "trade-off" between literacy and life expectancy. Unless the basis for such an evaluation can be established, all weighting remains arbitrary and misleading, and composition is impossible. The case for considering the two indices separately is exactly the same as the case for having an index independent of GNP.

If the interpretation of basic needs were taken literally, so that all basic needs, being "basic", would have to be met together and trade-offs between different basic needs were ruled out, a composite index would not be necessary. As long as the "package" of basic needs has not been fully met, no amount of additional satisfaction of any one component could compensate for the slightest deficiency in any other, so that a composite indicator would be ruled out. Once all basic needs had been met, again no composite index would be required, for the indicator for any one need would show that all had been satisfied. But we are not advocating such a literal interpretation of "basic needs".

RECOMMENDATIONS FOR FUTURE WORK

This brief survey has reviewed four alternatives to GNP per head as methods of calculating some of the dimensions of development. The adjustment to GNP approach has focused largely on improving GNP as a measure of economic welfare. Attempts to introduce other costs and benefits of development, which would move GNP toward a broader welfare measure, lack a logical basis and tend instead to result in a confusion of concepts. Research on "social" indicators has failed to produce an alternative which is as readily accepted and comprehended as GNP per head though they are useful for judging social performance. Systems of social accounts, which could integrate social indicators through some unifying concept, have not been able to overcome successfully all the difficult problems encountered.

Efforts to develop composite indices have ranged from a search for better measures of the physical production of goods and services, to a measure of the "quality of life", of "economic" or "social" welfare, of satisfactions, "happiness" and other objectives. The search for a composite index of social welfare, analogous to GNP as an index of production, has been a fruitless one so far, since it has proven virtually impossible to translate every aspect of social progress into money values or some other readily accepted common denominator. The great deal of work devoted to composite indices, however, suggests the need for a single number which, like GNP per head, can be quickly grasped and gives a rough indication of "social" development.

The current discussion of basic-needs oriented development focuses on the alleviation of poverty through a variety of measures other than merely redistribution of incremental output. Such a focus supplements attention to *how much* is being produced, by attention to *what* is being produced, in *what ways*, for *whom* and with what *impact*. Obviously, the rapid growth of output will still be important to the alleviation of poverty, and GNP per head remains an important figure. Required, in addition, are some indicators of the composition and beneficiaries of GNP, which would supplement the GNP data, not replace them. The basic-needs approach, therefore, can be the instrument for giving the necessary focus to work on social indicators.

As a first step, it might be useful to define the best indicator for each basic need. At present, the essential basic needs are considered (Haq, 1977) to cover six areas: nutrition, primary education, health, sanitation, water supply and housing. This would suggest that a limited set of core indicators covering these areas would be a useful device for concentrating efforts. Once defined, however, this set could then serve as a call for the collection of more adequate, standardized, comparable international statistics, and thus help to concentrate data gathering efforts on the most important indicators. It is not clear that because there are six basic needs, there need be only six core indicators. It may be that more than one indicator will be necessary to measure adequately progress in any one area of basic needs. Nevertheless, the basic needs concept serves as a useful device for integrating efforts of data gathering and analysis.

Once defined, these core basic-needs indicators would have the potential for important policy analysis relating, for instance, to international comparisons of performance and relative aid levels. Such indicators would be a more useful guide to the relative "gap" between rich and poor countries, and offer a different view on the speed with which this gap was widening or narrowing. They would be useful in understanding which countries were meeting their basic needs, and how their policies are related to the growth of output, trade, investment, etc.

The problem of selecting the appropriate index in each field is best taken up by technical experts in each sector. To give an indication, however, of the indicators which might be included, the following have been identified as a preliminary set:

Health:	life expectancy at birth;
Education:	literacy;
	primary school enrollment (as per cent of population aged 5–14);
Food:	calorie supply per head or calorie supply as a per cent of requirements.
Water supply:	infant mortality (per thousand births);
	per cent of population with access to potable water;
Sanitation:	infant mortality (per thousand births);
	per cent of population with access to sanitation facilities; and
Housing:	none.

The core indicators identified here attempt to follow the philosophy of the paper in stressing measures of results, rather than inputs. Following the conclusion of the United Nations Research Institute for Social Development (UNRISD), infant mortality is assumed to be a good indicator of the availability of sanitation and clean water facilities. While literacy is a good general measure of progress in education, the per cent of the relevant age group enrolled in primary school is included to measure country effort. Inputs measures have also been identified for water supply and sanitation as supplementary measures. It has not been possible, however, to identify a satisfactory measure of housing needs. The only readily available indicator is people per room, but this does not capture much of the quality of housing, only the number of rooms, which, in turn, is a very rough index of crowding.

If an acceptable system of weights could be developed, it might be possible to combine the core indicators into a composite basic-needs index. The chances of an acceptable system of weights being developed, however, are extremely small. Despite considerable research on composite indices, no one has come close to developing a rational weighting system. It is difficult even to suggest directions for further research.

Instead of attempting to develop a composite index of basic needs, a useful alternative may be to narrow the range of indicators from six to one or two, which correlate highly with basic needs development. This approach would serve the needs of those who desire a single number for making quick judgements on social performance, without introducing the problems of weighted composite indices.[4] The prospects for doing this are considerably enhanced by the fact that many of the so-called "basic needs" are, in fact, inputs rather than ultimate goals. Certainly nutrition, water supply and sanitation are valued because they improve the health status of the population. To a more limited extent, this is also true of housing and education. All of these can be considered to be inputs into the health "production function". They may be valued for reasons other than their influence on health status, but a high association between the various core indicators can be traced to their impact on health. Therefore, it could be argued that some measure of health, such as life expectancy at birth, would be a good single measure of basic needs. In a sense, life expectancy is a kind of weighted "composite" of progress in meeting physiological basic needs. It has the advantage of capturing the impact on individuals, not only of non-market factors but also of income net of taxes, transfer payments and social services, without raising all the difficulties of income per head measures, such as the appropriate unit (individual, household or family), the appropriate magnitude (capital, consumption, income), the appropriate set of prices (market prices, international prices), what to value as final goods and what as costs, etc. For these purposes, it might be regarded as superior not only to a composite index of social indicators but also to GNP and to indices of income distribution. It is possible for two countries to register the same GNP per head and the same ratio of income accruing to the bottom 20 per cent, and yet to have different average life expectancies. For some purposes, e.g. for distinguishing between meeting the basic needs of men and women, or of rural and urban populations, or for additional information if life expectancies cluster very near one another, it would, however, be useful to add a measure of progress in education, such as literacy. It is, of course, possible to have a long and miserable life, and one might wish to put an upper limit to the desired life span. But at low income levels, there is a high correlation between morbidity and mortality, so that life expectancy covers health as well as length of life.

In using a single indicator, it is, however, important to guard against two dangers: the danger to interpret the *result* in a unidimensional way, and the danger to interpret *inputs* in a unidimensional way. Life expectancy can be increased by measures that affect different age groups differently. Improved nutrition, for example, may affect life expectancy above one year, whereas women's education may affect infant mortality. The second danger is that the improvement of a health indicator such as life expectancy will divert attention to health measures generally, and doctors, clinics and nurses specifically, whereas the "production function" for life expectancy may include a number of thrusts not obviously related to health, such as improved jobs, earnings, environment, etc. Just as we now know that reductions in the rate of population growth are not simply functions of improved family planning, so improved health and longer life are not simply functions of improved health delivery systems. But as long as the indicators are not identified with unidimensional results or unicausal remedies, there is much to be said for a simple system of recording and monitoring.

NOTES

1. A fifth method would be to interview a sample of individuals and to ask each to place himself on a "happiness" or "basic needs" scale between, for example, 0 and 10, and to say whether he feels his basic needs had been met more adequately than at some specified date in the past. But this kind of survey is still rudimentary and does not provide us with the kind of information we should need for monitoring a basic needs approach.
2. This sample excludes the centrally planned economies and all countries with populations of less than one million. While the total sample includes 106 countries, missing data reduce the sample size for each correlation (see Table 22.1).
   We use r^2, the coefficient of determination, rather than r, the correlation coefficient, for two reasons: first, it gives a better idea of variation in income that can be attributed to the variation in the indicators, and *vice versa*; secondly, it enables us to produce an average r^2 without having to introduce the concept of absolute values.
3. For life expectancy, a semi-log function increases the r^2 from ·53 to ·75.
4. This assumes that such needs are legitimate; some might argue that it would be better to ignore such requests.

BIBLIOGRAPHY

Adelman, Irma and Morris, Cynthia Taft, *Economic Growth and Social Equity in Developing Countries*, Stanford, Calif. (1973).

Ahluwalia, M. and Chenery, H. "A Conceptual Framework for Economic Analysis", in Hollis Chenery *et al.* (ed.) *Redistribution with Growth*, London (1974).

Agency for International Development, "Socio-Economic Performance Criteria for Development", Washington, DC, (February 1977).

Baster, Nancy, "Work on Development Indicators by National Governments, Research Institutes and Individual Scholars: A Selective Review and Discussion of Issues and Problems", United Nations University, Tokyo, Japan (May 1977).

Beckerman, Wilfred, *International Comparisons of Real Incomes*, OECD, Paris (1966).

Clark, Colin, *Conditions of Economic Progress*, 3rd edn, London (1951).

Denison, Edward F., "Welfare Measurement and the GNP", *Survey of Current Business*, no. 51 (January 1971).

Drewnowski, Jan, "Social and Economic Factors in Development", United Nations Research Institute for Social Development, report no. 3 (February 1966).

Drewnowski, Jan and Scott, Wolf, "The Level of Living Index", United Nations Research Institute for Social Development, report no. 4, Geneva, Switzerland (September 1966).

Edelman, John A. "The ODC Proposal on a Quality of Life Index", World Bank Memorandum, (7 December 1976).

Gilbert, M. and I. Kravis, *An International Comparison of National Products and the Purchasing Power of Currencies*, OECD, Paris (1954).

Haq, Mahbub ul, "Basic Needs: A Progress Report", World Bank (10 August 1977).

Harbison, F. H., Marumburic, J. and Resnick, J. R., *Quantitative Analyses of Modernization and Development*, Princeton University, Princeton, NJ (1970).

King, Mervyn A., "Economic Growth and Social Development: A Statistical Investigation", unpublished paper.

Kravis, Irving, "The Scope of Economic Activity in International Income Comparisons", in *Problems in the International Comparisons of Economic Accounts*, NBER Studies in Income and Wealth, vol. 20, Princeton University Press, Princeton, NJ (1957).

Kravis, Irving *et al.*, *A System of International Comparisons of Gross Product and Purchasing Power*, The Johns Hopkins University Press, Baltimore and London (1975).

Kravis, Irving *et al.*, *International Comparisons of Real Product and Purchasing Power*, The Johns Hopkins University Press, Baltimore and London (1978).

Kundu, A., "Social Indicators: System and Norms", unpublished paper, World Bank, Washington, DC (14 January 1975).

Kuznets, Simon, "Problems in Comparing Present Growth Rates for Developed and Less Developed Countries", *Economic Development and Cultural Change*, no. 20 (January 1977) pp. 185–209.

Leipziger, D. M. and Lewis, Maureen A., "A Basic Human Needs Approach to Development", USAID, Washington, DC (12 September 1977).

McGranahan, D. V. and Richaud-Proust, C., "Methods of Estimation and Prediction in Socio-Economic Development", UNRISD, Geneva, n.d.

McGranahan, D. V., Richaud-Proust, C., Sovani, N. V. and Subramanian, M., *Contents and Measurement of Socio-Economic Development*, Praeger, New York (1972).

McGranahan, D. V., "Development Indicators and Development Models", *Journal of Development Studies*, no. 8, (April 1972).

Morawetz, David, "*Twenty-Five Years of Economic Development 1950 to 1975*", World Bank, Washington, DC (1977).

Morris, M. D. and Liser, F. B., "The PQLI: Measuring Progress in Meeting Human Needs", Overseas Development Council, Communique on Development Issues no. 32 (1977).

Nordhaus, William and Tobin James, "Is Growth Obsolete?" in *Economic Growth*, NBER/Columbia University Press, New York (1972).

OECD/DAC, "Socio-Economic Typologies or Criteria and Their Usefulness in Measuring Development Progress", Paris (7 April 1977).

OECD, "Performance Compendium—Consolidated Results of Analytical Work on Economic and Social Performance of Developing Countries", OECD/DAC, Paris (1973).

Olsen, Mancur, "The Treatment of Externalities in National Income Statistics", in *Public Economics and the Quality of Life*, Lowdon Wingo and Alan Evans (eds), (published for Resources for the Future and the Centre for Environmental Studies by The Johns Hopkins University Press, Baltimore (1977). "Toward a Social Report: II" in *Public Interest*, no. 15, (spring 1969).

Overseas Development Council, "A Physical Quality of Life Index", in *The U.S. and World Development Agenda, 1977*, Praeger, New York (1977).

Pison, A. C., *The Economics of Welfare*, Macmillan, London (1920).

Pyatt, Graham and Round Jeffery, "Social Accounting Matrices for Development Planning", World Bank (July 1977).

Schreiber, Gotz, "Measuring Economic Growth in Developing Countries: Problems, Results, Implications" – presented at the Fifth World Congress of the International Economic Association, Tokyo (September 1977).

Seers, Dudley, "Life Expectancy as an Integrating Concept in Social and Demographic Analysis and Planning", *Review of Income and Wealth*, 23 (September 1977).

Seers, Dudley, "The Meaning of Development", *International Development Review*, 11, (December 1969).

Seers, Dudley, "What Are We Trying to Measure", *Journal of Development Studies*, 8, (April 1972).

Sen, A. K., "Poverty: An Ordinal Approach to Measurement", *Econometrica* vol. 44 (February 1976).

Sen, A. K., "The Welfare Basis of Real Income, Comparisons: A Survey", *Journal of Economic Literature*, vol. 17, no. 1 (March 1979).

Sheehan, Glen and Hopkins Michael, "Basic Needs Performance: An Analysis of Some International Data", ILO, Geneva (1978).

Singer, Hans W., "Social Development: Key Growth Sector – Philosophy, Plans and First Results of the UN Research Institute", *International Development Review*, 7 (March 1965), pp. 3–9.

Streeten, Paul, "The Distinctive Features of a Basic Needs Approach to Development", World Bank, (10 August 1977).

Streeten, Paul, "Basic Needs: Premises and Promises", *Journal of Policy Modeling*, vol. 1, no. 1 (January 1979).

Stone, Richard, *Toward a System of Social and Demographic Statistics*, United Nations, New York (1975).

Terleckyj, Nestor, *Improvements in the Quality of Life*, National Planning Association, Washington, DC (1975).

UN-Economic Commission for Europe, *Economic Survey of Europe in 1969*, Part 1, New York, (1970), Ch. 4.

United Nations, Economic and Social Council, Committee for Development Planning. "Developing Countries and Levels of Development", (15 October 1975).

UNESCO, *The Use of Socio-Economic Indicators in Development Planning*, UNESCO Press, Paris (1976).

World Bank, *Atlas*, World Bank, Washington, DC (1976).

World Bank, "Basic Needs: An Issues Paper", Washington, DC (21 March 1977).

22 Trans-National Corporations and Basic Needs

The role of the trans-national corporation (TNC) in development is already large and is of growing importance, and policies have to be evolved that enable governments willing to admit it to harness its potential for the benefit of the development effort. We start with the premise that a fundamental objective of development is to meet the basic needs of the billion or so poor people in the world, that some governments are prepared to commit themselves seriously to giving high priority to this objective, and that they wish to explore the role of TNCs in such an approach.

One of the attractions of the BN concept is that it provides a powerful organizing and integrating framework for a whole range of otherwise disparate and apparently intractable issues. One of these is the role of the TNC. When we ask ourselves what contribution can TNCs make to meeting the basic human needs of the poor, the issues that are raised become, at least in principle, amenable to answers.

The basic-needs approach consists of three components: adequate personal incomes, basic public services and appropriate administration. The contribution of the TNC clearly lies primarily in the area of the basic-needs goods and services on which the personal incomes of the poor are spent, both producer and consumer goods, both final and inter-mediate products. It also covers the area in which the incomes of the poor may be earned, such as foreign trade, both in manufacturing and agriculture.

APPROPRIATE PRODUCTS

There has been a good deal of discussion of appropriate technology, and the charge has been raised that TNCs introduce excessively capital-intensive, and therefore inappropriate technologies into the developing countries. I shall return to this issue, but the first point to make is that the oversophistication and overspecification lies more often in the *product* than in the *technology*.[1] While the case for a "balanced diet" makes it impossible to substitute between very broadly defined product groups, such as food, clothing, household goods, transport, shelter, etc., the specifications of particular products within these broadly defined groups provide scope for choice. Food can be branded and advertised, packaged, highly processed and standardized to headquarter specifications, or it can be natural or semi-processed, variable in quality, locally grown, unpackaged. Transport can be by private cars, buses, motor bicycles, mopeds or bicycles. Shirts can be made with synthetic fiber, drip-dry, or with natural, locally grown fibre, washable, ironable. Agricultural machinery may be tractors or simple power tillers.

It is in the nature of the TNC that it possesses a monopolistic or oligopolistic advantage over its potential local rivals, for otherwise international investment would not occur. This oligopolistic advantage may take various forms, but one common form in consumer goods is the creation of goodwill through advertising and sophisticated marketing techniques, as in branded foods. Another form is the incorporation of research and development expenditure, as in pharmaceuticals. A third form is large-scale production with the restriction on rival entry that this entails. These monopolistic advantages enable the firm to reap quasi-rents or monopoly profits until the advantage is eroded by competition, when the firm has to renew its attempt to re-establish the advantage. The sophistication of the products, and the complexity of the technology determined by the products, are therefore not only a response to the high incomes and high savings in the mass markets of the developed countries, but they are of the very essence of the TNC. Very simple products cannot normally be protected through patents, trade marks, trade secrets or other forms of exclusion and are readily imitated. Even where they can be so protected, the appropriation of profits does not last long. Unless they are much cheaper to produce on a mass scale (as is the case with buses or mopeds), the TNC has no special advantage in producing them. It is for investigation why multinationals produce and sell simple basic-needs products such as bicycles, sewing machines, margarine, soap and washing powder, and whether small-scale domestic firms, if given access to capital, to other inputs, and to markets, might not be able to compete successfully. The presumption is that the TNC has no special advantage in supplying simple basic-needs goods and services and that transformation in the direction of reduced dualism is likely to reduce the scope for its operations.

The provision of an adequate diet and health is an essential part of the basic-needs approach. On present evidence, the branded, advertised and marketed food products and soft drinks of the TNCs do not appear to be capable of making a substantial contribution here. This is not the place to rehearse the scandals of some of the baby formula companies, or of some of the pharmaceutical firms, who have been accused of grossly overcharging for the active ingredients of drugs. Alan Berg concludes a careful survey of TNCs and nutrition by saying that, in spite of the substantial time and energy devoted by governments to involving big business, "there is little to show in the way of nutrition improvement. Nor are the prospects bright for reaching a significant portion of the needy with proprietary foods marketed in the conventional manner . . . the major impediment is the inability to reconcile the demand for corporate profit with a product low enough in cost to reach the needy in large numbers."[2]

In so far as "appropriate" products of a simple, not overspecified kind, using local materials and local labour, have not been invented, so that there are gaps in the product range, there is clearly need for R & D. But for the reasons given, the TNC will not have the incentive to devote its R & D to this purpose. For, having spent possibly substantial sums on an innovation, rapid imitation will soon erode its profits and it will not be able to recoup its expenditure. It is the very fact that the social returns on such innovations exceed the private, appropriable returns, and that markets in developing countries are more competitive, that leads to the minuscule research that is done on appropriate basic-needs products. An example would be a cheap, say $50 refrigerator. The argument points to alternative methods of financing R & D.

Similar considerations apply to simple producer goods, like hand tools and power-driven equipment, both for small farmers and for small industrial and service enterprises. The appropriate technology may be missing or, though in existence, may be unknown in the country. But it is hard to see how the TNC could have an incentive to spend funds on developing such products. There might be more scope in supplying capital goods required as inputs into the public provision of basic services (road-building equipment, equipment for geological surveys, medical equipment, drugs). And TNCs can be sources of tax revenue that can be used directly or indirectly for meeting basic needs.

Quite distinct and complex issues, not discussed here, arise for the TNC and the host country in the area of foreign trade. Labour-intensive manufacturing and agricultural production for exports provide opportunities for employment and income generation, and for acquiring skills, as well as tax revenue. On the other hand, excessive incentives in the form of tax concessions and subsidized inputs can lead to the phenomenon of "negative value added", just as it has in the more thoroughly studied case of high-cost import substitution. In both cases, profits to private foreign firms are consistent with social losses for the host country.

TECHNOLOGY

In spite of frequent charges that TNCs, compared with local firms, introduce excessively capital-intensive technologies into developing host countries, there is no evidence that *for the same product lines* TNCs use more inappropriate technology than local firms. Some evidence points to the opposite. The previous section argued that the real issue is not the technology for a given product, which is often dictated, at least within a range, by the specifications of the product, but the product choice itself. Thus the technology employed in a steel plant is largely determined by the degree of sophistication of the final products for which the steel is needed.

There has also been controversy on the location of the R & D activities, developing countries complaining that parent countries monopolize the bulk of this activity. However, R & D is a high-skill-intensive activity and this type of skill is even scarcer than capital in developing countries. Only where research depends on local conditions (as in much agricultural research, on soil and climate) is there a strong case for the location of the research in the developing host country.

There is a clear need to devote substantially more R & D to the invention and dissemination of appropriate, capital-saving technologies and products, and the solution of the problems of the developing countries, many of which have been identified. The difficulty, as already mentioned in the discussion of products, is that normally the TNC has no incentive to devote its resources to such research, because it does not offer the opportunity to recoup the full benefits derived from the expenditures, through monopoly pricing.

Nevertheless, there might still exist an unrealized potential of TNCs for transferring and adapting existing technology and for inventing new and appropriate technologies. In order to reap the maximum benefits, the developing countries would have to create the conditions for absorbing the contributions by the TNCs, possibly through joint ventures, conditions for training local counterparts, encouraging local research and fostering attitudes favourable to such absorption.

But, as far as simple, basic-needs products, and simple, capital-saving technologies, adapted to local climatic and social conditions are concerned, there is no escape from the conclusion that it is in the nature of the TNC that it will not devote R & D funds to this purpose. The small, competitive local firms in the developing countries, on the other hand, do not have the market power and the means to embark on such research. The conclusion for policy again points to alternative ways of financing relevant R & D, either directly through government finance or indirectly through governmental compensation for innovators, the social benefits of whose inventions exceed their private ability to appropriate the returns.

TNCs AND SMALL-SCALE LOCAL ENTERPRISE

It is controversial whether TNCs encourage or discourage local entrepreneurship in the "informal" sector. Some observers have adduced evidence on subcontracting, showing the stimulating impact of TNCs, others have produced evidence that local firms are bought out and local initiative has been stifled. The two positions are, of course, not inconsistent, for some types of activity might be encouraged, others discouraged. Government policies that have kept interest rates low and have rationed capital to large, including trans-national firms and that have discriminated in government procurement in favour of these firms have reduced employment, increased inequality and run counter to a basic-needs approach. The complexity of government regulations, the encouragement of collective bargaining, minimum wage legislation and similar measures also make it more difficult for small-scale domestic firms to compete with the TNCs.

THE CONTRIBUTION OF TNCs

It is sometimes said that TNCs passively adapt to the economic and political environment that governments create. Like the corner grocer, the TNC is said to respond to ruling prices and to cater for existing demand. Such a picture flies in the face of mounting evidence. TNCs have actively attempted to shape their environment, from attempting to overthrow a legally elected government (ITT in Chile), to bribing a president to reduce export taxes in order to break a banana cartel (United Brands in Honduras), to bribes to officials and royalty in order to sell aircraft (Lockheed, not a TNC, in a number of countries). Even if we rule out illegal, unethical and improper activities, it is clear that TNCs attempt to influence governments when negotiating about establishing their subsidiaries, about the terms of the contract, including such items as tariff protection, labour laws, tax provisions, etc.

If their role in shaping the environment has been systematically underestimated, their role in contributing capital has been overestimated. As much as three-quarters of foreign investment by TNCs is now financed locally, either by retained earnings or through raising local capital. The special contribution of the TNC consists in the "package" of capital, technology, management and marketing. One of the problems in assessing the impact of the TNC on BN is that some components of the package may have desirable, others detrimental effects. The host country may not have the foreign marketing facilities that the TNC provides, but the TNC's technology may aggravate local unemployment. Or the company may provide skills for production for domestic consumption, but the product may be suited only for the upper income groups. It is this fact, as well as more general cost considerations, that have led to the demand for "unbundling" the "package", and purchasing the components that cannot be produced domestically separately. But since the monopolistic strength of the TNC consists precisely in offering the whole "package" on a take-it-or-leave-it basis, it will be unwilling to agree to "unbundling".

TNCs AND LABOUR UTILIZATION

A BN approach calls for raising the productivity and earning power of the poor. One of the most important ways of doing this is to increase remunerative jobs. Can the TNCs make a contribution to job creation?

On past evidence, the answer is not encouraging. Estimates of overseas assets by TNCs in the Third World are unreliable but a plausible figure is that the stock of foreign capital in 1970 was $40 billion, of which half was located in Latin America and the Caribbean. This stock provided employment for approximately 2 million workers or roughly 0.3 per cent of the labour force.[3] The average capital cost of creating a job is therefore $20,000. It appears that, on past performance, TNCs cannot make a more than negligible contribution to employment creation.

A BN-oriented approach, by spreading purchasing power more widely, would, of course, reduce the incentives to produce sophisticated products requiring capital-intensive techniques. A turn to greater export-orientation would enlarge the scope for labour-intensive export industries, particularly for the location of labour-intensive processes or the production of labour-intensive components by vertically integrated firms in developing countries. But here again, technical innovation may shift the comparative advantage if, as seems likely, mechanization can replace these labour-intensive processes.

In spite of some opportunities, the specific advantages of TNCs in a BN approach would be considerably smaller. There would be less demand for sophisticated, mass-produced consumer and producer goods. The scope for advertising and shaping tastes by sophisticated marketing techniques would be reduced. The profitability of R & D-intensive technology would fall. Both the need of host countries for TNCs and the incentive of these companies to operate in developing countries would decline.

NOTES

1. Frances Stewart, *Technology and Underdevelopment*, Macmillan, London (1977).
2. Alan Berg, *The Nutrition Factor*, Brookings Institution, Washington (1973), p. 158.
3. United Nations, *Multinational Corporations in World Development* (1973).

Part V   Miscellaneous

23 Taxation and Enterprise[1]

Taxation—like economics—deals with two dangerous subjects which, combined, give an explosive mixture: a man's pockets and his ideals. Fuel has been added recently by the publication in England of the three important reports of the Royal Commission on the Taxation of Profits and Income.[1] These lucidly written documents, and especially the final one, will keep the fires of controversy burning for a long time to come, not only inside Great Britain but outside her shores. Although the commissioners have not reached revolutionary conclusions, many imaginative reform proposals were considered, discussed, and, occasionally rather regretfully, rejected. The general tenor is that the British tax system, although complex and defective in many respects, is, if not the best of all possible systems, at least among the least bad ones—and that most of its evils are necessary.

The commission was appointed in 1951 and issued its report in 1955. Its chairman was Lord Radcliffe, a distinguished lawyer, and among its fourteen members were four university teachers, four business men, three trade unionists, and one accountant. The report contained a substantial "Memorandum of Dissent" signed by Mr Kaldor and two trade unionists. This minority report is more daring and imaginative than the majority report and much of what I shall say will be drawn from or inspired by it. The most controversial issue that divided the minority from the majority was the question of whether we should impose a capital gains tax. This has been much discussed in the press and the learned journals and I shall not say much on the subject. The most fascinating aspect to me, with which I shall deal later, is the discrepancy between our widespread belief in the rough fairness of our tax system and the wide scope for tax avoidance which the minority report has brought to light.[2] I shall divide this essay into two parts. In the second part I shall reiterate the hackneyed question of whether free enterprise can survive taxation, but in the first part I shall turn the question round and ask whether taxation can survive free enterprise. It is to be hoped that not both answers will be negative, or else we should get a situation like that depicted in a cartoon in which two snakes eat each other until nothing is left over.

1

When I announced a talk to an Oxford undergraduate society under the title "Can Taxation Survive Free Enterprise?" various inquirers asked whether there had not been a misprint. Should it not be the other way round? I was reminded of Colonel T. E. Lawrence's reply to his proof-reader. The latter wrote into the margin of the *Seven Pillars of Wisdom*: "'Meleager, the immoral poet.' I have put 'immortal' poet, but the author may mean immoral after all." To this Lawrence replied: "Immorality I know. Immortality I cannot judge. As you please: Meleager will not sue us for libel." Similarly, I should say: "Of the attack of enterprise on the tax system I know. Of the effects of taxes on enterprise it is difficult to judge. As you please: the surtax payers will not sue us."

We all know the traditional complaint that free enterprise—indeed sometimes a free society—cannot survive our present penal rates of taxation. We are, it is often said, killing the goose that lays the golden eggs. The lament is as old as taxation. Indeed, David Hume wrote: "'tis to be feared that taxes all over Europe are multiplying to such a degree as will entirely crush all art and industry." Professor Lionel Robbins in a recent article argued that the tax machine more than any other thing is driving us towards collectivism. (Professor Robbins also expressed fears lest our Inland Revenue Commissioners, who assess jointly those whom God has joined together in holy matrimony, should encourage thereby "more casual associations"; having killed free enterprise and a free society, only free love would flourish.) I shall have to say a little about the traditional complaint in the second part, but should like to turn the tables and ask to what extent enterprise has undermined our tax system.

We are familiar with grumbles about expense accounts out of which the managerial classes are subsidized in our modern societies—as much in theoretically socialist Russia as in the theoretically more or less social democracies of the West. But if, after the glad hand of corporate (public or private) planning has taken over from the invisible hand of competition, expense-account splurging has replaced bank-account thrift, there exists, at any rate in England, a widespread belief in the fundamental fairness of the system. The minority report has shaken this belief.

As Mrs Jackson says in her article, we now have two quite separate systems of taxation: one for wage and salary earners, university professors among them (under that scheme you pay up, and no nonsense about it); the other for those who are in business or who own shares or other property. Under that scheme there is much more scope for enterprise and initiative to reduce your tax liabilities. It has been said that tax payments, particularly of surtax, for those who come under the free enterprise system are largely voluntary. This may be an exaggeration, but there are numerous ways in which tax can be avoided. I must stress that I am not concerned with tax *evasion*, that is, illegal tricks. Tax *avoidance*, "the art of dodging tax without actually breaking the law", is entirely above-board legally, and some say morally. We have it on high authority. Lord Tomlin, in the case of the *Duke of Westminster* v *CIR* (1935), said: "Every man is entitled if he can to order his affairs so that the tax attaching under the appropriate Acts is less than it otherwise would be. If he succeeds in ordering them so as to secure this result, then, however unappreciative the Commissioners of Inland Revenue or his fellow tax payers may be of his ingenuity, he cannot be compelled to pay an increased tax."

The main point is that tax liability depends on what you mean by "income". Under the enterprise system the determination of this meaning is to a large extent left to the taxpayer and his assistant, the high-powered, tax-avoidance industry that consists of lawyers and accountants— members of the most respectable and honourable professions. The secret is simply to transform as much of what unenterprising people would naïvely consider "income" into expenses, benefits in kind, and other deductible items, or into capital gains. Since none of these are taxed, you can slip through the net, however deeply it is dipped into the high incomes. Let me illustrate.

To live well on expense accounts, to occupy luxury flats owned by your company, to drive or be driven in company cars, to travel, and to entertain, is not as easy as it was before legislation a few years ago tightened the net somewhat. But it is still much easier for the man in business than for a civil servant, teacher, or a subordinate office worker.

Another operation, still at a relatively low level, is to blend your business life with your private life: make your home your office, your maid your office cleaner, your furniture your business stock and your wife your secretary. But you must be careful: although it pays to make your wife your secretary (because you can then deduct her household allowance as a business expense and thus get additional earned income relief) never make your secretary your wife if the sum of your incomes is at all substantial. She can live with you as your mistress and you can gain benefits by settling property on her or by making a seven-year covenant in her favour (a discretionary trust and a reliable trustee may even prevent the need to continue payments should she leave you). If, however, you are really determined to marry you should then get a divorce. If you earn £5000 per annum and live with your wife and three children, you pay £2375 tax. But if you get a divorce and an Order of the Divorce Court to pay £1,500 to your ex-wife and £500 directly to each child, the total tax paid by the five of you will only be £1,500. You save £875. After the decree is made absolute there is no reason why you should not again all live together happily.

There was a time when company directors played musical chairs, for mutual advantage could be derived from five-year contracts with generous damage or compensation for loss of office. When the directors are sacked and swap companies the sums are capital and untaxed, but allowed as deductions by the employer.

Another important way to reduce tax liabilities is to make losses. Companies are advertised which pride themselves on a "good loss record", and it pays to buy loss companies and put profits through them. Since losses are deductible from taxable income, they become attractive forms of enterprise. This, incidentally, should be borne in mind by those who lament that high taxation discourages risk-taking. Whether the risk-taking thus encouraged is always desirable is another question. No doubt universities and research institutes have benefited from these provisions. On the other hand they have encouraged advertising (thus indirectly subsidized by the government at the rate of £125,000,000 per annum), entertaining, and various types of "improvements" whose social benefit is not always clear. The novel by the former American business executive Cameron Hawley, *Cash McCall*, makes instructive reading.

A special case is that of what the commissioners call, with masterly understatement, the "hobby farmer", and the popular press more colourfully "the playboy-ploughboy". He buys a decrepit farm and then begins to improve it (deducting allowances in respect of capital expenditure from his business income), to eat its produce (untaxed benefit in kind), to enjoy it (untaxed psychic income), and to make losses (deductible from surtaxable business income). As a result of these transactions the value of the farm has gone up and if he then sells it the capital gain is untaxed. He can now start again. Though even the majority report suspects that this is going rather too far, its suggested test, namely determining whether the enterprise "lacks commercial inspiration", would not be easy to apply in a tax system that prides itself on not examining motives.

Trust funds provide an ideal method of escaping surtax and death duties, and have the incidental pleasant effect that your heirs acquire a vested interest in your life rather than your death. For a trust established less than five years before death has to pay full duties. It has been said, with not too much exaggeration, that the payment of death duties can be ascribed only to ill luck, ill will or ignorance. If you invest your fund money properly so that the assets appreciate, you can borrow from the fund to the tune of the capital appreciation. You can not only live on the loan but deduct interest payments from surtaxable income. The whole fund goes to your children and grandchildren tax-free.

Property income can, with patience, be converted into capital gains in a number of ways. If you own a house you can reduce the rent (which is taxed) but charge a large premium on the lease. If you buy shares, it pays to buy those with a low dividend yield but high prospective capital appreciation. It is no longer legal for the same person to sell securities "cum dividend" and buy them back "ex dividend", but you can achieve the same end through two separate and unrelated transactions.

The fact that certain groups of people (stockjobbers and finance houses), being taxed on capital gains as part of their trading income, can deduct capital losses from taxable income, and that other institutions (charities, pension funds) can reclaim taxes paid, provides opportunities for mutual aid. It thus pays stockjobbers and pension funds to buy "cum" and sell "ex" so long as the capital loss is less than the gross dividend or interest payment. It pays the ordinary investor to sell "cum" so long as the net capital gain is greater than the net dividend or interest which he sacrificed. Only the Treasury loses and the gain is split between buyer and seller. This operation is called "bond-washing", and can be carried out repeatedly with the same parcel of bonds during three critical weeks every year when such transactions are permitted. The Stock Exchange Council has recently expressed its disapproval, but it is not easy to see how bond-washing can be stopped.

But those who take their tax problems seriously do not stop here. There is also "dividend stripping". A finance house (one of those privileged institutions that can deduct capital losses, being taxed on capital gains) buys a private company with large liquid reserves. It extracts these reserves and sells back the assets or shares in a "new" company to its original owners at a loss. The loss gives rise to a repayment claim against the tax borne on the dividends. The shareholders in the private company make an untaxed capital gain. If this transaction is made with a charitable institution or pensions fund, the whole of the tax can be reclaimed.

Ingenuity has been exercised in an attempt to work out schemes for investment trusts that never pay dividends at all: all earnings are reinvested and shareholders take their profits in the form of capital appreciation. The recent tax concessions to overseas trade corporations open up entirely new fertile fields for enterprise and initiative in tax avoidance. But it would be tedious and, for most of us, unprofitable, to go on listing ways in which enterprise has undermined the nominally stiff tax system: family trusts and covenants (even gardeners have, until a few years ago, been paid by seven-year deeds); formation of private companies to avoid surtax on ploughed-back earnings, charitable subscriptions, allowances to kinsmen, elaborate loans joined to life insurance policies, and so on. Any comparison between the rise in incomes, the rise in tax rates and the negligible additional revenue from surtax and death duties provides evidence.

The clue to the whole trick is that our tax is a tax on income, but the definition of income is largely left to private initiative. Powerful accountants and first-class lawyers are set to work to reduce its meaning to a minimum. Legislation is trying to close loop-holes, but this often only gives rise to new ones.

What then are the lessons and what is the moral of this tale?

In the first place it explains the puzzle of plenty in the midst of (statistical) misery. According to the National Income Blue Book only sixty people in 1949 and five hundred in 1956 earned more than £6,000 net of tax. Yet, they can be seen everywhere. Mr Richard Bissell, the perceptive author of *The Pajama Game*, observed in the *Atlantic Monthly* (January 1956):

And before I went over I thought the English were busted. Maybe they are, but I never saw anything like the Rolls-Royces, Bentleys, the huge Daimlers. And certainly *never*, in New York or any place, have I seen so many chauffeurs. When I remark on this, everybody is giving me different explanations. It seems these cars belong to "the wrong people." (Who in hell are the wrong people?) Or it seems they belong to "movie people" (oh now, come off it, you chaps, the combined UK film industry only turns out one picture per annum, judging by their export business). Or to people who are "not eckshully rich in *paounds*, but . . ." (But what? lire, rubles, piastres?) So I can't figure it out; the whole bloody town is filled with hotshots putting on the dog, and they all talk with English accents too, so they can't very well be from Dallas. I wish I could figure out how to go broke like that and I'd have it made.

In the second place one might complain that the system is unfair. This is not a point on which I wish to dwell. Once nobody is allowed to fall below a decent minimum the case for greater income equality is less strong. One can even argue that the splashing and splurging of the expense-account élite adds colour and excitement to the drabber lives of the rest of us. The popular press, which knows what is good for us, gives us tales and pictures of gold-plated Daimlers, zebra-skin seat-covers ("mink is too hot!") and champagne baths on yachts. It may well be that the fun we get from reading about the antics of the rich exceeds the envy aroused by it. Nevertheless, we ought to remember that not all expenditure is equally glamorous and imaginative. Stockbrokers, company directors, and film stars ought to be screened for their contribution to our day-dreams. And it is probable that the (legal) avoidance of the few encourages the (illegal) evasion of the many.

Third, and more important, the system is wasteful. Too many scarce resources are absorbed by advertising, entertaining, bogus expenses, and the tax-avoidance industry. Too many good brains of barristers, solicitors, and accountants are side-tracked into reducing tax liabilities instead of costs, and more, not quite so well paid, brains are employed by the Inland Revenue to examine and oppose this army. The rest of us pay for these services, for the tax avoider's tax savings clearly exceed the fees of his advisers. Therefore the argument that the revenue gain from a capital gains tax or from a broader definition of the income base would be small is beside the point. The gain in efficiency through better allocation of resources would be substantial. If the mental qualities that are now absorbed in increasing deductible items could be switched to increasing exports, our balance of payments problem would be solved.

Fourth, one sometimes hears it argued that all these loop-holes are essential if private enterprise is to survive at all. If we really meant to put into practice the egalitarian intentions of our tax system, this would deprive the managerial élite of all incentives. If this were so (and I do not agree that it is) the answer would be to make the present system honest. If we decide that certain wealthy groups should get off lightly, we could reduce the tax rates and levy them on a wider base. We should include capital gains and much of what are counted now as expenses. The revenue would be the same, the tax would be the same, but the inequality would be seen clearly as the price which we pay for enterprise. This may be a difficult political move, but the alternative implies deception, sooner or later loss of faith in the equity of the system, and the spread of cynicism.

Finally, we hear much of the dilemma between equity and progress. I do not believe such a dilemma exists. We can use credit policy and accelerated depreciation allowances to promote investment and growth and distribute by fiscal means what is left over for consumption in any way we believe is right. But granted the existence of such a dilemma, the private enterprise system at present attacks both objectives. A reform would not have to sacrifice efficiency to equity, but would improve both.

2

The press, most notably in the form of the *Economist*, politicians, in the person of the Lord Chancellor Lord Kilmuir, and economists, outstandingly Mr Colin Clark, have argued that too large a proportion of our national income is taxed; that this leads to inflation and kills incentives to save, work and bear risks.

This is a big and dreary subject to which I have attempted to make one or two contributions in other places. The amount of speculation on this topic is in inverse proportion to the available evidence. As a result a good deal of nonsense is being written. Perhaps a few remarks may be justified to clear the air. The arguments are usually based on four fallacies:

(i) A statistical trick which exaggerates the proportion of national income taxed;
(ii) The fallacy that all taxation discourages risk and enterprise;
(iii) The fallacy that more risk-taking, of whatever kind, is always desirable;
(iv) The belief that private savings and private risk-taking are always preferable to public.

According to Clark's First Law of Income Dynamics, a society that taxes more than 25 per cent of its national income is bound to drift into inflation. This is accompanied by statistics purporting to show that we now take roughly 40 per cent in taxes. The war-cry has been taken up by others. But it has been shown by Dr Prest and Mr Marris[3] that the high percentage is the result of a statistical illusion. The argument of the 40 percenters resembles one that would complain that a society that consisted of 50 men and 50 women had an excessive proportion of women: for 50 is 100 per cent of the supply of men, hence the society consists 100 per cent of women. Total public expenditure, including transfers, subsidies, and so forth, is divided by the national income at factor cost, without transfer payments. This is no measure of anything. Certainly not of any burden, nor of "disincentives" (a tax on transfers is an incentive to work). Dr Prest, on more reasonable assumption, has reduced the ratio to 17 per cent.

On the question of the relation of taxation to risk-bearing (closely related to enterprise) I should like only to make a few categorical statements:

(1) Economic growth in the United Kingdom has been and is running at a record high. There is no evidence of stagnation.
(2) The present system, far from discouraging, clearly encourages

certain types of risk-taking (see previous section).

(3) It is false to believe that there is any peculiar virtue in risk-taking as such. The shouldering of many risks (for example, self-created ones) has no social merits. We want useful production, not risk-taking for its own sake.

(4) Where specific instances can be cited in which risks that ought to be borne are not, greater provisions to offset loss, tax loans to small and new firms, favoured depreciation allowances, and so on, can be used to stimulate desirable risk-taking. Averaging facilities should be increased so that fluctuating incomes do not suffer from the fact that more is lopped off on top than is regained at the bottom. But this does not constitute an argument for general tax reduction.

(5) The appropriate reward for risk-taking is largely conventional.

(6) Continued full employment has reduced some of the most deterrent risks of enterprise. But present full-employment policies are linked with the high and progressive tax structure.

(7) If the worst comes to the worst, the state or other public bodies could take over some risk-taking where it is desirable. Many risks are already carried by the state as an inevitable result of income taxation. (The belief that all reductions in private risk-taking resulting from the imposition of a tax are equivalent reductions in total risk-taking is another widespread fallacy.) There is neither a *priori* nor *a posteriori* evidence that this would bring us nearer slavery, collectivism, or totalitarianism.

Those who are worried lest the supply of risk capital should dry up, ought to welcome recent proposals that the state should buy ordinary industrial shares. Such action would set free substantial amounts of risk capital while management, where efficient, could be carried on without the disturbance of nationalization.

As far as the incentive to save is concerned, again the evidence does not suggest very deleterious effects. Even if they existed, there are few things that personal savings can do that company or public savings cannot do just as well.

The incentives of the working class do not appear to have been blunted— possibly because the complexity of the tax system leaves many workers ignorant of what they actually pay in taxes for extra effort. The problem of incentives for the managerial classes would become topical if the existing loop-holes were successfully closed.

Reform proposals can be grouped under three headings: radical reforms, slow reforms, and patching. Among radical reforms, the most interesting proposal is Mr Kaldor's expenditure tax. It would be a progressive tax on all consumption expenditure (whether out of income, capital, or capital gains), while savings would be exempt. The objections to it have been largely focused on its administrative practicability, although some theoretical objections have also been raised.

Another possibility would be to introduce a capital gains tax. Experience of other civilized countries shows that it is practicable, although the estimated yield might not be large. But as we have seen, revenue should not be the main criterion by which it is judged.

Finally there is the capital levy or a repeated capital tax which might reduce the large amount of capital inequality that still exists in spite of much greater (theoretical) income equality. Two-thirds of the property in Britain is owned by less than 4 per cent of the population. But there is a fundamental dilemma in a democratic society about a capital tax: it can be imposed only by a government with a popular mandate and a strong majority in Parliament. But in order to be successful it must be a surprise. Otherwise capital can be dissipated or given away in a bogus fashion.

Slower reforms would concentrate on reforming the laws relating to death duties, covenants, trusts. We might limit the amount that can be transferred between individuals and we can impose duties that rise progressively, not with the total estate, but with the size of the legacy to any given beneficiary—thus encouraging diffusion of property.

Finally there are endless ways of patching up the present system. To my mind the most important measures here are, first, a greater encouragement to dynamic firms through accelerated depreciation allowances—possibly up to a 100 per cent write-off in the year in which the investment takes place. For whatever one's views about the merits of small and new firms, compared with large and established ones, it is the rapidly growing firm that suffers under our present system. The second measure is the raising of the differential between rates on unearned and earned income, coupled with exemption from this higher differential of small unearned incomes and pensions.

A good tax policy should combine social justice, the promotion of economic progress, the maintenance of incentives, and stability. Careful thought can contribute to a much greater harmony between these aims than is often admitted.

NOTES

1. From the *University of Toronto Quarterly*, January 1958.
2. HMSO, 1953–5: First Report (February 1953), Cmd 8761; Second Report, (April 1954), Cmd 9105; Final Report (June 1955), Cmd 9474 (the last hereafter referred to as the report).

3. See the brilliant article by Mrs Anne Jackson, "Taxation and Hypocrisy", *Twentieth Century* (July 1955), on which I have drawn.
4. R. Marris, "A Note on Measuring the Share of the Public Sector", *Review of Economic Studies* (1954–5), pp. 214–19.

24 Gunnar Myrdal[1]

Gunnar Myrdal was born in 1898 in the village Solvarbo, in the parish of Gustafs, in the Swedish province of Dalarna. He attributes his faith in the Puritan work ethics and his egalitarianism to his sturdy farming background.

His early interests were in the natural sciences. However, at the university he started to read law in the belief that he would learn about how society functioned, but was disappointed and soon changed to economics, the method of which was more like that of the natural sciences. He was a student of the giant figures Knut Wicksell, David Davidson, Eli F. Heckscher, Gösta Bagge, and above all (Karl) Gustav Cassel. His personal friendship was warmest with Cassel, to whose chair in Political Economy and Financial Sciences at Stockholm University he succeeded.

At first a pure theorist, Myrdal's year in the United States as a Rockefeller fellow, following the crash of 1929, turned his interest to political issues. On his return from America he, together with his wife Alva, a pioneering emancipator of women and in many ventures a partner of her husband, became active in politics. Labour came to power in Sweden in 1932. He was involved in the work of a number of Royal Commissions and Public committees and, in 1935, became a member of Parliament. Together with his wife he pioneered modern population policy. His work in Sweden between 1931 and 1938 turned him from a "theoretical" economist into a political economist and what he himself described as an institutionalist. In 1938 the Carnegie Corporation selected him for a major investigation of the Negro problem in America, a project which resulted in *An American Dilemma* (1944). He returned to Sweden in 1942 and for five years was involved in political activities. He headed the committee that drafted the Social Democratic post-war programme. He returned to Parliament, and became a member of the board of directors of the Swedish Bank, chairman of the Swedish Planning Commission, and Minister for Trade and Commerce (1945–7). As Minister he arranged for a highly controversial treaty with the Soviet Union and was also involved in controversy over the dismantling of wartime controls. In 1947 he became executive secretary of the United Nations Economic Commission for Europe, to which he recruited an outstandingly able team of colleagues and where he inspired young people to give their best. After ten years with the Commission in Geneva he embarked on a ten-year study of development in Asia, the result of which was the monumental *Asian Drama* (1968).

Methodological questions occupied Myrdal's thoughts throughout his life. They were already present in the young Myrdal's inconoclastic *Political Element in the Development of Economic Theory* (1930). It was under the influence of the remarkable Uppsala University philosopher Axel Hägerström that he had begun to question the economic establishment.

Myrdal's doctoral dissertation on price formation and economic change (*Prisbildningsproblemet och föränderligheten*, 1927, as yet untranslated) introduced systematically expectations into the analysis of prices, profits and changes in capital values. The micro-economic analysis focused on planning by the firm. Many of these ideas were used in his later macro-economic works: *Om penningteoretisk jämvikt* (1931), *Der Gleichgewichtsbegriff als Instrument für Geldtheoretische Analyse* (1933) and *Monetary Equilibrium* (1938).

Much confusion had been caused by the lack of distinction between anticipations and results. The concepts *ex ante* and *ex post* greatly clarified the discussion of savings, investment and income, and their effects on prices. In anticipation, intention, and planning, savings can diverge from investment; after the event they must be identical, because the community can save only by accumulating real assets. It is the process by which anticipations *ex ante* are adjusted so as to bring about the bookkeeping identity *ex post* that explains unexpected gains and losses as well as fluctuations in prices. Only in equilibrium are *ex ante* savings equal to *ex ante* investment, so that there is no tendency for prices to change. Myrdal saw the chief contribution of this book as the formulation of this distinction.

By introducing expectations into the analysis of economic processes, he made a major contribution to liberalizing economics from a static theory in which the future is like the past or "other things remain equal", and to paving the way for dynamics, in which time, uncertainty, and expectations enter in an essential way.

What is common to his subsequent three important books, *The Political Element* (1930, 1953), *American Dilemma* (1944) and *Asian Drama* (1968) is the emphasis on realistic and relevant research, whether on economic problems, race relations, or world poverty, and with it, the efforts to purge economic thinking of systematic biases.

The work for *An American Dilemma* (1944) was done for the Carnegie

Corporation of New York, at the invitation of its trustees. They had turned to Myrdal as a student from "a non-imperialist country with no background of discrimination of one race against another". They requested that he produce "a comprehensive study of the Negro in the United States to be undertaken in a wholly objective way as a social phenomenon".

Starting on the study almost completely ignorant, he soon discovered that, in order to understand the black people in the United States, he had to study "the American civilization in its entirety, though viewed in its implications for the most disadvantaged population group" (Introduction to *An American Dilemma*, Section 4). The way to reach objectivity was to state explicitly the value premises of the study. These premises were not chosen arbitrarily, but were what Myrdal called the "American Creed" of justice, liberty, and equality of opportunity. But while these value premises were chosen for their relevance to American society, they corresponded to Myrdal's own valuations. As a result, he became closely identified with America's ideals and the study turned into a deep personal commitment. Indeed, he came to regard it as his war service. And the war gave additional importance to race relations as a source of national concern. The book, published before the end of the war, attempts to present a comprehensive, well-documented account, and an intensive, scientific analysis of the facts and the casual relations between facts at the end of the 1930s and early 1940s, with the discernible trend of future changes. The major contribution of the book is the analysis of more than six decades after Reconstruction as "a temporary interregnum" not a "stable equilibrium", and of the incipient changes, on which the prediction of the Black Revolt in the South was based.

Myrdal has never been easy to typecast. On many issues he fires at both sides of the conventional barricade and likes to emphasize the false shared premises of the combatants. Thus, in the discussion of the role of the purely *economic* factors in development, to the exclusion of cultural, social, political, and psychological, he criticizes liberal and conservative economics for assuming the non-economic factors to be fully *adapted* to economic progress, and therefore bundled away under *ceteris paribus* clauses, and the Marxists for believing that these factors are responsive and automatically *adaptable*, as a result of changes in what Marxists call the economic substructure, and therefore also beyond analysis and policy. From diametrically opposed premises, liberal conservatives and Marxist revolutionaries therefore arrive at the same conclusion: there is no need for direct action on non-economic variables (administration, educational systems, labour markets), for in the one case they are fully suited for the required change and in the other they will inevitably and automatically be shaped by the underlying economic change. Liberals and revolutionaries share common ground, which prevents them from seeing the need for the conscious planning of institutions.

While highly critical of the results of a free market system, Myrdal is not among those who dismiss economic progress as irrelevant or detrimental to human life. In his view, economic advance is a necessary condition for achieving social ends and he disagrees with those conservationists who believe that a better quality of life is possible only by abandoning economic growth.

The options before us, in Myrdal's view, are not confined to the models of capitalist or Soviet development. Social objectives can be pursued by a system of decentralized decision-making in which planning is combined with freedom. But here again, the added option is not one of the apolitical possibilities of the futurologists or science fiction writers, but is anchored in political feasibility. He stands nearest to the so-called "utopian" socialists, whom Marx and Engels contemptuously dismissed as "unscientific", but who paid careful attention to shaping social institutions and even human attitudes for a better society. According to the Marxists such planning was impossible or unnecessary: impossible before the revolution, because they formed part of the superstructure determined by the economic conditions; unnecessary after the revolution, when human attitudes and social institutions would be automatically adapted to the socialist society.

Apart from his work on racial problems, Myrdal is best known for his critique of conventional economic theory applied to underdeveloped countries. He calls for a reconstruction of such theory. First, we must free ourselves from the limitation imposed on our thinking by Euro-centricity. Many of our concepts, models, theories, paradigms are "Western" (and "Western" for this purpose includes Marxist and Soviet) in the sense that they fit, more or less, the reality of advanced industrial societies, but are quite "inadequate to the reality" of underdeveloped societies. (It is interesting to note that Myrdal's critique of the application of "Western" concepts to poor countries has caused a reappraisal of the applicability of these concepts to Western societies themselves. In development studies, as in history, there are bonuses.) Both positively, by the way concepts are selected as strategic variables, such as "capital", and negatively, by the way certain items are ignored, such as corruption, the limited experience of "Western" societies as well as opportunistically motivated schemas are reflected.

Myrdal's appeal for realism, or as he calls it, "adequacy to reality", is not primarily a critique of abstraction or selection or simplification. As a most sophisticated social scientist, he is, of course, not only aware but also insists that all theorizing must abstract and select. His criticism is that the abstractions follow the wrong lines, that the irrelevant features are selected.

It is pouring out the baby *instead of* the bath water. He subjects the commonly used concepts of employment, unemployment, income, consumption, savings, investment, capital, output, capital/output ratio, etc., to close scrutiny and finds that in large measure they dissolve when applied to underdeveloped societies.

Having dissolved them, the question arises whether they can be reassembled: whether capital, for example, cannot be given a new and wider meaning, including investment in forms conventionally accounted as consumption, or investment in a programme of family planning or in a land reform; and whether employment cannot be replaced by a richer and more realistic concept of "labour utilization". This would allow for the different attitudes of different castes towards work; it would allow for the effects of the components of the level of living, such as nutrition and health, on intensity of effort; and it would allow for the different types of labour markets. Myrdal has been less succesful in this reformulation and reconstruction than in his critique of existing concepts. His critique is often not accompanied by the presentation of useful alternatives. He has often remarked that "facts kick" against the hard crust of established models or paradigms. But the powerful hold of these paradigms, and the need to demolish established paradigms by providing alternative ones rather than simply by pointing to facts inconsistent with them, may explain why Myrdal's critique has not been more widely accepted in the profession.

A second line of Myrdal's criticism has been directed at the narrow definition of development as economic growth. He replaces it by the concept of the modernization ideals. The emphasis here is again on actual needs and valuations (much more than narrow interests) of real people and groups of people. The ideas must be relevant to the actual valuations of men and women and not the created abstractions of philosophers, statisticians, and economists. The United Nations accepted this approach in 1969 as the Integrated or Unified Strategy of Development, and the United Nations Research Institute for Social Development, on the governing council of which Myrdal sat, was entrusted with further research on it. The social indicator movement has also derived strength from it.

His third criticism is directed at the narrow definitions and limits of disciplines. The essence of the institutional approach, advocated by Myrdal, is to bring to bear all relevant knowledge and techniques on the analysis of a problem. According to this institutional approach "history and politics, theories and ideologies, economic structures and levels, social stratification, agriculture and industry, population developments, health and education and so on must be studied not in isolation but in their mutual relationships" (1968, vol. 1, p. x). In an interdependent social system, there are no economic problems, political problems, or social problems, there are only *problems*.

His fourth line of criticism is directed at phoney objectivity, which under the pretence of scientific analysis conceals political valuations and interests. Myrdal argues that this pseudo-science should be replaced by explicit valuations, in the light of which analysis can be conducted and policies advocated. He is not so naive as to believe that simple specification of these value premises is easy or even possible at all, and has shown how complicated and complex the nexus between values and facts can be. But he has constantly fought the inheritance of natural law and utilitarianism, according to which we can derive certain recommendations from pure, theoretical analysis. "The greatest good for the greatest number" or the "maximization of social welfare" are targets for his critique.

A fifth line of criticism throughout his writings is directed against biases and twisted terminology. He examines such expressions as "United Nations", "international", "values", "developing countries", "unemployment", "bilateral aid", "the free world", and lays bare the opportunistic interests underlying such use of language.

The features against which these lines of criticism are advanced are combined in the technocrat. He isolates economic (or other technical) relations from their social context; he neglects social and political variables and thereby, unconsciously, ministers to the vested interest that might otherwise be violated; he pretends to scientific objectivity and is socially and culturally insensitive. Certain types of planners and so-called experts who try to impose their technical models on a living society fit the picture.

But scholars may ask: is this not simply a question of method? Can the narrow technocrat not be replaced by one who introduces social variables openly into his formal models? Jan Tinbergen, Hollis B. Chenery and Irma Adelman have tried to do precisely this. Cannot the "Western" approach be saved in this way?

Myrdal's answer is Yes and No. In certain areas, a widening or redefinition of concepts can be allowed for. The productive effects of better nutrition can, in principle, be studied and the line between investment and consumption be redrawn for poor societies. The influence of climate (much neglected by most economists), of attitudes, and of institutions can be introduced either as constraints or as variables. An agricultural production function can be postulated in which health, education, distance from town, etc., figure as "inputs". "Capital" can be redefined so as to cover everything on which the expenditure of resources now raises the flow of output later, so that it is greater than it would otherwise have been.

But there are limits to such revisionism. These limits apply both to the analysis of facts and to the recommendations of policies. On the factual side, the reformulation runs into difficulties if the connection between expenditure of resources and "yield" is only tenuous, as in the initiation of a birth control programme or a land reform.

In the analysis of values, the construction of a social welfare function in Myrdal's view is not a logical task. The unity of the social programme of a party or a movement is not like that of a computer programme or a logical system, but more like that of a personality. It is discovered not only by deductive reasoning and the application of syllogisms, but by empathy, imagination, and even artistic and intuitive understanding. Just as we may ask "what would a person like this do or want if the situation were different in specified ways from what it is", so we may ask similar questions about classes, parties, groups, or even whole societies. Means and ends, targets and instruments, are very misleading ways of grasping this type of question, for the unity from which we infer recommendations is not logical but psychological.

It is important here to return to Myrdal's call for expressing our valuations explicitly before embarking on social analysis, precisely in order to make research more objective. What are these valuations in the modernization ideals? They constitute a complex system that includes rationality, planning the future, raising productivity, raising levels of living, social and economic equalization, improved institutions and attitudes, national consolidation, national independence, political democracy, and social discipline. All of these value premises and the valuations derived from them are subsumed under the quest for rationality. As we examine them, we cannot fail to become aware that these are the values of the Swedish welfare state, writ large. High material standards of living must be combined with welfare care for the ill, the poor, and the victims of the competitive struggle. They are the liberal values of a mixed economy, part public, part private. Myrdal, the great critic of the transfer of inappropriate "Western" concepts and values, has been accused of assessing, if only unconsciously, the experience of the underdeveloped countries against that of the modern welfare state, and of a certain lack of empathy for the possibility of doing things differently, by providing alternative roads to development. The Indian anthropologist T. N. Madan charged him with failure to practice what he proclaims, when Myrdal complains that:

large numbers of South Asians have only one set of clothing which is seldom washed, except in bathing. Typically, the same clothes are worn day and night since pajamas and even underwear are luxuries a great many people can ill afford. The hygienic consequences are easy to image.[2]

In particular, he has no place at all for what some of his critics regard as benign forms of corruption and nepotism. Traditional valuations are acceptable only if they do not conflict with the modernization ideals, otherwise they represent "obstacles and inhibitions."

No doubt, there is some justification for this accusation. As a proud, somewhat unSwedish Swede (he is admired and revered by some and detested by other Swedes, and the award of the Nobel Prize in 1973, in its fifth year, is regarded by some as too late, by others as too early), he finds it easier to identify with liberal Americans than with the English or French, and easier with Englishmen than with the Indian masses. It is partly for this reasons that *An American Dilemma* is an optimistic book, and *Asian Drama* a pessimistic one. He once said how kindred American aspirations and ideals, and the "American creed", were to his own beliefs, and how he could identify with these ideals when writing the book on the black problem; and how, in contrast, when he visited an Indian textile factory, the thin, half-naked brown bodies struck him as utterly alien. But more profound than this difference in personal allegiance is Myrdal's view that the American Creed was not only the set of value premises chosen for *An American Dilemma*, it also represented the historical trend; whereas the modernization ideals, though almost a state religion, do not necessarily reflect the trend of the future.

Optimism and pessimism, Myrdal would be the first to emphasize, should have no place in an objective analysis because they are wishful thinking or biased positions, convenient to those who hold them, and reflect "opportunistic" beliefs in what they select and "opportunistic" ignorance in what they omit. The scholar should be concerned with realism. In particular Myrdal brought out clearly the origins of and the interests behind the swings from colonial pessimism about the "idle natives" to the post-independence optimism of the 1950s and early 1960s, and back to the pessimism of the 1970s. He was an early critic of the euphoria of the "Green Revolution" (the high-yielding varieties in agriculture), a euphoria which ran against the stark critique of *Asian Drama*.

Asian Drama is an odd book. And it is odder still that no reviewer pointed out this oddity. A recurrent theme in the main body of the book is the reasons for biases in economic theorizing about South Asia. Some issues concerning substantive economic analysis of Asian development, on the other hand, are relegated to appendixes. Myrdal once said it is like a stocking turned inside out. For Myrdal, the important task is to purge, to cleanse of biases before analysing and reconstructing. He regards the existing structure as deeply contaminated by bias, behind which stand vested interests.

How then are biases related to interests? According to the colonial ideology, a hot climate, a backward social structure, and ethnic inferiority prevent economic advance. Economic progress is the privilege of a few races. The pessimism about the possibility of development was opportunistic for it lifted responsibility for promoting development from the colonial administration.

Independence saw the rapid growth of the "development industry". A massive body of research and communications grew up in the 1950s and 1960s, and the mood changed to one of optimism. The new independence, the desire of the ruling élites to emulate the West, and the rivalries of the Cold War fed this optimism. The false analogy of European reconstruction under the Marshall Plan was used as the paradigm for development. Since the communists had blamed the colonial powers for lack of development, the response was to drop the colonial doctrine. The existing body of economic analysis came in very handy. It neglected climate, it ignored attitudes and institutions as strategic variables, it regarded consumption as not productive, and it treated the state as exogenous. The conclusion: pour capital into the sausage machine, turn the growth handle, and out comes evergrowing output. The optimism is reflected in the changing terminology: from backward regions (not yet countries!) to underdeveloped countries to developing countries. "Diplomacy by terminology", Myrdal calls it. There is assumed to be a "trade-off" between equality and growth, and therefore equality, which hinders growth, has to be sacrificed or postponed, and with it goes any deep analysis of land reform, education, corruption, social discipline, and the interest and efficiency of the state.

In the late 1960s and 1970s, there occurred a return to a pessimistic mood, rationalized by the ineffectiveness of aid, by "wrong" domestic economic policies, and by reduced need for aid. At the same time, the underdeveloped countries called for a "New International Economic Order". Myrdal had stressed throughout his work the need for reforms inside the underdeveloped countries themselves, though the developed countries and international reform can make contributions to overcoming internal difficulties. In the prescient *International Economy* (1956) he had developed the idea that national integration led to international disintegration.

An important idea in Myrdal's arsenal is that of circular or cumulative causation (or the vicious or virtuous circle), first fully developed in *An*

American Dilemma. Traditional theory explains inequality between individuals, regions, and countries as the results of differential resource "endowments". But resources are the result, not the cause of income and wealth. Unimproved land, which is an endowment, is important for resource-based industries, but not for processing and manufacturing. It is the resource-poor countries, such as Israel, Hong Kong, Singapore, Taiwan, Japan and South Korea, that present the success stories of development. Capital, an important factor of production, is also much more the result than the cause of economic growth. The principle of cumulative causation postulates increasing returns through specialization and economies of scale, and shows how small advantages are magnified.

The principle goes back to Wicksell, who, in *Interest and Prices* (1898), had analysed divergencies between the natural and the market rates of interest in terms of upward or downward cumulative price movements, until the divergence was eliminated. Wicksell pointed out that if banks keep their loan rate of interest below the real rate of return on capital, they will encourage expansion of production and investment in plant and equipment. As a result, prices will rise and will continue to rise as long as the lending rate is kept below the real rate.

The principle of cumulative causation can be used to show movements away from an equilibrium position as a result of the interaction of several variables. But not any form of circular or mutual causation or interaction is cumulative and hence disequilibrating, for a series of mutually caused events can, after a disturbance, rapidly converge either on the initial or on some other point of stable equilibrium. In order to create instability, the numerical values of the coefficients of interdependence have to be above a critical minimum size. For example, an increase in consumption will raise incomes which in turn will raise consumption, and so on. But the infinite series will rapidly converge on a finite value. Only if the whole of the extra income or more were spent on consumption would the process be cumulative and disequilibrating.

The notion was applied by Myrdal most illuminatingly to price expectations in *Monetary Equilibrium* (1931) and to the relations between regions in *Economic Theory and Underdeveloped Regions* (1957). He showed how the advantages of growth poles can become cumulative, so that "unto those who have shall be given", while the backward region may be relatively or even absolutely impoverished.

Myrdal applied the notion also the sociological variables and their interaction with economic ones, such as discrimination against blacks, their incomes and their level of performance (low skills, low morals, crime, disease, etc.). In the analysis of development the relation between better nutrition, better health, better education, and higher productivity, and hence ability further to improve health, education, and nutrition, shows that the inclusion of non-economic variables in the analysis opens up the possibility of numerous cumulative processes to which conventional economic analysis is blind. It also guards against unicausal explanations and worldwide remedies or panaceas.

The revolutionary character of the concept of cumulative causation is brought out by the fact that interaction takes place not only within a social system in which the various elements interact, but also in time, so that memory and expectations are of crucial importance. The responses to any given variable, say a price, are different according to what the history of this variable has been. It is this dynamic feature of analysis and its implications for policy that distinguishes Myrdal's approach from that of economists who think in terms of general equilibrium.

In *Economic Theory and Underdeveloped Regions* (1957), (delivered as the Cairo Lectures), and later in *Asian Drama*, he used the concepts "backwash" and "spread" effects to analyse the movement of regions or whole countries at different stages of development and the effects of unification. It is a highly suggestive, realistic, and fruitful alternative explanation to that of stable equilibrium analysis, which is usually based on competitive conditions and diminishing returns, and concludes that gains are widely and evenly distributed. Some might consider these concepts as one of Myrdal's most important contributions.

Like the Marxists, Myrdal emphasizes the unequal distribution of power and property as an obstacle not only to equity but also to growth. But his conclusion is not Marxist. He regards a direct planning of institutions and shaping of attitudes (what Marx regarded as part of the superstructure) as necessary, though very difficult, partly because the policies which aim at reforming attitudes and institutions are themselves part of the social system, part of the power and property structure.

This brings us to Myrdal's critique of the kind of government he calls the "soft state". This critique has sometimes been misunderstood. It is plain that "softness" in Myrdal's sense is quite compatible with a high degree of coercion, violence, and cruelty. The Tamils in Sri Lanka, the Indians in Burma, the Chinese in Indonesia, the Hindus in Pakistan, the Moslems in India, the Biharis in Bangladesh—to take six states he calls "soft"—would not complain about excessively soft treatment. "Soft states" also use military violence, both internal and external. Their "softness" lies in their unwillingness to coerce in order to implement declared policy goals. It is not the result of gentleness or weakness but reflects the power structure and a gap between real intentions and professions.

Myrdal has applied his method also to the analysis of inflation combined with widespread unemployment in the developed countries of the West in the 1970s. He attributes "stagflation" to the organization of producers as pressure groups, and the dispersion and comparative weakness of consumers, to the tax system which encourages speculative expenditures, to the structure of markets and to the methods of oligopoly administrative pricing, and he condemns inflation as a socially highly divisive force.

The approach favoured by Myrdal is one of neither Soviet authority and force nor of capitalist laissez-faire but of a third way: that of using prices for planning purposes and of attacking attitudes and institutions directly to make them the instruments of reform. The difficulty is that any instrument, even if used with the intention to reform, within a given power structure may serve the powerful and re-establish the old equilibrium. Even well-intentioned allocations, rationing and controls may reinforce monopoly and big business. What looks like socialism in the first round feeds monopoly capitalism in the second or third. How does one break out of this lock? Myrdal does not draw revolutionary conclusions but relies on the, admittedly difficult, possibility of self-reform that arises, in both the American creed and in the Modernization Ideals, from the tensions between preferred and proclaimed beliefs and actions.

On the one hand, he thus stands more firmly in the neo-classical tradition than he might be prepared to admit and attributes considerable importance to avoiding "distortions" of interest rates and prices. On the other hand, there is an inconsistency in his advocacy of central planning and his contempt for most politicians and bureaucrats, which reveals an anarchistic streak.

Both *An American Dilemma* and *Asian Drama* are books about the interaction and the conflict between ideals and reality, and about how, when the two conflict, one of them must give way. Much of conventional economic theory is a rationalization whose purpose it is to conceal that conflict. But it is bound to reassert itself sooner or later. When this happens, either the ideals will be scaled down to conform to the reality or the reality will be shaped by the ideals. Even if the chances of success are only one in a hundred, Myrdal, never afraid to express unconventional and unpopular views in plain language, will have been a leader, in thought and action, towards a reality shaped by enlightened ideals.

NOTE

1. From the *International Encyclopedia of the Social Sciences*, vol. 18.
2. *Asian Drama*, p. 552 and T. N. Madan, *Economic and Political Weekly*, vol. 4, no. 5 (1 February 1969), pp. 289–90.

WORKS BY MYRDAL

1927	*Prisbildningsproblemet och föränderligheten*, Almqvist & Wiksell, Uppsala and Stockholm.
1930	*Vetenskap och politik i nationalekonomien*, Norstedt, Stockholm.
1930	*Das Politische Element in der nationalökonomischen Doktrinbildung*, Junker and Dünnhaupt, Berlin.
1931	Om penningteoretisk jämvikt, *Ekonomisk Tidskrift*.
1933a	*The Cost of Living in Sweden 1830–1930*.
1933b	Der Gleichgewichtsbegriff als Instrument der Geldtheoretischen Analyse, *Beiträge zur Geldtheorie*, Friedrich von Hayek (ed.), Vienna—Expanded version of Myrdal (1931).
1933c	Konjunktur och offentlig hushållning. Bihang till riksdangens protokoll 1 saml., Bilage III.
1933d	Das Zweck-Mittel-Denken in der Nationalökonomie. *Zeitschrift für Nationalökonomie* 4.
1934	*Finanspolitikens ekonomiska verkningar*.
1934	Myrdal, Alva, and Myrdal, Gunnar *Kris i befolkningsfragan*, Stockholm.
1939	*Monetary Equilibrium*, Hodge, London.
1940	*Population: A Problem for Democracy*.
(1944a) 1962	*An American Dilemma: The Negro Problem and Modern Democracy*, Harper, New York—(a paperback edition was published in 1964 by McGraw-Hill).
1944b	*Varning för fredsoptimism*, Bonniers, Stockholm.
1945	*Warnung gegen Friedensoptimismus*, Europa Verlag, Zurich.
1953	*The Political Element in the Development of Economic Theory*, translated by Paul Streeten, Routledge & Kegan Paul, Harvard University Press, Cambridge, Mass. (originally published in German).
1955	*Realities and Illusions in Regard to Intergovernmental Organizations*, Oxford University Press.
1956a	*Development and Under-development: A Note on the Mechanism of National and International Inequality*, National Bank of Egypt, Cairo.
1956b	*An International Economy: Problems and Prospects*, Routledge & Kegan Paul, London.

1957	*Economic Theory and Under-developed Regions*, Duckworth, London; Harper, New York.
1958	*Value in Social Theory: A Selection of Essays on Methodology*, Paul Streeten (ed.), Routledge & Kegan Paul, London.
1960	*Beyond the Welfare State*, Yale University Press, New Haven.
1961	"Value-loaded Concepts", in Hugo Hegeland (ed.), *Money, Growth and Methodology and Other Essays in Honor of Johan Åkerman*, Lund: Gleerup, pp. 273–88.
1962	*Challenge to Affluence*, Pantheon, New York.
1968	*Asian Drama: An Inquiry into the Poverty of Nations*, Twentieth Century Fund, New York.
1969	*Objectivity in Social Research*, Pantheon, New York.
1970a	*The Challenge of World Poverty: A World Anti-poverty Program in Outline*, Pantheon, New York.
1970b	"The 'Soft State' in Underdeveloped Countries", in Paul Streeten (ed.), *Unfashionable Economics*, Weidenfeld & Nicolson, London, pp. 227–43.
1973	*Against the Stream: Critical Essays on Economics*, Pantheon, New York.

For a full bibliography, see Harald Bohrn (editor), *Gunnar Myrdal: A Bibliography*, 1919–1976, Stockholm: Acta Bibliothecae Regiae Stockholmiensis, 1976.

Author Index

Page references in *italics* are to the notes and references.

433

Subject Index

STRÈÈTEN: Development perspectives